POLITICAL INDOCTRINATION
IN THE U.S. ARMY

from World War II to the Vietnam War

Christopher S. DeRosa

POLITICAL INDOCTRINATION IN THE U.S. ARMY

from World War II to the Vietnam War

University of Nebraska Press · Lincoln & London

Library of Congress Cataloging-
in-Publication Data
DeRosa, Christopher S.
Political indoctrination in the
U.S. Army from World War II
to the Vietnam War /
Christopher S. DeRosa.
p.   cm.—(Studies in war, society,
and the military)
ISBN-13: 978-0-8032-1734-8 (cloth: alk. paper)
ISBN-10: 0-8032-1734-X (cloth: alk. paper)
ISBN-13: 978-0-8032-2486-5 (paper: alk. paper)
1. United States. Army—Political activity.
2. United States—Politics and government—
1945–1989.   I. Title.   II. Series.
UA25.D42   2006
355.1′23—dc22
2005035112

For Katie

CONTENTS

ACKNOWLEDGMENTS

I had a wonderful time writing this book and owe many thanks to all the people who made it such an enjoyable and enlightening process. I had the privilege of being a student of the late Russell F. Weigley at Temple University. He set for me the highest standard as a scholar. I am grateful for his encouragement, his invariably good humor, and his generosity with his time and talent. I could not have wished for a better mentor or teacher, and I treasure my memories of him. Richard H. Immerman read my chapters carefully and helped me place my research within broader contexts. His wise counsel was always accompanied by his infectious enthusiasm. He is the biggest reason why Temple is such a great place to be.

I first became interested in the subject of political indoctrination in the military in one of David Alan Rosenberg's memorable and stimulating classes. I thank him for his critical guidance as this project took shape. As the outside reader on my dissertation committee, Brig. Gen. Harold W. Nelson, U.S. Army (ret.), provided me with a host of good ideas and valuable criticisms. I thank Temple University for supporting my studies with a teaching assistantship and my dissertation with a grant.

At every archive I visited I encountered helpful and knowledgeable professionals, nowhere more so than at the United States Army Military History Institute at Carlisle Barracks in Pennsylvania. In particular I appreciate David A. Keough's thoughtful assistance at many points in my research. At Monmouth University, I am lucky to have the help of the able and tireless Linda Silverstein at the Guggenheim Library. I am indebted to the University of Nebraska Press's readers for their many helpful suggestions and to Elizabeth A. S. Demers, Heather Lundine, Beth Ina, Christopher J. Steinke, Tish Fobben, Carolyn Einspahr, Sabrina

Stellrecht, and Alison Rold for shepherding this book through to the light of day. I also thank copyeditor Paul S. Bodine for his thorough work on the manuscript. Any errors in the book are mine alone.

I could not ask for a more welcoming and friendly environment than the one I have found in my new home in Monmouth University's Department of History and Anthropology. I thank all my colleagues and in particular my chair, Brian Greenberg, for bringing me into the fold.

I owe warm thanks to Bill Ashbaugh, Julie Berebitsky, Alexandra Friedrich, and Rich Veit for all their encouragement and good advice and to Yvette Florio Lane for her support and for her insightful comments on the manuscript. The greatest pleasure of being an historian is to have friends and colleagues such as these.

I appreciate the generous help provided by Gina Isaacs. I thank Celia Feinstein, Jim Lemanowicz, Robin Levine, and Kathy Miller for their many kindnesses. I am grateful to Peter Dizikes and Murray Markowitz for their friendship. Thanks also to my in-laws, Marilyn Parkin and Ernest Parkin III, and to my grandparents, Joseph and Yolonda DeRosa, for all their good wishes. My deepest thanks to my parents, Joseph and Esther, and my brothers, Jon and Ben, for their support. I thank my daughters Vivian and Quinn for the joy they bring to my life every day. Most of all, I thank my colleague, best friend, and wife, Katie Parkin. The ways in which she has helped me in every aspect of this endeavor are simply staggering. Her belief in me is the most precious thing I have.

INTRODUCTION

After drilling troops during the American Revolution, Baron Friedrich von Steuben was said to have noted that while you could tell a Prussian what to do and expect him to do it, you had to tell an American why he ought to do something before he would comply. Few of the officials who ran the United States Army's "Troop Information" programs from World War II through the Vietnam War failed to invoke von Steuben's observation in defending their mission. They saw themselves as explainers rather than persuaders, different from the enemy's propagandists not by degree but on fundamental principle. "Propaganda" seemed to them at odds with the democratic, individualistic genius of American society.

Nevertheless, the management of opinion lay at the heart of the Troop Information (or, later, "Command Information") mission. Between 1940 and 1973, millions of young Americans passed through the ranks of the U.S. armed forces. For officials who harbored doubts about the nation's ideological commitment to its battles, these draftees and volunteers made up a captive audience ripe for political indoctrination. For over three decades, the military subjected soldiers to an array of films, radio programs, pamphlets, and weekly lectures designed to stir their patriotism and activate their contempt for first fascist, then communist enemies.

Military sociologists, political scientists, and scholars of mass communication have analyzed the Troop Information program's effectiveness, but few historians have devoted much attention to the way the armed forces conducted political indoctrination. In this history of the formal political indoctrination of U.S. soldiers, I draw on the records of the army and the Department of Defense's information offices, the content of the indoctrination materials themselves, and the recollections of soldiers to analyze the political messages that the nation conveyed to its army over the three decades of American conscription. I examine how the Troop Information program took root as an army institution, how its indoctrination technique evolved over time, and how it interacted with America's larger political culture.

For the most part, the indoctrination campaign was mild in scope. The army's decision at the end of World War II to house Troop Information together with its better-funded, better-staffed public relations office damaged the program's prestige. In the field, commanders considered Troop Information a low priority, and many thought it a nuisance. The indoctrinators' conflicting impulses to inculcate patriotism and to shun propaganda as un-American further limited the program's reach. Still, their respect for freethinking individualism helped keep them within safe boundaries. Only rarely did they indulge in crass, overtly propagandistic appeals.

Nevertheless, the efforts to impose a political consensus on soldiers raised both practical and ethical questions. Did political indoctrination actually work? The social scientists who monitored the programs searched mostly in vain for evidence of success. Even the military's best-crafted propaganda, such as director Frank Capra's World War II *Why We Fight* films, failed to budge soldiers' opinions on issues closest to their immediate self-interest. The influence of families, peers, schools, and civilian political culture seemed to weigh far more heavily than military propaganda in forming soldiers' more abstract political beliefs. It is possible that the military establishment lost little, in the end, when it left the task of persuasion to the engines of opinion in society at large.

More importantly, the military maintained its cherished political neutrality better when it did so. When the nation attempted to use the army as a school of citizenship it forced it to take positions in Americans' unsettled political debates. The army was the destination of the majority of the millions of draft-era enlistees, and hence that service is the focus of the book. One army information chief remarked to his officers in the 1950s that it was their duty to salvage those soldiers who had "missed their schooling." Their program was "the last time that organized society can impress upon them their responsibilities as citizens." The idea of the army as a school of the nation had no real counterpart in the other services. The navy and marines tended to doubt that abstract ideology was an important motivational agent and accordingly stressed building pride in the unit or the service more than in the nation. They offered decentralized information programs and deemphasized broad political themes. Though the air force shared information materials with the army, its view of itself as an elite, technologically advanced organization made for a different approach to indoctrination than a would-be teacher of remedial citizenship. If the army also often lacked interest in propaganda, however, it could less easily avoid civilian and Pentagon propagandists' interest in the army.[1]

It was not until World War I that Americans seized upon the army as a potential "school of the nation," and not until World War II that the military implemented a political indoctrination program from the outset of a conflict. Political indoctrination did not became an army institution until the Cold War, when Pentagon officials sought to provide American soldiers with ideological armor as impregnable as communist soldiers, they assumed, possessed. The program's inability to find a usable set of common political ideals in this period revealed the illusory nature of the apparent political consensus in the postwar United States. Citizen-soldiers, like their civilian countrymen, contained multitudes; what activated the patriotism of one could be diametrically opposed to the beliefs of another. This inherent conflict metastasized in the early 1960s, when Maj. Gen. Edwin A. Walker, commander of the Twenty-fourth Infantry Division stationed in the Federal Republic of Germany, tried to indoctrinate his troops with his personal brand of right-wing politics. After his recall, ultraconservatives attacked the army for being soft on communism. The controversy showed that anticommunism could not be taught as part of a national consensus though it also formed the very grammar of American party politics.

The Vietnam War presented the information program with its greatest challenge. Hampered by a turgid bureaucracy, information officers (IOs) struggled to come up with fresh or inspirational approaches. Grave doubts about the conduct and purpose of the war pitted the program's message against draftees' deeper indoctrination as American citizens, making plain the weakness of the military's propaganda as a motivational tool. By the early 1970s it was clear that army culture had rejected formal political indoctrination. In abandoning the draft the country also abandoned the concept of its army as a forge of patriotic citizenship. The events of the 1960s cooled the nation's anticommunist ardor to the point where it was willing to leave the volunteer soldiers to their own politics and loyalties, concluding apparently that there never had been a place for political indoctrination in an army of a democracy.

POLITICAL INDOCTRINATION
IN THE U.S. ARMY

from World War II to the Vietnam War

Anxious to Work Bodily Destruction

Political Indoctrination in World War II

Shortly before the United States entered World War II, it set up a political indoctrination program for its draftees and volunteers. With little in the way of an inheritance from World War I, those who labored to counteract enlistees' flagging morale had to invent programs and procedures almost entirely anew. As in many other aspects of the nationwide undertaking, the creators of the war orientation program met their mission with an optimistic spirit of innovation. The army mobilized accomplished filmmakers, writers, and social scientists to craft occasionally stunning propaganda. It charged officers with the "indoctrination of hatred" in lectures to the troops. Implementation of the program revealed, however, that commanders often considered it a waste of time, and though troops enjoyed the films they sometimes found the weekly sessions oppressive. As the social scientists learned, these methods were only marginally effective. Propaganda, no matter how well made, could not overrule men's instinct for self-preservation.

After the fall of France in June 1940, and before the Germans turned on their Soviet allies a year later, the global peril was evident enough for the United States to raise an army for the defense of the western hemisphere, if nothing else. Although dwarfed by the outpouring of patriotism after the empire of Japan's attack on the U.S. fleet at Pearl Harbor, the reintroduction of Selective Service in 1940 produced its own wave of patriotic and willing volunteers and draftees. However, it also swept into the ranks many reluctant citizen-soldiers who blamed their boredom, confinement, and endangerment on what they took as America's decision to fight Great Britain's war. On August 12, 1941, Congress voted, quite narrowly, to extend the soldiers' term of service past the original year. Some disgruntled draftees, believing that the extension was a breach of contract and convinced that the international situation was not really that grave, spoke openly of going "Over the Hill in October" when their initial year of enlistment ended. *New York Times* reporter Hilton Howell Railey investigated the matter confidentially for the army and claimed that such talk was alarmingly common in the camps.[1]

Given the reports of significant discontent, Gen. George C. Marshall, the army chief of staff, instructed the War Department's Bureau of Public Relations to prepare a lecture series for the soldiers on the purpose of the war. Given the prevailing attitude that morale was best maintained by the time-honored device of keeping soldiers busy, there was little in the way of an established apparatus to carry out Marshall's order. The decision to indoctrinate draftees politically thus came in response to this immediate morale problem rather than out of the army's past experiences. Nevertheless, the World War II programs had antecedents in America's previous wars.

Antecedents of Political Indoctrination
The army's political indoctrination programs always claimed a lineage reaching back to George Washington, who on occasion tried to raise his army's spirits with inspirational words invoking the political goals of the Revolution.[2] Washington's distribution of pamphlets and other political speeches was opportunistic, rather than programmatic, morale building. The first nation in modern history to attempt to manufacture soldiers' political attitudes systematically was revolutionary France in the 1790s. To thwart counterrevolutionary activity in its armies, the government's Committee on Public Safety tried to educate the troops as to whom they owed their true allegiance. Soldiers received political journals, learned songs with patriotic lyrics, and attended ceremonies celebrating the revolution. With these tools, the government tried to undermine the soldiers' immediate loyalties, especially toward their officers and generals, and replace them with a purer, abstract devotion to the *patrie*.[3]

Not until half a century later, in the American Civil War, did the United States became a nation-in-arms on the scale of revolutionary France. Associations of private citizens, concerned with soldiers' dedication to the Union cause, circulated pamphlets and newspapers in the armies' camps. At the same time the administration of President Abraham Lincoln made some limited attempts to curtail soldiers' access to hostile pamphlets and newspapers. The materials soldiers received, however, were not generated under government or army auspices. The North's political parties vied for soldiers' hearts, minds, and votes just as they would any segment of the electorate.

Democrats argued that men in uniform could not act as freethinking citizens. They feared a moblike "bayonet vote" that would uniformly favor the commander in chief. The Republicans, confident of their campaign's popularity with the troops (and, not inconsequentially, their superior ability to communicate with the armies), upheld the political integrity of the citizen-soldier. In their campaign materials Republicans flattered the soldiers' judgment and played on their contempt for Copperheads (peace Democrats). One of their 1864 pamphlets, entitled, *A Few Plain Words with the Rank and File of the Union Armies,* stated: "Napoleon wittily warned governments to 'beware when bayonets should learn to think;' but with us far from being a subject of fear, it is our glory and pride that the war for the Union has been upheld by a million of 'thinking bayonets.' . . . This election touches you, because in becoming *soldiers* you did not cease to be *citizens.*" Given these differing approaches, it was hardly a surprise that when they went to the polls the soldiers endorsed the Republicans' prosecution of the war to an even greater degree than did the civilian electorate.[4]

The American military itself did not set up a program to indoctrinate troops politically until late in World War I. As in the Civil War, the government provided channels through which civilian propaganda could reach soldiers. In 1917, however, President Woodrow Wilson's administration did not merely pass on the products of patriotic leagues and party loyalists. It centralized control of the propaganda under its own agency, the Committee on Public Information (CPI), led by progressive journalist George Creel. The CPI produced films, pamphlets, posters, and slide shows that promoted American war aims and crafted a frightening portrait of the enemy. It deployed seventy-five thousand speakers, known as Four Minute Men, to cover the countryside, making four-minute speeches or singing patriotic songs. Early in 1918 the

War Department asked the CPI to reissue some of the Four Minute Man presentations to company commanders to deliver to the troops. Creel remembered that "We went far beyond the request and furnished hundreds of officers with regular Four Minute Men bulletins as well as with the Committee's pamphlets. All were expected to make 'morale talks' to their men, yet nothing was done to aid them, and the publications of the Committee were their one hope." In 1917 and 1918 the CPI and the Signal Corps produced newsreels and longer films and sent them, "free of charge, to the encampments in the United States as well as to the picture-shows on the firing line in France."[5]

The potential effects of military life on citizen-soldiers worried segments of the American public, and they urged the Wilson administration to guard against socially unacceptable behavior in and around the camps. In response the government set up the Commission on Training Camp Activities (CTCA), an organization under whose umbrella various civilian groups (such as the Young Men's Christian Association and the American Library Association) strove to make army life more wholesome. Nancy K. Bristow, in her 1996 book *Making Men Moral*, located these moralizing efforts in the Progressive Era tendency of white middle-class Protestants to exalt their own value system as the American standard. Like the settlement houses established to aid immigrants, the CTCA simultaneously provided comforts to soldiers and demanded social conformity.[6]

Political indoctrination was not a primary concern of the CTCA. Rather, its first mission was to safeguard soldiers' sexual purity. The fact that venereal diseases impaired military efficiency goes only so far in explaining the zeal that animated the organization on this point. As Bristow described it, the CTCA's methods for actively policing soldiers' sexual behavior included forming civilian leagues to harass camp followers and distributing pamphlets and films to dramatize the dishonor that befell sexually active men—a fate far worse than death on the battlefield. The CTCA discouraged drinking, close dancing, the reading of improper books, and the watching of improper movies. Never before had a civilian agency tried to exert such control over soldiers' lives.[7]

Although many of the reform-minded organizers who flourished in the early part of the twentieth century feared that their social work would be thrust aside when America entered the war, some, including the CTCA officials, realized that the war would be a vehicle well suited for promoting their values. In this way the Great War and the progressives were made for one another. The administrators of the American Expeditionary Force and their civilian allies made unprecedented efforts to impose order on the process of raising an army. They created the Selective Service system to manage the flow of inductees, then sorted and rated the recruits with intelligence and psychological tests. Volunteers and draftees made up a sizable captive audience for experiments in citizenship training and social engineering.

Not all interested observers agreed with the CTCA's premise that camp life degraded soldiers. Prewar advocates of universal military training and service invited young men to their encampment in Plattsburgh, New York, with the idea that paramilitary training was a character-building experience. Some Plattsburghers, such as Theodore Roosevelt, claimed that mixing men in the training camps would help them overcome class and ethnic differences and forge instead a common identity as equal, democratic, and robust citizens. Former army chief of staff Leonard Wood was just as optimistic about the benefits for industry if universal military training could accustom a workforce to regimented life and condition it to obey orders.[8]

Whether their purposes were democratic or undemocratic, supporters of the conscription movement assumed that the army could properly teach citizenship to Americans. Many progressives wanted American education to level class distinctions amongst students and bring them up as political equals. When the army assumed the role of a "school of the nation" through the World War I draft the goals of its civics training was quite different, however. Implicit in its vision was the idea that military discipline promoted good citizenship, not the other way around. This model was the opposite of philosopher John Dewey's blueprint for democratic education, which advocated teaching democracy by immersing students in its practice.[9]

In May 1918 the army established its own Morale Branch to tend to the soldiers' mental well-being, with Brig. Gen. Edward Lyman Munson from the Medical Corps as chief. Since the previous January Munson had lobbied for a means to formalize the manufacture of enthusiasm.

[5]

Morale, he argued, could not be left to chance; the army had to manage it systematically, for "The soldier will not fight at his best for a cause of which he knows little or in which he does not fully believe."[10]

The Morale Branch could not, in the brief time allotted to it, realize the breadth of Munson's vision. Despite a disclaimer that the vast majority of morale problems were local and therefore outside the purview of his organization, Munson's conception of morale work was almost limitless in scope. Holding a low opinion of the intellectual ability of American soldiers, he argued that a proper morale program would constantly monitor and correct their behavior. Munson advised close control over the books and papers in camp libraries. It seemed to cause him some anxiety that "When the soldier is reading, he is beyond the direct influence of his commander and comrades." On matters of hygiene it would not be enough to scare the troops with talks about venereal diseases; they would have to be trained to suppress the sexual impulse itself.[11]

The morale chief hoped his work would follow the men into their civilian lives. "Besides teaching men how to die for their country," Munson wrote, "the army will not do its full duty toward them unless it teaches them how to live for their country in the sense of better citizenship." To that end he recommended that "The Americanization work in the Army should coordinate with that being conducted in civil life, though naturally going much further and securing better results." Munson argued that a morale program was not just a wartime measure but the military's permanent stake in shaping the nation's character. He went so far as to predict that his various strategies for controlling people would be of more use in "civil life in respect to industrial morale" and would help solve "the disturbing economic, social and political problems springing from human relations in industry."[12]

Throughout the 1920s the army continued to incorporate this variety of "citizenship" as a small component of soldiers' training. After the war large budget cuts reduced the General Staff's commitment to comprehensive morale work. Yet citizenship training still took place in forty-minute classes at the discretion of the camp commander (the 1928 *Citizenship* training manual recommended rainy days as a good time to Americanize the troops). Instructors "carefully selected" from the company officers led group discussions on the nation's system of government and the men's numerous obligations as citizens.[13]

The authors of the army's lesson plans viewed the state of the nation with pessimism. Citizenship instructors were warned that "A study of the census reports of the United States, particularly during the past 50 years, reveals a condition that to every thinking man and woman is fraught with grave danger." Until recent times, the authors continued, most immigrants to the country were "of Anglo-Saxon origin, that race of people which has been working on the problem of self-government for nearly 2,000 years." Now, the authors feared, the nation, and by extension the army, was flooded with non–Anglo Saxons, who had no idea of what it meant to be an American.[14]

In the Great War the army had dealt sensitively with the ethnic and religious customs of its numerous foreign-born soldiers. After the war, however, the army course taught that American citizenship resided only within narrow ideological limits. Socialist-derived concepts such as "class consciousness" and "class activity" were not merely outside American norms; they were so un-American as to not be "tolerated." Lesson Six, "Individual Initiative," informed soldiers simply that "'Socialism' kills." The authors argued that "A surfeit of food, clothes, comfortable homes, and much time for idleness can easily become the first step to the overthrow of civilization."[15]

Although in the previous decade the nation had fought, with great fanfare, a war to "make the world safe for democracy" the authors of the *Citizenship* manual doggedly insisted that "the United States is a Republic, not a democracy." Troops attending the discussion sessions heard this point repeated many times. The ninth lesson, "Representative Government," held up "democracy" ("Results in mobocracy") and "autocracy" as the two destructive poles between which societies had to steer. Such lessons discouraged the new, unwanted Americans from defying the established social order. To wit, the lessons emphasized the "laws against the abuse" of free speech more than the right itself.[16]

Citizenship training seemed more intent on making obedient civilians than obedient soldiers. Its concerns about the composition of the country's racial stock and its probusiness lessons reflected the conservative backlash that swept the country in the wake of World War I. In the Red

Scare of 1919–20 employers and government officials cracked down on labor organizers and socialists, jailing or deporting thousands. Nativist attitudes and ill-founded racial categorizations enjoyed respectability in large parts of the scientific community. The National Origins Act of 1924 established strict quotas to limit arrivals from eastern and southern Europe. The military itself had a hand in formulating the restrictive immigration policy. In his history of anti-Semitism in the U.S. Army, Joseph W. Bendersky found that an ultraconservative clique centered in the Military Intelligence Division argued consistently against admitting to the United States any but their preferred Nordic racial stock. Officers of this persuasion invited racialist and nativist speakers to the Army War College and circulated their literature to their fellows. Formal indoctrination at the troop level, however, never got much further than the 1920s citizenship classes. In the latter half of the interwar years, morale work revolved more around recreation and administrative issues of pay, leave, and promotion.[17]

In theory, if not always in practice, the army's socialization efforts during World War I were more invasive than necessary, judging by the sole criterion of military effectiveness. They did not assume, however, that the army had to justify the war's aims to its soldiers or court their approval of military service. It was only in World War II and the Cold War that the enemy powers articulated their own challenges to America's political vision in an ideological form. The successive confrontations with fascism and communism convinced the government that new soldiers required increasingly potent political indoctrination.

Indoctrination and Motivation

With such a modest legacy from the interwar years, the morale officers of the 1940s started almost from scratch. In imitation of the British Army, the U.S. Army made orientation sessions a weekly affair. The authors of the program's support material included the preeminent nationally syndicated columnist Walter Lippmann, who wrote on United States foreign policy (and had written propaganda for the army in World War I as well) as well as Raleigh C. Travelyan, who wrote on English history. The World War I veteran and military critic Samuel L. A. Marshall made the most significant contribution: *The War in Out-*

line, a lesson plan that became the basis of the orientation program's initial approach. *The War in Outline* contained a chronology of the war and historical documents from both sides, including the Bill of Rights and treaties made by the Axis powers.[18]

Marshall arranged the *Outline* to lead the reader to the conclusion that the Allied war was just, but it contained few overtly argumentative passages and no emotional appeals. "Since individual speakers or discussion leaders should make their own presentations of the topics," the preface stated, "the facts here are presented in an abbreviated style." For example, the Spanish Civil War between the supporters of the Spanish Republic and Francisco Franco's fascists stirred the passions of the American left, but the *Outline* explained it in these plain terms: "Hitler intervened, with Mussolini, in Spain in 1936. A total of about 45,000 Nazis and 175,000 Facists [*sic*] served the Spanish Dictator (Franco). Spanish battle fields were used as testing grounds for new German weapons (planes and tanks), and the new tactics of machine warfare. This action had the further purpose of extending Nazi influence in the Iberian peninsula—an area of critical importance in Europe and in the Mediterranean region."[19]

Marshall evidently assumed that commanders needed no argumentative, persuasive, or dramatic materials to interest their men in the goals of the war. This assumption fit well with Marshall's own theory of soldierly motivation. However, there is also good reason to rate the political dimension highly in assessing soldiers' motivation in war, and until World War II it was common to do so. Army researchers in that war argued that ideological factors mattered little in explaining a soldier's commitment to the war in general and combat in particular. They discovered that the troops forbade one another from voicing idealistic or patriotic interpretations of the war: "Probably the strongest group code, except for . . . flagrant disloyalty, was the taboo against any talk of a flag-waving variety. Accounts . . . indicate that this code was universal among American combat troops and widespread throughout the Army. The core of the attitude among combat men seemed to be that any talk that did not subordinate idealistic values and patriotism to the harsher realities of the combat situation was hypocritical, and a person who expressed such ideas a hypocrite." As one soldier told the

researchers, "There's no patriotism on the line." John Ellis, in his book
The Sharp End, contended that while patriotism and politics had some
importance to soldiers, "Many of the men for whom such beliefs were a
sufficient motivation had been wiped out in Spain, and anyway they are
never more than a tiny handful in any conscripted mass army."[20]

In his 1947 study *Men Against Fire: The Problem of Battle Command in Future War*, Marshall used after-action reports to critique the
American soldier's fighting performance. He argued that true combat
motivation depended on the cohesion of a small group of men who
were well supplied with relevant tactical information. Ideals alone were
of distinctly limited value. Bill Mauldin, the favorite cartoonist of the
World War II GI, said as much when he wrote of soldiers' camaraderie,
"That kind of friendship and spirit is a lot more genuine and sincere
than all the 'war aims' and indoctrination in the world." Other analysts
theorized that attachment to a specific "buddy" was the key to performance under fire. In *Wartime: Understanding and Behavior in the
Second World War*, Paul Fussell wrote that soldiers would "attack only
if young, athletic, credulous, and sustained by some equivalent of the
buddy system—that is fear of shame."[21]

The theory that soldiers fought essentially for the other members
of their "primary group" enjoyed widespread acceptance in the postwar era. Historians applied its logic to past events and discovered that
largely nonideological soldiers had waged and won America's wars.
Bell Irvin Wiley's studies of Civil War soldiers suggested that "Johnny
Reb" and "Billy Yank" rarely had lofty national goals on their minds.
Later, Mark Edward Lender, in his study of the New Jersey Line in the
American Revolution, argued that American soldiers resembled their
mercenary European counterparts in their poverty, lack of property, and
dependence on army pay.[22]

At the end of the 1960s, perhaps spurred by American soldiers' apparent lack of ideological commitment to the Vietnam War, analysts
began to challenge the primacy of primary groups. Charles Moskos,
in his *The American Enlisted Man* (1970), agreed that overt appeals to
patriotism left soldiers unmoved but argued that the soldiers he interviewed in Vietnam possessed a "latent ideology." No matter how reluctant to parrot an official line they functioned effectively only so long as

they had an underlying confidence in the righteousness of their cause, or at least in the rectitude of the social system that spawned the cause. Their sense that America was the greatest country in the world was a far better guarantor of their obedience than their faith in America's specific war aims in Vietnam.[23]

In the past twenty years historians have reclaimed the politically committed American soldier. Charles Royster's study of the Continental Army demonstrated the importance of patriotic symbols and ideological arguments to Revolutionary War soldiers. Recent books by James M. McPherson and Joseph Allen Frank have depicted the Civil War soldier as highly politicized. Articulated political opinions do not play as prominent a motivational role in Gerald F. Linderman's nuanced portrait of the World War II combat infantryman, however. He credited prayer as a sustaining factor in combat, but abstract political beliefs had much less value than the support or shame that comrades could bestow. Nevertheless, even if the American soldier in World War II voiced few explicit political motives, it is possible that political indoctrination contributed to his underlying sense of his country's propriety. Even if the troops themselves would have none of it, it may have been useful for them to think that at least the government believed its own justification for imperiling them.[24]

A Bureaucracy for Political Indoctrination

The generally nonaggressive nature of Samuel L. A. Marshall's *Outline* anticipated the conclusions many later drew from his *Men Against Fire*, that American soldiers did not fight out of a sense of patriotism or for an abstract ideology. At the time, however, other supporters of the program thought the *Outline*'s bare-bones approach was insufficient, and the orientation effort intensified throughout the first two years of mobilization and war.

It soon became apparent that the army's orientation program and other internal informational services required a bigger bureaucracy than the Morale Branch, which had been carrying out those duties since its re-creation in June 1940. In early 1942 the army grouped the information functions of the Morale Branch under a new Special Services Division. Under this name the army released Frank Capra's famous *Why We*

Fight films. Frederick H. Osborn, a successful businessman and a leader of the American Eugenics Society, was commissioned as a brigadier general to command the division.

The selection of a noted eugenicist to head Special Services (which had the task of puncturing Nazi claims of racial superiority) hearkened back to the army's citizenship training and racialist lectures at the War College in the 1920s. However, in 1940 Osborn was trying to distance American eugenics from Nazi racism, even claiming that the eugenic ideal rejected race and class bias. The eugenics movement had no discernable impact on the content of Special Services programs. In *The Story of American Freedom*, historian Eric Foner argued that World War II created a pluralistic and tolerant national mood, at least toward ethnic whites, that abjured the World War I era's drive to Americanize different ethnicities. As the nation confronted enemies espousing racist ideologies, racialist theories lost credibility in the scientific community, and the multiethnic rifle squad became a cliché of war movies. If Osborn reflected prewar army conservatism and white Anglo-Saxon homogeneity, Capra, the son of Italian immigrants, was more obviously representative of the division's personnel and product. Like the Roosevelt administration's civilian propaganda outlet, the Office of War Information (OWI), the military's internal information program attracted a healthy share of liberal writers, artists, and entertainers. These volunteers were committed to a patriotic battle against intolerance and prepared to push the broadly liberal definition of American war aims embodied in Roosevelt's Four Freedoms.[25]

In October 1943 the Troop Information and Education programs (often known as I&E or TI&E) were transferred from the Special Services Division to the newly created Information and Education Division. By the end of the war it had a staff of 281 personnel manning four branches: the Army Education Branch, the Research Branch, the Orientation Branch, and the Army Information Branch, with subdivisions of film, radio, and print media sections in the last.[26]

Dr. Samuel A. Stouffer, a sociologist, headed the Research Branch, which compiled studies on the attitudes of American soldiers and rated the effectiveness of the orientation material. Stouffer taught at the University of Chicago, where he had earned his doctorate in 1930, and used statistics and polls to analyze public attitudes. He had recently studied the drop in the rate of American marriages during the Depression and after the war would become president of both the American Association of Public Opinion Research and the American Sociological Society. Stouffer valued utility and guarded the integrity of his branch by insisting that the researchers be "close to policy but not make policy." He sought "free-flowing" meetings with the division's policymakers and encouraged his staff to develop personal contacts in all offices of the army and the War Department. His experience working for the National Resources Planning Board convinced him that academic researchers could work for the government only if they adopted the government's timetable as their own. Findings, he had learned, would only be of use while they were fresh. He therefore pushed the Research Branch to focus only on those areas of soldier opinion that the army was in a position to act on.[27]

The Education Branch was responsible for getting deficient soldiers up to the minimum educational standards required by their military occupation. The other branches were responsible for publishing army newspapers such as the daily *Stars and Stripes* and the weekly *Yank: The Army Weekly*, broadcasting radio shows, making orientation films, and developing lecture and pamphlet material.

By the end of the war *Stars and Stripes* published over a million copies a day in Europe and seventy thousand copies in the Pacific, while *Yank* published over two million copies a week overall. The division considered these papers to be "information" materials, designed to boost soldiers' morale by keeping them abreast of the news, rather than "orientation" material whose purpose was to adjust a soldier to his new life or influence his political attitudes. This distinction broke down early in the war when production of orientation films became the responsibility of the Information Branch. Soon the general term *information* applied to everything from a World Series radio broadcast to an anti-Nazi film. Indoctrination materials became known euphemistically as "Troop Information." Nevertheless, the division rarely used its most widely circulated items, the service newspapers, as vehicles for political indoctrination. In 1944, I&E officials fought off a plan to transfer control of *Stars and Stripes* to the army's Bureau of Public Relations, arguing that the paper properly supported morale rather than "propaganda."[28]

The I&E program relied on entertainers, writers, and publicists to reach its military audience. A bevy of Hollywood worthies staffed the film section, and civilian radio industry veterans manned the radio section. Arthur W. Page, American Telephone & Telegraph's vice president for public relations, acted as a civilian troubleshooter for Osborn's staff and had the ear of his longtime friend Secretary of War Henry L. Stimson. Writers as diverse as William L. Shirer (known for his reports from Berlin from 1938–40), Theodore Geisel (later famous as Dr. Seuss), and the aforementioned S. L. A. Marshall lent their talents to the information effort. Only late in the war did the War Department establish an Army Information School at Carlisle Barracks, Carlisle, Pennsylvania, to train information officers.[29]

To counsel personnel charged with I&E duty the Information Branch produced a *Guide to the Use of Information Materials*. For the benefit of army broadcasters, news editors, and discussion leaders the *Guide* described the preferred way to handle the presentation, tone, and substance of a host of items that might affect the political beliefs of soldiers, or as the authors called them "opinion forming elements."

The first sentence of the *Guide* stated unequivocally that the first principle of American information was that it be the truth. The second sentence immediately acknowledged the limits of this commitment: "But, as in all other matters pertaining to security in wartime, common sense must be exercised, and common sense is action according to circumstances and not according to rules." By the second paragraph the authors of the *Guide* were struggling to reconcile their first principle to the requirements of propaganda work: "Truth becomes falsehood unless it has the strength of perspective."[30]

Here was one of the basic problems facing an I&E program: how to go about indoctrinating soldiers with an exclusively tailored set of opinions when the freedom to hold and express different opinions stood so high among the propagandists' and the soldiers' core political values. Despite the questionable dedication to truthfulness the World War II–era *Guide* was notable for its frankness in discussing the indoctrination method. This is especially apparent when they are compared to later guide books, produced after the Cold War paradigm assigned the words *propaganda* and *indoctrination* to the communist enemy.

Allies were not to be criticized for any military failing or cultural difference: "Let us say less until we have done more." Similarly, the fighting power of the enemy was to be respected because experience in World War I indicated that troops who thought they faced high-quality German units fought better than those who thought they were up against weak forces. Information specialists were not, however, permitted to use the enemy's own colorful, impressive names for their equipment and units, except for the terms *panzer* and *Luftwaffe*, cases in which people's vocabularies were already set (10, 21).

To emphasize the totality of America's war effort policy required that army information give no serious attention to tentative peace offers short of unconditional surrender. Likewise, no Allied military action was to be described as a "reprisal" or revenge: "In war's new testament, if your enemy shoots your toe, you shoot his head" (6).

Claiming that Americans in World War I concentrated so much of their antagonism on Kaiser Wilhelm II that they had no wariness left for the German people after the war, the *Guide* advised that criticism of the enemy heads of state be broadened to include the entirety of enemy society. American soldiers were not to think that only leaders started wars or that enemy soldiers were just regular fellows like themselves who had been forced into harm's way. Even in the 1944 edition of the manual, after Italy's surrender, army information policy guarded against sympathy for the people of Italy until they had made a material contribution to Allied victory (10).

On issues touching the home front, information personnel were encouraged to treat all questions of race and national origin with an even hand. In practice this meant that discussion leaders, editors, and broadcasters would not use offensive terminology or indulge in racial stereotyping, but would also take care not to offend racist sensibilities by challenging segregation in the armed forces or in American society.

On the subject of American politics, policy scrupulously tried to avoid charges of interference in the democratic process. Any political party that fielded a candidate in at least six states was entitled, theoretically, to equal time and treatment in army informational materials. In 1944 the Democratic, Republican, Prohibition, Socialist, and Socialist-Labor parties met this requirement (7). In the postwar era, however, the armed forces extended equal treatment only to the two major parties and dropped all mention of minor parties.

Far left parties at home may have received some minimal protection, but policy concerning the treatment of the Soviet Union's political system was a trickier matter. Here the need to build confidence in major allies clashed with the ideological stance of the information materials. The *Guide* argued that "It is not necessary or desirable to defend communism in order to enlist the sympathetic interest of the American soldier in the defense of the USSR." The best thing to do was to avoid the subject of communism when possible. To explain the Soviet Union's 1939 attacks on Finland and Poland the *Guide* advised information officers to stress the resulting military situation. "Without attempting any moral judgments on the matter," it concluded, "it is enough to state the military fact that had the USSR not acted so, the Allied cause would be weaker today" (20).

The most explicit and revealing passages in the *Guide* fall under the heading "Indoctrination of Hatred." The authors explain to the information disseminators that the question of indoctrinating hatred of the enemy must be considered a practical training issue, not a moral one. "Since killing is the primary means by which the enemy is compelled to submit to one's own discipline, one of the ends of training must be to so indoctrinate the soldier that he is not only willing but anxious to work bodily destruction upon the foes of his country. That state of mind is not possible unless the soldier is motivated by hatred in the hour when he is at grips with the enemy" (12). Nevertheless, hatred was not an end unto itself. Passions ought not be inflamed to a point where they could not be sustained. Therefore it would have been "reckless" to use a great deal of harsh invective to stimulate emotions. Better simply to build up a soldier's confidence in his own cause and then allow hatred to come through naturally when the actions of the enemy were presented. For example, the "military murder of [James H.] Doolittle's fliers" (i.e., those air men executed after being captured during the air raid on Tokyo on April 18, 1942) was more useful in making "the name of the Japanese army stink" than any elaboration on the subject could. "It is part of our business as soldiers to see that the rank and file of the United States Army do not forget" such incidents. To that end information personnel were instructed to make use of "Horror Pictures and Stories," so long as they could be authenticated and had some relevance to the situation facing the soldiers. As a useful example the *Guide* suggested that pictures of "emaciated Greek civilians, either dead or dying from enforced starvation" had immensely greater value than any dry recitation of statistics describing the German attempts to shut off food shipments to Greece (12).

The Research Branch found that despite military and civilian propaganda, hatred of the enemy cultivated in American soldiers was superficial, especially in comparison to the genuine vindictiveness harbored by British, French, and Soviet soldiers, all of whose countries had suffered German attacks. Even though soldiers were sometimes motivated by hatred it ranked as at best a tertiary factor in the will to fight. Both prayer and the thought that "you couldn't let the other men down" stood higher among servicemen's motivating forces.[31]

The absence of vindictiveness was consistent with what the Research Branch described as Americans' relatively low level of personal commitment to the war. Americans were willing to do their part—but only their part. American GIs in World War II were reluctant, at the outset, to make the war their own. They tended to see it as a "detour" rather than the central event of their lives, especially with economic opportunities beckoning as the nation emerged from the Great Depression. For many the "total" nature of the war justified their involvement, but only in so much as it called for their "fair share" of the work. The troops' overwhelming confidence in ultimate victory abetted this limited sense of commitment.[32]

The burden of replacing this emotional distance with anxiousness "to work bodily destruction" fell to the unit commanders through the devices of lectures and discussion sessions. Immediately, the program encountered the problems that plagued Troop Information throughout its history. First, the restrictions of army life sometimes seemed to stand in direct contradiction to propaganda about the blessings of freedom and democracy. Perhaps worse, a large number of commanders considered lecturing on world politics a waste of time and ignored the instruction to hold weekly sessions. In the Burma-India theater, for example, only one unit out of thirty-five surveyed in March 1945 was holding the scheduled meetings. In an April 1945 survey of fifty-seven units in Europe, only thirteen reported that orientation meetings were held once a week, and nineteen reported that they had not held a session in over three months. When the Special Services Division dispatched Arthur W. Page, AT&T's public relations specialist, to England to help with Troop Information for the invasion of France, he encountered resistance from officers reluctant to hold the sessions. When he visited liberated Paris in February 1945 he still found commanders avoiding their I&E duties. Despite reports such as these, as well as anecdotal evidence that front-line soldiers never received the programs, the Research Branch's studies indicated that a unit's combat or noncombat status did not influence the frequency of discussions.[33]

Some of those who did conduct the sessions read aloud the preparatory material word for word, without adapting it for presentation, or at high speed in order to dispose of the requirement as quickly as possible. Commonly, the commander passed off the nuisance duty to an officer for whom he had little other use. One infantry regiment commander later associated with the program recalled that "The yard-stick in many units for an I&E officer was—if he couldn't be used for anything else—there wasn't a balloon officer or they would have made him that—but if he couldn't run a mess, he couldn't fight a company, or platoon, if he couldn't handle a supply, if he couldn't count socks, why they said 'that's just the man for I&E.'"[34] The result was often a decrease in both physical and mental attendance, a phenomenon that might be termed "the substitute teacher effect."

The pamphlets produced for soldiers in support of the program were likely of little help to commanders trying to win soldiers' hearts and minds. The army pitched these pocket-sized booklets to the lowest common intellectual denominator. Textually simplistic, their value was in their colorful graphics and straightforward messages. One such pamphlet was *Invisible Weapon*, written to convince soldiers that the Lend-Lease agreement was not an American charity for greedy allies. On the first page were silhouettes of pistols and rifles and a caption suggesting that while the soldier knows what these things are the United States has another weapon too. Page two read: "Another very powerful weapon which is INVISIBLE because it's an IDEA." Page three asked, "What is the BIG IDEA?" Page four answered: "It's LEND-LEASE." Page five had a cartoon of a man gleefully emptying a safe full of cash. "Is Lend-Lease this? . . . NO." Turning the page explained what Lend-Lease was. "IT'S THIS!": a bulbous cartoon fist smashing Hitler's face.[35] This graphic argument was unlikely to impress any servicemen who were politically sophisticated enough to harbor doubts about Lend-Lease. Neither the lectures nor the pamphlets provided the sort of effective indoctrination the army wanted. With the chief of staff George C. Marshall's blessing, Osborn's division made its major effort with film.

Why We Fight

When the army transferred volunteer Frank Capra from the Signal Corps to the head of the film section of the newly formed Morale Branch, the famous Hollywood filmmaker asked his new superiors if he was "in the propaganda headquarters of the U.S. Army?" His commander informed him that while *propaganda* was a dirty word to the public, his mission to explain the "why" of the war was indeed far more serious than the Morale Branch's "innocent façade" would suggest. Despite the fact that he had always regarded documentaries as "ashcan films made by kooks with long hair," Capra pledged that the army's new political indoctrination films would be "the best ever made."[36]

Control of filmmaking in the army belonged to the Signal Corps, whose main facilities were located in Astoria, New York. The Signal Corps greeted the arrival of Capra and other Hollywood soldiers with all the enthusiasm one might expect of an entrenched bureaucracy threatened with a hostile takeover. The system in Astoria was geared to make simple technical training films on subjects such as cleaning rifles and dressing wounds. The chief of staff knew the passionate, argumentative films he wanted to show America's young soldiers required different talents. Capra, for his part, believed "It would have been stupid, if not disloyal, to allow the inspirational *Why We Fight* films to be made by Signal Corps colonels to whom soldiers were 'bodies'; colonels who were automatically hostile to the power of ideas."[37]

One idea Capra had was to survey new soldiers about their most urgent questions and film President Roosevelt speaking directly to those issues. Roosevelt agreed to appear, if the filmmakers could learn what the recruits wanted to hear from him. The Research Division dispatched pollsters to gather the data, but ultimately Capra's team decided to let the enemy do the talking. The main strategy of his films would be to use the enemies' own words against them. There was widespread agreement throughout the information program that the Nazis' own utterances were a rich source of ammunition. Of his preinvasion indoctrination work, Page said, "we took things Hitler had said and explained them in G.I. language." To this same end Capra purchased civilian newsreels from New York's Pathé News, managed to win from an unhappy Signal Corps jurisdictional control of the Department of the Treasury's collection of enemy newsreels, and moved the lot of them into a cooling tower belonging to the Department of the Interior. On May 2, 1942, the army styled the director's unit the 834th Photo Signal Detachment of the Signal Corps and placed it under command of the chief of the Special Services Division to resolve the problem of multiple commands claiming control of film. When the operation outgrew the Washington DC cooling tower, the Special Services Division permitted the film section to move to the more conducive filmmaking environment of Los Angeles, California.[38]

Propagandists are often among the most thoroughly indoctrinated in the ideals they espouse. Studio talent alone could not produce effective films for military use, as such brilliant filmmakers as Ernst Lubitsch and John Huston discovered when they tried their hands at it. A large part of what made the *Why We Fight* series successful was Capra's genuine confidence in both the American people and the rectitude of the unfettered, enterprising American spirit. Some of his most memorable commercial films, such as 1939's *Mr. Smith Goes to Washington* or 1941's *Meet John Doe*, depicted people who overcome selfishness to affirm that which is best in their natures. *Why We Fight* similarly urged Americans to put aside the lure of isolationism to act in the common and righteous interest. Capra's own rise from a family of financially struggling Sicilian immigrants to the Hollywood marquee was to him proof enough of the validity of the American Dream. His ability to overcome an audience's resistance to sentimentality made Capra the perfect artist to reach skeptical soldiers.[39]

All the more reason, then, that Capra's "confidence was murdered" when the script treatments he assigned to seven civilian Hollywood writers came back "larded with Communist propaganda." Capra fired the writers and started again, realizing that "the project was so sensitive that it could only be carried out by controllable men in uniform." In Hollywood Capra's motto had been "one man, one film." Naturally he chafed under the authority of military discipline. But the prospect of subversive scriptwriters made him an enthusiast of rank in no time. Someone with his experience in the film industry probably would not have accidentally hired actual communist writers. More likely, the first drafts did not match the level of stridency he wanted. Although their makers regarded the films as factual and informational, others thought *Why We Fight* overly manipulative.[40]

In October 1942 Capra and his superiors screened the newly completed first film in the series, titled *Prelude to War*, for the chief of staff. Marshall was impressed enough to warrant another screening, this time with the president in attendance. Roosevelt was likewise impressed. Marshall would say later that he ordered that no soldier leave the United States without seeing *Prelude to War*. To show the film in civilian theaters as well, the military had to overcome the trepidation of the civilian Office of War Information (OWI), which regarded *Why We Fight* as too propagandistic. Although both OWI and the Special Services Division drew on liberal writers and artists who believed "truth" was on their side, the OWI staff in the early part of the war was more resolute in its insistence that it did not indulge in propaganda. As historian Allan Winkler has argued, the agency's idealism eventually bowed to the cheerleading role demanded by the president in his pragmatic "Dr. Win the War" incarnation. Once the army got clearance to go public, approximately 45 million Americans in and out of uniform saw the first installment of *Why We Fight* (it won the Oscar for "Best Documentary" in 1942). The film is by no means invisible in modern scholarship, but given its unique exposure and effectiveness it is worthwhile to analyze *Prelude* in some detail to isolate the elements that separate it from the general run of indoctrination efforts.[41]

Prelude to War demands the immediate attention of the audience with martial bugles blaring over the opening credits and the disclaimer that, save for animated charts and maps, every image in the movie was authentic, whether from newsreels or captured enemy footage. The disclaimer was not entirely accurate. Scenes depicting the assassinations of Japanese moderate politicians were obviously reenactments, as were some others. And though Capra declared that he would hang the enemy with their own words, his team took many editorial liberties in grafting simplified translations of speeches and writings onto unrelated footage.

For example, Adolf Hitler, Benito Mussolini, and an unidentified Japanese demagogue are each depicted as shouting, "Stop thinking and follow me." The triple repetition was dramatically effective, but the narrator shifted from direct quotation to paraphrase without notifying the audience. In another scene Adm. Yamamoto Isoroku's warning that in order to best the United States it would be necessary to dictate peace terms in Washington was shorn of context and matched with a clip of Yamamoto speaking forcefully on a different subject. The sleight of hand sets up one of *Prelude*'s most chilling moments. "Yes," said the narrator over an image of marching Japanese troops superimposed on a picture of the Capitol, "the conquering Jap army down Pennsylvania Avenue, that's the ultimate goal," and after reminding the audience of the Rape of Nanjing, added "imagine the field day they'd enjoy marching through the streets of Warshington."[42]

The voice belonged to actor Walter Huston, who narrated most of the *Why We Fight* series. Huston displayed easygoing warmth, good comic timing, and a deadpan sarcasm, which made him sound more like an in-the-know co-conspirator than a preachy advocate. Throughout, his spoken text and Alfred Newman's score supported the visual imagery adroitly. Newman used classical selections of proven potency as well as familiar, traditional music to manipulate the audience's emotions. For instance, whenever the film returned to America, Newman represented the United States with bright, cheerful, optimistic music, while martial drum beats announced subjects pertaining to the Axis powers.

The producers employed a subtle technique in the narration by substituting a second voice for Huston's, that of scriptwriter Anthony Veiller, at two key moments. One was an accelerated rundown of the enemies' control of print and broadcasting in their respective countries; and the other was the voice-over during the main animated map sequence. Veiller spoke in a sharp, clipped staccato in contrast to Huston, who had already established himself as the audience's guide through the film. The second voice removed the selected portions of the film to a seemingly reportorial level, as if this new information was coming from another, more authentic or credible source.

Walt Disney Productions supplied the animation for the map sequence, which pictured the Axis powers as a liquid darkness engulfing different neighbors as Veiller outlined their plans of conquest. The black shading overran each continent at a quickening pace until it stood poised to pour into North America from both the Pacific and the Atlantic. There, said Veiller in one of the series' crasser moments, the Germans would link up with "their buck-toothed pals" and divide the Americas between them.

The bigoted description was out of step with the general tone of *Prelude to War*. Even so, the filmmakers were not reluctant to make negative generalizations about enemy peoples. *Prelude* described Germans, for example, as having "an inborn national love of regimentation and harsh discipline." *Why We Fight* portrayed enemy people not as victims but as contemptible agents who eagerly "threw away their human dignity, gave up their rights, and became part of a mass, a human herd." As the *Guide to the Use of Informational Materials* suggested, the series attempted to make it clear that enemy soldiers were not objects of sympathy nor were the civilians in enemy nations innocents to be pitied. As John W. Dower pointed out in his 1986 book *War Without Mercy: Race and Power in the Pacific War*, the government especially adhered to this characterization in the portrayal of the Japanese.[43]

Another tactic used to group enemy peoples unsympathetically unfolded in the film's treatment of children. *Prelude* depicted children in Germany, Italy, and Japan as goose-stepping young automatons in training. Many scenes featured uniformed children marching, drilling, saluting, and practicing military skills. These images were contrasted with those of American children ("kids" in the language of the film) playing on swings and slides and, ironically, contributing their pennies to help Japanese earthquake victims, the very children preparing to kill them. Twice, scenes of martially appointed children dissolved into scenes of grown men executing the same drills and activities.

Nor were mothers eligible for any chivalric sentiment the American soldier might have left. Women, according to the series, were also part of the enemy's massive war machine. They were married en masse and set to the task of producing as many warriors as they could bear.

One rationale for indoctrinating hatred of a people rather than of a leader was that the war would likely have continued even if Hitler or Premier Tojo Hideki had suddenly died, so a focus on leaders could have given soldiers false hope in easy routes to victory. Another advantage of painting with a broad brush was simplicity. In the effort to produce soldiers anxious to work bodily harm, the army did not wish to introduce conflicting ideas or concepts that had multiple valid interpretations. *Prelude to War* tried to draw the lines as starkly as possible at the outset with a quotation from Vice President Henry A. Wallace, stating that the struggle was between the "slave world" and the "free world." The film represented the two ideological camps with a pair of globes, one a glowing white (showing the western hemisphere) and the other a dull black (showing the eastern hemisphere). Individual freedoms and Christian values characterized the free world. To keep dual appeals to political freedom and religious tradition from tripping over one another, the script merged them into a single creed of pious democracy. The film identified "Christ" as the principal historical proponent of freedom, at the head of a table that also included Muhammad, Simón Bolívar, and Abraham Lincoln.

Nor were the filmmakers inclined to dilute the description of the threat to Christianity-Democracy by dwelling much on the Nazis' all-consuming hatred of the Jews. They depicted the Nazi attack on religion wholly in terms of its conflict with Christian churches. In one sequence from *Prelude to War* bricks smashed through a church's stained-glass window, "the last obstacle" to tyranny, to reveal a poster of Hitler behind it. Capra and his team assumed that showing Nazi effrontery toward Christianity was a surer way to inflame passions than mentioning the more thoroughgoing attack against Jews and communists, whom the Nazis had identified as their primary foes.

Although the filmmakers were unaware of the full extent of Germany's horrific extermination campaign, the Nazis' special animus toward Jews was well known. In a montage of headlines announcing the silencing of German religious leaders, only one rabbi was visible in a lengthy series of priests and pastors. Perhaps because they feared an anti-Semitic backlash from their viewers, the scriptwriters risked only small gestures such as these to build common cause between Christian and Jewish allies.

Like the filmmakers, authors of OWI materials and writers for army publications alike hesitated to test their theme of democratic pluralism against public anti-Semitism. Joseph W. Bendersky found that even at the end of the war editors of *Yank: The Army Weekly* and *Stars and Stripes* preferred German atrocity stories with unspecified victims: "Conspicuous by its absence in these stories and editorials was the word 'Jew.' One could not detect the slightest hint that Jews had been the prime target of Nazi genocide or indeed that they had been victims at all." In the wake of victory in Europe 51 percent of American soldiers surveyed agreed that Hitler "did do Germany a lot of good before the war," and 22 percent thought "Germans had some good reasons 'for being down on the Jews.'" American propagandists were willing enough to engineer citizens' opinions about the purpose of the war, but ethnic, racial, or religious prejudices were not among their priority targets.[44]

For Americans general knowledge of Nazi anti-Semitism did not suggest the Nazi-Jewish struggle was central to the war. When the western Allies overran the concentration camps of Buchenwald and Dachau in Germany in 1945, Gen. Dwight D. Eisenhower took the opportunity for some spontaneous indoctrination. He ordered available U.S. troops to tour the camps along with journalists and civilian officials. His aim was both to establish witnesses to Germany's crimes and to remind the soldiers what they were fighting against. The experience tended to reinforce the diversity of Nazi depravity rather than its fixation on Jews. The western camps contained prisoners from all over Europe, held on political as well as racial grounds. The camps whose main purpose had been the annihilation of the Jews were in the east, and hence liberated by the Soviets. In *The Holocaust in American Life*, Peter Novick argued that for most Americans the Nazis' mass murder did not crystallize as an event directed primarily against Jews until the 1961 trial in Israel of one of its architects, Adolf Eichmann. Even after the war, then, the information program made little use of some of the enemy's most repulsive ideas.[45]

Prelude had purposes beyond painting the enemy unsympatheti-cally. Another theme that Capra promoted was American internation-alism. Disarming any lingering isolationists in the audience called for a light touch rather than a heavy hand. To this end the director made excellent use of a 1939 Pathé Opinion Poll newsreel asking the "per-son in the street" whether the United States ought to get involved in a European war. The responses were nearly all in the negative. Some of the naysayers could be interpreted as ethnic stereotypes (especially one man with a heavy Brooklyn accent), others the viewer may have assumed were white middle-class Protestants. In any case none of the respondents are shown to their advantage; Capra makes them objects of gentle fun.

Isolationism was not stupid or evil, the film suggested, but just the natural, if wrong-headed, stance of the live-and-let-live American whom the film calls "John Q. Public." Subtly, as the narrator derides America's reluctance to get involved in Europe, the filmmakers insert a fleeting clip of a Barnard College antiwar rally. As Barnard was a women's college, the film instantly associated isolationism with femininity. In general, however, *Prelude* eschewed the accusatory *you* and adopted the blame-sharing *we* when depicting American isolationism and antiwar senti-ment, as in "We turned our backs on the League of Nations."

These controversial issues involved the army in a realm it tradition-ally and properly sought to avoid: advocacy of positions still in dispute in American politics. Certainly those on the outside of the New Deal alliance that swept Franklin D. Roosevelt to second and third terms in 1936 and 1940 would find much to disagree with in *Prelude*'s asser-tion that America dealt with the Depression in a completely positive, democratic way. The film heaped praise on the Civilian Conservation Corps, the Social Security Act, and the Public Works Administration and sneered at the "farce of Prohibition." All were endorsements of the policies of the sitting administration.

Its concern for such specific issues was only one of many features that made *Prelude to War* so sharp a contrast to the world's most fa-mous propaganda film, Leni Riefenstahl's film of the 1934 Nazi party rally in Nuremberg, *Triumph of the Will*. Capra's film was packed with pyrotechnics, humor, quick cuts, busy imagery, and sudden mood shifts. His Hollywood tenure taught him that faster was always better. The orientation films he directed and produced have the pacing and the crammed-screen look to satisfy an audience with a short attention span. *Triumph of the Will*, conversely, attempted to mesmerize its audience with striking images of power displayed in long shots of masses of people marching, working, and listening to speeches.

Capra watched *Triumph* before commencing work on the *Why We Fight* series.[46] In his effort to use the enemy's own words against him, he lifted several shots from *Triumph* for *Prelude*. The Nazi leaders whom Riefenstahl dignified in her film became frothing barbarians in their *Prelude* cameos. Wide shots of massive blocks of people that she used to impress her viewers become chilling scenes of regimentation in Capra's editing hands.

Finally, *Prelude to War* was notable for what it omitted. Capra downplayed the Japanese attack on Pearl Harbor, the most convenient touchstone for American war spirit. The filmmakers may have been afraid of lessening the impact of a self-explanatory event by trying to milk more outrage out of it. Another explanation might be that the army wanted to minimize the Pacific War in order to focus the troops on its preferred "Europe first" strategy.

In other cases the filmmakers wisely made no attempt to enlarge questionable offenses or to defend unsavory actions when they had better ammunition to choose from. Hence, they made no mention of incidents in the Battle of the Atlantic, where the United States pursued an aggressive brand of nonbelligerency. Nor was there any attempt to defend, or even any mention of, the Soviet Union's opportunistic 1939 nonaggression pact with Germany. Building confidence in the Russian allies would require a separate film.

The next two films in the series, *The Nazis Strike* and *Divide and Conquer*, continued the portrayal of the enemy established by *Prelude*. These sequels were less directly argumentative in tone. They took for granted the audience's acceptance that the material presented was a recitation of objective facts. Capra moved into a supervisory role (to concentrate on his next directorial effort, the sixth film in the *Why We Fight* series, *The Battle of China*), and others took their turns in the director's chair. The change was apparent in some clumsy moments, as when in the middle of *Divide and Conquer* the film cuts to a briefing by a stiff army intelligence officer.[47]

The Battle of Britain, the two-part *Battle of Russia*, and *The Battle of China* enlarged on themes introduced by *Prelude to War*, with descriptions of the Allied peoples' bravery being paramount. *The Battle of China* contained the harshest visual images of the entire series, especially those depicting the Rape of Nanjing. In December 1937 Japanese soldiers forced their way into the Chinese city of Nanjing and committed atrocities that claimed the lives of between 100,000 and 350,000 people.[48] The film showed Japanese troops executing two prisoners and conducting a mass burial of civilian victims. It also showed the corpses of Chinese children and the grossly wounded bodies of survivors. Although graphic, the footage was still an understatement of the subject matter. The last film, *The War Comes to America*, recapped the series with a special emphasis on America's road to war as a fait accompli. But by the time it was completed America had already come to the war, and the debate over abstention from Europe's conflicts was a receding memory.[49]

Capra's Captive Audience

The army's Military History Institute has surveyed thousands of veterans, mostly from World War II and the Korean War, about their wartime experiences. Although the respondents were asked to examine events decades old, many retained a sharp memory for the details of what for most was one of the great upheavals of their lives. The institute's lengthy, open-ended World War II survey asked veterans specifically for their reaction to the *Why We Fight* films. Most respondents never saw or did not remember seeing the films. Certainly, the Special Services Division's dissemination of its films was far from complete; many soldiers probably never did see them. At the same time, many others likely saw I&E films before embarking on far more vivid, and possibly traumatic, experiences, so it is not surprising that the details of their training, political or otherwise, faded from memory. Moreover, the fact that veterans forgot elements of the Information and Education program does not prove that it was inconsequential or ineffectual. It might mean instead that the program worked subtly enough not to be an irritant to most soldiers.

Capra's movies, however, were vivid enough to excite comment from many veterans. Most of those who liked the films did so for more than their entertainment value. A soldier in the Second Armored Division called them "entertaining, educational, and motivational." A 1943 draftee who saw the whole series noted that it "sure inspired me to help in the war effort." James H. Cornell, who volunteered at age twenty because he "wanted to be part of something so important," fought in the Hurtgen Forest and was captured during the Battle of the Bulge. He found *Why We Fight* "interesting and informative. Inspiring for young minds." Reynold W. Ross, inducted at age twenty-seven a month after Pearl Harbor, noted that the films "provided a training break," but also "pointed to things people tend to forget." As a prewar draftee, Corp. Thomas Molle was part of *Why We Fight*'s original target audience. He approved of the film because he "felt it was necessary to show why we had to take sides."[50]

Respondents did not limit their positive reviews to their original recollections of it. "Excellent series, very professional," commented one veteran, "until today I was/am impressed by [the] series." An antiaircraft artillerist called the films "very timely and informative (I now have a copy on video tape)." The motivational intent of the films was not lost on the veterans who recalled them favorably (even though, at the time, the Research Branch found that most viewers did not realize *Why We Fight* was a device of persuasion). A veteran who served at Maxwell Air Force Base in Alabama during the war characterized *Why We Fight* as a "good promotional film to keep soldiers focused on their purpose." For John Schell, who enlisted in 1942 because at age eighteen he was already "tired of the stares from men in service," the series "served as motivation—idealistic, but good." Roger Lee Farrand, an eighteen-year-old volunteer in 1943, remembered that the films "reinforced all other propaganda and proved totally convincing."[51]

Others found the practice of celluloid indoctrination more problematic. Some, like George P. Nestor, an officer in the Twenty-sixth Regiment of the First Division, considered the whole effort a "waste of time, money, and men." Most of the critical veterans, however, based their objection on the film's status as "propaganda." One 1943 draftee who went on to serve in the First Division called the films simply "a big spread of propaganda." "It was a real Hollywood 'propaganda' special," said artillerist Russell Davidson, who equated *Why We Fight* with the patriotic fare the film industry cranked out for the home front. Wilbur D. Cook, drafted at age eighteen in time to see action in Germany toward the end of the war, thought the men had been "taught to hate in order to fight" by the films.[52]

Respondents from the segregated army's black Ninety-second Division had obvious reason to be skeptical of Capra's glorification of American democracy and to object to the films' implicit defense of the status quo. Capt. Rufus Winfield Johnson, who taught classes for men seeking civilian job skills (the education half of I&E), tried to offer his troops a "translation" of the films to which they could relate. Otherwise, he doubted they were "meaningful to Negro soldiers deprived of their rights at home." Indeed, *Why We Fight* failed to impress Pvt. Edgar Piggott, for whom it was just "another training film," or Sgt. Emeral E. Hayden, who dismissed it as "propaganda." Willard F. Harper, who volunteered as a college sophomore, described his reaction as "passive, because I knew it was for propaganda purposes to incite the soldiers to fight the 'Japs' and 'Germans.'"[53]

Propaganda on the Air

Just as the Special Services Division recognized early on that it might effectively use film to convey its message, it also seized the opportunity to broadcast Troop Information material over the radio. Arthur W. Page joined officials of the J. Walter Thompson advertising firm, the Columbia Broadcasting System (CBS), and General Foods (a major sponsor of radio programming) on a subcommittee of the Joint Army-Navy Committee on Welfare and Recreation to plan troop information and entertainment on the radio. In November 1942 the Allies invaded North Africa to dislodge the occupying German forces. On December 15, within a month of the commencement of the operation, the army began broadcasts from the "American Expeditionary Station" in Casablanca. On the first anniversary of these initial broadcasts, the army formally organized the radio effort as the Armed Forces Radio Service (AFRS) with headquarters established in Los Angeles, California. AFRS's mission was to provide information and entertainment to United

States soldiers. In the intervening year the government had erected two powerful transmitters, one in Los Angeles for shortwave broadcasts to Alaska and the South Pacific, and another in New York City to transmit shortwave signals to Europe. By the end of the war AFRS operated 177 transmitters and broadcast over 54 foreign stations. On October 14, 1944, AFRS was classified as a joint activity of the army and the navy, although its staff of forty-four remained under the army's Information and Education Division.[54]

With the establishment of AFRS a propaganda battle for the mind of the American soldier was joined over the air. Troop Information conveyed via radio no doubt made less of an impact than that contained in films but still offered advantages over pamphlets and lecture-discussion sessions. Professional entertainers created and performed both orientation films and radio programs, whereas lectures were delivered by officers who earned that duty by virtue of rank rather than charisma. Radio, like films and later television, made fewer demands on its audience.

Despite having less visceral impact on the audience, radio should not be seen as simply an inferior medium to film, that is, sound without picture. The 1930s and 1940s were American radio's "golden age." Americans listened to music, drama, sports, comedy, and adventure shows on radio. They were also accustomed to the radio as a medium for news and political argument. Roosevelt famously broadcast "fireside chats" to rally support for his administration's agenda. The medium therefore lent itself to indoctrination work in important ways. Radio information programs were easier to produce than films or pamphlets. Filmmaking required large studios, sets, cameras, and editing equipment. To screen the movies a unit needed access to a movie theater or to a projector and screen. Pamphlets and posters had to be typeset, printed, and shipped, often overseas. Radio shows, dependent only on preexisting broadcasting equipment, a studio mike, and the imaginations of listeners, could be hurried from script to the airwaves in less time and at less expense than it to took to deploy the other media. For example, a "commentator"-type information program, with no music or sound effects, could be readied in a single day.[55]

Because of the lack of physical restraints on broadcasting, radio outstripped other forms of propaganda when it came to reaching troops overseas. The continued use of Voice of America to influence allies and enemies well into the late twentieth century testifies to this efficiency.[56] Still, in World War II, radios remained somewhat scarce and bulky items. Furthermore, if all that was required of the audience was passive reception, then the broadcasters had no means to compel troops to listen in. Unlike the screening of an orientation film or the presentation of a Troop Information lecture, radio shows were not discrete events with mandatory attendance, but were instead crafted to fill the soldiers' spare hours, to be stumbled upon voluntarily and hopefully to be insinuated, like soap operas, into the listener's routine.

In fact, radio soap operas went to war, just as Hollywood did. AFRS broadcast shows in the indoctrination effort in a soap-opera format, using actual professional soap-opera radio personalities. One AFRS series, *The Victory Front*, even featured the appropriately soap-operatic title *Life Can Be Beautiful.*

Life Can Be Beautiful related the story of elderly Papa David, a kind, wise, stereotypically Jewish man who owns a New York City second-hand bookshop, and his employees: bravely "crippled" lawyer Stephen Hamilton, and the main character, Chi Chi, an all-American girl (by which the producers meant a grown woman).[57]

Part One of *Life Can Be Beautiful* opened with ballpark-quality organ music and a message from actor Conrad Nagle ("speaking for the United States Government"), thanking the actors for their participation. Chi Chi is closing the bookstore when Trina, a meek refugee from the Nazi-occupied Netherlands, comes in. The Dutch girl timidly admits that she came in for a Bible and is amazed to find that Bibles can be sold openly and without fear in the United States. Chi Chi asks why Trina would have such fears. The refugee relates, with her initially halting English suddenly rising to the occasion, how the Dutch once enjoyed such freedoms but the Nazis have now eliminated them. Further, "cripples" and Jews have been taken to institutions and killed, and girls like Trina have suffered an unspeakable fate worse than death. These horrors shock Chi Chi, who realizes that under such a regime, Papa David and Stephen could be killed. Papa David is Jewish, she thinks aloud, but quickly adds, "of course I'm a Gentile," in order to allay any negative response from any parochial audience members. Again, Trina intimates that Chi Chi herself would not be killed but preserved for some other unspoken fate—the threat of sexual violation at the hands of the Nazi Huns was weighted with leaden obviousness.

The second through the fifth installments traced the course of Chi Chi's subsequent nightmare, in which Nazis do to America what they had done to the free nations of Europe. In her dream, Nazi undercover police stationed in America trick Chi Chi into admitting that Papa David sells Bibles. A squad of armed troopers occupies the bookstore, displaying weaponry and bad German accents.

Stephen, the lawyer, ineffectually quotes the rights Americans possess under the German Occupation Treaty, to which the German commander replies with mocking laughter. Both Stephen's physical disability and his designation as a lawyer link his faith in treaties with the weakness and naiveté personified by former British prime minister Neville Chamberlain, who had tried to limit German territorial ambitions with a strategy of appeasement.

Chi Chi is forced to cook for the Nazi chief as a prelude to her sexual enslavement. Finally, the bullying commander confronts the entire bookshop group, and in deference to traditional villains' etiquette explains at length why the Germans were able to conquer the Americans. His themes: Americans think too much and love their individuality to a fault. The Germans had the advantage of unity. Because they were not of one mind regarding the war Americans let isolationists distract them, failed to take the threat seriously, and did not buy enough war bonds, leading the country to ruin.

The long-winded German commander is too broadly drawn a caricature, especially in his chortles over his wicked plans, to convey any real menace or inspire hatred. Rather, the treatment suggests that German commanders were oafish figures not to be taken seriously. When he finally delivers his speech about why America lost, the transition from drama to "message" is all too apparent. Furthermore, the dialogue and pacing of *Life Can Be Beautiful* made it immediately identifiable as a soap opera. Possibly AFRS intended the show to target specific segments of the civilian population that formed soap operas' regular audience as well as soldiers.

One device used in *Life Can Be Beautiful* highlights the differences between the approaches and sensibilities of the radio shows and the *Why We Fight* films. The AFRS show used the time-honored technique of putting women in jeopardy, a popular method of inciting anger in World War I, but generally eschewed by Capra's unit.[58] In *Life Can Be Beautiful* the lustful enemies were waiting for their opportunity to invade America and rape the wives, daughters, girlfriends, and mothers of the servicemen. The threat to "their" women, also illustrated graphically in at least one wartime poster in which a diminutive Japanese soldier carries off a naked, white, blonde woman, might have been effective in eliciting outrage, even in the case of the cartoonish Chi Chi. The enemy-ravisher struck simultaneously at the welfare of loved ones, activated the soldier's chivalric obligation to defend helpless females, and threatened to emasculate him by possessing his woman. Perhaps the single most powerful motivation in the defense of one's "home" is the idea that one's wives, sisters, mothers, and daughters are the enemy's sexual quarry.

An element in the series that reflected more consistency with the film section's approach was the emphasis on the Nazis' hostility to Christianity. The offense of the bookstore owner was not, directly, that he was Jewish but that he was selling Bibles. By stressing the Bible the series linked the interests of Jewish and Christian Americans, without dramatizing the Nazis' defining anti-Semitism. By having the main character state explicitly that she was a Gentile, *Life Can Be Beautiful* suggested that the normal American protagonist was not Jewish but might safely support and interact with Jewish neighbors and fellow citizens. In this instance the show was bolder than the government's better-known propaganda outlets. The virtue of its approach was that it did not directly ask the audience for empathy that it might not have been prepared to offer. Instead, it somewhat obliquely introduced the idea of a workplace free of prejudice as a regular American occurrence.

Relying on the threat to Christianity was a strategy that not only helped to simplify the indoctrination message; it also revealed assumptions about what Americans truly held dear. The attack on the church struck not only at shared democratic political values but at Americans' private religious sensibilities. American propagandists in World War II did not lean exclusively on a democratic civic "creed" as a source of national identity. Robert B. Westbrook, in his essay "Fighting for the American Family: Private Interests and Political Obligation in World War II," argued that the nation's opinion makers recognized that Americans would not respond to a call "to work, fight, or die for their country as a political community." According to Westbrook the most compelling appeals were "to defend *private* interests and discharge *private* moral obligations." For example, in Norman Rockwell's popular illustrations of the "Four Freedoms" only the painting representing the freedom of speech (in which a man rises to speak at a meeting) depicted the political community. The illustrations of the freedom from want, freedom from fear, and freedom of worship offer scenes from the private sphere.[59]

Though the military's internal information program never completely steered clear of politicized appeals, it too converted abstract appeals into ones with more personal meanings to soldiers. Hence the simplest way to describe Hitler's political, racial, and ideological aims to Americans was to describe him as wanting to be worshipped like Christ or to replace or overthrow Christ. The implicit assumption was that arrogant blasphemy would provoke more outrage than totalitarian statism, notions of Aryan racial superiority, or ambitions of global domination.

Although "informing" soldiers was one of the main reasons for establishing AFRS, the broadcast day was by no means an unabated Troop Information bombardment. In practice the morale-building "entertainment" portion of its mission occupied the bulk of airtime. Among the more successful shows were *Command Performance*, *GI Jill*, *GI Journal*, *Juke Box U.S.A.*, *Jubilee*, *Mail Call*, *At Ease*, and *Sound Off*. Most were music shows. In the popular format of *Mail Call*, for example, servicemen's stateside relatives sent letters in to the station requesting particular songs. The disc jockey would read selected letters and play the requests.

One cannot entirely separate the information mission from the entertainment mission because, like *Life Can Be Beautiful*, much of the Troop Information material for AFRS was part of a library of entertaining items for station managers to draw from, in contrast to the lecture pamphlets and orientation films that the specific, discrete information sessions used. Because soldiers did not typically write in and request more war orientation shows, one must turn again to veterans' surveys to examine how the orientation program in its various media was received.

Soldiers' Reactions to Troop Information

"I'm not sure what those were," answered one World War II chaplain when asked for his opinion on the army's Troop Information programs. The response was not atypical. Thomas Deming of the Tenth Mountain Division remembered I&E as "Poor. Seems as if it never existed." The program was "SNAFU most of the time," agreed a fellow mountaineer.[60]

Before the set-piece landings on the Normandy beaches, U.S. information czars had sufficient time to plan troop information for the invasion forces. Osborn sent Arthur W. Page as a civilian advisor to Col. Oscar N. Sorbert, the morale chief for the European Theater of Operations (ETO). Page and Sorbert coordinated I&E session topics to match carefully timed news releases and noted that soldiers' attention to the program increased as D-Day drew nearer. Once the invasion commenced, however, such precision was no longer possible. The Research Branch's studies notwithstanding, after D-Day the Information and Education Division seemed to have difficulty reaching front-line units.[61]

According to Jesse A. Brewer, an officer of the Ninety-second Division, Troop Information was "Good in the U.S., poor overseas." A soldier who saw action in France and Germany reported that I&E "only trickled down to us on rare occasions," and a veteran of the North Africa campaign assumed that I&E "was just for rear echelon." Raymond C. Chariton's airbase on Guam simply did not have the facilities to support anything but a "very limited" Troop Information program. Another soldier in the Pacific theater recalled, "It wasn't until the end of the war that [we] ever received any of these programs." Northham Stolp of the Eighty-second Airborne Division summed up the opinion of many of his fellows when he concluded that I&E was "fair in non-combat situations—didn't have enough during combat—should have had more info to work from."[62]

Other veterans echoed Stolp's complaint about the dearth of information. To them, the information officers provided not oppressive or even irritating propaganda but a valuable link to the war's larger context.

[36]

Mark J. Alexander, another paratrooper, thought Troop Information inadequate and that more "would have helped morale of the troops." Attil A. Pasquini, a 1940 draftee who served in the Twenty-seventh Division, thought it was "Great, but we didn't see enough of it." For Leroy A. Lewis, official information in the Italian campaign was "Not really much of a factor," so his comrades "tried to furnish our own."[63]

Not everyone who wanted more information wanted the kind the orientation writers provided. Norris H. Perkins of the Second Armored Division had never heard of Troop Information but remembered that "any news dispatch was very eagerly read." George Nestor, the soldier who thought that *Why We Fight* was a "waste of time, money, and men," also claimed that the army did not give troops enough information. Given his opinion of the film, it is unlikely that Nestor would have wanted more nationalistic pamphlets, lectures, and films. Edgar Piggott, another viewer unmoved by Capra's productions, pointed to the type of knowledge some felt was lacking: "It helped to know who was next to you, and what was going on." A veteran from the Twenty-seventh Division thought Troop Information was "lousy" because each soldier only knew where his own unit was going. Asked if soldiers ever developed their own ways of finding out about their situation, ETO veteran Howard S. Hoffman replied, "Nope. Not that I know of. Nobody knew what the hell was going on. I mean we knew if we had to take a town or go into, you know, fire at a particular place, but we didn't have any idea of what the big picture was, other than that we're pushing for the Elbe River or we're pushing for crossing the . . . going into Rome, pushing for Rome, something like that. But no knowledge of the big picture; they never told us what the hell we were doing or even where we were." In *Men against Fire* S. L. A. Marshall argued that in order to function combat troops needed to be aware of the presence of their fellows. "Information," he wrote, "is the soul of morale in combat and the balancing force in successful tactics." This insight may have a corollary beyond the tactical level. Troops might have been comforted to know that their unit was not carrying an unusual burden and that there were large forces engaged to either side of them. Men like Nestor, Piggott, and Hoffman at least would have been more interested in progress reports than background on the war.[64]

The GI's thirst for information could evaporate in combat. Gerald Linderman has observed that for men at the front the war narrowed to their immediate circumstances. He relates a story of a Marine on Guadalcanal who informed his fellows of an Allied success in Europe, only to be met with bemused indifference. Even idealized images of home, strong motivators early in a tour, became emotionally distant memories as a soldier came to inhabit fully his life in the present. For the front-line troops who could not spare the mental investments required by homesickness or war news, more patriotic justifications emanating from the rear would have been unwelcome even if they had been forthcoming. "It is not that men would not have cared deeply about such things back home," John Ellis argued, "but simply that modern combat took *everything* out of a man so that his mind was entirely occupied with the problems of eating, drinking, staying awake and staying alive."[65]

The reactions of the men who had greater exposure to the Troop Information program ranged fully from hearty approval to curt dismissal. Albert C. Zerr, a 1945 volunteer at age thirty-one, "regarded as sacred" the utterances of the I&E Division. Merritt Bragdon, Joseph P. Ghilardi, and Francis J. Harnahan, young draftees in 1943, all rated Troop Information as "very good" or "informative," perhaps indicating that by the middle of the war the program was hitting its stride. However, these veterans saved their highest praise for the *Why We Fight* films. Bragdon called them "Very eloquent and convincing. I believed it and still do." In Ghilardi Capra's films evoked a feeling of "extreme patriotism." Harnahan reported that "The film made me feel that the duty that I was performing was necessary for millions of peoples' freedom."[66]

William F. Houser, who enlisted in 1940 and served twenty years, held the opposing view. Despite favoring universal military training and service Houser thought Troop Information a "waste of time and money." Russell Davidson, a veteran of the campaign in Europe, was more specific in his objection. Troop Information was "Too vague, too condescending, [and] too conservative." He also felt the army had not provided soldiers with "nearly enough" data on the histories of the countries to which they had been sent. A veteran from the Twentieth-seventh Division commented, "I personally thought 'our' love of Russia was overdone." His opinion echoed a complaint commonly leveled at the program in the early part of the Cold War.[67]

In his memoir, Lester Atwell, a private in the Eighty-seventh Division, related his German-American sergeant's angry reaction to the troop information film *Know Your Enemy*. "It had shown the German people, innocent to the eye, waltzing in their beer gardens; suddenly the waltz stopped and a cathedral was blown to bits. Every German was a spy and a sniper. . . . Sergeant Brauer said hotly in his Teutonic accent, 'I have seen that film many times and it is a lot of s—! I have one brother in the German Navy and two in the German Army. You think they are like that? That they wanted war? They are chust like us! Like you and me. People are the same all over, everywhere.'" While he believed "some of it" Atwell felt that "propaganda's always a little overdone."[68]

When Irving E. Pape, a veteran of the ETO, objected to "propaganda" he referred not to political characterizations but to exaggerations of American fighting power. He told interviewers from Rutgers University's World War II oral history project: "When we were first in training we were given a lot of propaganda films. Now propaganda can be the truth as well as the advertising puffery. One of the things that they told us was that 'You have the best weapons in the world. We're giving you the best weapons. We're giving you the best training.' Well, it turned out it wasn't quite so. The Germans had the best tanks. They had the best artillery in the 88, which was a fantastic weapon. We didn't have anything like that."[69]

Franklyn A. Johnson remembered getting his "comeuppance" at German hands in the battle of Kasserine Pass in North Africa in February 1943. He saw political and combat indoctrination serving the same end: "we had been told 'Well, you know, the American soldier, he's ten feet tall. We'll knock these Nazis off without any problems.' Well, that's good propaganda. You've got to hype up your soldiers, you know, and convince them that there's a bastard named Adolf Hitler over there, and we're going to get him . . . but we were not well enough trained for that job, up against experienced soldiers."[70]

Robert G. Theobaben, who served in the Pacific, was among the critics who thought political indoctrination did not go far enough. He remembered the information program at Camp Wheeler in Georgia:

Every Saturday we had a film—Why We Fight or Venereal Disease. In hindsight, I'd say we spent much more time on films associated with illicit sex than why we why should kill the Germans and the Japanese. Our political indoctrination was limited to a few films entitled The Rape of Nanking, Bataan Death March or German Blitzkrieg. I know Sergeant Simmons never gave us a lecture on politics and the war, and I cannot remember our second lieutenant doing it either. The army at that time presumed that if they taught a soldier how to fire a rifle and use the various weapons . . . he would use them that way in combat.

He contrasted American neglect of political motivation unfavorably with the attention Chinese communists paid it, but noted, "The VD films were a different thing. They were graphic, particularly on the consequences of syphilis and gonorrhea, and one could easily be persuaded that a life of celibacy was the only way to go. If the Army had put half the effort into political indoctrination that it put into keeping the soldiers celibate, we would have defeated the Japanese a year earlier."[71]

For Charles B. MacDonald, who commanded an infantry company in the ETO, the official pronouncements simply could not capture the purpose of the war. He managed to receive *Stars and Stripes* and the two-page mimeographs summarizing the Armed Forces Radio news from his division's Special Services. But it was not until he saw "the unleashed joy" of a crowd of liberated Czechs at the end of the war that he realized "what no one had thus far been able to put into words—what we were fighting for. And I found a lump in my throat which I could not swallow."[72]

Some soldiers were aware that the program operated under some logistical constraints. A veteran of the Battle of the Bulge and a former prisoner of war thought information specialists "Did as best they could," though the effort was "sometimes not good enough." An infantryman in the Twenty-eighth Division displayed awareness of the program's ideological constraints as well when he noted, "It was slanted, but they tried to let us know." Some men distinguished between the quality of the *Why We Fight* series and the rest of the orientation materials. Pvt. Loren Randall Tinker served in the Twenty-eighth Division during the war and served again in Germany in the mid-1950s. He thought *Why*

We Fight was a "great movie" but the rest of the program "poor." Stephen B. Morrissey, who enlisted in 1935 and later earned a commission out of West Point in 1940, thought the films influenced viewers to "respect and fear" the Germans and Japanese. He considered the larger orientation effort a good idea that was diminished by poor support from the chain of command (above the small unit level). However, it was more than command support that bothered Morrissey. He thought attempts to "motivate troops ideologically" failed because they did not "appeal to basic psychology."[73]

In *For Cause and Comrades*, James M. McPherson wrote that soldiers of the Civil War "needed no indoctrination lectures to explain what they were fighting for, no films like Frank Capra's 'Why We Fight' series in World War II." Compared with their Civil War counterparts, soldiers of the 1940s were seldom as voluble about their political motivations. Yet the U.S. Army in World War II did not lack men for whom patriotic exhortations "merely reinforced the ideas they had absorbed from the political culture in which they had grown up," just as they had done for McPherson's subjects.[74]

"I didn't need the propaganda!" insisted Northham Stolp. "I was way ahead of them and knew why! . . . we had to stop the Axis before they owned the world." Looking back on *Why We Fight* one 1943 volunteer said, "I did not need the film to inspire me—I had already made up my mind about dictators." Benjamin H. Feldman of the Tenth Mountain Division remembered that he "didn't have to be motivated" because as a patriotic twenty-six-year-old volunteer he "hated Nazis and Japs." Charles F. Stewart Jr. was likewise "ready to fight before I saw the film." In particular he "felt like he had a score to settle" with the Japanese. The way Charles R. Cawthon of the Twenty-ninth Division saw it, "In the ranks there was little of the 'Cheer, boys, cheer' and 'Rally 'round the flag.' The World War II soldier, on the whole, I believe, went to the battlefield more at the urging of duty and sober conviction. The challenge of Pearl Harbor was unqualified. The war grew out of a complex of political and economic conflicts, but for the soldier, it all boiled down to the fact that a mortal blow had been aimed at his country and survival was at stake."[75]

The attack on Pearl Harbor was not the only source of inspiration in the civilian political culture. "O! We were patriotic," wrote Carl M. Becker of his youth before being drafted to fight in the Pacific. "If our patriotism had flagged, my classmates and I could have taken our cue from our hometown." In the town in question, Miamisburg, Ohio, the newspapers, war workers, soldiers' parents, and war bond buyers made it plain that the community had gone to war. Joseph S. Sykes, who went into the army with his National Guard unit in 1940, was willing to fight because of his appraisal of German ambitions: "My father having come from England, I thought we waited too long to get involved. Hitler . . . was in dire danger of taking on the U.S. on *his* terms." Richard Mote, a paratrooper drafted at age eighteen, considered Troop Information to be entertaining propaganda. His schooling had convinced him that the Nazis posed a serious threat. "In the seventh grade I did a book report on *Mein Kampf*. I *knew* Hitler had to be crushed."[76]

The Research Branch was mindful that a soldier's "prior indoctrination" as a civilian might limit the Information and Education Division's influence on his attitudes. If one had heard antifascist messages in school or on the radio, hearing similar ones in an army camp might have no measurable effect. Furthermore, soldiers may have acquired in civilian life skeptical attitudes toward government-issue opinions. The Research Branch suggested, for instance, that overexposure to propaganda in World War I made Americans especially suspicious of internationalist arguments in the interwar years.[77]

Whatever effect World War I propaganda had on American attitudes toward war and peace, most World War II servicemen were too young to have any off-putting memories of it. Other experiences with civilian political indoctrination may have been more important. The Civilian Conservation Corps (CCC), created by the government to employ young men during the Great Depression, enrolled three million volunteers in the decade before the war. Once the United States entered the conflict the CCC's camps promptly emptied as the workers volunteered for military service or received their draft notices (Congress discontinued the program in 1942). Although the CCC planners tried scrupulously to ban military training and trappings from the camps, some similarities to service life were inevitable in sites administered directly by army officers. As in the army, enrollees lived communally in an all-male environment and performed demanding physical labor punctuated by daily parade ground assemblies and patriotic rituals. Camp education differed from the army's mandatory Troop Information and Education in its emphasis on reading, writing, and vocational skills and its lack of direct political argument. Classes and camp newspapers (which resembled service newspapers) stressed what one historian of the program called "CCC values and life lessons." At least the CCC introduced future servicemen to the experience of attending classes when weary from days of heavy work. Instructions provided to the program's "Education Advisors" even anticipated the tips given to army lecturers on avoiding controversial political arguments.[78]

The remarks of one career soldier suggest that some soldiers were motivated not by any specific indoctrination experience but by what political sociologists describe as "diffuse" political support. He was willing to fight, he said, not only because Japan attacked the United States but because he was "brought up to love my country." Indeed, this generalized loyalty, which did not depend on any particular national policy or leader, seemed a firmer bedrock for many soldiers' justification of the war than anything army propaganda could supply. The government even drew this generalized support from the citizens who had the least reason to give it. Respondents from the Japanese-American 442nd Regimental Combat Team often cited high among their motivations a desire to prove their loyalty to the very country that had proved so disloyal to them. Pvt. Sam S. Ozaki marveled at his wartime behavior: "I have often wondered why we volunteered for a segregated infantry unit when we had been stripped of our rights and were still in a concentration camp. . . . I think we were all very naïve and brainwashed into thinking we had to prove we were good loyal American citizens." Asked why he fought, Shukichi Yoshino, a Hawaiian drafted in 1944, responded, "to fight against Nazism, [and to] protect freedom and democracy."[79]

The Information and Education Division made little attempt to promote or justify the government's policy of removing Japanese Americans from the West Coast to internment camps. In a 1944 guide produced for troops serving in Hawaii it even counseled: "You're going to meet a lot of Japanese during your stay. . . . Now get this straight. Most of these went to American schools. They learned to pledge their allegiance to the same flag you salute. They like American soft drinks. And one of their favorite radio comics is Bob Hope. They're Americans. What's more, many of them have husbands, sons, and brothers fighting for Uncle Sam. These Japanese-Americans (Nisei) aren't just talking patriotism. Their battalions proved, in the battle of Italy, that they are willing to die for it. Don't sell them short."[80]

Nevertheless, Troop Information could claim little success in cultivating this patriotism among the men of the 442nd. "Never gave it much thought," admitted one of the unit's officers, "I guess there was a TIP [Troop Information Program]." An Reserve Officer's Training Corps (ROTC) student who ultimately had to enlist from an internment camp in Utah remembered discounting Troop Information when he read an exaggerated account of enemy numbers in Italy. Shuki Akiyama, a Hawaiian, remembered seeing *Why We Fight* but thought it was "lousy." Katsuki Tanigawa, who had been anxious to volunteer, thought his orientation on Italy was "comical but of little value" and the whole information program ineffective, "except for VD lectures—most [other] subjects were not of very much interest to us." The willing service of so many Japanese-American soldiers in World War II, despite the internment policy, testified to the strength of previously established political loyalties.[81]

The I&E Division did not concern itself with what opinions about their products the soldiers might retain later in life. Whether orientation materials were well crafted, like the Capra films, or poorly made, like *Life Can Be Beautiful*, there is no evidence that their authors worried about what long-term effects making soldiers "anxious to work bodily destruction" might have on them. The Research Branch recommended a series of postwar information efforts to counteract dangerous attitudes cultivated during service, but they were forgotten after victory.[82]

The fact that anyone even considered a possible need for a "de-programming" campaign indicates that at least some of the researchers assumed that propaganda had a powerful effect. In his thoughtful exploration of men in battle J. Glenn Gray assumed that the state's indoctrination of hatred was successful. Negative images of the enemy, he argued, evoked strong responses from soldiers. If the image represented an abstract, total evil, then it resulted in "enmity in battle that is probably unsurpassed." The army's propagandists would have been surprised to be credited with such persuasive powers. On the contrary, their studies of their own programs indicated there were strict limitations on what they could make people think.[83]

Measuring Indoctrination

The Information and Education Division tried throughout the war to put the disparate reactions to its programs into systematic perspective. Continuously, the Research Branch subjected the division's materials to a battery of sophisticated tests. For example, it studied the effects of a "commentator" radio program as opposed to a dramatic "documentary" program with actors and music in the style of *Life Can Be Beautiful*. The social scientists had two programs made, both designed to convince the listener that the war in the Pacific would not be a brief or simple undertaking. The programs had roughly the same effect on the opinions of the test audience.[84]

One could not conclude from this study, however, that commentator programs were just as effective as dramatic programs. Each film, pamphlet, or radio program presented a unique set of variables to the researchers. A statement that resonated with the soldier in one context might have alienated him in another. Given the limits on the amount of testing the Research Branch could conduct in wartime it could not determine conclusively that one medium or method of presentation was superior to another.

For example, one study asked whether giving one side or both sides of an argument was more effective. Some researchers thought that by airing the opposing point of view a propaganda pitch could steal the thunder from an audience member inclined to resist its message. Others suspected that a one-sided presentation was stronger. The branch again tested materials made to curb overconfidence in the war with Japan. Results revealed no change in the overall level of persuasion achieved, but the two argumentative methods did work differently on different individuals. Two-sided arguments proved more acceptable to better educated personnel and those who initially thought the Pacific war would be over quickly. The two-sided presentation offset this gain by confusing less educated men who already thought it would be a long war. Not even these conclusions were generally applicable. The data collectors discovered that many men placed great importance on the Soviet Union's promise to enter the war against Japan, a point neglected by the two-sided presentation. Stouffer's team theorized that if the two-sided argument had taken this point into account, the results of the study might have been entirely different. In short, making any sort of valid generalization about how to indoctrinate soldiers was frustratingly difficult.[85]

Despite this fundamentally insurmountable obstacle, the Research Branch made some ingenious attempts to isolate useful or detrimental elements in the information catalog. In particular Stouffer's team conducted tests to rate the reactions of soldiers to orientation films. One method of evaluation was to monitor viewers' reactions while a film was in progress. During the screening the viewer pressed one button to indicate he liked what was on the screen and another to indicate he disliked it. The buttons were wired to a polygraph to record the results. Researchers instructed the soldiers to indicate visceral satisfaction with the presentation, not approval or disapproval of the people or events on screen. Nevertheless, getting the men to confine themselves to the sort of button pushing required by the experiment was a problem.[86]

Most often, viewers hit the "like" button during action scenes and the "dislike" button when a "talking head" came on screen. Viewers pushed the "like" button far more often than the "dislike" button. In general, soldiers liked orientation films, especially the *Why We Fight* series. Seventy-seven percent of respondents in one survey "very much" liked *The Battle of Britain*, while only 2 percent liked it "not at all." How much an audience enjoys a presentation is not necessarily an indication of how deeply it has been influenced. In fact, one concern of the Information and Education Division was that some films were so entertaining that they jogged the viewer out of a learning frame of mind. Measuring the data retained by the troops required other tools.[87]

The method most commonly employed was to show a film to a group of about a thousand soldiers and compare their responses on questionnaires to those of a control group of soldiers who had not seen the film. The questionnaires asked soldiers to recall data presented by the films and report on their attitudes toward the subject matter. As often as possible the two groups were from the same base and similar in terms of age and racial composition. Differences in audience members' educational backgrounds formed a key area of inquiry. The branch found that the material was more effective with less educated men. The research team anticipated this result: "Nonacceptance by more intelligent men of some of the interpretations by the orientation films studies would seem quite likely since the films did not involve a purely dispassionate presentation of a series of facts, but instead were often 'slanted.'"[88]

The Research Branch studied the films individually and cumulatively, checking for both short- and long-term changes in opinion. They also examined possible opinion "boomerangs," to ensure, for example, that a film did not cultivate so high a regard for an ally that the audience thought the help of the United States was no longer needed.[89]

The Research Branch began with the assumption that the goals of the films were to create a firm belief in the cause for which America fought; foster trust in comrades, leaders, and allies; instill resentment toward the enemy; and finally leave the impression that through military victory would come a better world order. The films were successful to the degree that they promoted these opinions. Obviously, however, the filmmakers had considerable leeway in emphasizing the various goals.[90]

The scientists found that the orientation films, particularly the seven of the *Why We Fight* series, substantially increased the viewer's "factual" knowledge. For example, the third film, *Divide and Conquer*, makes the point that the Nazis bombed Rotterdam after the Dutch had surrendered. Only 17 percent of the control group were aware of this item, but 62 percent of those who saw the film were able to recall it on the questionnaire.[91]

The films also had some small influence on soldiers' attitudes about war issues. Men who had seen the fourth film, *The Battle of Britain*, were less likely to say that America was propping up the British war effort. Men who had seen *Prelude to War* were more apt to believe that the Germans would deprive them of the freedom of religion should they ever conquer the United States. In a key area the percentage of men who agreed that Soviets had been secretly "preparing" while allied with Germany rose 11 percent after viewing *Prelude*. The researchers made allowances for the gray area between what was a factual issue and what was a matter of opinion. For instance, the fact that more soldiers believed, after seeing the film, that there *was* such a thing as a Battle of Britain, was considered as a gain in both departments.[92]

Nevertheless, the percentage of "right" answers on attitudinal questions was not so great as on the objective questions, and the films demonstrated no ability whatsoever to change behavior. For example, although a soldier viewing the films might be slightly more likely to hate the enemy than one who had not, he was no more willing to say he would volunteer for combat or overseas duty. Nor was he more likely to agree that he was serving the country better in the army than he could have been in his civilian job. A study of soldiers in units with "active" and "inactive" I&E programs also found no statistically significant difference in these crucial attitudes.[93]

The Research Branch offered a variety of explanations for the failure of the orientation program to more substantially affect attitudes. It suggested, for instance, that the Information and Education Division had a harder job indoctrinating soldiers than its counterparts in World War I because in 1917–18 propagandists could offer "positive" reasons for the war and positive outcomes of victory. This attitude is surprising now, when World War II is enshrined as a wholly positive national undertaking but understandable in light of the unfulfilled idealistic goals announced in World War I. In retrospect, the researchers theorized, exposure to a mass media propaganda blitz in the Great War had only set the public up for disillusionment when victory failed, after all, to make the world safe for democracy. The experience helped condition Americans to regard cynically any grand claim that the war would create a better world. In the interwar years isolationists inveighed frequently against interventionist "propaganda."[94]

The propagandistic nature of the materials could not, however, bear much responsibility for their rejection. Only a relatively small percentage of the viewers (27 percent in one study) correctly identified the purpose of the films as motivational, and only a few of them objected to them on those grounds. Perhaps, the analysts theorized, "previous indoctrination as civilians" had already done as much as propaganda could do to influence the citizen-soldiers' feelings about the war.[95]

Other factors that mitigated the films' influence included "lack of specific coverage" and "conflicting motivation." Stouffer's staff found that if the film did not make specific mention of an item they wanted to impress upon the audience then the troops would not infer it from other suggestive information. For example, *Prelude to War* stated that the Luftwaffe had the world's largest air force. The film successfully increased the number of viewers who could remember that fact, but the same men were much less likely, on the basis of that information, to upgrade their estimate of German military power or Germany's threat to the United States.[96]

Even under normal circumstances most people resist changing long-held opinions on the evidence of a few contrary facts, even telling ones. Recent draftees had even more reason to resist the connections that the filmmakers wanted them to make. Most soldiers had no personal interests that ran counter to a specific description of the size of the Luftwaffe, or the valor of the British in the Battle of Britain. They did, however, have great personal stake in whether or not they would be sent overseas, how long they would be in the army, or whether or not they would have to fight. Fear of death or injury could "offset anything presented in the 'Why We Fight' films." The researchers hypothesized that "If they wanted to be out of the Army soon, if they hoped they would not be needed for combat, or if they hoped even in combat that they would not run many risks, they would have strong motivation to resist evidences for a long and difficult war."[97]

Fifty-minute films could not create a lust for combat in the face of the instinct of self-preservation. The recalcitrant Yossarian in Joseph Heller's novel *Catch-22* exposes the conflict of interests when he refuses to fly any more bombing missions. Asked if he wants his country to lose, he replies, "We won't lose. We've got more men, more money and more material. There are ten million men in uniform who could replace me. Some people are getting killed and a lot more are making money and having fun. Let someone else get killed."

"But suppose everyone on our side felt that way?" his superior asks.

"Then I'd certainly be a damn fool to feel any other way. Wouldn't I?"[98]

Soldiers targeted for persuasion not only resisted risking their lives, they resisted *arguments* that legitimized the risking of their lives.

[49]

Stouffer's researchers found that a man's doubts about the righteousness of the war were not static; they increased with proximity to the fighting front. The closer a soldier got to danger the more he adjusted his world-view to accommodate his instinct for self-preservation.[99]

Propagandists, as well as opponents of propaganda, operated from the assumption that belief systems guide human behavior. Therefore, influence over thought meant influence over people's action. Belief in the efficacy of propaganda accounts for the negative connotation it acquired after World War I. Political scientist Harold D. Lasswell's *Propaganda Technique in the World War* (1927) depicted a public helpless but to take its marching orders from wily opinion leaders. The findings of the Research Branch supplied evidence for a far different view: that people's self-interested behavior guided their opinions. Confronted with these results social scientists after the war examined more closely the active role of the audience in selecting and interpreting the messages aimed its way.[100]

From its own extensive studies, then, the Information and Education Division knew by the end of the war that it could not make soldiers more "anxious to work bodily destruction" or less interested in avoiding it. That did not mean that political indoctrination was without other rationales. If political appeals cut little ice in a soldier's willingness to fight, they paid off somewhat more handsomely in instilling political knowledge and opinions. The potential effects in these areas were attractive enough for I&E to survive the demobilization and take up a permanent residence in the Cold War–era army.

2

The Morale and Whatnot of the Army

Indoctrination Institutionalized in the Postwar Army

Once it became apparent that the Allies would prevail in their struggle with Germany and Japan, the Information and Education Division had to address the guardians of an armed peace rather than war-fighting troops. The propagandists tried to harden troops earmarked for the occupation of Germany against too much sympathy for their defeated foes. They also tried to overcome the strong anticommunist impulses of troops who had to work with Soviet allies. However, the indoctrinators found themselves behind the ideological curve on both counts. The rapid postwar realignment made allies of the Germans and enemies of the Soviets. As the Troop Information program reoriented to anticommunism it also became a permanent army institution, housed with the army's better-supported publicity office. These developments put the army's Troop Information specialists on the defensive during the Cold War. Coupled with the continuing skepticism of many officers and soldiers, political indoctrination gained permanency in army life, but fell short of gaining legitimacy.

Rationales for Continued Indoctrination

Scholars from a variety of fields who have studied the military's political indoctrination program have generally reached the same conclusions as its own Research Branch: it had little effect on soldiers' belligerency. There were other reasons besides creating a fighting mood, however, to carry on political indoctrination after the fighting was done. Army officers valued a good attitude in its own right and hoped it would buoy a soldier during the stress of service life. Even if it could not manufacture the will to *fight*, the indoctrination effort could contribute to the will to *war* by quelling dissent and depriving the soldier of the intellectual refuge that the war was fought for someone else's benefit.[1]

Anthony Kellet in his 1982 study *Combat Motivation* distinguished between the sort of motivation that brought a soldier to battle and the kind that sustained him once he was there. According to Kellet ideology had a role in the former. Even if one were to agree that formal indoctrination weighed little in the heat of combat, there is more to performance in war than the extreme experience of actual fighting. A soldier can perform his duties to the best of his abilities, or only well enough effort to avoid punishment. He can march efficiently or drag behind. He can remain at his post or desert. In any war an army must complete countless actions that are not acts of violence but are necessary to victory.[2]

Related to this "good attitude" rationale is the premise behind the uninspired greeting card: it's the thought that counts. This rationale holds that even a poor attempt to indoctrinate soldiers might have productive outcomes for the army because the troops expect, and are therefore comforted by, some form of political direction from "authority." The Research Branch found that most soldiers "liked" orientation discussions and films, despite officers who often appeared less than enthusiastic and even disrespectful toward Troop Information and Education duty. The social scientists acknowledged that idealism and cynicism were not mutually exclusive. No matter how ham-fisted the effort to "inform" them, the soldiers at some level appreciated it at the same time they scoffed at it because it was important that someone, if not they themselves, believed the government's justifications for the hazards they faced.[3]

John A. Lynn, in his history of the army of revolutionary France, has suggested that the most important function of the "political education" of the troops was not in the content conveyed but in the act of conveyance. Lynn contended that "Most soldiers in most armies have at best only a partial understanding of the causes and goals of the war they are fighting, but they do have a sense of whether or not their efforts are valued. The most crucial wartime opinion is this appreciation of soldiers' sacrifices and triumphs." Ideologically rendered war aims might have been more important to the home front than to the fighting front, but civilians' attempts to court the opinions of soldiers in the field at least showed that the civilians cared.[4]

The "good attitude" rationale for political indoctrination still assumed that propaganda influenced behavior. Other rationales went beyond this justification. The Soviet Army, for example, carried on political indoctrination despite the absence of any evidence of influence over troops' attitudes. By repeatedly placing before its soldiers the tenets of the state religion, the government communicated to them the bounds of acceptable behavior, whether they agreed with them or not. Another benefit that accrued to the indoctrinators was that by monitoring which parts of their program met with the most resistance they could find out what soldiers really thought. Herbert Goldhamer, in *The Soviet Soldier*, argued that indoctrination also provided an opportunity for the ruling Communist Party to project its own unpopular actions onto its enemies, fulfilling the regime's psychological need to see itself in a heroic light. Sociologist Morris Janowitz saw political indoctrination in the Western armies as serving a similar end. The military establishment tried to convince soldiers (and the public) of its moral virtue because it needed to reassure itself.[5]

Alfred Thomas Palmer's 1971 study "'Why We Fight,' A Study of Indoctrination Activities in the Armed Forces" also emphasizes the ancillary benefits of the programs. He notes that simply having a program made "influential backers of Troop Information in Congress, the Executive, and elements of the private sector . . . 'feel better about the Armed Forces,'" regardless of its actual effect. Palmer offers as the chief rationale for the programs their influence on foreign opinion. He discovered that in countries where American servicemen were stationed the host citizens became avid consumers of Troop Information materials. In particular the Armed Forces Radio and (later) Television Service (AFRTS) attracted a foreign audience sometimes estimated as many times larger than that of Voice of America, the radio propaganda source actually intended for it. To Palmer Troop Information was therefore valuable as a back channel in postwar diplomacy: "If, for example, we desire to transmit our resolve to stand firm in Berlin to the Russians and East Germans, what could be more effective than to state this in the form of communication to American troops over AFRTS facilities in Berlin?"[6]

These possible psychological and diplomatic benefits of indoctrinating soldiers did not come without cost. Most important, the practice had the potential to complicate and even destabilize civil-military relations. Stephen B. Wesbrook, another thorough student of the programs, dismisses as "naïve" fears that political training could motivate an officer to become involved in domestic politics. He cited the fact that Congress gave the military a "free hand" in such training as proof of the propriety of the undertaking. The approval of some legislators, however, proved no adequate safeguard for the military's essential political neutrality.[7]

Historian Lori L. Bogle argues as much in her 2004 book, *The Pentagon's Battle for the American Mind: The Early Cold War*. She demonstrates that the Pentagon's attempts to instill religious nationalism in the American people as a Cold War measure eventually led to unfortunate politicized alliances between officers and the radical right. Yet it was not only extremism that ran afoul of proper civil-military relations. Simply attempting to establish what was or was not part of the American consensus could lead the indoctrinators to take sides in domestic political debates. Benjamin L. Alpers, in his article "This Is the Army: Imagining a Democratic Military in World War II," describes how the army's orientation materials became part of a military and civilian campaign to assure the public that mobilization would not degenerate into militarism. He cautions that propaganda that promoted a democratic military eroded Americans' traditional suspicions of standing armies: "Fears that the military might be inherently undemocratic, that what is good for the military might necessarily be bad for democratic life, have receded to the margins of American political life."[8]

Under the circumstances of the Cold War, the civilian public did indeed embrace a peacetime military establishment of unprecedented size. The army institutionalized its information programs in order to navigate this new arrangement, not only to communicate with the draftees and short-term volunteers who continued to make up its ranks, but to maintain its new status with the public as a necessary bulwark of the American way of life.

Improvised Indoctrination

Not until late in World War II did the army begin to train its own information specialists and establish its permanent infrastructure for political indoctrination. In the meantime, the men and women who performed information functions generally had military tasks relevant to their civilian experience. Admen crafted propaganda, newsmen handled public relations, old Hollywood hands made films, and radio professionals manned the airwaves. Nevertheless, experienced or not, the people charged with communicating the army's message lacked any common training or doctrine on which to rely. As a result, they were thrown back on their own creativity, often with disparate results.

Despite some consistencies between the ideological approach of radio shows like *Life Can Be Beautiful* and Col. Frank Capra's flagship film effort, the information campaign was not strictly thematically organized or coordinated from Washington. The centrally produced material was careful to cultivate the soldiers' sense of outrage, but also careful not to go too far ahead of the audience emotionally. Local efforts and contributions from other organizations that played overlapping roles, like the Office of War Information (OWI), were rough hewn by comparison, and in some cases may even have contradicted the goals of the overall campaign.

The work of 1st Lt. Jane Temple, a Women's Army Corpswoman stationed in the public relations office of Battery General Hospital in Rome, Georgia, provides examples of the improvisational efforts of a local information specialist. Temple wrote the hospital's internal information newsletters and press releases and eventually scripted shows for the CBS radio series *WACs on Parade* as well as for the base's own show, *Battery General Presents*, which aired on station WRGA in Rome. Her 1945 pieces reflect a war weariness that was likely inspired by the patients at Battery General but was at odds with the Information and Education Division's desire to concentrate the nation's reserves of enthusiasm against the listing Axis Powers and then to enforce victory through lengthy occupations.

On March 7, 1945, *WACs on Parade* presented an untitled Temple play narrated by "McConnor," a hospitalized soldier. McConnor had teased his buddy Bill about his devotion to his girlfriend, Doris, and his pursuit of the American dream house. Now, blinded from wounds received in combat, Bill refuses to write to Doris. Because he has heard Doris described at great length, McConnor is able to recognize her in the hospital and direct her to Bill. She still loves him, and they marry.

Temple sought to ease veterans' anxieties that their wounds or experiences placed beyond their reach the things for which they had fought, including their own home and a woman, "blonde, 5′2″, and comes just up to his shoulder." The writer's proximity to her subjects lent credence to her dramatization of their concerns. Her portrayal also supports the argument that American soldiers in World War II fought not to make a better world but to preserve a status quo that promised them the good life.[9]

In his memoir of the Pacific War historian William Manchester admitted that he and his fellow soldiers would have been bewildered had they known in advance of the postwar rights revolution. "That [gay rights] just wasn't one of the rights we were fighting to protect. We weren't exactly prejudiced. . . . We hadn't thought about it. That didn't make it unique. We weren't fighting for the emancipation of housewives, either, or for the right of blacks, who performed menial, if safe, tasks far behind the lines, to bleed alongside us. Like most soldiers in most wars, we were fighting for the status quo ante bellum. And like the others, we were doomed to disappointment."[10]

Of particular concern to soldiers was the availability of jobs. A majority of servicemen thought it possible that their mass return to the job market would set off another depression. Social critics and government propagandists fretted that in war women had become dangerously more independent, economically and sexually. For the nation to make good on the private goals for which the soldier fought, opinion makers hectored women to relinquish industrial jobs and fulfill the role of the idealized sweetheart that had inspired the men in wartime, thereby soothing veterans' anxieties about their return.[11]

However clichéd was *WACs on Parade*'s yearning for domesticity, its emotive style and concern for the soldiers whose sufferings had not ended with the Axis surrender set it apart from the official materials. The simple acknowledgment of wounded and hospitalized soldiers was impossible in the atmosphere of unrelenting determination presented by the centrally produced items.

The format of *Battery General Presents* was to intersperse monologues or skits with popular songs in such a way that the spoken material segued into the song titles. Actors, rather than an announcer, read the between-song bits. On September 6, 1945, a Temple character ("Voice II, tough building up throughout") delivered a remarkable speech that concluded with this statement:

> That slug from a chopper spoiled a few of my ideas, but here's one that didn't spoil! I got a kid. . . . When he grows up, I want the world to be just tough enough for him so he can learn to take it. None of this sissy stuff for him. BUT GET THIS STRAIGHT! I DON'T WANT HIM TO HAVE TO FIGHT ALL OVER AGAIN THE WAR HIS OLD MAN'S BEEN FIGHTING! DO YOU GET ME? I DON'T WANT ANOTHER WAR FOR HIM! That's all I've got to say! SO DON'T LET IT HAPPEN AGAIN! (song: "Don't Let it Happen Again")[12]

In the immediate postwar period the official army materials urged soldiers to remain vigilant, to carry out occupation duties enthusiastically, and to await discharge patiently, with the warning that failure to see the victory through would risk losing the peace. Superficially, the wounded soldier's appeal accorded with the goal of continuing service. But he addressed his comments not to those on occupation duty but to the civilian world at large. The responsibility for war and peace lay not with him and his fellows, he suggested, but with the undefined authority to which he appealed.

Temple was careful to have the soldier lay a masculine groundwork for his impassioned antiwar plea. A mother might be expected to wish a peaceful world for her child out of loving, sentimental weakness, but this father wanted no sissy stuff. The world was to remain the tough place he knew before his military service—absent the war, he thought things should go back to how they were. These apologies notwithstanding, Temple's naked demand for peace retained emotional power.

War weariness was not a sentiment the army appreciated. Films such as *Two Down, One to Go*, featuring army chief of staff George C. Marshall making an on-camera appeal to the troops not to relent, attested to the fear that euphoria after victory over Germany would produce a letdown against Japan.[13] Later, after victory in the Pacific was assured, the problem became sustaining enthusiasm during the occupations.

Know Your Enemies: Old and New

Several agencies exercised overlapping information duties under the Office of Military Government for Germany (OMGUS). Psychological warfare personnel ran Information Control, a program designed to steer German newspapers toward support for de-Nazification and the democratization of the American Zone. "Why are we here?" asked a booklet for Information Control personnel. The answer: "Because Goebbels had all the media under his control for 12 years." The army did not define a clear border between psychological warfare and information and education. Crafting propaganda for the enemy was a "psy-war" function, and crafting it for American troops was the job of I&E. Once the Germans technically ceased to be the enemy, however, the areas of responsibility were less distinct. Gen. Dwight D. Eisenhower, the Supreme Allied Commander in Europe, was happy to concede the entire mission to the Office of War Information. If the OWI could not be America's voice in Europe, he told an economy-minded Congress, then the army would have to do the job, and far less efficiently.[14]

However, Republicans in Congress, eager to shed the tiresome role of loyal opposition, found the apparently nonessential OWI a good place to pick a fight. Seventeen Democrats joined 120 Republicans in support of a House proposal to slash OWI's budget. Representative Leon H. Gavin, Republican of Pennsylvania, complained that he was "suspicious of the whole outfit. . . . Now I'm asking you, why do we have to have 3,701 foreigners on the OWI payroll? What is the trouble with some sound and clear-thinking Americans?"[15]

Victory eroded dedication to propaganda work in other ways. One fear was that soldiers on occupation duty would let their guard down and fraternize with the subdued enemy. The Information and Education sections of units in Europe issued booklets and handbooks that tried to define the rules and limitations of interaction with the German populace. American officials frowned upon friendships and romances between Germans and the troops. The bizarre contingency anticipated by a Third Army question-and-answer book indicates the soldiers' determination to circumvent these limitations: "Q: There is a German girl . . . her parents are not mixed up in the Nazi party . . . I would like to adopt this girl . . . is there any chance I can marry her while I'm still

[58]

in the Army? . . . A: You cannot marry the girl. You cannot adopt the girl."[16]

The army made the point even more emphatically in the fifteen-minute film *Your Job in Germany*. Supervised by Frank Capra and directed by Theodore Geisel ("Dr. Seuss"), *Your Job in Germany* was one of the last government-produced propaganda films of the war. With the crisis passed, the Signal Corps was able to reassert itself against the Hollywood mavericks and regain control of filmmaking from Capra's detached unit. Nevertheless, *Your Job in Germany* bore the marks of the other efforts supervised by Capra's team.[17]

Occupation soldiers, said the film's narrator, would see a peaceful Germany with pretty scenery, but they should not be lulled by it, for they were in enemy country. "Be alert. Be suspicious of everyone—you are up against German history." The narrator described how after World War I, Americans made the mistake of blaming the bloody struggle on Kaiser Wilhelm II rather than on German culture's lust for conquest. Germans raised in the Hitler Youth still believed they were part of a master race. "They are not sorry they started the war, only sorry they lost it." Soldiers were not to debate Germans or try to educate them; "others will be sent to do that." Nor were they to fraternize with the Germans. Over a scene of a crowd of Germans a giant hand appeared on the screen, superimposed over the indistinct sea of humanity. "This is the hand that heiled Hitler, the hand that dropped bombs, the hand that held the whip over slaves, the hand that withheld food, massacred, killed, crippled—don't clasp that hand!"[18]

Not all the indoctrination materials were as morally certain as *Your Job in Germany*. In 1944 the War Department enlisted the cooperation of the American Historical Association to produce a pamphlet series entitled *G.I. Roundtable*. Each pamphlet was designed to provide the basis for a discussion session. Unusually, the authors actually intended to stimulate open-ended discussions rather than lead the troops to a particular conclusion. For example, the pamphlet *What Shall Be Done about Germany after the War?* discouraged the notion that Germany started World War II because the victorious powers imposed harsh terms in the Treaty of Versailles after World War I. However, it did not explicitly encourage soldiers to favor a hard occupation; it cited the pitfalls of leniency while at the same time noting that Germany could never be permanently disarmed, divided, or even occupied. They would try to indoctrinate Germans with democratic values, but the Allies could not "force freedom on a people."[19]

G.I. Roundtable blamed Germany's leading industrialists and the professional military officers for the rise of the Nazis, but ordinary Germans did not escape opprobrium entirely. They were "half persuaded, half terrorized" to follow the Nazis, and members of Germany's militias and paramilitary organizations had no recourse to the "superior orders" defense. The installment *What Shall Be Done with the War Criminals?* was remarkable for its frank discussion of Germany's mass murder of European Jews. Whereas in the *Why We Fight* films the Nazis' obsessive enmity toward Jews went unmentioned, the *G.I. Roundtable* writers could ask troops whether anything in the history of human cruelty matched the Nazis' "butcheries of Jews, Poles, Russians, Italians, Greeks and other people." Pressing home the shocking nature of the crime, the pamphlet described "acts of torture and murder of thousands of men, women, and children . . . in death houses specially constructed for the use of live gas or fumes as a lethal weapon" and "the forcing of victims to dig their own graves."[20]

In his memoir of his service in Europe Lester Atwell recorded just the sort of discussion the authors of *G.I. Roundtable* hoped to spark. When he and his buddy Phil disagreed about the postwar motives of the Soviet Union, Atwell changed the subject: "All right then, well listen. What do you think we should do with the Germans once this war is over?" John Ellis observed that while "few soldiers had much interest in the ideological aspects of their war" the one thing that did concern them was "what was to be done when the war was over." The sheer yearning for the end of the war "forced men to speculate upon exactly what should happen when this golden day dawned." Phil for one had evidently put a lot of thought into the matter. He suggested that the Germans be forced to rebuild the cities they had destroyed, especially with labor gangs culled from ss troops. "Leave one badly smashed-up city as a monument so they'd never forget. Have one day a year when every student through grammar school, high school and college would have to sit and look at all the war films showing what

Germany did to the other countries, and then what happened to dear old Deutschland as a result."[21]

As Atwell and his buddy moved amongst the conquered German civilians in March 1945 they pressed the issue of war guilt. When one woman lamented what Hitler had done to her country they answered that the German people had to take responsibility for Hitler, and pointedly asked what had happened to the Jews who had lived in the area. Even as they did so, they saw the occupation as falling short of its aims. "'The fact remains we were poorly indoctrinated,' Phil insisted. 'We should have had a separate Army of Occupation ready to move in right behind us, made up of specially-trained men.'"[22]

The Information and Education Division had reason to resist the conclusion that it had done a poor job of indoctrinating the occupation troops. In a follow-up to the survey that had found that 22 percent of the troops surveyed in Europe thought the Germans "had some good reasons for being down on the Jews," the Research Branch discovered that 29 percent of responding troops stationed stateside answered the same way. In fact, on seven out of eight questions the percentage of soldiers with undesireable attitudes pertaining to German relations was as high or higher among troops in the United States as among the troops occupying Germany.[23]

Officials, like Atwell's friend Phil, who wished to keep American troops even warier of the Germans found themselves pitted against an American tendency to minimize the past and look to the future. Despite the misery wrought by the Nazis' racist ideology and militarism Americans' bitter feelings toward the Germans could evaporate quickly. Historian Petra Goedde, in her 2002 study of relations between ordinary Germans and occupation soldiers, found that the American troops adopted a protective attitude toward Germans as they forged personal ties with German women and children. Through these relationships men exchanged a wartime image of Germany as a male aggressor with a peacetime image as a feminized victim. Meanwhile, impatience as well as sympathy characterized American attitudes toward "displaced persons." Some American officers and enlisted men found the impoverished and homeless concentration camp prisoners revolting. Tadeusz Borowski, the acerbic Polish writer, doubted young American soldiers could ever comprehend the depths of German depravity: "these strong, cheerful men, full of joy of living and the expectation of great opportunities lying around the corner, these sincere, direct men, with minds as clean and fresh as their uniforms . . . felt an instinctive contempt for the people who had lost their businesses and their jobs and dropped to the bottom of society. But their attitude toward the courteous German bourgeoisie who had managed to preserve their culture and fortunes . . . was one of understanding and friendly admiration." Although the troops' widespread disregard for the antifraternization rule flummoxed the high command the Research Branch, at least, was not surprised. It had predicted a softening of attitudes against Germans and recommended intensified information efforts to counteract it. Even before V.E. Day research found that more American soldiers liked Germans "just as people" than liked the French.[24]

The Information and Education Division failed to stem fraternization. In retrospect, the Research Branch considered its approach too negative: "There was a distinct lack of an attempt to outline in positive terms the mission of the Army in its occupation functions." Furthermore, fraternization itself tended to increase warm feelings toward the Germans. In the end, instances of friendly contact were probably inevitable and arguably more helpful than damaging to the occupation mission. The researchers reported that despite diminished animosity "the men showed practically no change in their overwhelming support for a tough policy." That is, American soldiers could distinguish their personal relations from larger political questions.[25]

As there was a *Your Job in Germany*, so there was also a *Your Job in Japan*. Hundreds of thousands of American soldiers and civilians also took part in the occupation of Japan. As in Europe there were many instances of kindness and spontaneous generosity on behalf of the conquerors. There were also displays of overweening arrogance, as Americans requisitioned fine houses, flaunted wealth and power, and exploited women driven into prostitution. In his history of the occupation John W. Dower described how inexperienced Americans "were empowered to tell more elderly Japanese how to conduct their business and rearrange their minds" and prone to judge Japanese by their ability to speak English. Remarkably, however, the wartime hatred for the

Japanese dissipated as quickly as had that for the Germans, even though it had been by most accounts deeper and more intense.[26]

Troop Information had a different purpose in Japan than in Germany. In a largely failed effort, army information writers sought to keep the American soldier's guard up against the defeated Germans and to discourage fraternization. The mission in Japan was nearly the opposite, to disarm hostile attitudes and minimize barriers to working relationships. At the army's Civil Affairs Staging Area in California, training materials tried to defuse wartime characterizations of the Japanese as monkeys or vermin. Though the training film *Your Job in Japan* contained atrocity footage and shared the unforgiving tone of *Your Job in Germany*, it argued that Japan's aggression stemmed from recent militaristic propaganda, not from racial or cultural imperatives. In November 1945, Gen. Douglas MacArthur's occupation headquarters still found the tone too harsh and sent the film back to the Information and Education Division. The revised version featured images of Americans interacting with Japanese civilians to soften its portrait of the Japanese.[27]

Political indoctrination may have aided the rapid de-escalation of hatred toward the Japanese. The Research Branch does not appear to have studied the effects of the Japanese program to the same extent as the German program, probably because the Allies took four additional months to defeat Japan. The researchers had a few months to examine occupied Germany before the war ended, and the army scaled back its operations across the board. The largest immediate postwar morale issue for the occupation forces was, in any case, not soldiers' opinions of the former Axis nations, but their desire to leave them as soon as possible.

The first postwar chief of the information program (the "Chief of Information" or "CINFO") was Lt. Gen. J. Lawton "Lightning Joe" Collins, the famed commander of the VII Corps in the drive across Europe. One of the toughest problems during his stint in the information business was how to deal with the bring-the-boys-home sentiment that ballooned as victory approached. After V-E Day the government announced it would discharge unneeded soldiers in the order of points accumulated for combat service, parenthood, and noncombat service. The War Department had surveyed the opinions of soldiers overseas to determine the weight given to various types of service. Despite the attempt to take their feelings into account the points system (along with other demobilization snags) aroused soldiers' ire. Many did not believe that any of their fellows had really been polled. Early in 1946, while on a tour of the Philippines, Secretary of War Robert P. Patterson was quoted in a way that made him seem ignorant about the point system's cutoff date. Exasperated soldiers held angry meetings and demonstrations in both Europe and the Pacific.[28]

The charged meetings, "near mutinies" in the eyes of some officers, represented a failure for Troop Information. The program had not been able to counter men's emotional responses with convincing assurances about the discharge policy. "Dreadful period," recalled Collins:

> [Patterson's comment] was seized upon by agitators in the service, whom I always felt were affiliated in some way with the communists' agitation to break down the Army and to demobilize rapidly. I'm not one of those that looks for communists under the bed every night and everything of that sort, but there's no question in my judgment that a lot of trouble we had after the war in the camps, where our men were waiting to come home, was communist inspired. There's no question about it, and if I recall rightly the leader of one of those groups out there in the Philippines was subsequently identified as being either a Communist Party card carrier, or certainly affiliated with them.[29]

Citizen-soldiers who had served willingly enough to defeat the Axis powers now longed to resume their civilian lives. Not unreasonably, they wanted fresh draftees to take over the duties of occupation. The CINFO's suspicion that it took communist agents to stir up the troops reflected an overly optimistic view of the patience of men who saw their mission as accomplished and their personal contribution as more than sufficient. Collins was no paranoid ideologue, however. Officers high and low throughout the armed forces shared the suspicion that communists were trying to weaken the victorious American military. Edward S. Sullivan worked for King Features Syndicate and was employed by the OWI during the war as a propaganda analyst in its Far Eastern section. In addition to his chief duty of monitoring radio broadcasts from Tokyo Sullivan kept watch on outgoing propaganda as well. On March 27,

1945, an item caught his eye that made him report: "if this ist out-and-out commie propaganda, i'll eat admiral kings report without mustard. seems to me very odd that this item shudve been picked for our use."[30]

The item's offense was the use of the phrases "global culture" and "international cooperation," which signaled to Sullivan advocacy of a communist-dominated world government. The analyst notes with gravity that the item originated in Brooklyn, New York, and that its author was "well known in east as a red . . . seems to me the mans theories would be nice in the best of all possible worlds with moscow as capital, but have no place in U.S. wartime propaganda."[31]

Sullivan had focused overzealously on some generalized language about what was actually a widely shared assumption: that there would have to be some international security mechanism in the postwar world. However, his sense of political estrangement from the intellectuals who wrote America's propaganda material was not merely the product of his own imagination. For four years the task of the information authors was to convince Americans hostile to communism that the Soviet Union was a trustworthy ally and that its system of government, while different, was compatible with a future peaceful world. Even as victory and the consequent division of the global spoils soured Americans on the prospect of cooperation with the Soviets, the American propagandists could not so easily shift gears. They had indoctrinated themselves into a corner.

America's Red Army Ally

While vigilant Americans began to reorient their suspicions toward their communist ally, the Information and Education Division, in contrast, continued to soothe the soldiers who harbored antipathy for the Soviets. The persistence of the friendly stance lasted just long enough to occasion unpleasant scrutiny, but not long enough to destroy the program or to devastate the reputations of its personnel.

The Communist Party of the United States of America (CPUSA) had gone to considerable lengths to soften its image in the mid-1930s. Promoting a Popular Front to make common cause against fascism, communists downplayed their hostility to the mainstream labor movement and the Roosevelt administration's New Deal recovery policies. Simultaneously, as the intractable Great Depression made critiques of American capitalism more acceptable, communists forged alliances with the left, recruited their largest membership, and succeeded at least partially in Americanizing the image of their movement.

The Nazi-Soviet Pact of 1939, and CPUSA's corresponding support for it, destroyed the Popular Front and permanently alienated mainstream allies. Communism regained some of its respectability, however, when the Germans' June 1941 invasion of Russia forced the Soviets back into the antifascist camp. Communists and anticommunists alike understood the temporary nature of this confluence of interest and were determined to terminate the truce on the eve of the peace. The information programs were not quite as ideologically nimble, however, and found it difficult to keep up with these hairpin turns. It was not until two years after the war, for example, that the army restricted and made "every effort" to "completely withdraw" the widely distributed *Why We Fight* film *Battle of Russia*. In this regard, the authors of the information program, often writers with liberal, academic backgrounds, resembled the authors of texts for the nation's secondary schools. Historian Frances Fitzgerald, in her study of history schoolbooks, demonstrated that textbooks were often a few years behind the latest-breaking political interpretations. She noted that American history textbooks as late as 1950 still struck a note of wartime triumphalism and did not reflect the nation's pessimistic anticommunist anxiety until the middle of the decade.[32]

In April 1945 the division published a pamphlet, *Your Red Army Ally*, to prepare the men headed east to the Elbe River, the designated line where the Allied fronts would halt and meet. Calling their coming encounter with Russian troops a "historical occasion," the pamphlet told American troops of the Red Army soldier: "He is your friend. He is your ally. He has fought hard in this war, just as you have, to bring about a United Nations victory."[33]

To facilitate the initial encounters the booklet provided a glossary of phonetic greetings and the Soviet soldier's most likely responses. The description of the Russians was meant to engender respect for their seriousness and to encourage the good behavior of the Americans. "You will notice that a Red Army sentry keeps his weapon either at the ready, at order, or at shoulder arms. He does not sit down, or lean against anything. He does not eat, drink, smoke or sing while on post. He talks only in the line of official business." One mentally supplies the unspoken parental admonishment: "unlike some sentries we know."[34]

In a section entitled "Why He Fights" *Your Red Army Ally* elicited sympathy for the plight of the Soviet people, citing their "justifiable hatred" of the Germans: "Twice in one lifetime, they have seen their land ruined by foreign invaders. The Germans have slaughtered their people literally by the millions, carrying other millions off to brutal slavery." Yet in common with comparatively undamaged Americans, "These men too want to return to their homes, to work in factories and farms, and to build up a comfortable, happy life." Just as the American was meant to admire the Red Army man, he was told that he was himself admired, or more precisely that his Russian counterpart appreciated America's "trucks and jeeps, telephones and radios, Spam and boots."[35]

The Information and Education Division aimed *Your Red Army Ally* at an unsophisticated soldier. It encouraged the reader to take pride in the most elementary and obvious aspect of his own country, that is, its material, industrial might. It sought to build respect for the Russians on such tangible and easily understood qualities as stern demeanor on sentry duty. It rested its case for common cause on uncomplicated shared hatred. The enlisted man with more sophisticated questions about the nature of the alliance with the Soviets found no answers here.

The information writers lavished considerably more care on materials meant for officers. To prepare them to interact with Soviet officers, in 1945 the army produced a lengthy pamphlet entitled, *The USSR: Institutions & People: A Brief Handbook for the Use of Officers of the Armed Forces of the United States*. The handbook offered the disclaimer that it merely supplied accurate information about the Soviet Union: "It should be distinctly understood that no judgments of any kind are here made or intended by the issuing agency." The authors did not wish to give the impression that favorable information indicated approval of communism. Even so, neutrality itself was an unsafe stand. Within a few years information that "intended no judgments" about the Soviet Union's form of government would practically serve as grounds for a congressional investigation.[36]

The USSR began by citing "physical similarities" between the United

States and the Soviet Union. Stalingrad was similar to industrial Pittsburgh, Moscow's counterpart was New York, and Leningrad was like Chicago. In between these metropolises, both nations had great rivers and large agricultural tracts. Each country's population was racially heterogeneous and possessed of pioneer spirit and wanderlust, especially in comparison to the peoples of western Europe. But these commonalities had to be weighed against strong "psychological dissimilarities." Though many Americans might have suffered in the war the handbook cautioned that "The burning sense of bereavement and loss, both personal and national, was very likely to make the Soviet people approach the business of peace-building with a grim intensity which may be difficult for an American to understand unless he reminded himself constantly of the reasons which have brought it into being." Or, as the authors put it in a section entitled "The War as the Soviet People See It": "Much of this chapter may strike the American officer as being unfair . . . to the war effort of the United States. . . . But the purpose of this chapter is to convey to the American reader the probable state of mind of his Soviet 'opposite number.' . . . Insofar as this *Handbook* is concerned, it is left to each American reader to achieve the delicate balance between truth as he sees it and as it is seen by other people with whom he has to maintain working and social relations." In this spirit the authors speculated that the Soviets believed that they were ignored in their honest attempts to build a coalition against Germany in the 1930s. From this perspective the Molotov-Ribbentrop Non-Aggression Pact was seen as a purely defensive maneuver; and despite these qualifications, the handbook made no mention whatsoever of the Soviets' 1939 invasion of partially occupied Poland.[37]

The USSR urged the sort of contextual understanding of the Soviet position that revisionist historians of American diplomacy would later adopt. Rather than suggest that Marxism propelled the Soviet Union down a path of world domination that had to be met with unyielding resistance, it made a case for cooperation.[38] The authors approvingly paraphrased Soviet premier Josef Stalin's justification for alliance with the Western capitalists: "He has told the Soviet people that the Allies are fighting a war of liberation and therefore a just war. He has also pointed out the differences between the Nazi regime and American-British regimes, citing . . . elemental liberties, trade unions, labor parties, and parliaments . . . in the latter." Moreover, because the Western allies met Stalin's rigorous criteria for virtuous societies "this allied unity is not a transitory affair" and might last into the postwar period.[39] The idea that Americans had to make allowances for Soviet behavior was another soon to be outmoded sentiment.

Nevertheless, the *Handbook* critiqued the Soviet system as a one-party dictatorship. The authors of the guidebook wanted officers not only to adopt the opinions presented in the material but to be able to win arguments when those opinions were challenged. To this end, they did not present the Soviet system in the one-sided, good-versus-evil manner that had seemed appropriate for Germany and Japan. Instead of telling officers that the Soviet Union had no economic freedom, the book distinguished between employing the labor of others, which was strictly forbidden, and minor forms of enterprise, which were allowed. The American officer, if he had committed the handbook to memory, would not have embarrassed himself by saying Soviets had no private property, only to have an agitator, a diplomatic rival, or a disgruntled soldier reply that Soviet citizens could in fact own some things, including a "home, clothing, or a milk cow." Rather than argue that Soviet workers were all treated the same regardless of productivity the authors admitted that pay was supposed to be scaled to their contribution. The Soviet Union did have a meritocracy, said *The USSR*, but bosses manipulated it in their own favor.[40]

Likewise, the Soviet government provided for freedom of conscience regarding religion and suspended "anti-religious propaganda" during the war. Nevertheless, "Communists . . . still regard religious belief as an error which scientific propaganda is expected to correct." Generally speaking, the authors of *The USSR* strove to make the same points about the Soviet regime that its harsher critics made, only they took pains to avoid blanket statements that could be disproved.

During the war American propagandists adhered to a policy of portraying enemy peoples as willing participants in their nations' march to conquest. *The USSR* handbook was more circumspect when dealing with the attitudes of the Soviet people—sensibly so, as the Cold War's diplomacy depended somewhat on understanding each contestant's self-image. In the cases of Germany and Japan, by contrast, the point was moot.

The authors' treatment of Soviet trade unions is a case in point. They argued that as "administrative units of the government" such unions were unlike American ones, but they cautioned that "The average Soviet worker . . . seems to regard them as representing his interests." Likewise, "The people of the Soviet Union believe that they have a democratic form of government," having "developed concepts of democracy which differ from those which Americans customarily accept." Specifically, they saw political dominance of the Communist Party as a limitation on freedom but not the absence of freedom. Soviets allowed public debate on issues about which the party had not determined a policy. Soviet citizens stressed their economic security and freedom from exploitation as the true basis of liberty.[41]

The authors took seriously the Soviet peoples' commitment to their political principles. Unlike the enemy "human hordes" of the *Why We Fight* films, this ally/rival population was credited with almost noble loyalty to its government: "This patriotic national sentiment . . . has broadened the base of popular support for the regime, has given it added strength during the war, and promises to perform the same function in the post-war period."[42]

The information program's ambiguity regarding the Soviet Union dramatically changed the tenor of the criticism directed at it. During World War II Congress expressed doubts about the propriety of indoctrinating the sons of democracy, and some civil libertarians regarded the *Why We Fight* series as insulting propaganda. With the onset of the Cold War it would be more than fifteen years before voices raised against propagandizing American troops reached sufficient volume to register in the national consciousness. Indeed, the chief complaint about information programs from 1945 on was that they were not strident enough. Nor was the critique limited to the foreign policy issue of how the propaganda should describe the Soviet Union. Recalling his information service, General Collins noted:

> The only problem that we had with this was from the conservatives, either on the hill or out in public life, who thought we were being too liberal in our outlining to the soldiers what the American system was.

[70]

[Director of the internal information program, Brig. Gen. Charles T.] Buck Lanham happens to be a liberal. I think I'm still a liberal despite some things that have given me pause subsequently, but both Lanham and I had a liberal outlook toward the information that ought to be given to our soldiers about what democracy consists of, and we were attacked by people who claimed we were teaching an illusory democracy you see.[43]

Attacks on the program's liberalism continued into the 1960s. Because Americans generally consider military culture to be conservative, one might assume that its political indoctrinators would likewise espouse conservative views. In some cases Troop Information content did lean unmistakably rightward. Conservatives were correct, however, in their perception that the information services attracted their share of liberal staffers. In fact, the office charged with providing anticommunist instruction to the troops was likely among the most liberal sectors of the army. Therefore, even officers convinced of the need for anticommunist vigilance did not look favorably on the program. Right-wing general Charles A. Willoughby, MacArthur's intelligence chief in occupied Japan, went so far as to suggest that information jobs and service newspapers were havens for subversives and cowards. In the opinion of one military intelligence officer who worked on the Truman administration's anticommunist loyalty program, "A liberal is only a hop, skip, and a jump from a Communist. A Communist starts as a liberal."[44]

During and immediately after the war, conservatives often held government propaganda in suspicion, both on principle and as a carrier of liberal ideas. In Great Britain as well, conservatives attacked liberal and leftist instructors in the British Army Education Corps, blaming them for influencing the soldier vote against Prime Minister Winston Churchill on the eve of military victory in 1945. Later, with the advent of the Truman Doctrine and explicit confrontation with the Soviet Union, American conservatives increasingly saw internal and external propaganda as a vehicle for their own agenda. What they first viewed as a money-wasting government excess they came to see as a potent tool, crucial in the battle against communism, and more dangerous than ever in the hands of liberals and leftists.[45]

Office of the Chief of Information

Given Collins's wartime exploits and his later service as army chief of staff, his days as chief of information consume little of his oral history. His information job description, and the shape of army public relations generally, owed much to the recommendations of Arthur W. Page. In November 1944, while still working for with the Information and Education Division, the AT&T vice president for public relations began compiling a report on the army's public information machine. His advice was that in order to sell its point of view to the public the army would do better to designate a PR chief from its own ranks than to hire an outside expert such as himself. A civilian publicity specialist would not only have to learn the culture and procedures of the army, he or she would be continually surprised by sudden turns of policy and events. An army officer, however, would be familiar with the ways of the service, and if he was of sufficient rank would be trusted to attend policy planning sessions at the highest level. That way, an army chief of information would learn of any controversial undertakings in time to lay the groundwork of public opinion, and be able to caution his colleagues on the likely impact of their decisions on public and congressional sentiment. Although an insider, this official would enjoy a status similar to Page's own within AT&T. Page also hoped that if the army cycled some of its best officers through public relations duties it would break down resistance to the practice.[46]

Page's recommendation that an officer hold the information post was also practical. In the postwar army, orientation programs for soldiers could no longer be the province of the Capras and the Pages, talented civilians cheerfully volunteering their time. The creation of the permanent post for the head of the Office of Information was the first important step in institutionalizing troop indoctrination as an army function. However, Page's recommendations, which included the selection of a three-star general with a respected combat record, make it clear that the army conceived of the CINFO primarily as a public relations director and his organization as a public relations department first and distributor of troop information second. In fact, Page's report persuaded the army to consolidate three World War II departments—Information and Education, the Bureau of Public Relations, and the Legislative and Liaison

Division (the army's lobbyists)—into the new office. In a less detailed report for the navy Page also recommended consolidating public relations and internal information.[47]

Page himself saw little or no distinction between the tasks. The public relations departments of large corporations like AT&T placed considerable emphasis on the morale and opinions of the "internal" audience. As big businesses in the first decades of the twentieth century grew in power and influence they began to rely on public relations specialists to court the favor of customers, politicians, and their employees. A consequence of a multiplant business empire with national, or even international, reach was that many industrialists felt alienated from their workers. Some were nostalgic for the lost culture of the small shop when the employers worked alongside their employees. In this romanticized setting, bosses gave paternal oversight and in return enjoyed their underlings' filial loyalty. Roland Marchand called this agonizing over employee loyalty, especially prevalent after World War I, "the Lament."[48]

Marchand argued that the Lament discouraged employers from identifying their corporations with armies. Immediately after allied victory in World War I the image of the industrial powerhouse as a dynamic military outfit seemed a fitting one. It depicted the laborers as disciplined troops, flattered the industrialist as a bold general, and implied that efficient, top-down authority governed the whole enterprise. Cravings for employees' loyalty and affection seemed to demand a different image, however, that of the family. At the same time that they tried to convince the outside public that the corporation was a benevolent community institution publicists told workers that they were not cogs in a ruthless machine, but family members. They used some techniques similar to those of the army's information programs, such as the print media. Employee magazines, like information pamphlets, sometimes veered into moralizing, and Marchand's evidence suggests that few workers took them to heart.[49]

Though they could not discourage soldiers from regarding the army as an army, military leaders along with corporate leaders valued the idea of family—not so much through some paternal bond uniting the organization and troops but in the feeling of brotherhood among soldiers in a small unit. Industrial workers went home each night to their real families, whose intimacy undercut the familial pretensions of the corporation. Soldiers, especially those stationed far from home, had to rely on comrades for intimacy and support much more deeply than workers relied upon one another. Basic training severed the new soldier from many civilian adhesions, and the threat of actual combat further alienated the soldier from the concerns of his relatives at home, while strengthening the bond with men facing the same risks. By situating Troop Information in the public relations office, rather than making it organic to training, the army put its program for communicating purpose to soldiers at a remove from the forge of loyalty.

If the output of the information program did not necessarily help to make the army seem like a family it did make it seem more like a corporation. In his 1960 study *The Professional Soldier*, Morris Janowitz described the numerous ways in which the postwar military establishment commingled with and came to resemble civilian institutions such as corporations. He identified the institutionalization of political indoctrination (along with changes in recruitment and career patterns, the overlapping of civilian and military managerial skills, and the increased reliance on persuasion rather than coercion) as one of the key elements in this process. The army, like early-twentieth-century businesses, contained some individuals who rejected the premise of the exercise. Marchand characterized public relations as a "feminine" development for corporations that were formerly steeped in a "masculine" culture of straightforward production. The army as well had officers for whom postwar changes such as mandatory TI&E went too far in softening service life.[50]

Because of this resistance, and the different concerns of soldiers and civilians, Public and Troop Information never fused completely into a single mission. The original pairing of public relations and internal indoctrination created a permanent tension between the two missions over the next three decades. Public Information ("PI" in army parlance) competed with Troop Information for the limited resources made available to such secondary military missions. In any budgetary argument public relations officers had the upper hand over the internal information officers. After World War II the value of Troop Information was no more widely accepted in the ranks than it had been during the conflict.

Any new wrinkle introduced into established command practices might be expected to encounter initial resistance, if only because it took time away from things commanders had learned from experience to consider essential. Nor did experience with Troop Information breed eventual respect. Many commanders still considered it a nuisance duty, a waste of time, or at best a good enough idea under ideal circumstances but impractical to implement in real life. In fact, despite operating continuously from World War II through the Vietnam War, Troop Information never overcame its status as a new invention of dubious value.

Conversely, most officers could immediately conceive of a powerful need for a Public Information apparatus. As an organization that had toiled in relative obscurity before the war the postwar army was naturally sensitive to press criticism. Whether one was a general officer snagged in a debate over national policy or a commander dealing with an off-base community newspaper, PI officers could be put to use. A press "flack" was a welcome addition to the staff of any commander who lived in fear of being embarrassed in the papers. The most important aspect of the PI program, however, was to argue the army's case in the intensifying interservice competitions for roles and budgets in the postwar period.

The advent of atomic weapons, along with weariness after a long war, rekindled hopes that the United States might base its security largely on an airpower deterrent and minimize ground forces and the unpleasantness they entailed. It seemed clear that the navy and soon-to-be-independent air force required budgets that could sustain the most modern and technologically sophisticated weapons. As so often before, however, the army needed to justify its existence to the taxpayers and their congressional representatives (albeit with less opposition than at other points in U.S. history).

This public relations mission could pull into its vortex even resources that OCINFO earmarked for Troop Information. In 1951, for example, OCINFO invited newspaperman Richard P. Taffe to rejoin the army and serve on its staff. Taffe described himself as a "not so secret flag-waver" and assumed he had been recruited in part because he knew what it was like in the trenches: he been wounded in the Pacific with the Eighty-first Division, where he also doubled as I&E officer for his unit. The deputy information chief told him he would be addressing the internal audience. His subjects "could range all the way from why they ate beans twice this week to what the President had in mind for the strategic employment of the forces in Korea." Yet soon enough Taffe was also writing articles aimed at the civilian public. His piece for *Collier's* about the army's 1952 maneuver in the wake of an atomic bomb test (Exercise DESERT ROCK) went directly to the issue of the army's postwar role. "Troops can attack through the ravaged area immediately after the blast," Taffe wrote. Or in the words of a general he quoted approvingly, "You can't research the infantry out of business."[51]

Housing Public Information and Troop Information under the same administrative roof was logical in some ways, but it was not necessarily the only option. An immense military organization has many functions that are "informational" in character. An army imparts information to its troops on how to clean, maintain, and discharge their weapons; commanders share information to plan strategies and tactics; and battlefronts transmit information to rear areas. Instead of being paired with public relations the type of information disseminated in troop indoctrination could just as easily have been linked to the practical type of information used to teach soldiers about drill, tactics, and equipment. As political indoctrination was supposedly part of training in any case, such an organization might have institutionalized it as part of primary training instead of relegating it to secondary status.

One need look no further than the navy for alternatives to the army's arrangement. Political indoctrination in the air force was similar to that in the army even after the air force gained autonomy in 1947. Its program generally used the same materials as the army but had a smaller budget and held instruction sessions less frequently. The navy and Marines conducted indoctrination much differently. The marines went to the greatest lengths of any of the services in avoiding politicized indoctrination. Their program emphasized unit pride and marine elitism rather than American and enemy ideologies. Because the army's leadership put greater stock in the need for political training, the marines' bare-bones program could not serve as much of a model. The navy was not as hostile to the concept and, like the army, encouraged relatively frequent political instruction. The navy, however, did not go as far in implementing Arthur Page's advice to centralize information functions. Instead, it integrated its program into its ongoing leadership training and ceded control of content to the local commander. That meant more attention to troops' immediate concerns but less adherence to the basic themes of patriotism and anticommunism generally favored by the senior commanders and civilian Cold Warriors. Had the army also tried to root Troop Information more deeply in training it might have avoided some of the friction with Public Information, though at the expense of control over the program.[52]

What is remarkable about the institutionalization of political indoctrination in the U.S. Army is that the War Department, and later the Department of the Army, apparently never considered other organizational options. During World War II, the army discovered that it needed to communicate in several unfamiliar ways as a deluge of draftees and volunteers overstrained the traditionally available channels. The original name of the office that rose to meet these challenges, the Special Services Division, bespoke the ad hoc nature of its organization and the variety of its duties. After the war, as the Information and Education Division, it continued with more or less the same grouping of responsibilities with little reevaluation.

In part, the army paired PI and TI as well as merging mundane information with political orientation because all these missions required personnel who had writing and speaking ability. Further, through both Public Information and Troop Information the army conveyed its agenda to a segment of the public. Because the soldiers came from and returned to the civilian public at large, what the army told one audience could not be wildly different from what it told the other. If the arrangement sacrificed an opportunity to integrate indoctrination and training, then having Public Information and Troop Information emanate from the same office ensured consistency of content and voice.

Collins, in any case, gave PI more of his attention. He recalled that after Page had made his recommendations about the need for a military chief of information

> I heard rumors that I was going to be Chief of Information and I wanted no part of it. I finally went in to see General Eisenhower who was then Chief of Staff and I told him that I'd heard these rumors that

I was going to be Chief of Information. I said, "Well, I always felt that my forte was commanding troops." He glared at me and said, "Joe, what in the hell have you been doing for the last two years?" So I stuck my tail between my legs and walked out the door. The next day orders came out designating me as Chief of Information.[53]

Collins became the first CINFO on July 1, 1946. Between higher-profile posts he had trouble, looking back at his career later, remembering exactly what title he had held from the summer of 1946 until July 29, 1947, when he became deputy chief of staff of the army.[54] The army's readiness to use Collins as Page suggested can be interpreted in two ways. It may have been a way of putting a talented officer in a holding pattern. After World War II the army had a glut of famous generals qualified for top command whom it could not easily accommodate in the peacetime organization.

Another possibility is that the army, expecting that Collins would eventually be chief of staff or North Atlantic Treaty Organization military chief (another post for which he was considered), gave him the Information and Education Division as part of the grooming process. As information chief, in the role that Page imagined, he would deal with the press, gauge congressional reactions, and learn to swim in Washington's murky waters of intrigue—all valuable experience for a potential chief of staff. Collins himself would at least admit that CINFO was one of the jobs he was glad to have had before assuming the top job.[55]

If indeed Eisenhower or anyone else had ever considered the Office of the Chief of Information (OCINFO) as a good place in which to groom future members of the Joint Chiefs of Staff, the idea never caught on. Though many capable officers wore the CINFO hat no others would go on to be chief of staff or occupy any post of comparable influence. Perhaps the reason that CINFO did not become a regular stop for top military commanders on the road to strategically vital posts was that, through the efforts of publicists like Page himself, public relations had by mid-century become a specialized business, requiring practitioners with specific training and expertise.

In 1946, however, Collins viewed the job of CINFO as being mainly about coordinating public relations while also keeping an eye on the

internal aspect. He had charge of three departments covering Public Information, Troop Information, and Troop Education, the last of which,
consisting of courses teaching basic or vocational skills, was comparatively apolitical in nature. Collins set about countering negative articles
and managing newspapermen, believing as he did that an aggressive
rebuttal of all criticism was the best defense against a hostile press. He
persuaded columnists to give him ample forewarning of adverse publicity by promising to "get them the facts" and was proud that both
parties kept their bargain during his tenure as chief. His main task, as
he saw it, was consultative: "if some matter was being discussed by the
Secretary, or at the Army Policy Council that was not directly involved
in legislation, I was supposed to say, 'Well look, have you thought of
the impact of that on the hill, how is that going to affect Congress, or
if it is some legislation, how is it going to affect the public at large or
within the Army, what's going to be the effect on the morale and what
not of the Army?'"[56]

The dismissive phrase "I was supposed to say" may indicate lack
of interest on Collins's part, but he did not always make light of the
"morale and whatnot of the Army." Later information officers would
remember the World War II and immediate postwar period as one in
which troop indoctrination sessions were turgid, unimaginative affairs.
Collins, however, considered his internal program to be effective, largely
because of his internal information deputy, Brig. Gen. Charles T. Lanham. During the war Lanham had commanded the Twenty-second Infantry Regiment in the Hurtgen Forest, where he won the admiration of
the war correspondent traveling with the unit, Ernest Hemingway. Collins credited Lanham with making sure his office communicated with
the troops and supporting Collins's dedication to keeping the troops
informed about their tasks.[57]

During Collins and Lanham's tenure, the Office of the Chief of Staff
ordered the Information and Education Division to reduce its staff to
thirty officers and sixty-one civilians, with further cuts planned. They
drew the line at the elimination of the Research Branch, deemed by both
the War Department and the Manpower Board to be "one of the least
essential functions of the War Department." Lanham supplied Collins
with evidence that contracting even a single attitude study to a civilian

organization would cost almost as much as the Branch's annual budget. Given these belt-tightenings, it was not surprising that in 1947 the Research Branch estimated that only a third of the troops stationed in Europe were getting weekly Troop Information meetings or that only 57 percent of soldiers surveyed had heard of the Troop Information program.[58]

Later, as army chief of staff, Collins endorsed a bigger role for propaganda. Toward the end of March 1952 he testified to the House Appropriations Committee in favor of a Department of State request for $170 million for a "campaign of truth." The State Department designed this information venture to counter Soviet propaganda. Proponents of the campaign argued that since 1950 the Soviet Union had been spending the equivalent of a billion dollars a year on a "hate-Americans" campaign. Unlike previous communist propaganda that trumpeted the advantages of their sociopolitical system or attacked capitalism generally, this new effort attempted to persuade "the individual Russian to hate the individual American."[59]

Collins urged that the State Department counteract "Yankee Go Home" propaganda in countries where the United States had stationed troops. The budget was to include $24 million for books to counter Soviet books, $5 million for influencing sentiment in Japan, and $5 million for anticommunist films to influence "the Near, the Middle and the Far East." At least one news commentator approved, suggesting that Collins's advocacy of the program was a "tribute to his growth, both in office and stature," whereas before the general had been chary about the value of a propaganda offensive.[60] Nevertheless, though he cheered the State Department into battle, the role the army's own Troop Information program would play in such a campaign never animated his interest.

As chief of staff, Collins was fairly attentive to the concerns of the information office, perhaps more so than any of his successors before William C. Westmoreland became chief of staff in 1968. More than a year after the State Department proposed an all-out propaganda offensive, Collins turned his attention to the army's internal program. On November 27, 1953, the *Washington Post* reported his criticism of American soldiers' lack of historical knowledge. Saying that troops needed to "be indoctrinated . . . with American military history," he encouraged the army to undertake a new effort to study its traditions. Although this statement did not constitute a lot of official attention, later information officers came to prize such rare acknowledgments of their existence by the army chief.[61]

Collins's late encouragement, in the waning days of the Korean War, was not enough to establish information as an army priority. Nor was it enough to fend off the avalanche of bad publicity that the troop indoctrination program received when the public learned that a tiny group of American soldiers held by the communist enemy refused to be repatriated to the United States in the war-ending prisoner exchanges. Neither Collins's personal fame nor his administration of the Office of the Chief of Information in 1946–47 gave the program much of a boost in the battles for budget, mission, and jurisdiction that almost all military departments waged in the postwar United States. Instead, the most enduring aspect of his stint as CINFO was the development of an information school.

The Army Information School

In 1943 the Information and Education Division began offering a few courses at the School for Personnel Services at Washington and Lee University in Lexington, Virginia. The courses covered only some aspects of Troop Information and did not address Public Information. Perhaps the need to train public relations personnel gave impetus to the establishment of an exclusive, official school to train specialists in all aspects of the information mission. Not until after the war did the school come to fruition. In January 1946 the War Department issued War Department Circular number 28, establishing the Army Information School (AIS) at Carlisle Barracks, in Carlisle, Pennsylvania. Again, the foundation of the school conformed to the plan outlined in Page's report, and Page served as the school's chairman of the board of regents.[62]

Carlisle Barracks was a venerable installation that had recently housed a number of diverse army schools. The first commandant was Brig. Gen. Williston B. Palmer, who like new information chief Collins came fresh from a prestigious combat command in Europe. In his oral history Palmer recalled that his appointment as commandant predated the existence of the actual school. With no background in information,

Palmer had to assemble a faculty, oversee the development of a course of instruction, and find a physical site.[63]

Palmer's memories of this period reveal an officer who was level headed about troop morale matters but no particular enthusiast of either internal propaganda or public relations. Asked whether the army had a legitimate role in informing the public or molding public opinion on matters of military policy, he replied: "No. I don't think so. . . . When you are explaining why you have these outfits, obviously you get into a certain amount presenting that side of the story. But it's not the Army's business. . . . Military policy is something set by the civilian authorities, as far as I understand it. . . . Now it is perfectly true that the Navy and the Air Force are whooping it up for their specialties, so possibly we ought to whoop it up for ours, too; but it's never appealed to me very much."[64]

Also unappealing to Palmer was the idea of the army as "school of the nation" to its citizen-soldiers. Palmer remarked that the elements of good morale were "pretty cut and dried" and consisted mainly of a sense of mission. He did not mean the larger, national mission but that the army ought to convey to each soldier a sense that he was part of an important unit, that his job was an important one in that unit, and that he was "not just being thrown around like a potato." The type of motivation that Palmer valued obviously had to be tailored to a unit's specific circumstances, and the unit commander, rather than a central authority, was in the best position to supply it.[65]

Despite his ambivalent attitude toward I&E the new commandant moved quickly to build the Army Information School. He requisitioned the post at Carlisle Barracks, and by February 27, 1946, future information officers began training in central Pennsylvania. Collins attended the opening of the school and in his remarks said: "The day is past when we can put second raters into the jobs of public information and information and education. First class persons must go into these jobs."[66] The first class may or may not have been first-rate people, but in any case they were not all destined to be career information specialists. The AIS was one of several schools housed in Carlisle, including the Military Police School, the Chaplain School, and the Adjutant General School. The creation of a new organizational structure did the same thing for the army's junior officers that the offices of CINFO and Commandant, AIS, did for its top brass: it provided a holding pattern for personnel who were left without an immediate function in the postwar army. The AIS was not a place where dedicated IOs came to be informed about the latest indoctrination techniques. Instead, officers gained exposure to public relations in accordance with Page's belief that every officer ought to have some PR training. Page himself lectured to the first graduating class and several others. Army areas also used the school for "quota-filling" by sending the same man first to the AIS, then to the MP school, and so on (though presumably not to the Chaplain School).[67]

The first class contained two hundred students whose course of instruction ran eight weeks. In March 1946, Charles T. Lanham addressed the class with a talk specifically on the internal program, which he noted was now exclusively to be called "Troop Information" (as opposed to orientation, which he thought smacked "too much of propaganda"). Noting that Palmer's introduction was the first nice thing anyone had said to him since taking over "the Slings and Arrows Division," Lanham warned the students that most of the army was unfriendly to the program. They would therefore have to have the "moral courage" to "slug it out toe to toe with all of the advocates and disciples of intolerance, or prejudice, of the dead hand of the past." Anyone, he said, could recite what was wrong with the program, but when one pointed out all the things it did one could see that it was in fact valued. He called on students to respect the chain of command and the army's political neutrality, but also encouraged them to seize the role of the army's "intellectual aristocracy" and attack the "little bundle of prejudices" that soldiers brought into the army whenever they impaired teamwork.[68]

By June 1946 the school had increased the course work to twelve weeks. By the end of the first year the AIS had graduated 1,824 officers and enlisted men as information specialists. Enlisted men's courses generally ran about half the number of hours afforded officers, so enlisted classes graduated at twice the rate of officer classes. Later, the length of the program was increased to fourteen weeks for officers while remaining six weeks for enlisted men. Within eight years, 10,578 men and women had passed through the courses.[69]

The school fell within the command of the Second Army, headquartered in Baltimore, Maryland. This arrangement subjected the faculty to the attention of Col. Frederick S. Doll, a Second Army intelligence officer. Doll pursued Palmer throughout his tenure with complaints that AIS was "full of subversives" and that Col. Fred Herzberg, in particular, was a communist. Herzberg, a dentist and a graduate of Northwestern University, was an orientation lecturer in Italy during the war and had been invited to stay on afterward as information instructor. Finding no evidence to substantiate the charges, Palmer and Lanham confronted Doll in September 1946 and forced him to admit that he had based his accusations solely on the facts that Herzberg favored the fair treatment of black soldiers and that he was Jewish. At that point, Gen. Manton S. Eddy, the Second Army commander, called off Doll. In 1947, however, Gen. Albert C. Wedemeyer succeeded Eddy and permitted the smear campaign to linger. Wedemeyer shared Doll's politics and circulated among other commands his conviction that the information program was infecting soldiers with socialism.[70]

The army to which AIS graduates would administer was far different from the one Wedemeyer had known when commissioned in 1918. In World War II what had previously been a comparatively homogeneous and intimate organization swallowed millions of racially and ethnically diverse citizen-soldiers, who were mobilized under the banner of pluralistic democracy and dedicated to the overthrow of the self-appointed master races. Despite rapid force reductions after the war the army did not return to its previous insularity. The nation maintained the largest peacetime force in its history—over a million soldiers—as Congress first extended the wartime Selective Service Act and then, in 1948, enacted another one. The same year, Truman issued Executive Order 9981, ordering the armed forces to integrate racially, and Congress passed the Women's Armed Forces Integration Act, which gave women the opportunity for limited careers in the military. The peacetime draft helped ensure that the army would continue to consist in large part of short-term citizen-soldiers. The majority of these men, whether draftees or volunteers, eager or reluctant, entered the army with an attitude similar to their wartime predecessors in at least one respect: they interrupted their lives to discharge a patriotic duty, not because soldiering was their preferred lifestyle.[71]

In part to accommodate this attitude, the government and other opinion makers promoted the World War II army as "democratic," not only in allegiance but in culture. Continuing the trend in the late 1940s, the army attempted to become somewhat more "soldier friendly" by reducing sources of friction in officer-enlisted relations. Most notably, it softened the more severe aspects of military law with a new Uniform Code of Military Justice that featured legal protections for soldiers based on civilian practices. This "democratic" posture appalled many career soldiers, who saw in these small cosmetic changes (to say nothing of the larger social changes of integration) the beginnings of a crisis in military discipline. Herzberg's efforts to introduce the topic of better race relations to future information officers, and the willingness of superiors like Palmer and Lanham to support him, indicate that the recently born OCINFO was more of the new army than the old. Officers who identified Troop Information and its mission to soothe soldiers' doubts about service with this supposed new laxity hindered the branch's acceptance in the postwar army.[72]

Palmer's first successor as commandant of AIS was also a brigadier general. After 1954 colonels served in the post, perhaps reflecting retirements in the ranks of World War II general officers. Under the commandant were two deputy commandants (colonels), one for administration and the other for instruction. Under the deputy commandant for instruction were two directors (lieutenant colonels), the director of Public Information Training and the director of Information and Education (I&E had come to refer solely to Troop Information). At first the school maintained separate academic departments under each director of training. Students took courses in both departments but graduated with a specialty in one or the other. Probably because an information officer in the field would have both PI and TI duties, in 1951 the school did away with the departments and reconstituted them as seven academic "fields" under the two directors jointly.[73]

The seven fields were History-Economics-Government, News Writing, Pictures, Education, Radio and Television, Oral Communications, and Policy and Operational Procedure. Each had its own director and a staff of instructors. Some of the first individual classes included "Officer-Enlisted Relations" and "The Mind of a Democracy." The school stressed hands-on experience and practice rather than simple classroom instruction. To learn the ropes of leading discussion, I&E students had to brief the post's "Information Hour" discussion leaders and were graded on their performance. The school selected some officers to go to the University of Chicago for specialized discussion-leading techniques. To teach the operation of a base newspaper instructors in the newswriting subdepartment gave every student a "dummy paper" to edit with full responsibility for every aspect of production. Enlisted men got five surprise tests on current affairs, but, pop quizzes apparently being beneath their dignity, officers were exempted.[74]

Following another of Arthur Page's suggestions, Palmer initiated a four-year project in which students compiled a 1,000-page army almanac. The book was to serve as a reference bible for PI officers, I&E officers, and civilians, and contained accounts of campaigns, army history, customs, etiquette, standard procedures, and the like. In 1950 I&E students participated in LOGEX 50, a combined map maneuver and logistics exercise. The class divided into committees to prepare reports on the exercise. Their assignment was to do a complete information and education workup for the participating soldiers, including a four-page newsletter, to emulate the way information officers would cover a real operation and explain it to troops.[75]

Students competed for plaques that recognized outstanding I&E efforts, and the "I&E Department's Little Art Players" performed skits that depicted the operation of the educational program, the information officer's role as a staff member, and methods for handling different types of interviews. One of the subdepartments (History-Economics-Government) led a tour of the nearby Gettysburg battlefield (and felt the need to provide "background music and Union and Confederate flags waving to give the proper effect").[76]

The AIS showed an immediate interest in the developing technology of television. Recognizing TV's potential as a disseminator of information and propaganda the school installed a visual aids workshop in the basement of Hoff Hall (today's Upton Hall), where the AIS was located, and tested the effectiveness of televising the curriculum's classes. Although the army ultimately refrained from replacing live instructors with televised classes the experiment indicated an open-minded, imaginative school eager to interact with the outside world.[77]

Credit for this attitude belonged in part to a well-qualified faculty composed of military and civilian teachers. For example, the director of instruction for I&E in the early 1950s, Lt. Col. Guy Lothrop, boasted a West Point education with graduate work at Columbia University, the Sorbonne, and the General Staff College at Fort Leavenworth, Kansas. The army invited students from foreign nations to teach and learn from information specialists in allied armies. Although rapid turnover in assignments made it impossible to keep track of what the program's graduates were doing, faculty members made frequent trips into the field to get feedback from working information officers.[78]

For example, freshly minted IOs found themselves at a loss when confronted with bookkeeping and expense reports. The curriculum soon incorporated instruction on how to manage I&E's "appropriated" and "non-appropriated funds." Besides the aforementioned exchange with the University of Chicago the school sent liaison officers to Columbia University's Teachers' College, where in 1950 and 1951 they helped develop Columbia's *Hours of Freedom* teaching series for the military.[79]

On June 1, 1948, the Department of the Army redesignated the AIS as the Armed Forces Information School (AFIS). It was one of four schools to undergo service unification with the birth of the Department of Defense (DOD). Airmen and sailors joined army officers and enlisted men in Carlisle and took courses together. The teaching methods did not distinguish between students' service of origin in their approach to the material. The idea of a unified school was that all students would learn in the same way, presumably to smooth differences among the different branches of defense and to promote shared procedures as much as possible. The position of commandant would now rotate among the services, with Rr. Adm. Thomas Binford succeeding Palmer's successor, Brig. Gen. Edward J. McGaw, in December 1950.[80]

Commandant Binford served the AFIS for four years, until 1954, a period of change for the program. During his tenure the Army War College moved to Carlisle, and to make room the information school vacated its home in Hoff Hall and moved to Fort Slocum in New Rochelle, New York, along with the Chaplain School. The school reopened on April 19, 1951, optimistic that its new location, only sixteen miles from New York City, would provide valuable opportunities for its students to learn their trade in the media capital of the world.[81] Of particular value was the chance to interact with the major Armed Forces Radio Services station in New York.

The AFIS prided itself on being a model of interservice cooperation, entirely free of the acrimony that characterized the services' interaction in other arenas. Unfortunately for information's champions, the source of this harmony was that no one considered the turf worth disputing. Again, the navy and air force viewed the training program with less interest than did the army. Officer Class Number 6 and Enlisted Class Number 12, which graduated together in August 1950, comprised thirteen army officers, one Women's Army Corps officer, and only two each from the navy and air force. Only six sailors, two airmen, and one marine joined forty-six army enlisted men and seven WACS.[82]

Finally, the Department of Defense pulled the plug on the unified school. On March 17, 1954, the Department of the Army issued General Order Number 18, renaming the institution the Army Information School. The school celebrated its independence with a star-studded series of speakers, including Eisenhower, Collins, Eleanor Roosevelt, James Cardinal Spellman, Generals Jacob L. Devers and Albert M. Gruenther, historians Henry Steele Commager and Douglas Southall Freeman, and journalists Edward R. Murrow and Eric Sevareid.[83] The newfound independence was short lived, however. Despite relenting temporarily in the matter of the AIS, the Department of Defense regarded troop indoctrination as a militarywide function that should be coordinated at the highest level. The services argued that information programs had to be tailored to specific needs best assessed and dealt with by each individual service. So far as information was concerned, they presented a unified front against unification.

In the meantime, the school adapted to the Korean War. Emphasis in the newswriting subdepartment shifted to supervising existing newspapers rather than creating new ones. The administration cut class hours to get IOs into the field faster.[84] On the whole, the Army Information School presented a competent faculty and an innovative curriculum to its students. It incorporated ideas from civilian educators, media professionals, and its own officers in the field.

It did all this without any deep commitment from the military to support the Troop Information program. The restrained attitude of the army's new information institutions toward the internal indoctrination mission made the program ripe for close Department of Defense oversight. The army's office assumed a defensive posture toward the DOD, which it maintained through the Vietnam War. The Pentagon was more sanguine about propagandizing troops. Throughout the Cold War it held the program's ideology fast to the anticommunist line. Because it was farther removed from soldiers in the field, however, it became harder for those who set the indoctrination agenda to gauge how their messages were received, or if they were received at all. In a 1949 survey, the percentage of soldiers who said they had attended "last week's" Troop Information session stood at a robust 73 percent, but 40 percent of them characterized the sessions as only "sometimes" or "never" worthwhile. Postwar equivalents of the World War II Research Branch wielded less influence than their predecessor, and the dissonance between propagandists and their audience grew.[85]

Troop Information gained permanence in the army but not acceptance. Therefore, when the Korean War broke out it was no better prepared than any other branch of the U.S. military machine. Like the rest of the armed forces its personnel learned to function during the crisis. These factors combined to create an organization that could not boast of much confidence or sense of purpose and retained few links to its experience in the last war. Not knowing exactly what they wanted to do afforded the Korean War's information officers a certain flexibility. The solutions they improvised reflected the process of institutionalization that the program had undergone during the five years between wars, including the restrained ideological responses of the copywriters; the low-intensity, liberal leadership of Collins, Lanham, and Palmer; and the open-mindedness of the AIS. But in a frustrating and tense conflict these solutions would satisfy few Americans.

3

OAFIE's Voice

Political Indoctrination in the Korean War

The army's formal attempts to influence soldiers' views about the Korean War were relatively modest, especially measured against the McCarthyite excesses after the war. Despite its limited scope, the information program of the early 1950s faced several difficulties. At the outset of the conflict the authors of the Troop Information materials harbored unrealistic expectations about what they could achieve. Later, however, they found a more moderate tone in which to convey political messages to skeptical soldiers. The inexperienced discussion leaders responsible for disseminating information had to overcome the difficulty inherent in staging supposedly open discussions while simultaneously stifling any signs of dissent. Furthermore, the program's content itself contained an internal contradiction not easily ignored. By trumpeting as a peculiarly American virtue the fact that the government does not tell its citizens what to think the Troop Information program constrained its own ability to do just that. The army tried to accommodate the beliefs of its citizen-soldiers as much as it tried to shape them. After the war, when stories of American prisoners of war (POWs) collaborating with the enemy rocked the country, critics urged the military to replace its circumspect approach with a simple brand of hard-core anticommunist nationalism. Yet the very diversity of the civilian critiques of the information program cast doubt on Americans' acceptance of one-size-fits-all patriotism.

A New Bureaucracy Goes to War

The victory of the Allies in World War II freed the Korean peninsula from forty years of Japanese rule but also made it a battlefield of the Cold War. As relations between the United States and the Soviet Union hardened into open hostility, each side helped a friendly faction secure power in their respective zones of occupation. Most Americans had little awareness of the local and nationalistic forces moving Korea toward civil war, nor had the American military regarded the peninsula as a vital strategic investment. So, when the communist Democratic People's Republic of Korea invaded the south on June 25, 1950, it took American policymakers by surprise. In another sense, however, the attack did not surprise them in the least. Not only did they interpret the invasion as Soviet aggression by proxy, but they also recognized in it the incrementalism of Germany's provocations in the 1930s. The lessons learned in the last war seemed to mandate immediate confrontation.

The information program quickly rallied to produce pamphlets, radio programs, and films for the new war. Political indoctrination in the army came under the umbrella of the Office of the Chief of Information (OCINFO). The information branch had two realms of responsibility: public relations and Troop Information and Education. As in World War II the "education" half of TI&E taught basic skills and trades. The "information" half of the mission administered political orientation in the form of the Troop Information program. Unlike the Special Services Division in the late war, however, the internal program in the Korean War did not distinguish bureaucratically between politicized, motivational "orientation" and mundane "information." In the early 1950s the military classed everything from anticommunist training to instructions on collecting pay as "information."

In 1950 the Department of Defense, armed with new centralizing powers, created the Armed Forces Information and Education Division (AFIED) to oversee the army's OCINFO and the other services' internal information programs. The army's major general William K. Harrison Jr. became AFIED's first director. Originally a division of the department's Personnel Policy Board, AFIED became the responsibility of the Office of the Assistant Secretary of Defense (Manpower and Personnel) in 1951. In 1952 it changed its name to the Office of Armed Forces Information and Education (OAFIE).

In contrast to its usual struggles with the services, the Department of Defense, through OAFIE, gained considerable control over the army's troop indoctrination. Because the army housed the indoctrination program in an office that considered it a distant second in priority to public relations it had little invested in its autonomy. OAFIE, conversely, was unburdened by public relations duties; the Department of Defense had a separate Office of Public Information unconnected to internal information. Thus, the internal information program was OAFIE's raison d'être. Perhaps more importantly, the army's wariness concerning political indoctrination compelled it to loosen its grip on the process when confronted with Department of Defense's untroubled enthusiasm.[1]

The limited nature of the Korean War presented challenges different from those of World War II. Information officers had to convince draftees that their service was a fair and just obligation of citizenship when they could plainly see how many draft-age men escaped selection. No nationwide effort demanded participation by sheer momentum. The United States had not suffered direct attack, nor was it self-evident that the global position of the United States would be threatened by a North Korean victory. Most American soldiers knew little of the allied Republic of Korea and had no racial or ethnic ties with Koreans for the information writers to exploit. Given the precarious peace between the superpowers the United States had to be cautious and flexible in its war aims, which made it difficult to give soldiers a clear statement of purpose or a promise of a better world to come through their efforts.

One avenue open to the program's operators was the anticommunist line. Communism had aroused widespread suspicions in the United States even before the Russian Revolution in 1917. Faced with a powerful Soviet state that espoused, at least theoretically, the overthrow of the capitalist democracies, opposition hardly softened after World War II. Despite communism's acute unpopularity in the postwar United States it nevertheless came to shape mainstream political debate. The Republican Party had not been able to muster a presidential majority since the onset of the Great Depression. By the time they had finished serving their term as the loyal opposition during World War II, Republicans had been out of power for more than a decade, while Democrats had led the nation's embrace of global power. Eager to contest the Democrats' preeminent position in foreign affairs the Republicans attacked the Truman administration for reversals in the Far East, especially for the communists' 1949 victory over the nationalists in China's civil war. At the same time, the Democratic administration of President Harry

S. Truman adopted loyalty programs for government employees and tried to deport foreign-born suspected communists. By accepting the premise that communists were invariably agents of an enemy government, rather than often simply domestic radicals, liberals and centrists ensured that anticommunism was not just the stance of the right.

Within the anticommunist consensus, however, politicians tried to outdo each other in their depth of anticommunist commitment. As Steven J. Whitfield observes in *The Culture of the Cold War*, "Citizens were expected to enlist in the Cold War. Neutrality was suspect, and so was a lack of enthusiasm for defining American society as beleaguered." Civilians therefore became accustomed to dramatizations of communism's threat as part of their daily political bread. Because of this conditioning anticommunism provided a readily understood vocabulary for making the case for the Korean War.[2]

The Troop Information program employed four basic media: radio broadcasts, films, printed material, and direct verbal presentations at meetings. Although the Troop Information branch shared the Armed Forces Radio Service schedule with general entertainment and morale-boosting shows, it did its best to squeeze TI&E content between more popular programs. OCINFO and OAFIE created or commissioned more than three hundred short radio shows. Films produced for Troop Information included both the instructional and motivational variety. Printed material was the largest part of the information arsenal and included pamphlets, posters, comic books, and overseas guidebooks. One series of pamphlets formed the basis of the "Armed Forces Talks," sixteen hours of lecture and discussion that was delivered to the soldiers during basic training.[3]

The Pentagon seized the creative initiative for writing and producing the various information materials. OAFIE more or less set the Troop Information agenda, with only the broadest pronouncements by Department of Defense superiors for guidelines. The army's OCINFO adopted the defensive posture of reacting to OAFIE's initiatives—accepting, rejecting, or urging modifications of its proposals. OAFIE itself did not boast as prestigious a stable of writers, artists, and filmmakers as the Special Services Division had but instead hired outside writers, often academicians, to produce the information material. The government subjected civilian participants to a background check to prevent communist agents and fellow travelers from infiltrating the program.[4]

Only when an information idea was fairly well developed did OAFIE pass it down to OCINFO. The army office's review occasionally led to substantive changes in Department of Defense proposals. However, because OAFIE possessed a research branch and was responsible for studying the effectiveness of the information programs it generated much of the evidence used in its own evaluation. Anything to which OCINFO agreed had to go up the ladder for final approval by the Organization and Training Division at the General Staff level, which was not deeply involved in the creative process.

The development of the Columbia University *Hours of Freedom* series illustrates the process in action. In December 1950 Dwight D. Eisenhower, then president of Columbia University, placed the university's facilities at the disposal of the Department of Defense. A legacy of World War II had been a warmer relationship between the military and the academy. Whereas after the 1918 scholars were somewhat embarrassed by their promotion of wartime propaganda academics of the early Cold War maintained extensive ties to the national security apparatus. This engagement was most prominent in the sciences, but humanities professors also remained involved in troop indoctrination through the information school's exchanges with the University of Chicago and Columbia's Teachers College. Taking up Eisenhower's offer, the military asked Teachers College to prepare a series of ten "citizenship training" pamphlets called the *Hours of Freedom* (it took an hour to present and discuss each pamphlet in a Troop Information session). The pamphlets covered the following topics: Responsibility to Serve, The Worth of the Individual, Freedom of Religion, Freedom of Expression: The Press, It Takes Courage, Citizen Control of the Government I and II, The Threat to Freedom, The Role of the Law, and Community Relations. Their creators trumpeted the series' "attention-getting devices" and argued, dubiously, that the emphasis on discussion would negate the need for experienced lecturers.[5]

Columbia took over a year to complete the pamphlets, at which point OAFIE persuaded OCINFO to have the army stock an initial supply. Nevertheless, the army's information officers shelved the *Hours of Freedom* after field testing. Reports forwarded from six continental armies convinced OCINFO that the *Hours of Freedom* series was too expensive and time consuming to implement on a regular basis. Reported comments such as the following must have given OCINFO pause: "a clever teaching device . . . though many trainees found them a dissipation of time."[6]

The *Hours* taught American citizenship in much the same way as the nation's secondary schools, and consumed ten of the sixteen basic training hours allotted to Troop Information in the process. Despite the great time demand, some observers thought the talks were not overtly political enough and contrasted them unfavorably with the existing programs. Said one, "they made no attempt whatsoever to explain why the threat of communism to the American Way of Life has caused the basic trainee to enter the military services of his country."[7]

The criticism was partly accurate. The Columbia *Hours of Freedom* seemed geared for a peacetime army. It wasted far too much time explaining topics such as how a bill becomes a law and gave precious little attention to why the soldier had to risk his life in Korea. Some of the critics reacted to the absence of unsophisticated anticommunist bombast and claimed Columbia's liberal faculty had skewed the program too far to the left. Though such an agenda is difficult to detect, the material still lacked any visceral quality that would have made it more memorable to soldiers in their twenties than it had been to them as students in their teens.[8]

The *Hours'* "Civics 101" approach may have been the wrong way to conduct political indoctrination, but the correct way was not instantly identifiable. Nevertheless, over the course of the Korean War the military's information materials matured discernibly. By 1952 the pamphlets in use had a consistent, moderate tone notably absent from the initial efforts.

Fighting Words

In August 1950 the army issued a *Four-Hour Pre-Combat Orientation Course* to present to basic trainees. A rushed effort, the course crammed into four hours material that would later be afforded sixteen. The format of the booklets was nearly uninterrupted text, encouraging the discussion leader simply to read the pamphlet aloud. Its summary of international current events tried to make soldiers angry. Commu-

nists had taken "a slap" at the United States, demonstrated "pure inso-
lence," and were in fact "a gang of second-raters." The pamphlet went
on to denounce any domestic opposition to the war as subversive "puny
whimperings" (belying the course's celebration of Americans "standing
tall" through their freethinking political freedom). The last hour of the
course repeated almost verbatim the historical summary featured in the
first hour.[9]

The course's recommended presentation depended entirely on impractical staging demands. For instance, the instructions prompted
the instructor to ask the assembled soldiers what they thought was the
greatest weapon at their disposal. When someone answered "the ba-
zooka" or "the atom bomb" the instructor was supposed to say, "Men,
the most effective weapon of war is *man*!" At this point a curtain was
to rise on a stage behind the discussion leader to reveal a heavily armed
soldier in full battle dress, representing the audience members themselves. A bright spotlight would "accentuate his warlike appearance."
The pamphlet did not say what to do if a stage, curtain, or spotlight
should be unavailable (3).

The course attempted to explain initial military setbacks and, especially,
to counter boastful enemy propaganda. It tried to dispel rumors rampant
at the outset of the war that the army's equipment was old and unreliable. The pamphlet stressed that soldiers should not interpret phrases like
strategic withdrawal as euphemisms for military debacle (15).

The greatest drawback of the early material was that it tried to over-
whelm the subject with bombast and showmanship. This approach
might have worked in the hands of a charismatic leader. When Lt. Gen.
Matthew B. Ridgway took over the Eighth Army in late December 1950
he sought to instill a fighting spirit in his troops, in part by issuing a
message to every man explaining "Why are we here? What are we fighting for?" He wrote: "The real issues are whether the power of Western
civilization, as God has permitted it to flower in our own beloved lands,
shall defy and defeat Communism; whether the rule of men who shoot
their prisoners, enslave their citizens, and deride the dignity of man,
shall displace the rule of those to whom the individual and his individual
rights are sacred; whether we are to survive with God's hand to guide
and lead us, or to perish in the dead existence of a Godless world."

Infantryman Harry G. Summers Jr., who later authored the influential critique of American strategy in the Vietnam War, *On Strategy*, thought Ridgway's arrival marked "the most remarkable transformation I have ever seen of turning an army around, on the strength of his character alone." And after the general's message, "no one had the slightest doubt why they were in Korea."[10]

Ridgway's personal review of conditions at the front sparked his inspirational exhortations. Prepackaged tough talk, on the other hand, was unlikely to be as effective in the hands of the mostly inexperienced information officers to whom commanders often delegated lecture duty. In this instance, ios were ill served by the Army Information School's emphasis on Public Information (PI) rather than Troop Information (TI, or TI&E) duties. However, even if the curriculum had favored the TI&E mission, the army did not have enough Army Information School graduates to cover all the units eventually mustered for the war. Most of the discussion leaders still had to learn their task through trial and error.

The Backseat Drivers

The information managers did not have to wait long to get feedback on their programs. Americans evinced some interest in the conduct of the Troop Information program even before controversies over the behavior of POWs thrust it into the national spotlight. Many of the critics were World War II veterans. OAFIE's staff spent a great deal of time fielding the inquiries and advice of the interested public and responding on behalf of director Maj. Gen. John M. Devine.

Though the quality of civilian advice was uneven, not all of it was unsolicited. Just as the army sought civilian help when facing the morale problem of 1941, so OAFIE sought outsiders' opinions from within the military and without. Most of the appraisals they received were uncomplimentary. A report from a civilian advisory committee indicated that "the Troop Information programs appear to be missing their mark by a wide margin." The men and instructors were apathetic about the compulsory sessions and considered them a waste of time.[11]

In January 1951 civilian Charles O. Porter, a former information officer who served in World War II, insisted that the Korean War's TI discussion format was overly rigid and unable to address the concerns of the audience. He thought the program required qualified leaders who could run a presentation similar to a "Chinese criticism meeting," in which soldiers could discuss economics and politics and "air their views and ask embarrassing questions."[12]

In a follow-up letter to Marx Leva, the assistant secretary of defense (legal and legislative affairs), Porter suggested that the group leaders be college graduates with liberal arts backgrounds. Under the prevailing system the officers who had to present Troop Information material regarded the job as nuisance duty, akin to kitchen patrol. One sergeant read his men the pamphlets in "an unbroken monotone, including the italicized instructions to the instructor." The restrictive policy on soldiers' questions "ripped the guts out of the whole thing." Leva replied that commanders, not teachers, had to lead the discussions or the soldiers would not pay attention at all.[13]

Joe Michaels of WFDR radio made several suggestions that received serious attention in the information branch as well. "The enemy has a 'cause'," he wondered, "why not us?" A proper indoctrination program, he argued, required feature-length films, posters with threatening slogans, and the distribution of "real literature" such as *1984* and *Darkness at Noon*, all to inculcate in soldiers "a sincere and knowledgeable hatred for communism." He also recommended that outside teachers be given total independence from unit commanders, making them for all purposes political officers.[14]

While Michaels was overambitious in recommending "real" literature as training material, Lt. Gen. LeRoy Lutes, commanding officer of the Fourth Army, probably underestimated the U.S. soldier in his recommendations. He argued that because "we have such a large number of men in service who think in very simple terms . . . they must be approached on these terms. . . . The Russians use the catechism method on most of their rank and file, why don't we? Long lectures to large groups do not get over to the men. Catechism instruction in small groups would." Lutes enclosed a sample catechism for OAFIE's study along with some of his own reactionary political speeches. "If you use it," he warned, "don't let some pink modify it or insert language that is vague."[15]

Another World War II veteran with experience in the information realm proposed that the Americans imitate the South African "Battle School": "30% commando tactics, 20% theory of leadership, and 50% disguised political indoctrination." The author contrasted this model favorably with his experience in the U.S. Navy, where he was "fed pap that the war was fought for the privilege of munching a hot dog at Ebbets Field."[16]

Col. Harrod G. Miller, a training officer with the Signal Corps, spoke for many when he summarized: "Results of the [Troop Information] program do not appear commensurate with present expenditure in time and money." The problems as he saw them were that assignment as discussion leader was an unpopular, extra duty and that the classes were too large. As these problem were unlikely to change, Miller recommended that the program be radically altered to explicitly embrace controversial, engaging topics such as "Socialized Medicine in England" and "Complete Integration of Negro Troops." He recognized that soldiers rejected attempts to give such topics a "candy-coating."[17]

The perception that political indoctrination was failing was sufficiently widespread to encourage at least two universities, Duke University and the University of Colorado, to propose replacing the military's program. In March 1951 Duke vice president Paul Gross pitched a "democratic indoctrination program for the armed services" that for a budget of about $200,000 would study indoctrination techniques used in the past and in other countries, survey five thousand soldiers about their attitudes toward "Russian Communism," and create a curriculum ("perhaps using the comic-book technique to some extent") based on the results. The University of Colorado's Committee for University Research based its proposal "upon the belief that the present information program of the armed services is not altogether achieving its purposes." By interviewing soldiers in installations nearest to Boulder, Colorado, the researchers would ascertain "what unanswered questions these men have concerning the world situation" and then convene a "large and distinguished panel" of national leaders to answer them. "After the questions have been collected from the servicemen themselves, and the answers accumulated from the panel of outstanding citizens, the third phase would involve transmitting the collected information back to the training camps." The Colorado team made the whole process seem rather easier than the information officers had found it to be, and in its reply the Pentagon pointed out that the proposed efforts paralleled ones they had already undertaken. The Duke proposal drew a polite rejection from Secretary of Defense George C. Marshall, who nevertheless had Devine meet with a Duke professor to explain his office's mission.[18]

That these outside recommendations received the attention they did was due not only to the organization's openness to suggestions but also to the fact that the indoctrinators were still struggling to find a consistent voice. Defending his office both from critics who wanted to broaden the political debate in the sessions and those who wanted them to become more stridently orthodox, Devine articulated his understanding of the mission. Propaganda and political indoctrination, he informed most critics, were the tools of the enemy. OAFIE would not imitate the models of the Chinese, Soviet, or South African programs but would adhere to uniquely American values. The information services, he claimed, merely armed the soldiers with the facts. Truth was the information officer's watchword.[19]

Devine was not being facetious. Information officers, by inclination or necessity, often took to heart the national ideology they espoused to the troops in their charge. A determination to use propaganda on citizen-soldiers coexisted with a high regard for the same men's freedom of thought and spirit of independence. For all its drawbacks, the program administered by such true believers was far more suitable to an American audience than the enemy indoctrination systems admired by Lutes and Porter. Chinese "criticism meetings" theoretically permitted troops a frank airing of views but in practice simply demanded, through constant badgering, rigid ideological conformity. Political indoctrination in the Soviet Army was a relentless bombardment of lectures, movies, meetings, and other exhortations. One analyst concludes that this overbearing approach dulled Soviet troops into political apathy and sowed resentment by frequently imposing on their leisure time. In contrast, the American indoctrinators' "just the facts" philosophy limited the intensity of OAFIE's indoctrination. It also helped the organization achieve a more rational, moderate voice as the war entered its second year.[20]

Maj. Gen. Gilman C. Mudgett, who succeeded CINFO Floyd L. Parks toward the end of the war, later reflected on this developmental period.

The Troop Information program, he recalled, "was developed by enthusiastic people who knew nothing of leadership problems and was unpopular." Demoralized information officers often found themselves in the "dungeon" separated from the unit commander. Mudgett wanted the army to convince information school graduates of their vital importance to the sprawling military machine around them. Though the unit commander presumably had a sense of his own importance, Mudgett wanted to impress upon him the need for the information mission. One of the problems with the material was that the commander had instructions but not options. The *Troop Topic* pamphlets, Mudgett insisted, were meant only as suggestions. As the Korean War went on, OAFIE and OCINFO did modify their written material enough to make this point somewhat better than they had at the outset.[21]

In the same remarks, Mudgett revealed his willingness for the army to embrace the role of "school of the nation." To the charge that teaching citizenship was the task of schools and churches, he argued that the army could not ignore soldiers who had "missed their schooling" or had at best a "fourth grade education." He saw OCINFO's mission as "the last time that organized society can impress upon them their responsibilities as citizens and the Army must accept that challenge."[22]

After the war, in the mid-1950s, OAFIE became the primary advocate of using the troop indoctrination program as a school of American citizenship. The army shied away from such a role. OAFIE's position at the Department of Defense level exposed its leaders to public demands for zealous anticommunism. OAFIE's own true believers found friends in political circles eager to support aggressive indoctrination.

The influences on OCINFO were different. Political concerns also weighed heavily on information chief Parks and his superiors, but they manifested themselves as fear of adverse public relations, rather than doubts about soldiers' civic education. Information officers heard from the top brass whenever a newspaper story depicted a soldier as ignorant of his job or questioning his purpose.[23] In 1952 the army tried once and for all to put a stop to embarrassing publicity on the information front by issuing orders that all soldiers be "informed up to 'phased minimum standards.'" Commanders were to ensure that all troops be able to give unhesitating answers to questions within the following areas:

A: Present mission—why he is in his particular station and in his particular job.

B: The history of his unit

C: The names of his commanding officers

D: The price of the equipment he handles regularly

E: Why U.S. troops are fighting in Korea[24]

The "phased minimum standards" order described other topics upon which troops ought to have been better informed, all of which were already covered by some part of the Troop Information program. Most importantly, however, at all levels of instruction, commanders were to reemphasize the five listed areas. In this instance, it seemed that the army did not want to create better informed citizen-soldiers so much as the impression of better informed citizen-soldiers.

Rocky press relations no doubt exacerbated the army's sensitivity to adverse public relations during the peak of the Chinese offensive in December 1950 and again during the wearisome defensive stalemate of 1953. In the latter instance, reporters complained that Eighth Army personnel shoved them around at airports and slapped demeaning restraints on their movements. In protest they boycotted a press event staged for Gen. Matthew B. Ridgway's return visit to Korea as army chief of staff. Army press censor Lt. Col. Melvin B. Vorhees recalled that young reporters, unfamiliar with the press censorship of World War II, considered the Korean War restrictions unprecedented and draconian. Some composed a "Correspondent's Battle Hymn" in reaction:

> Mine eyes have seen the censor with my copy on his knee
> He is cutting out the passages that mean the most to me
> This sentence hurts morale as it's defined in Section 3
> This sentence must come out
> Glory, glory to the censor . . . this passage must come out[25]

OCINFO became embroiled in a separate controversy when Vorhees published his account of the news watchdog's life in his 1952 book, *Korean Tales*. Maj. Gen. Phillip "Pinky" Dorn, the deputy CINFO, refused Vorhees clearance for the work, but ironically the censor defied him and published it anyway. The main thrust of the book was that in the final analysis the censors had done nothing more than protect vital military information. However, the author could not resist the temptation to write several disparaging passages about former the commander in chief, Pacific, Gen. Douglas MacArthur. Dorn objected in particular to a passage that said Ridgway "was unable to compete with MacArthur in the hazardous field of public propaganda statements"; the official position of the information office was that Americans did not indulge in propaganda.[26]

Leading the Discussion

The dual mission of engaging troops in lively discussions while stifling opposition and avoiding negative publicity required that the discussion leader be well trained. When possible, prospective session leaders attended the "Forty-Hour Discussion Leader's Course" at the Defense Information School (formerly AIS). The course made a few suggestions for making a successful presentation but served chiefly to provide a set of guidelines for avoiding controversy and getting through the sessions as smoothly as possible.

The course began with a history of Troop Information in the wars of the United States. It argued that the present program was similar in spirit to George Washington's addresses to his men before the Declaration of Independence and the raid across the Delaware. The purpose of the course's historical preamble was to convince the future discussion leaders that this kind of program has always been part of American military activity and was not some untried, recent concoction. "Troop Education and Information is not a frill," the course instruction book pleaded somewhat desperately. It warned that the poor World War II program had allowed soldiers clamoring for discharge to force the nation to disarm in the face of a new enemy, as if in a "red haze."[27]

According to the forty-hour course the discussion leader was inevitably torn between being too boring and falling prey to "the explosive nature of ideas." Trying to put the dilemma in terms they thought unit commanders could understand, the program's authors asked them to conceive of discussion leading in the same way they might lead a rifle platoon into combat (44).

The diagram that accompanied the passage illustrated the objective of the troop information program: the "Better Citizen Soldier," whose path was shown barricaded by "Ignorance" and "Opposing Ideas" as well as fortified "Apathy." If the Troop Information program attacked on the left it might have gotten bogged down in the "Dull" and "Uninteresting" swamps. If it approached on the right, the program would have run afoul of the "Explosive Personal Crusade" minefield. The booklet marked out the most promising route of attack: a three-pronged assault along the roads labeled "Best for the U.S.": "Truth" and "Common Sense" (45).

Restating the discussion-leading mission as a combat firing problem may have broken the ice with some instructors, but it merely delineated, rather than solved, the dilemma of how to be simultaneously interesting and uncontroversial. The course claimed that the discussion hours would refute "the mistaken idea" that soldiers surrendered their freedom of speech upon entering the military. In order to have sessions that compared favorably with contemporary radio programs such as "University of Chicago Round Table" the authors urged leaders to see that individuals in their charge were free to speak their minds so long as they remained within the bounds of "military courtesy, military security, discipline, and commonly accepted standards of decency" (48).

However, the course also instructed information officers to permit no criticism of army regulations, to avoid appearing to promote reform in the area of race relations, and to divert the group from discussing any political questions. Matters of government policy were "discussible" but not "debatable," an unhelpful distinction at best. The course further warned that the Communist Party U.S.A. would try to infiltrate the program, so discussion leaders had to be on the alert for "loud mouths" or "glib individuals" who might try to convert the uninformed into communist sympathizers. Such troublemakers were to be reported, but the discussion leader was not to become a "one man FBI" (48–51).

Besides representing a stunted view of free expression, the assumption that any vocal soldier was a potential communist infiltrator invited the discussion leader to view the troops with suspicion. Here was an open manifestation of the distrust that justified troop indoctrination in the first place. The military did not trust its incoming soldiers to be good citizens. A certain amount of distrust is implicit in all training; that is, the military could not trust a draftee to know how to use weaponry, survive in the field, or obey orders. Nevertheless, to inculcate pride and initiative the army had to place its confidence in the men up to a point. Yet in the Cold War, as in the World Wars, allegiance to America's war aims was an area in which the state was reluctant to extend its trust.

Armed with a suspicious attitude and hindered by a narrow definition of propriety, the Korean War session leader would find it difficult to conduct anything more than a trite, watered-down discussion. Most topics that generated interest quickly ran afoul of the prescribed limits and put the instructor in a quandary. He had to risk either losing the soldiers' interest or watching the lecture degenerate into a series of morale-dampening complaints. If the sessions became too leaden to salvage, the best emergency tactic the forty-hour course had to offer was "The Baseball Game." In a gimmick familiar to most schoolchildren, the instructor divided the audience into opposing teams and asked questions based on the previous lecture. Correct answers earned bases, incorrect answers counted as outs (95). In American school life, however, the Baseball Game was a device employed more often by substitute teachers than their regular counterparts, no doubt because it was more useful for pacifying students than actually instructing them.

The Baseball Game was only one example of the use of sports in the Troop Information program. Service newspapers and AFRS broadcasts featured extensive sports coverage, so soldiers could follow interunit contests as well as their favorite teams from the civilian world. Enthusiasts and detractors have long considered participation in athletics as a crucible for the formation of values, while critics of the nation's sports culture claim it encourages chauvinistic attitudes. Proponents of "character building" through sports, especially coaches and successful athletes, commend them for nurturing the values of loyalty, discipline, and physical courage. For a military organization such values were more important than any risk of chauvinism. In *The Rites of Men: Manhood, Politics, and the Culture of Sport*, Vandra Burstyn describes how a procession of presidents in the postwar period invoked the nation's robust athletic culture as a vital foundation for America's success in international competition. It is hardly surprising, then, that the armed forces provided soldiers with recreational opportunities to play sports.[28]

The information services, however, interacted with soldiers not as players but as fans. In the twentieth century, newspapers and radio networks brought the nation's top amateur and professional athletics to a mass audience. In the fishbowl world of sports the trials and triumphs of the contestants became accessible morality plays for the millions who followed them. For chaplains requiring nondenominational material for moral instruction sports culture provided a frame of reference readily understood by soldiers of different religious backgrounds. The authors of the *Duty, Honor, Country* series, written for chaplains, illustrated the featured moral teachings not with biblical parables but with stories from the widely known mythology of American sports history. For example, one entry in the series invited the chaplain to contrast an anecdote about the unsportsmanlike Lenin with the apocryphal, quasi-religious tale of Babe Ruth healing a sick child with the promise of a home run. The pamphlet also contained the "Ten Commandments of Sportsmanship."[29]

The army used sports not only to instruct but to divert. Noam Chomsky has argued that Americans' fascination with the details of pro sports has the effect of distracting adults from more important matters. Fans invest tremendous mental energy in mastering sports' intricacies and nuances but seldom develop comparable expertise about the serious business of the polity. As a by-product, spectator sports encourage in some fans the habits of passivity and thoughtless chauvinism, mind-sets useful for taking orders and hating the enemy.[30]

In the case of the Troop Information program ensuring that the fighting men had plenty of sports to think and talk about helped distract them from the arbitrary and unpleasant aspects of army life. In OAFIE's *Armed Forces Newspaper Editor's Guide* for semiautonomous military publications, prospective journalists learned that sports often occupied a full quarter or more of the available space in a successful paper, and that the quality of the sports page could make or break their newspaper.[31]

The Armed Forces Radio Service did its part to feed its listeners a steady diet of sports, though its mission in any case was more entertainment than troop indoctrination. For instance, on Monday, July 1, 1952, the New York AFRS offered the following programming: AFRS *Sign On and Music, Conference Period, News, Sports Briefs, Hometown High-*

lights, U.S. Armed Forces News/Show Business, Sports Lights, Feature Page, Sports Page, AFRS *Parade of Sports, A Date with Rosemary Clooney, News,* and AFRS *Sign Off.* AFRS devoted 41 to 43 percent of a typical broadcast day to sports shows.[32]

As with the teaching methods espoused in the *Forty-Hour Discussion Leader's Course,* the widespread use of sports was part of an attempt to convey information in a palatable way that stressed smoothing over differences and avoiding conflict. The pamphlets produced in late 1951 and 1952 brought this attempt to fruition.

At the Lectern

Despite the observations of the civilian critics not all officers complained about the mandatory sessions. A captain in the 955th Field Artillery Battalion reported that he "conducted extensive troop training utilizing battalion officers to show training films and conduct classes in all aspects of Army duties." However, Troop Information won little enthusiasm even from commanders who complied with the directives. Morton Wood Jr., an officer in the First Cavalry Division, recalled: "I gave lectures (I&E) and ran films at Ft. Myer. Didn't pay much attention." Nor did he mention continuing the practice as a replacement rifle platoon leader in Korea. Another officer, who volunteered at the outset of the war, remembered: "I gave lectures to the troops and I thought they were asinine and useless, a waste of time."[33]

This attitude dismayed some information specialists, while others seemed to agree with it. It is tempting to make the casual assumption that as the ones who delivered the official patriotic and anticommunist lines the lecturers must themselves have been strongly committed ideologues. In actual practice, however, anticommunist crusaders did not dominate the information ranks, which contained conscientious liberals as well as committed conservatives, and irreverent cutups as well as ideological knuckle-rappers.

The training background of those who performed TI&E duties varied widely. Venico C. Gacono was a reservist glad to be activated in time to help the nation's cause in the Korean War. On the recommendation of his commander he went to the information school at Carlisle Barracks in 1951 to specialize in information, and received three college credits for political science in the process. True believers and trained specialists like Gacono worked to implement the program alongside men like Arthur Brown, a 1944 enlistee who became part of his post's TI&E section because he had served two tours in Korea before the war. In describing his military instruction Brown mentioned basic, advanced mechanized, transportation, and ordnance training but none for information.[34]

The survey comments of veteran specialists also discourage the idea that the military entrusted TI&E to carefully screened "political officers." A theater manager in civilian life Sgt. Jack R. Dillon became his battalion's NCO for Information and Education, in charge of finding places to show movies. When asked if he had been aware at the time of domestic opposition to the war he responded, "Yes—we were part of it!"[35]

One reminiscence of Gerald L. Trett of the Ninety-eighth Engineer Aerial Photo Company is just the sort of episode that rankled ultraconservative critics of the program. Trett considered TI&E "the official bullshit dropped from on high about not much of anything." He got his information assignment because "anybody could simply read off the stuff but 'they' preferred to have it 'delivered' as interestingly as possible. Being the man in the company with the highest education . . . and able to talk on my feet . . . I was the unlucky recipient of the honor and did my best." Trett's "moment of glory" came in 1954 when in front of an observer from Eighth Army headquarters, he gave a talk on Washington's shifting support for France's failing struggle to regain control of Vietnam: "So I said to my group, 'Now, you recall, guys, that some time back I gave you all these brilliant reasons why it might become necessary for American forces, like us, to get involved in Indochina, to defend our freedoms from the Commies who are trying to take over. But you can forget that: we're not going. And we're not going because our esteemed Commander-in-chief came in from the golf course long enough to discover what his deterrent-happy Secretary of State was threatening.'" His commander rebuked him for embarrassing his unit, but Trett relished the laughter of his listeners, who told him afterward, "'Best yet, buddy!' We were in the army and knew it."[36]

Trett supplemented the official materials with items gleaned from the Sunday *New York Times*, as did John E. McGregor, an instructor at the Medical Leadership School at Fort Sam Houston, Texas. McGregor explained: "I often considered I was using propaganda written by some staffer in Washington—so we used material from *Times-Newsweek* and major newspapers."[37] Even some IOs who did want to make a good impression on superiors still shaped the program's messages to reflect their independent views.

In fact, the army's information chiefs wanted field officers who were conscientious enough to supplement or replace official pamphlets and films with the material that was most suitable to their unit's situation. In the political environment of the early 1950s, however, the independent judgment of information officers became a point of vulnerability for the army. During the Korean War, ultraconservative anticommunists organized a series of complaints—including the "loss of China," the relief of Gen. Douglas MacArthur, and the decision to limit the Korean War—to create a fear of widespread communist penetration of the executive branch. To increase the pressure on government liberals, Senator Joseph McCarthy's aides developed the tactic of investigating overseas libraries maintained by the State Department's International Information Agency. Roy Cohn and David Schine latched onto the presence of books by left-of-center authors on library shelves to smear the authors, librarians, and State Department officials without having to produce any evidence against them or even contemplate the merits of the books. They claimed that the libraries contained thirty thousand books by "pro-communist" authors.[38] Attacks on the army's base libraries did not boil over until after McCarthy's demise, and the right-wing charge that the program was soft on communism did not influence TI&E content until after the war. In the meantime, the information writers adopted a milder approach.

Voice of Reason

Pamphlets written after the first year of the war were noticeably different from their predecessors. Common sense and logic characterized the OAFIE's new, mature voice. These later pamphlets aimed for a conversational and almost insinuatingly reasonable tone. The authors used a technique of sympathizing with their readers at the outset, then turning the tables to undermine their skepticism. A common approach was to start with a statement such as "These training exercises probably seem silly to you now" and then, after begging the reader's patience, explain why they were important in the long run. The calmer tone was a much closer approximation to the way Americans received trusted information. Of course, the public was also accustomed to hearing harangues, but it recognized them as *arguments*. People accepted calm, qualified words, like those used on radio news and the pages of major dailies, as *information*.

A voice of reason is a major component of Calvin F. Exoo's "cultural hegemony" model for the formation of public opinion. A student of politics and the media, Exoo described the creation of public opinion as a top-down exercise of "cultural hegemony" in which the elite rule not by coercion but by controlling discourse. To control public discourse, he wrote, one must capture "good sense." To make information favorable to the ruling class seem commonsensical it must be wrapped in "genuinely worthy ideals." Freedom, for example, is especially valuable to the elites when specifically defined as the freedom to own and use property of all sorts. Freedom is also generally worthwhile enough to be successfully used in the service of cultural hegemony. One need not reject more participatory models of opinion forming to recognize the benefits that propagandists derive when speaking with "good sense." The very fact that a message has to be couched in such accommodating terms suggests how the public receives it does much to shape its meaning. The materials OAFIE produced after a year of war were aligned more closely with "good sense" than the earlier efforts.[39]

The change in style is apparent when the *Overseas Orientation Course*, produced in November 1952, is contrasted with the older *Four-Hour Pre-Combat Orientation Course* that it replaced. The later course, like the first, gave a summary of recent international history in the introduction, but gone were all the fighting words that characterized the 1950 course. The new introduction made the exact same points concerning the evils of communism but without rancor or obvious attempts to manipulate the audience. As a result, "international communism," rather than the discussion leader, was made to look unreasonable.[40]

The counterpropaganda pamphlet *Truth Is Our Defense* was another example of Troop Information's calmer voice. The instructor using this pamphlet did not ridicule enemy propaganda as the *Four-Hour Pre-Combat Orientation Course* had, nor did he bore the soldier with unlikely claims about its dangers. Instead, the lecture acknowledged the intelligence of the United States soldier and admitted that the enemy's technique was crude. However, it insisted that those crude efforts might have been more effective under harsher circumstances. After all, simply because one has a strong fortification does not mean one never patrols the ramparts.[41]

The *Separation Series* pamphlets also made successful use of the moderate voice. By 1952 the information needs of the army had changed so that some of the concepts previously inculcated, such as confidence in equipment and cost awareness, had been replaced with new ones, such as the penalties for being absent without leave and the importance of an honorable discharge. The *Separation Series* gave soldiers a series of orderly steps to follow when leaving the armed forces. In commending the troops on a job well done the pamphlet admitted that "It may sound like flag-waving, but . . ." the individual soldier had validated his citizenship and rendered his country an invaluable service.[42] The initial admission of "flag-waving" permitted the writer to wave the flag as much as desired.

A key element in Troop Information's shift in tone was that the earlier material was more or less aimed at the lowest common denominator of intelligence, whereas the later lectures aimed considerably higher.[43] The problem with appealing to the army's least informed soldier was that it left the majority feeling insulted. Further, the lowest common denominator likely did not read army pamphlets. Indeed, though such works can help one understand the intentions behind the indoctrination program, soldiers seldom read them. The program's printed material would most likely have reached troops through a lecturer in an Armed Forces Talk or "TI Hour." The restrained pamphlets, whose language was no more complex than earlier versions, made a more direct appeal to a reasonably intelligent audience.

Although generally reinforcing the conservative aspects of the prevailing American political orthodoxy the mature Troop Information efforts strove to remain neutral in party politics. The *Armed Forces Newspaper Editors Guide* forbade military papers from printing editorials on election campaigns or including "editorial comment, criticisms, analysis, or interpretation of news of such campaigns." Likewise, the army monitored the political content of the daily news summaries to ensure evenhanded, neutral treatment. OAFIE's guide, *Voting Information 1952*, was a straightforward explanation of election laws in the different states and did not even mention the candidates up for election.[44]

Other pamphlets seemed intent on heading off political arguments before they arose. The Troop Topics pamphlet *The Soldier and the Community* was aimed at soldiers stationed stateside. It stressed the impact that soldiers' behavior might have on the public's opinion of the military and illustrated it with a hypothetical example of how strife with civilians could adversely effect local elections, with ramifications for the military base in question. Always publicity conscious, the authors warned men not to tell tall tales that might discredit them with knowledgeable locals. They advised troops that while anyone could take "good natured 'ribbing' about one's hometown . . . most people take offense when outsiders try to tell them how to run their affairs. Actually, it's silly for any stranger to try to do this." Immediately thereafter the lecture compared a Yankee twang to a Southern drawl, hinting that the booklet's authors were chiefly concerned with preserving amicable relations between the integrated army and the segregated South. In the information offices' hierarchy of values, maintaining smooth public relations and avoiding controversy ranked ahead of winning the goodwill of the African-American citizens under the command of the recently integrated army.[45]

The information offices offered similar warnings to those stationed abroad. Most of the overseas guidebooks cautioned soldiers not to act the ugly American by flaunting wealth or criticizing local customs. In keeping with the needs of a coordinated international war effort, the guides instruct soldiers not to argue politics with allies.[46]

The impulse to smooth over differences did not permeate all Troop Information material. More than anywhere else, the information branch was at its most politicized in its *Duty, Honor, Country* material, four series of pamphlets produced for use by chaplains. Whereas the position of most of the information lectures was that the army was not interested in reforming soldiers or changing their prejudices, the chaplains had a stated mission to improve the troops' moral character. Insofar as the military of the 1950s reflected national demographics, chaplains administered to an increasingly devout army. Religious participation rose sharply during the Cold War. In 1940 fewer than 50 percent of Americans belonged to a church. By the mid-1950s close to two-thirds of the population were affiliated with one. A revised version of the Bible sold 26.5 million copies in 1952–53, and Americans ranked religious leaders among their most respected officials. Francis Cardinal Spellman, the archbishop of New York City, aligned the Catholic Church so forcefully with anticommunism that historian Stephen J. Whitfield called him "more than anyone else . . . the chaplain of the Cold War." Spellman specifically called on the military's Catholic chaplains to inoculate the troops against domestic subversives.[47]

The first booklet of the first *Duty, Honor, Country* series revealed the authors' agreement with the notion, popular in right-wing political circles, that the moral character of the nation was in steep decline. In his history of the postwar conservative intellectual movement George H. Nash writes that, for neoconservatives, the "deepest lesson of World War II" was its confirmation of the existence of evil. In the face of such monstrous manifestations of evil, they thought, American culture had taken a far too relativistic attitude toward what the conservatives, and the chaplains, called "sin."[48] The Troop Information booklet devoted considerable attention to "the need for wholesome thinking," the evils of "smut and profanity," and the destructive habits of cursing and swearing (it emphasized the distinction between the two). Of particular concern was curbing the soldier's willingness to commit adultery. Instructively, despite the presumptuous nature of moral training, the mature voice of later Troop Information material was here again in evidence. Most information materials concerned not sinning but rule breaking. Conformity to the rules was the desired end, and regard for the rules was simply a means. Although the chaplain ostensibly addressed the character that informed soldiers' behavior the lessons attacked sin on practical as well as moral grounds. Swearing made one look stupid; adultery risked venereal disease. Again, the use of sports analogies helped make the teachings more conversational and accessible.[49]

Nevertheless, the writers of chaplains' guides could not bring themselves to shun completely the fire-and-brimstone approach. In contrast to the other *Duty, Honor, Country* series, the third series was written in the first person, which had the effect of making the moral lessons sound like religious catechisms. The third series' section on "My Right to the Truth" was among the more aggressive propaganda pieces in OAFIE's and OCINFO's pamphlet arsenals. It began by asserting that all men had a God-given right to the truth and that Americans were particularly blessed in this regard because of the freedoms they enjoyed. The pamphlet then detailed the various threats to the individual's right to the truth, which included rumor, censorship (as practiced by the enemy), and the American press's alleged lack of proportion. It assailed the free press for its pursuit of sales over dedication to accuracy.[50] In the name of the right to truth, *Duty, Honor, Country* sought to undermine the soldier's confidence in all sources of information except those emanating from the military.

Information on Radio and Film

In the Korean War, as in World War II, radio propaganda had to be delivered passively; the troops could not be compelled to listen as they were at the mandatory discussions. Throughout the early 1950s, Troop Information and Education fare usually made up between 2 and 4 percent of AFRS's broadcast day. To fill its small allotment, OAFIE commissioned a wide array of radio shows, many of them political in nature. Troop Information shows came in four discernible types. The practical sort of programs, such as *Don't Be a Sucker*, which warned soldiers not to lose their pay in confidence games; features, such as *Alaska, the Northern Rampart*, which were apolitical in nature; and the two types of programs that could be described as political: American history shows and anticommunist dramas.[51]

The American history programs were fairly elementary, resembling either grade school or high school history classes read over the radio. The anticommunist dramas were more ambitious and hearkened back to *Life Can Be Beautiful* and other anti-Axis propaganda skits that aired during World War II. The information agencies stocked twenty-six programs in this series. The plots were based on "actual incidents within Russia or its satellites in which an individual freedom was forcibly denied." In each case, however, the setting of the story was transferred from behind the Iron Curtain to the familiar setting of "Springfield, U.S.A." in order to demonstrate what would happen if the communists took over.[52]

Typical of the series was *No Escape*, "the story of what might happen to any girl if Communists took over America." The program tried to provoke the indignation of soldiers not only at the violation of Springfield but at a woman placed in jeopardy. *The Toss Up* demonstrated how the communists would rig a basketball game for political purposes. Another, *Freedom's Laughter*, warned that under a communist regime humor would be outlawed. This grim scenario recalled archcapitalist author Ayn Rand's 1947 testimony before the House Committee on Un-American Activities, in which she maintained that Russians no longer smiled, except "privately and accidentally."[53]

The AFRS quarterly reports revealed that these political shows were decidedly unpopular. Throughout 1951 and 1952 political shows debuted and disappeared each quarter of the year; the programmers were apparently determined not to let them overstay their welcome. In August 1951 OAFIE compiled data on all the fan mail received from soldiers for various AFRS programs. The political shows did not get any letters.[54]

Troop Information films bore more resemblance in tone and content to the written material than did the radio programs. No doubt this was partly due to the fact that the films were intended for use in conjunction with the lecture pamphlets. The most widely used film, *Why Korea* (1951), gave essentially the same lesson in recent world events as the *Overseas Orientation Course*, only with film's more visceral impact. Likewise, the film *Fighting Words* (1951) stressed the same warnings about the enemy's propaganda war as the pamphlet *Truth Is Our Defense*. Other films dealt with mundane topics such as *Dangerous War Trophies* (1952) and *1952 Voting Information* (1952). The content of the films does not seem to have deviated much from the print material they complemented.[55]

Gauging the Soldiers' Reactions

The success of the Troop Information program in the Korean War is difficult to gauge if only because any effect it had on troops would have been subtle. The information agencies improved their presentation of material throughout the war, but they could never fully eradicate the stigma of being a time-wasting annoyance that distracted soldiers from more useful aspects of training. Even if they had achieved armywide bureaucratic and command acceptance the information managers faced a seemingly insurmountable intellectual obstacle: how to hold a meaningful discussion session when provocative topics were mostly off limits.

In a postwar study of the program's effectiveness, OAFIE found that both officers and enlisted men responded well to Troop Information, if not with "overwhelming approval." Ninety-four percent of the personnel studied said that their units held Armed Forces Talks or Troop Information hours. Further, 60 percent were at least "somewhat" favorably inclined toward the sessions. College-educated men had a significantly lower rate of approval, however, and education had a negative correlation with the program generally. The best-received materials were not the pamphlets but local unit newspapers and *Stars and Stripes*, although soldiers considered such sources better for "military news" than for "the news of the day."[56]

The study revealed some problems with the implementation of the program. In the Far East as many as 36 percent of personnel had never seen any of OAFIE's films. Despite the injunction that commanders were supposed to conduct the discussion sessions, only 30 percent of the troops under study had an officer exclusively as their discussion leader, whereas 57 percent had only enlisted men heading the sessions (6 percent had some mixture of officers and enlisted men).[57]

The study's results indicated that the information offices did an adequate if imperfect job of distributing materials and convincing units to hold TI&E sessions. OAFIE's researchers administered a "Brief Information Test" to see how well their audience absorbed their messages. The test asked not only questions such as "Who is the Secretary of Defense?," which a soldier might answer correctly even without the benefit of a Troop Information program, but also ones that reflected the "phased minimum standards," such as "What is the price of combat boots?" ($7.20). Some questions were subjective, requiring soldiers to repeat elements of the information party line, such as the main thing to know about civilians is that they noticed the conduct of soldiers.[58] Performance on the Brief Information Test improved with the respondent's length of service in the armed forces. Though this trend reflects the impact of extended exposure to the Troop Information program, it also reflected soldiers' exposure to a host of other influences in service life. The results shed little light on the program's ability to cope with a mass wartime induction of citizen-soldiers.

Research on the effectiveness of the program often found that a majority of soldiers approved of it, but evidence of attitudinal change was harder to come by. A study of 380 enlisted personnel who watched the film *Face to Face with Communism* (about a sergeant who unwittingly stumbles upon an American town staging a demonstration of a communist takeover) revealed that 59 percent of the viewers "liked" the film, 35 percent thought it was "so-so," and only 6 percent disliked it. Of those who disliked it, several said the film did not go far enough, and of those who thought it was "so-so" many approved of anticommunist films, just not that particular one. High approval numbers may have simply reflected soldiers' long-held attitudes. In a major study of the change in soldiers' opinions after the first six weeks of service, the Research Branch discovered that high percentages of draftees, volunteers, and reservists entered the service with low opinions of communism and high opinions of American actions in Korea. For example, 89 percent of draftees said they had "nothing at all" or "very little" good to say at communism. Ninety percent thought communists were or might be trying to "overthrow the American form of government." After six weeks of training, the military's indoctrination program had made no statistically significant impact on these percentages: 86 percent still had nothing or little good to say about communism, and 87 percent still thought the communists at least might be trying to overthrow the American form of government. In the first six weeks of exposure OAFIE made no headway in whittling down pockets of resistance to the anticommunist consensus. The only large shift in opinion after six weeks was that the percentage of volunteer soldiers who said it was "wise to help" the Republic of Korea dropped from 62 percent to 36 percent. Draftees who thought it wise to enter the war dropped from 46 percent to 37 percent over the same period. Just as the Research Branch had found during World War II, the closer a question struck at a soldier's personal situation, the more his answer would be colored by his overriding interest in staying alive.[59]

Another possible way to rate Troop Information's effectiveness is to examine the memoirs and surveys of Korean War soldiers collected by the U.S. Army Military History Institute, Carlisle Barracks, Pennsylvania. For example, one survey question asked whether or not the soldier had been shown any orientation films or given any lectures and, if so, what was the soldier's opinion of them. Most (more than three out of four) answered that they did not get such presentations, did not remember getting them, or had no comment.

These responses provide some idea of the logistical difficulty of getting the indoctrination program up and running, even though Troop Information was, at least in principle, an established command function. However, it must also be assumed that many servicemen received some Troop Information in one form or another, but it simply made no strong impression on them. Some of these men simply forgot about what was a minor aspect of their training during their years at war. As historian Stanley Weintraub recalled: "While we were crossing the Pacific we were given handouts and bulletins about what was going on in Korea. . . . There was no euphoria whatever about going over. There wasn't any idealistic commitment felt by people there. I was gung ho for it more than the others, because I think I was more aware of the history."[60]

In other cases, the information program may not have been ready to accommodate the first wave of troops sent to Korea. Matthew R. Thome, a soldier in the Twenty-fourth Division, assumed that he encountered no films or lectures because "The division deployed to Korea within a few [days] of the attack on South Korea." Artillerist George E. Sites Jr. likewise explained: "[There was] no time for this. We were shipped over in August 1950." Others remembered getting only inappropriate materials. "No Korea films," noted James O. Christensen of the 388th Engineer Pipeline Company, "only film on how to survive an atomic bomb." November 1950 draftee Allan D. Carlson echoed the criticism leveled at American equipment generally at the outset of the war: "The only training films we were shown were left over from WWII."[61]

The fluidity of the front in the early part of the war also likely interrupted the regularity of meetings and film screenings. In the First Cavalry Division, which fought in the withdrawal to the Pusan perimeter in 1950, only nine of 60 soldiers surveyed recalled their TI&E sessions, and most of these joined the division after the withdrawal. When, after more than a year of fighting, the front stabilized around the future demilitarized zone, a soldier was more likely to encounter the program as it was designed. Recalled Robert J. Barnes, who was drafted in 1951 and served with the Fifty-first Signal Battalion: "Every other day we had a lecture on how the war was going, because at that time they were trying to stop the war." A 1952 ROTC graduate from Ohio State University reported: "I was the TI&E officer for my [unit] in Korea and gave a lecture on why we were there each month." Lewis Sanders, an ordnance specialist who was not drafted until 1954, remembered "weekly films and discussions."[62]

The purpose of the information program puzzled some soldiers who required no explanation from the government for their service. Herbert H. Braden, for example, who served stateside during the war, regarded TI&E as superfluous: "My reaction was that there was only one explanation—we were soldiers and we were under orders from the Congress." Arnold Tiscarino, a 1948 volunteer, likewise had "No reaction at all, I felt that we were trained to obey what our country wanted us to [do] blindly." For some soldiers the irrelevance of the government's justifications stemmed from their sense of duty. As artillerist Henry A. Pernicko explained: "Unlike today, we did not question our leadership. We accepted the fact that we had a job to do. The films didn't impress." For others, the war's political dimension was simply too abstract a concern given their immediate danger. Describing his feelings under fire, Lieutenant Ent said: "I didn't feel I was defending the port of Pusan, or the rights of the South Koreans, or the interests of the United States. I was simply trying to stay alive." Others were simply resigned, like Francisco Talavera, a volunteer with the Twenty-fourth Division, who summarized his reaction to orientation thusly: "We just get on the boat from Japan with no choice." "Foregone conclusion," noted one lieutenant; further explanations were "Nothing that would change the concepts or results." These men, whether out of stoicism or an all-too-keen awareness of their powerlessness, rejected a major premise of Troop Information: that American soldiers always demanded to know "why."[63]

If the surveys of veterans are any indication, however, a substantial number of soldiers did appreciate hearing the rationale for the war. "They were necessary!" construction engineer Joseph C. Bracale claimed regarding the programs. "Korea had to be explained to be understood." Andrew J. Dolak, who enlisted from the reserves and spent thirteen months in Korea, also believed the films and lectures were "educational. I was better informed on why we were there."[64]

As if such responses would not be music enough to information officers' ears, some soldiers even found the presentations inspiring. "They gave me a patriotic feeling to answer the call of duty," said one 1952 draftee. A 1951 draftee, perhaps indicating some distance from his initial response, reported, "Prior to disembarking from Ft. Lewis Washington for Korea we were shown some patriotic type films made for the army. They stirred the intended feelings of patriotism." Confirming what researchers during World War II had also discovered, political indoctrination seldom moved Korean War–soldiers to actual fighting enthusiasm. The response of Pvt. Richard E. Donaldson was about as much as the IOs could hope to achieve: "My reaction was that it was time for something to be done."[65]

Indoctrination might not eliminate doubts about the war, but in some cases it might help soldiers weather them. As one corporal commented, the instruction "strengthened my belief that no matter how unpleasant, [the war] was the correct decision." In the words of William J. Wehman, drafted near the end of the war, the program "Made me realize that even though I didn't relish combat I would do my duty." Chester Savory, a reservist sent to Berlin during the war, observed of the TI&E programs that "Most were very basic and intended to overcome soldier reaction that they didn't know what they were fighting for." Savory seemed to perceive that the problem of soldiers not knowing "what they were fighting for" was an attitude to be "overcome," as much as a cognitive blank space that needed filling with the appropriate information. If the military's political indoctrination could not change a man's beliefs, it might at least deprive him of one rationale for self-preservation or, in some cases, an excuse for grousing.[66]

There were also soldiers who responded readily to the anticommunist argument and particularly stressed the ultimate threat they believed communism posed to the United States. Lyle Rishell, a platoon leader in the Twenty-fourth Infantry Regiment, thought the war necessary. "If [the United States] failed to confront aggression in Korea, the USSR would continue its provocative acts," he asserted. James D. Stone, an activated National Guardsman, wanted to "go and do my part in keeping freedom free." He had a positive reaction to the TI&E message: "That's why I wanted to keep communism there, and not have it take over the U.S.A." Pvt. Donald F. Paul concurred with the one lecture he remembered getting concerning Korea: "We were there to halt communism." "I agreed with them," an August 1950 draftee said of the orientation materials. "They told us we were there to keep the communist[s] from coming here." Other men internalized the cause of the Republic of Korea, as opposed to focusing on the threat to American shores. After exposure to the program, one engineer said he "Felt sorry for the Korean people," and a stateside soldier in the Chemical Corps acknowledged a mission to "preserve freedom for Oriental peoples."[67]

Most Korean War soldiers came of age during World War II and in the late 1940s, and had therefore had many chances to become acquainted with unremitting anticommunism. For many, anticommunist indoctrination in the armed forces only reinforced messages they had become accustomed to receiving in civilian life. Robert F. Roser, who served in Japan during the Korean War, noted that "My college background and past Catholic School training drilled that we must stop communism at any cost." Robert R. Bayless, a World War II combat veteran who volunteered again in 1949, thought he and his fellows "Did not need T.I. films. We knew why we were there." Another infantryman in the Twenty-fourth Division "Assumed our country was correct in defending South Korea" and did not question his mission because he had "heard about the spread of communism." Unsurprisingly, Viktor Tkaczenko, a Ukrainian political refugee who joined the army to gain citizenship, described the anticommunist lectures as "very just."[68]

Sometimes, even when a soldier found the army's political arguments unconvincing his prior indoctrination remained unshaken. "I viewed most training films as heavy-handed," said an ROTC officer activated in 1952, "but I knew stopping the communists in Korea was important— not fun but necessary." An enlisted man simultaneously described his skepticism toward TI&E content and his adherence to the same basic orientation it promoted: "I did not entirely subscribe to the [North Korean] aggressor view presented. Though I thought it was better to fight in Korea instead of [California]."[69]

If the program's ideological chauvinism could put off some skeptics, it was liable to disappoint the most committed cold warriors. For example, William G. Cave, a World War II veteran reactivated with his National Guard unit, deemed the lectures and films insufficient. "The importance of Russia was downplayed. China was not mentioned. North Korea had big friends." Engineer Thomas Beck thought "we did a good job," but "we didn't go far enough." The information presentations made one patriotic draftee want to "Drop the bomb and end it fast." A Signal Corps corporal dissatisfied with the limited nature of the war dismissed the TI&E output as "just political," apparently meaning, in this case, toothless. Gen. Douglas MacArthur and the Republican right wing urged a wider war in Korea, including the use of Chinese nationalist forces and attacks on mainland China. Conservative troops who agreed with them rightly recognized that despite its anticommunist line the Troop Information program did not subscribe to the "no substitute for victory" outlook and that it did not sanction any war wider than the one the Truman administration was willing to wage.[70]

At the opposite end of the spectrum were soldiers who rejected TI&E as obviously manipulative. These critics generally offered bored dismissals rather than angry or contemptuous denunciations. A refrigeration specialist in Korea remembered that films "were shown to us and talks [given] while in Japan. To tell the truth I was sort of not with it. I suppose I was more impressed with what they told us about chances of survival." John L. Yack, stationed in Seoul during the war, remembers his reaction as "Ho hum—more government propaganda." Propaganda, a term much encountered by Cold War Americans, also served as the one-word characterization of TI&E by September 1950 draftee Robert D. Mitzel. Charles H. Rose described his pre-embarkation indoctrination sessions as "Fairly unintellectual." Leon O. Anderson of the elite Eighty-second Airborne Division (not deployed to Korea) described a benign if inconsequential program: "Most of us who could think took them at face value and were able to read between the lines." Edward

G. Abraham, an immigrant from Canada who served in the Twenty-fourth Division, was more condemnatory: "Lectures were basically of the 'evils of communism' type. TI&E classes were mandatory but not well received. They detracted from training and were not effective."[71]

Some soldiers thought propaganda worse than ineffective. Curtis James Morrow was a black volunteer who at the outset of the war counted Boston Massacre martyr Crispus Attucks among his heroes and looked forward to his "turn to fight for freedom, liberty, and justice, for all." In Korea, however, his sergeant quickly upbraided him for what he deemed a naïve outlook. If he wanted to stay alive, the sergeant told him, he should forget the "propaganda you been indoctrinated with." Soon, Morrow adopted the sergeant's stance as his own:

> We heard all the bullshit about fighting the spread of communism to protect our land of liberty. What the hell did we know about communism? What had the commies ever done to black people (that is, before we came to Korea)?
>
> Have the communists ever enslaved our people? Have they ever raped our women? Have they ever castrated and hanged our fathers, grandfathers, uncles, or cousins? Hell, blacks couldn't even vote in certain parts of the very country we were here fighting and dying for. Man, the Chinese, the North Korean, and every other fighting man in this war must be telling each other that we . . . must be the biggest fools in the world.

In the end, Morrow held "the propaganda the military fed us" partly responsible for turning black soldiers into cannon fodder in a war he did not believe was theirs.[72]

Of those survey respondents who expressed an opinion about the orientation effort, the ones who appreciated it, agreed with it, or wanted it to go further outnumbered those ones disliked it. On this basis, at least, the program could have claimed a measure of success. Most veterans, however, had no comment about their TI&E experience, positive or negative.

What acceptance the program did gain was due in part to the relative mildness of the form of political indoctrination it practiced. Its agenda of anticommunism and basic conservatism, often filtered through liberal interpreters, already enjoyed widespread acceptance in civilian society. Because the impact of political indoctrination was limited and merely reinforcing, army officials might well have concluded that shaping the political values of citizen-soldiers was best left to the engines of opinion in civilian life. Events conspired to cause a large number of Americans to conclude otherwise.

Indoctrination and Prisoners of War

At the end of the war thousands of North Korean and Chinese prisoners held by the United Nations refused to be repatriated to their communist homelands. That story weighed little with the American public, however, against the shocking revelation that twenty-one U.S. soldiers were among the prisoners in enemy hands who also refused to be exchanged, a major propaganda coup for the enemy. It had been over a century since an American war had ended without the United States dictating the peace terms, including the disposition of prisoners of war. For that reason, the American public could not entertain the notion that this small group of men might have been motivated by disparate reasons; the episode demanded an overriding explanation.

At first, much of the public was sympathetic to the twenty-one non-repatriates and attributed their behavior to a fearsome and mysterious practice: purported Chinese "brainwashing." American civilians mounted what could be described as an informal, last-ditch "Troop Information" campaign aimed at the nonrepatriates. The United Nations Repatriation Group (UNREG) assigned a team of "explainers" to talk with the men and persuade them to return. UNREG made an off-the-record statement to the press that only two or three of the recalcitrant soldiers had actually embraced communism. The others, UNREG suggested, were victims of blackmail, afraid of retribution for acts they committed while prisoners, or too frightened to double-cross their captors. The statement described the men as homesick but scared. It suggested that letters from home might sway them.[73]

Many Americans with no personal connections to the nonrepatriates addressed letters to them by name, pleading with them to reconsider their decision. The petitions used a range of arguments and ran a gamut from off-centered to affecting. A sixty-six-year-old California man wrote to a soldier many years his junior, "I assume you are an independent thinker, and I myself have read Edward Bellamy's books, and admit that our current system of production and distribution is not the best." He nevertheless enclosed some articles arguing the merits of capitalism.[74]

A high school student in Chicago, Illinois, reminded a nonrepatriate that Americans had a choice of political candidates, "but in a COMMUNIST country you have only one dictator to vote for." Another writer urged the men to "read the Lord's prayer," and confided, "It isn't money worth auto. It's auto worth money. There is a big difference."[75]

"An American mother" from North Carolina stressed the bountiful nature of life in the United States:

> My Marine son bought a green Chevrolet with the money he saved . . . we have a television set. It's like a movie in our own living room all day. I believe you'd enjoy it. There are so many good things to enjoy in the U.S. . . . I loved seeing the world series on it. . . . I'd love to hear from you, Sam. As I get older I realize you young people are our dearest possession. . . . God Bless you dear child. If I could say something that would make you decide to come to your home and country, I would be so grateful.[76]

She enclosed a Christmas card, a photo of a baseball game, and a sports article, "Dodger Pilot Wonders about Quick Calls." A Michigan writer also promised, "I'll send you the rest of the world series in the next letter." Another correspondent said simply, "We love you and want you back," and enclosed "pictures of American girls."[77]

A statement allegedly written by the nonrepatriates cited all these letters as part of "a small sample of slanderous and intimidating attack against us." Decrying the United Nations' "corrupt and filthy measures," they asked that all future mail be censored by the Neutral Nations Repatriation Commission in order to forestall such "malicious acts" and intercept all "mendacious and deceitful propaganda."[78] The adjective-laden style typical of communist propaganda casts doubt on authorship of the missive.

The sampling of American values and aspirations discernible in these letters to the nonrepatriates differs markedly from the military's political indoctrination message. Given the number of sports references in the letters, the Troop Information managers had likely calculated correctly in giving such a prominent place to sports and sports metaphors in their programs. But only the Chicago high schooler's "one dictator to vote for" letter would have formed an acceptable basis for a TI&E discussion hour. To be sure, simple abstractions like the high schooler's contrast of North Korean and U.S. political systems might intensify soldiers' patriotic feelings, but so too might such diverse items as green Chevrolets, pictures of girls, the Lord's Prayer, and debating Edward Bellamy. The letters to the nonrepatriates suggest that a people's patriotism is not necessarily limited to the principles they ostensibly share. The strongest sources of patriotism can be sensual, materialistic, or incoherent. The troop indoctrination process reduced the rich, highly personalized set of motivations to a homogenized package of bromides that could apply to everyone. The letters to nonrepatriates showed that official patriotism measured a small thing when compared to each American's own powerful sense of home.

Despite information chief Mudgett's concern that the army would have to teach citizenship to soldiers who had missed their schooling, as long as he was CINFO the army deemphasized the need for officially prescribed patriotism. In notes he prepared before a 1954 lecture at the Army War College, he described the future goals of the Troop Information program almost exclusively in terms of unit pride, paying little attention to Americanism or anticommunism. Esprit de corps, he argued, resulted from competition and shared danger. The information branch could help foster it by individualizing units, offering interunit competitions, promoting regimental bands, and teaching unit histories. Mudgett stressed the need to insert these measures into army life without fanfare: "A 'spirit' is not achieved by public announcement that a program has been launched to capture it."[79]

In 1955 Mudgett organized an ad hoc committee to study the deficiencies of the Troop Information program. The committee reported that though they had "an ideological goal to be achieved, on a national level," information officers would do better to focus on military performance. It strongly recommended that the army abandon regularly scheduled TI&E sessions. Giving an hour a week to lectures and discussions only caused "resentment" all around, in part because of the program's reliance on "mediocre discussion leaders." The investigators also advised OCINFO and OAFIE to drastically reduce the number of publications they issued.[80]

Simultaneously, other voices called for a dramatic expansion of political indoctrination. Maj. William E. Mayer, an army psychiatrist, was a member of a team assigned to interrogate prisoners returned in Operations LITTLE SWITCH and BIG SWITCH in 1953. Appalled by what he heard in the debriefings, Mayer became a vocal critic of American soldiers' behavior as POWs. Beginning in 1954 Mayer made hundreds of public speeches denouncing the POWs, garnering attention from Congress and the press. Apparently unfettered by his responsibilities as a medical officer, he appeared on radio and television shows, authored pamphlets, and disseminated tape recordings of his lectures.[81]

In the main, Mayer claimed that about one-third of the men in enemy hands became communist sympathizers or collaborators. His figure was at variance with the army's own findings, that of 4,428 repatriated prisoners, only 192 could possibly be charged with serious misconduct. Mayer blamed what he took to be the catastrophic collapse of prisoners' resistance on American society. Young Americans were vulnerable to communist brainwashing, he argued, because of eroding moral and ethical standards in the nation's education system, business practices, religious life, and family relationships.[82]

The army issued careful statements disassociating itself from Mayer's lectures. The psychiatrist was free to criticize the "institutions and mores of American life. . . . Such matters, however, are not within the specified responsibility of DA [Department of the Army]; in the official sense, DA has no opinion of these matters, regardless of how strongly individuals in DA may feel about them." A dossier that army intelligence compiled on the orator provides a truer picture of the department's opinion of him. Friends and associates considered the major

> brilliant, articulate, suave, charming, with unusual ability as a public speaker. However he is also characterized as restless, unstable, unreliable, undependable, fickle with women, self-serving, deceitful, opportunistic, disloyal to associates and immediate superiors, psychopathic, a manipulator, and fond of excitement, glamour and intrigue. . . . Pro-

fessionally, he is not highly regarded as a psychiatrist and, though afforded the opportunity, has not been certified by the American Board of Psychiatry and Neurology.

Nevertheless, his particular brand of charisma made him a favorite on the hard-core anticommunist lecture circuit.[83]

Audiences less prone to alarm were still shocked when, on October 26, 1957, a less strident critic, journalist Eugene Kinkead, wrote a "Reporter at Large" article in the *New Yorker* (subtitled, "The Study of Something New in History") that appeared to substantiate Mayer's outlandish claims. Kinkead expanded the article into a book, *In Every War But One*, published in 1959. He eschewed the term *brainwashing*, likely because it attributed too much agency to the Chinese wardens and not enough to the servicemen he wished to censure. Instead, he used the term *indoctrination* without qualification.[84] After the POW controversy, Americans were even less inclined to use the word *indoctrination* without a negative connotation.

Among Kinkead's revelations were that the prisoners were unprepared for the communists' good cop–bad cop interrogation tactics (126); failed to resist as effectively as other United Nations captives, in particular the Turkish POWs (165); and sometimes refused to maintain their own health, often succumbing to "give-up-itis" and dying (148). The officials Kinkead interviewed were united in the belief that army life had become too soft on draftees and discipline too lax. Their chief complaint was that changes instituted in 1945 gave the enlisted man channels to protest illegal actions by superiors (176).

Although Kinkead pointed out some instances when POWs displayed political ignorance, he did not urge the army to make its political education more thorough. Instead, he insisted that future American POWs maintain a rigid silence (138). He thought it both futile and dangerous to debate with communists, whom he considered invincible sophists (192).

In 1955 the armed forces instituted a code of conduct for all personnel. The code was meant to be internalized; the first of its six brief articles asserted "I am an American fighting man," and the rest laid out a series of sacrifices and promises that the soldier was obliged to under-

take and uphold. Although Kinkead lamented the decay of discipline
that led to such a pronouncement, he approved of its requirement that
captives give only their name, rank, service number, and date of birth
(20).

The Troop Information program in the Korean War had not been
completely silent on the subject of what a captured soldier might face.
A 1951 OCINFO pamphlet entitled *Behind Enemy Lines* raised many of
the problems for which Kinkead claimed the soldiers were completely
unprepared. The authors guessed that prisoners would be greeted by an
officer "who will tell you that you have not been captured, but 'liberated' from the armies of capitalistic warlords." The pamphlet warned
soldiers only to give their names, ranks, and service numbers, but realistically predicted that they would be forced to say something more than
that. It therefore prescribed evasive tactics, most of which consisted of
playing dumb or acting dazed. Unlike Kinkead's theory that any talking
placed one on the path to collaboration, *Behind Enemy Lines* saw the
utility of giving answers such as "I think so, but I'm not sure" or "Let
me see, it was last week. No, it must have been two weeks ago."[85]

Nor was the army completely ignorant of the political pressures to
which the communists would subject prisoners. The pamphlet cautioned that "your interrogator is a Communist and many of his questions will be political in nature. . . . Remember that he respects only
manual laborers. . . . If you have been a 'white collar' worker, it will
be in your interest to avoid admitting it." It also specifically forbade
potential prisoners from making broadcasts or appearing in photos or-
chestrated by the enemy.[86]

Even if the army's training did not discuss prisoner conduct exten-
sively, however, the POWS' performance was much better than Mayer
or Kinkead credited. In 1963 Alfred D. Biderman, a researcher who
had worked on prisoners' issues for the air force, published *March to
Calumny: The Story of American POW's in the Korean War*, a book that
rebutted most of Kinkead's charges.[87]

Biderman objected to the right's political uses of the POWS, both
within the army and without. He doubted that more draconian treatment of enlisted men would materially improve their conduct as prisoners, and he denied that contemporary American mores and institutions

had made young Americans any more likely to collaborate than prisoners in previous wars (8). As Kinkead was the most prominent critic of the POWs, Biderman wrote his own book as a point-by-point refutation of *In Every War But One* (14–16). In this endeavor he created the impression that Kinkead called for social reform, like Mayer. Actually, Kinkead concentrated almost solely on army reform. Like Kinkead, Biderman addressed the general question of American behavior in the POW camps rather than the specific cases of the nonrepatriates.

Biderman pointed out that Kinkead's and Mayer's critiques amounted to "anti-American" anticommunism (114). They accepted at face value the enemy's claims about his own prowess and ignored the atrocities, torture, and squalid living conditions inflicted on the American captives (239). Biderman similarly rejected the indoctrination measures Kinkead and Mayer advocated to solve the "problem." American anticommunism was already at saturation point, he contended. Military attempts to add more resulted only in crude propaganda that insulted the soldier (178). In Biderman's view the Code of Conduct was a product of distrust, and therefore no improvement. Its simplistic style betrayed low regard for the serviceman's abilities, and it made obvious that the army's chief reaction to a man's capture was suspicion (240).

March to Calumny was a useful corrective not only to *In Every War But One* but to simplistic thinking about troop indoctrination generally. Neither the Americans nor the Chinese could manipulate a soldier ideologically as easily as many supposed. A man who collaborated with the enemy almost never changed his ideological stripes, though he may have leaned on the enemy's self-justification in order to justify his own behavior to himself (75). A man who resisted did not do so because he had been recently clad in strong ideological armor but because of his own sense of pride. Biderman likened the pressure to collaborate to that a bully exerted on a schoolyard victim. The aggressor demands that the victim insult himself or his mother, and the victim resists so long as his honor demands as measured against the pain inflicted on him (81–82). Formal indoctrination could not construct a defense as resilient as the reluctance to humiliate oneself; worse, political instruction could interfere with it and other natural defenses such as ridicule (59).

To Biderman, Americans were "anti-ideological." They drew strength from a sense of superiority that was invulnerable to argument precisely because they did not couch it in argumentative, ideological terms. "The [returnees'] most common attitude was not only relatively apolitical, it was antipolitical. The almost universal way of referring to Communist indoctrination and indoctrination matter was 'all that political crap.' (It was 'crap' not only because it was Communist, but because it was political. The same attitude is the bane of the Information and Education Officer in our Armed Forces)." Biderman insisted that despite their heavy exposure to the Nazis' propaganda and articulated ideology, German prisoners in World War II were "relatively easy marks for both Western and Soviet political indoctrinators" (258).

Analysts of American politics also note its anti-ideological character. Samuel P. Huntington, for example, argued that Americans have no "carefully articulated, systematic ideology" but rather "a complex and amorphous amalgam of goals and values." Published contemporaneously with the POW scandal, Louis Hartz's *The Liberal Tradition in America* (1955) described Americans as a people who could treat divisive issues simply "as problems of technique" because they shared a consensus on the ethics of their Lockean political values. This consensus accounted for Americans' reverence for the Supreme Court—a place where problems were adjudicated according to agreed-upon rules. Hartz argued that the very pervasiveness of this consensus prevented it from being thought of as an ideology, hence the "American Way of Life" was a "nationalist articulation of Locke which usually does not know that Locke himself is involved." From the vantage point of the mid-1950s, Hartz contended that even the New Deal had ultimately resisted its opponents' attempts to paint it in ideological rather than pragmatic terms. Hartz was describing the era's political leaders and critics; the ranks of the military contained many men with even less patience for ideological abstractions.[88]

Americans' reluctance to articulate their political beliefs in abstract terms explained some of the difficulties the army information program faced in the Korean War. Even better materials and instructors could not surmount certain resistances, and perhaps it was better that they could not. By the time Biderman's book was published in 1963 the armed forces, with OAFIE director John C. Broger in the lead, had absorbed different lessons from the Korean War. Gone were the modest gains in rationality achieved by the pamphlet writers. Mudgett's emphasis on apolitical unit pride was likewise reduced to insignificance by the onslaught of politicized materials promoting Americanism and anticommunism. In the Cold War the army embraced political indoctrination more fully than the other services, but after the Korean War its approach was increasingly at odds with the Department of Defense. Although Mudgett's concern with esprit de corps implied strong input from commanders and IOs in the field, Broger's anticommunist campaign called for more centralized control over indoctrination. The watchword for OAFIE became "no more Koreas." In the Korean War, Americans met communists in battle for the first time in the Cold War and came away convinced that "anti-ideology" was no defense against subversion and brainwashing. Beginning in the mid-1950s the information branches embarked on a campaign to supersede soldiers' instinctive antipolitical defenses with a robust, militant, yet contrived national ideology.

4

An Arsenal of Democracy

The Armed Forces' Cold War Information Materials

In the Cold War, anticommunism became a corrosive force in American politics. The lessons of World War II sharpened Americans' already ample hostility toward the foreign political doctrine. Furthermore, the lesson of Germany's unchecked aggression in the 1930s seemed to demand confrontation with any provocative move by the Soviet Union or its allies. However, the Soviets' distressing possession of atomic weapons meant that such confrontations would tend toward frustrating stalemate. Thus stymied, the Americans, by the end of the Korean War had turned their anticommunist crusade upon themselves.

Though the nation enjoyed virtually complete agreement on the undesirability of communism, differences as to the proper degree and display of one's anticommunism nevertheless presented endless opportunities for conflict. Exploiting public concern over national security, conservatives of all stripes employed anticommunism as the cudgel of choice with which to beat back progressives' gains during the New Deal. In *The Story of American Freedom*, Eric Foner wrote: "For business, the anti-Communist crusade became part of a campaign to tar government intervention in the economy with the brush of socialism. Anticommunism became a tool wielded by white supremacists against black civil rights, employers against unions, and upholders of sexual morality and traditional gender roles against homosexuality, all allegedly responsible for eroding the country's fighting spirit." Given these political uses of anticommunism, the concepts that Americans used to define their own system became likewise fungible. In the simple juxtapositions of the era's propaganda, "democracy" became simply that which opposed communism. "Freedom," as Foner noted, could be used for such incongruous purposes as defending the overthrow of elected governments, harassing dissidents, and describing the governments of allied dictatorships.[1]

Between the Korean War and the Vietnam War, the military's internal information programs joined newspapers, schools, and citizens' associations in a widespread anticommunist mobilization. Delineating a dramatic global contest of ideologies, they portrayed democracy and communism as mirror opposites wherein every democratic virtue had a corresponding communist outrage. The propagandists were as intent on building robust "Americanism" as they were on hammering at communism. They posited a civic religion based on rituals of participation. Their amalgam of nationalist and anticommunist dogmas even threatened briefly to escape military bounds and add its force to parallel efforts in the nation's schools and churches.

Yet only part of America's national identity was shared and public. Of necessity, the indoctrinators lumped together the self-images of a pluralistic society to fashion a single politically and militarily acceptable American identity. In so doing, they took positions on issues that divided liberals from conservatives, men from women, northerners from southerners, and African Americans from white Americans. Troop Information's formalized ideology became like muzak played in public spaces, tolerable to all but embraced by few. Cold War Americanism mirrored the apparent political consensus of postwar America. An agreed-upon national identity was an idea with persistent appeal yet difficult to mobilize for any specific goal.

Indoctrination in Civilian Life

First Lieutenant Joseph V. Wittmann Jr., a soldier stationed in Berlin in the 1950s, remembered that Troop Information had been "VERY well-received by myself and the troops." The program "Gave all of us a 'Purpose,'" and "a reality which, sadly, was woefully lacking in the general media the Nation was exposed to." This veteran's comment is surprising because Troop Information in the 1950s rarely broadcast political messages to the troops that they could not have heard in civilian life from a variety of sources. One might go so far as to say that, Wittmann's memory notwithstanding, for an American sensible to the "general media" during the Cold War, these messages were nearly impossible to avoid.[2]

Americans entering the military during the Cold War already held communism in low regard. They saw the doctrine chiefly as the negation of personal freedoms, but also as a totalitarian form of government, an aggressor, and an undesirable economic system. In their schools, religious meetings, and youth activities they encountered political imagery that explicitly delineated America's position in an ideological standoff. High school textbooks of the mid-1950s not only acquainted future soldiers with the anticommunist line but even followed them into the service. As this chapter relates, Kenneth W. Colegrove's 1957 *Communism versus Democracy*, a text written for high schoolers, became the basis of the military's indoctrination materials toward the end of the decade. Future enlistees also had generous helpings of anticommunism in the news media and popular culture.[3]

Churches and patriotic groups disseminated anticommunist pamphlets similar to those used in the army information program. In 1950 the American Legion sponsored an "All American Conference" in New York in which sixty-six civic, religious, and labor organizations representing 60–80 million members pledged to wage a concerted campaign against communism. Popular magazines such as *Life*, *Look*, and the *Saturday Evening Post* regularly published features on the Soviet-American rivalry and the threat of domestic subversion. The Cold War civilians Lieutenant Wittmann thought lacking in purpose made bestsellers of Whittaker Chambers's *Witness*, J. Edgar Hoover's *Masters of Deceit*, and Mickey Spillane's *One Lonely Night* (in which detective Mike Hammer slaughters a large number of communists). Though not especially popular, anticommunist movies were plentiful. Perhaps the best-known examples are 1952's *Big Jim McLain*, starring John Wayne as a heroic investigator for the House Committee on Un-American Activities, and *My Son John*, starring Robert Walker as the red sheep of a patriotic, religious family. Television networks aired documentary specials examining the Soviet threat, and *I Led Three Lives*, a counterespionage drama based loosely on the real-life career of F.B.I. agent Herbert A. Philbrick, lasted three years in syndication, 1953–56. Adolescents could read comic books in which superheroes fought communist agents. In 1951, "Children's Crusade against Communism" trading cards urged children to "Fight the Red Menace." Clearly, the military's anticommunist materials would have seemed familiar to a soldier with prior exposure to images such as these.[4]

Beyond the continuities of propaganda found in civilian and military life, however, is the question of whether larger forces of political socialization minimize the impact of both sorts of messages. For social scientists, the Research Branch's discovery that the influence of indoctrination on World War II's citizen-soldiers had been weak threw cold water on the interwar belief in propaganda's potency. Direct messages from the government to the public had less impact on opinion than originally estimated, and analysts began to document other factors in the formation of people's political convictions. Leonard W. Doob, in his 1964 study *Patriotism and Nationalism*, suggested that the rise of mass communications in a country creates a competition for peoples' attention "so keen that suddenly the trend away from the face-to-face contacts characteristic of traditional and insular nations is reversed, and the need for such contacts increases." Therefore, despite the proliferation of communications technologies, word of mouth still ranked high among the means of spreading opinions. Respected friends and fellow members of clubs and associations could transmit their convictions to the people who trusted them. Interpersonal exchange in the home one grew up in was also of obvious importance. Propagandists had to contend with the past influence of parents on their subjects. Families spread political opinions through explicit teaching and, more commonly, through the parental statements that children overheard and adopted.[5]

Sociologists generally rank only school on a par with family as a determinant of political values. In his critique of the army's political training programs, Stephen D. Wesbrook differentiated between "education" and "indoctrination," and argued that too often the army had indulged the latter at the expense of the former. Education, as he envisioned it, would use civic lessons and "world events orientation" to equip soldiers with the means to reach their own conclusions about why they served and fought. Indoctrination, in contrast, employed useless "chauvinistic inspiration" and "threat propaganda." Even in its mildest incarnations the information program could not separate the goals of education from indoctrination because an outlook that conformed to the army's goals was the only acceptable outcome of the process. Nevertheless, there were significant areas of overlap between education and troop indoctrination.[6]

Just as the army made citizenship lessons a part of military training, so many American schools featured as part of the larger curriculum a "civics" class devoted to explaining the United States's system of government and the duties of its citizens. Interestingly, analysts who tried to isolate the effect of high school civics classes came to much the same result as observers of the army programs: the effect on students was minimal. In a study of three Boston-area high schools, for instance, Kenneth P. Langton and M. Kent Jennings (who claimed that school was in fact the largest variable in determining a person's political socialization) found civics courses to have no impact on students' political orientation. They speculated that at least for white students from better-educated families, the classroom lessons perhaps merely reinforced ideas they had already internalized. That is, even for adolescents years younger than soldiers, prior indoctrination explained their indifference to new lessons on Americanism.[7]

Political sociologist Jack Dennis argued that the success of a political regime depended on widely shared assumptions and "diffuse support." Diffuse support for a government involves a nonspecific loyalty, one not built on any explicit or absolute factors, like those presented in civics classes and troop indoctrination sessions. Because it does not rely on fully articulated definitions or axioms, diffuse support can weather any particular upheaval. As we saw in chapter 3, Albert D. Biderman argued that it was just this sort of amorphous sense of political rectitude that sustained "anti-ideological" American prisoners in the Korean War. Both Dennis and David Easton found that citizens could develop diffuse support for the political system in early childhood. Children as young as seven years old made contact with the concept of government and formed a benign and enduring impression of their own. Even as teenagers encountered difficult or conflicting political information, it was hard for them to shake that first, favorable opinion. Easton and Dennis even argued that, by adulthood, it was too late for a citizen to build the sense of political efficacy necessary to have confidence in the system.[8]

It is not necessary to see Americans as uniquely resistant to formal political indoctrination, however. In a communist system, no aspect of behavior is considered apolitical. The Soviet Union bombarded its citizens with political propaganda from womb to grave and placed special importance on persuading soldiers to adopt the state ideology. Communist Party officials viewed ideological conformity as the highest military virtue. Soviet officers who saw political indoctrination not just as an aspect but the essence of command got promoted. Yet in spite of the intense conditioning Soviet soldiers experienced before and during service, research suggests that they were largely unmoved by the massive propaganda effort and usually responded with only unenthusiastic participation. As in a Western democracy, boredom with the programs, family and ethnic ties, and habits formed in civilian life all militated against the acceptance of an overarching belief system imposed from above.[9]

American loyalties were therefore manufactured by means more subtle than a formal indoctrination programs. It is a propagandist's tenet that people will only accept new information if it is in a form they have been conditioned to receive. It was no wonder that World War I propaganda chief George Creel entitled his account of the Committee on Public Information, *How We Advertised America*. After the school model, the most obviously usable American channel of indoctrination was advertising. Americans were accustomed not only to advertising's form but to its content of alluring products and gratified consumers. When sociologist Charles C. Moskos Jr. pressed Vietnam War soldiers to describe what about their nation set it apart from others they frequently couched their answers in materialistic terms. They cited high standards of living, high-paying jobs, and the availability of cars and other consumer goods as the best things about the United States, which many in Vietnam thought of as "The Land of the Big PX." Cultural historians have noted the same pattern. Robert B. Westbrook, in his essay "Fighting for the American Family: Private Interests and Political Obligation in World War II," has argued that the nation's opinion makers recognized that Americans would not respond to a call "to work, fight, or die for their country as a political community." According to Westbrook, the most compelling appeals were "to defend *private* interests and discharge *private* moral obligations."[10]

Although Westbrook rated the World War II propagandists' conversion of the political into the private as successful with the general public, one cannot say the same about exhortations to soldiers. The military's internal propaganda was always weighted heavily toward political rather than private appeals. During the Cold War, anticommunists relished the chance to compare American workers' material situation with that of their counterparts in the Soviet Union. For the true believers who crafted the army's information materials, however, private interests and materialism were insufficiently noble to constitute the real Americanism.

Troop Indoctrination and American Politics

Though the U.S. Army prided itself on abstaining from the maelstrom of American party politics, it asked its Cold War–era soldiers to embrace a public and participatory definition of good citizenship that had been outlined in civics classes. Its information materials maintained a scrupulous neutrality between the Democratic and Republican political parties, especially in matters pertaining to elections. Political neutrality did not mean that the information agencies were apolitical when November rolled around, however. The Department of Defense's Office of Armed Forces Information and the army's Office of the Chief of Information attached great importance to soldiers' participation in the political process. The act of voting, no matter for which party or candidate, legitimized the concept of citizenship advanced by the organizations' patriotic materials.

A 1962 Troop Information fact sheet described voting as "a public trust," scolding the reader, "if you ever once failed to vote . . . if you ever once shirked your duty . . . SHAME ON YOU!" Despite this encouragement, military voter turnout could be disappointing. One election for which military participation numbers are available was the 1966 mid-term elections. Only 18 percent of the army's eligible voters cast ballots, compared to 52 percent for the air force, 41 percent for the Marine Corps, and 34 percent for the navy. Why the other services outperformed the army is unclear. Perhaps even with a diminished emphasis on citizenship training, the navy, air force, and marines' self-identification as elite organizations helped their members sustain a sense of political efficacy that the GIs did not feel. In any case, 18 percent was a poor showing for a would-be school of the nation. If the troops could not be motivated to cast a ballot, inspiring them to accept greater responsibilities of citizenship became all the more daunting a task.[11]

In election years information officers organized registration drives on "Armed Forces Voters Day," plastered Uncle Sam "I Want You" voting posters around bases, and gave colorful certificates to units that achieved high voter turnout. The short film *Ballots That Fly* explained how simple it was to vote. Even later, during the Vietnam War, when the program was less interested in Americanism than it had been in the 1950s, voting remained a priority. For the 1968 election, some IOs hand-delivered the easy-to-use federal postcard application for absentee ballots. Troop Information flyers told tales of narrowly won elections. For the 1970 mid-term election, the army appointed an attractive enlisted woman as its "Miss Military Voter" and sent her on a tour of bases to get out the vote.[12]

The exhortation to vote was only occasionally accompanied by urgings to vote carefully or intelligently. In the Civil War Democrats feared soldiers would heavily favor the sitting Republican administration. In World War II the opposition party had a similar anxiety. In the Cold War, despite a sizable peacetime army and three wartime presidential elections (1952, 1968, and 1972), neither party particularly feared or counted on the soldier vote. Nor did OAFIE or OCINFO reveal any desire to have soldiers vote one way or another. The ritual of participation was the important thing. For the same reason, a Department of Defense information bulletin on civil defense declared that Americans ought to build bomb shelters because they were "participants in the affairs of the nation," not because they thought it might help them survive a nuclear war.[13]

The demand for participation in approved civic affairs was a hallmark of the Cold War. It was seen most dramatically in the burgeoning church membership of the 1950s. As Stephen J. Whitfield has noted, "The theology of the 1950s was based far less on, say, Aquinas's proofs for the existence of God than on the conviction that religion was virtually synonymous with American nationalism." Religious belief and participation, in general, differentiated Americans from officially atheist communists, and were more important than the religious specifics.

Indeed, arguing the particulars was divisive and unhealthy. For this reason, President Dwight D. Eisenhower positioned himself as an almost nondenominational spiritual leader for a nation devoted to a "vague Judeo-Christianity." In her history of civic religion and national security, Lori L. Bogle found that the chaplains screened air force recruits and pressured those unaffiliated with a religion to choose one. As with voting and civil defense, faith itself was the vital thing.[14]

The American self-image promulgated by the armed forces was neither wholly liberal or conservative, progressive or reactionary. Some civilians assume that the army is either a depository or a breeding ground for conservatism. Cold War information materials (especially the chaplains' guides) provide some grounds for this assumption, especially when their authors argued that the nation suffered from a decline in moral standards and traditional sources of strength, a common tenet of conservative politics as well. Not surprisingly, they tried to imbue soldiers with a socially conservative outlook. Indeed, service life without a fair degree of social conservatism is difficult to imagine. OAFIE's materials on international affairs reinforced the basically conservative positions that nation-states do not naturally give way to more peaceful and stable arrangements, that they would continue to settle their affairs with wars, and that a nation ensured security only by possessing military might.[15]

However, the indoctrination program stressed broadly liberal themes as well. It endorsed not only America's international engagements but the interventionist, evangelical role it had assumed. Discovering in one study that some "nine-tenths of the men prefer to describe the American economic system by words other than 'capitalism,'" the indoctrinators did not endorse wholly unregulated economic competition. Their materials routinely praised trade unions. Anticommunist pamphlets rebutted the critique of American capitalism by pointing to the government's activist role in the economy as a sign of progress. The assumption of progress itself indicated the liberalism in OAFIE's political alloy.[16]

Taking its liberal and conservative aspects together, the information arsenal reflected postwar America's seeming consensus on political ideas. Gunnar Myrdal, in his analysis of race and American democracy, identified Americans' shared political beliefs as a "creed." Participating in civic affairs by voting, building a bomb shelter, affiliating with a church, or memorizing the Code of Conduct (the behavioral rules issued after the Korean War POW controversy) were acts of faith in the indoctrination program's quasi-religious ideology. The metaphor of a creed is apt in the sense that few Americans saw any legitimate alternatives to their political system. Fine-tuning of the system was possible, but only within the understanding that American political institutions were essentially good and built correctly. The creed's adherents were not always fired by religious fervor. The program found it difficult to inspire men with an ideology that, as Louis Hartz has argued, they did not acknowledge as such. Or as Whitfield put it in *The Culture of the Cold War*: "That ideology was not a lever with which the politically informed could act; it was more like a lounge chair in which they could repose." On the one hand, faith in a self-correcting system demanded little activism from citizens; on the other hand, as with any creed OAFIE's consensus was vulnerable to turbulent disagreements in interpretation.[17]

The organization's handling of racial issues was a case in point. Information officers trumpeted the benefits of integration to recalcitrant white soldiers, but they advocated it on the grounds of military efficiency rather than social justice. They knew no actual consensus existed among the troops about what social justice meant relative to arranging the laws and customs of their multiracial society. Hence the program's writers took steps to avoid offending racist sensibilities, despite the fact that segregationists could never be satisfied with the racial equality achieved in the postwar army. OAFIE planted its flag in the unoccupied middle ground.

Information materials also displayed discomfort over women's roles in the army. A 1968 chaplain's pamphlet informed those harboring chauvinist attitudes that women "have taken their place in the business world, have been accepted into the professions, have made their contribution in science and have become an integral part of our military services." However, as if to minimize their threat to the male soldier's world order, it also provided a lengthy discourse on the proper comportment of a "lady." The military lady "is not overly worried about her appearance or whether her figure is in style this year. Her womanly self-respect keeps her from neglecting herself or becoming careless about how she appears to others. She naturally takes advantage of the good features she has in her hair, bone structure, ability to wear certain colors and so on, and presents an attractive appearance."[18]

An accompanying film, *The Lady in the Military Service*, relayed the story of Wendy, a hardworking sergeant who nevertheless earned the disapproval of Captain Lindsay (also a woman) because she "no longer bothers to wear her hair becomingly, and forgets to use lipstick." The captain declines to confront her subordinate, trusting that Wendy's brother Bob, a sergeant first class, will straighten her out. "Bob is outraged to see Wendy chew out a young WAC Pvt. in 'tough-guy' fashion" and cancels their lunch date because "He came to see his sister, but the hard-bitten soldier Wendy seems to have become 'isn't anybody's sister.' Bob stalks out of the office, and leaves Wendy hurt and bewildered." Not only did the film make clear that the army wanted Wendy to be a sister as much as it wanted her to be a soldier, it also managed to portray Captain Lindsay as too incompetent to talk to her own sergeant. As late as 1972 chaplains' guides still warned army women to "avoid taking on masculine traits."[19]

From McCarthy to Militant Liberty

Specific attacks on communism, practically the program's raison d'etre in the 1950s, were no more satisfactory to all audiences than its treatment of race and gender topics. The latter failures merely produced uninspiring propaganda. Critics who judged Information's anticommunism inadequate, however, could make troublesome foes. This was especially so after Senator Joseph R. McCarthy (Republican, Wisconsin) catapulted himself to national prominence with his infamous 1950 speech in Wheeling, West Virginia, accusing the Truman administration's State Department of harboring communists. He demonstrated that with sensational enough charges, anticommunist politicians, activists, and editors could profitably harass even trusted government agencies.

The U.S. Army was one of the key targets of McCarthy's campaign of anticommunist hysteria. In 1947 the House Committee on Un-American Activities (HUAC) pioneered the security investigation as a publicity-generating device with its hearings on the communist influence of Hollywood. Pro-Soviet propaganda films made during the war drew particular attention. Walter Huston, the voice of the *Why We Fight* films, starred in two of the most notorious: 1943's *Mission to Moscow* (playing U.S. ambassador to the USSR Joseph E. Davies) and *The North Star* (penned by leftist playwright Lillian Hellman). Director John Huston, the actor's son, who also made films for the Signal Corps during the war, locked horns with HUAC before emigrating to Ireland in 1952.[20]

Not surprisingly, the Troop Information program's favorable stance toward the Soviet Union until 1945, to say nothing of its proximity to HUAC's Hollywood targets, resulted in unfriendly congressional scrutiny in the changed climate of the early Cold War. From the end of World War II through the mid-1950s the army discharged a steadily increasing number of soldiers as security or loyalty risks. Considering how many lives, livelihoods, and reputations the witch-hunting demagogues and informers wrecked, the military's information program was not hit especially hard. In 1946, responding to complaints from HUAC, the army prohibited "subversive" or "disaffected" soldiers from working in Information and Education. That I&E received the same status in this regard as cryptography, flight training, and officer candidate schools indicates the extent to which the army intended its loyalty measures to insulate the troops from unwanted political opinions while also shielding technological secrets from enemy agents.[21]

In 1948 HUAC made its most sensational findings in its investigation of State Department official Alger Hiss. In 1950 McCarthy followed suit and focused his initial accusations on Secretary Dean Acheson's Department of State. It was as part of this effort that the senator's aides scoured the shelves of the department's overseas libraries, attacking the authors they considered communist sympathizers. Aside from providing McCarthy's lieutenants with an extended European jaunt the library expedition kept their quarry on the defensive—no State Department official was prepared to answer for every book in a collection maintained in a foreign capital. In 1962 Senator Strom Thurmond (Democrat, South Carolina) resurrected this tactic when he grilled army officials on the contents of books in far-flung post libraries. At the height of McCarthyism, however, the information program escaped the senator's direct gaze.[22]

When the execution of Julius and Ethel Rosenberg in 1953 renewed concerns about "atom spies," McCarthy and his fellow witch hunters

concentrated on alleged communist penetration of the army's technologically sensitive installations. In particular, they tried to find an espio-
nage ring at the research center at Fort Monmouth, New Jersey, where
Julius Rosenberg had been an inspector during the war. The Signal
Corps, which housed its guided missile and radar laboratories at the
base, therefore took the brunt of the attack.[23]

Senator William E. Jenner (Republican, Indiana), rather than McCarthy, chaired the investigation of Troop Information and Education practices. With Republican victory at the polls in 1952 Jenner succeeded Pat
McCarran (Democrat, Nevada) as chairman of the Senate's Subcommittee on Internal Security. If he did not become as inflammatory a figure as
McCarran or McCarthy it was not for lack of trying. As arranged by the
Judiciary Committee in 1953, Jenner's subcommittee was supposed to
handle the bulk of the investigations into communist activity, but Mc-
Carthy's Subcommittee on Government Operations quickly encroached
upon its functions. Jenner nevertheless carved out areas of specializa-
tion for his investigations, such as education. The senator from Indiana
pressed for the dismissal of teachers even without the burden of proof
of communist ties.[24]

Jenner reviewed the army's World War II orientation program in the
context of his investigations of educators. His subcommittee dredged
up evidence that suggested a lieutenant colonel and a few other soldiers
in the Information and Education Division had at one time belonged to
the Communist Party of the United States of America. It also charged
that communist writers had infiltrated the *Stars and Stripes* and inspired
soldiers in the Pacific theater to agitate for rapid demobilization following the war. Bella V. Dodd, a former communist, also testified about the
World War II program. Dodd joined the party in 1943, became disillusioned, and was expelled in 1949. She then became an informer, chiefly
against leftists and former comrades in the New York City public school
system. She told the senators in 1954 that "many" communists had
been "very eager" to infiltrate the army's indoctrination program for
the purpose of convincing soldiers that "the Soviet Union was a democracy." The subcommittee needed no further proof to claim that during
the war conspirators within the army had purposefully indoctrinated
troops with communist propaganda.[25]

The charges Dodd leveled against the program were similar to those proliferating throughout American intellectual life. Some Stalinists in CPUSA did take their marching orders from Moscow. However, at the time, right-wing anticommunists defined a communist agent not simply as a spy in the employ of a foreign government but as anyone they thought created a receptive atmosphere for left-wing political positions. They sought leverage in every forum in which Americans formed their political ideas and used anticommunism as a pretext to purge American political discourse of liberal and prolabor attitudes. David Caute, in his encyclopedic *The Great Fear*, estimated that over six hundred professors and teachers lost their jobs, mostly on the vague grounds of "sympathy" with communism rather than active party membership. Meanwhile, fearful of sharing their fate, an untold number of educators refrained from exposing students to the left half of the political spectrum.[26]

The 1950s soldier subjected to anticommunist propaganda in the army information program likely found it consistent with his civilian schooling. Frances FitzGerald has described the history textbooks of the 1950s as ideologically seamless, presenting students with a perfect, unchanging America facing off against the ultimate enemy of freedom. By the middle of the decade, texts regularly hectored children to anticommunist vigilance, some going so far as to praise informing. Yet right-wing anticommunists were unwilling to settle for this anticommunist consensus. FitzGerald notes that after conservatives campaigned against left-of-center school history textbooks in the 1930s and 1940s, "By 1950 or so, the merely conservative groups had been so successful that they had nothing more to complain about: the texts had become reflections of the National Association of Manufacturers viewpoint. This surrender by the publishers, did not, however, end the war; it merely moved the battle lines farther to the right." Ultra-right groups kept the pressure on the textbooks. The John Birch Society, formed in 1958, even linked the alleged failings of the Korean War POWs to school texts that were not sufficiently hostile to communism.[27]

Jenner's attack on the Troop Information program was a skirmish compared to the larger Army-McCarthy battle centering on Fort Monmouth. When McCarthy's inquiry failed to identify any spies at that installation, his investigation meandered toward an army dentist named Irving Peress. Peress had received a promotion despite declining to list his political affiliations on his personnel security forms. In fighting McCarthy, the army had a reservoir of public goodwill upon which to draw and, ultimately, an ally in a president who was widely identified with the organization. Now that it was in power, Eisenhower's party had little use for McCarthy's attacks on government institutions. The army instructed its officers to stonewall McCarthy's committee on the Peress investigation. Moreover, it revealed that the senator and his aide, attorney Roy Cohn, had threatened the army with investigations if it did not give favorable treatment to G. David Schine, another of his assistants. The army refused, and the resultant televised hearings in 1954 put McCarthy's unattractive qualities on display and probably contributed to his subsequent loss of popularity.

The army's victory was not without its casualties, however. A wave of security checks accompanied the Peress matter, giving anticommunists an opportunity to recycle the false accusations against another army dentist, former information officer Fred Herzberg. By 1954 Herzberg was a reservist. Never alerted to the campaign that reactionary military intelligence officers waged against him in the 1940s, the accusations of communist subversion took him by surprise. In this regard he was one of thousands of politically active people the United States who found themselves labeled subversives without being able to face their accusers or know the evidence against them. Luckily for Herzberg, Generals Charles T. Lanham and Williston B. Palmer once again rose to his defense. Their intervention was a rarity in an era when trustees, school officials, sponsors, and employers all too often preferred to cut ties immediately with associates accused of communist sympathies.[28]

Although the Troop Information program and the army survived their clash with McCarthy and Jenner with their reputations intact, they had in effect been issued a warning. The mood of the country opened a window for a more thoroughgoing political indoctrination program. McCarthy had spent his personal power in ill-advised battles, but anticommunism remained a powerful force. Just as ultraconservatives continued to set the agenda for national discussion of democracy and communism, so the opportunity was still ripe for doctrinaire anticommunists to proselytize the army's captive audience of draftees and volunteers.

In the mid-1950s the strident tone seen briefly in the early Korean War pamphlets came back with a vengeance. It seemed as if the aggressive chaplains' guides, which had been exceptional among the wartime materials, became the model for the postwar materials. For example, a lengthy 1958 sourcebook called *Foundations of American Democracy* contrasted point by point America's "Creed of Christian Civilization" with the "Creed of Communism." The creeds asked the soldier to compare "Father, Son, and Holy Spirit" to their opposite numbers: Marx, Lenin, and Stalin.[29]

Two men fueled the program's pursuit of a national ideology with religious trappings, Adm. Arthur W. Radford, chairman of the Joint Chiefs of Staff under President Eisenhower, and John C. Broger. Broger, an ardent anticommunist and a graduate of Southern California Bible College, operated the Far East Broadcasting Company, an outlet he used to beam Christian and anticommunist radio propaganda at Asian countries. He met and impressed the equally religious Radford when the admiral was commander in chief of the Pacific fleet. While Radford advanced to the nation's top military post, Broger began working with the military's indoctrination program, first as an outside contractor and, starting in 1956, as deputy director of OAFIE. When Broger pushed for a "dynamic" democratic ideology to match that of the communists, he had a powerful patron.[30]

Broger contended that communists had succeeded because each was well versed in a simple, accessible ideology that they could explain to others. In contrast, the forces of Western democracy were often "incoherent and lacked the verbal ability to explain or defend completely what liberty is and thereby have forfeited the field to the Communists." The United States and its allies could only overcome communism if they rendered their political philosophy as a codified system.[31]

Broger's zealotry took a numerological form. He based his new indoctrination program, "Militant Liberty," on ten basic freedoms and ten corresponding responsibilities. "Ten is a good round number," Broger explained to a reporter. "We've tried to keep them to ten because that many is easy to remember. Giving twelve words to each freedom totals a hundred and twenty—anyone can memorize that—plus the same number for the responsibilities, of course. That's two hundred and forty." In an expanded version, Broger had "run them up" to seventy-two basic rights, seventy-two responsibilities, and seventy-two consequences from forfeiting a right by evading the associated responsibility. How well a nation cultivated these enumerated freedoms in six basic areas of performance earned it a ranking from minus 100 (communism) to plus 100 (democracy) on the "Militant Liberty" scale. The idea was to get all Americans thinking along on a single, easily grasped ideological axis, conceived for an audience with an eighth-grade reading level.[32]

In 1955 the Department of Defense hired the Jam Handy Agency of Detroit, Michigan, (merchandisers of Coca-Cola) to package Militant Liberty. The agency came up with a compact, portable "Battle for Liberty" kit, enabling any instructor to become a walking anticommunist indoctrination shop. Reflecting Broger's fondness for like numbers, the kits contained seven slide films, seven audiotapes, and seven pamphlets. From the first, Broger and Radford planned to use the kits not only in the Troop Information program and military academies but also in preschools, grade schools, high schools, colleges, veterans' groups, religious groups, and any other amenable civilian organizations. Given what they saw as the sad state of national character (and, presumably, a perilous slippage from a plus 100 ranking), the Battle for Liberty kits could not have been deployed fast enough.[33]

Broger and Radford's foray into American education represented a new type of military intrusion into civilian life. After World War II the civilian public accorded the military a sustained respect unlike anything it had previously enjoyed. Millions of veterans comprised a ready pool of civilian sympathizers. Additionally, the Pentagon had a significant ability to cultivate its own image via Hollywood war films. By loaning or withholding equipment (and often actual soldiers), the military enjoyed virtually unchallenged power over the scripts of war movies. It tended to use its prestige defensively, however, to wring deference from Congress's appropriations committees or to remove movie scenes that portrayed fictional military personnel in a negative light. With Militant Liberty, the Pentagon was not just burnishing its own image but insisting, on grounds of national security, that Americans adopt its own version of citizenship. Writing in the 1950s, Samuel P. Huntington saw the Joint Chiefs as recklessly overstepping their professional boundaries in this episode. In another context, he argued, Militant Liberty "would be put down as the naive, amusing, and harmless work of an eccentric. Issuing from the Pentagon, however, it was a warning symptom of the derangement of American civil-military relations: at one in the same time a measure of the civilian abdication and a devastating example of what can happen when generals and admirals . . . venture into political philosophy."[34]

Pentagon officials referred to the Korean War prisoner of war and nonrepatriate controversies when they explained their sympathy to Militant Liberty. "It hit us hard, what happened to many of our servicemen when the Communists turned the political heat on them," said one general. "To outsiders, it was a human tragedy. To us it was an earthquake." A colonel in the Office of the Secretary of Defense lamented that "The schools just aren't doing their job to teach our kids the elementary facts of American life." Assistant Secretary of the Army Hugh H. Milton II asserted that when communist interrogators confronted U.S. soldiers, many "were distressed to find that their American beliefs had little logical structure . . . many came to believe there must be some American dogma equivalent to Marxism concerning which they unfortunately happened to be ignorant."[35]

Even with the Pentagon's support, however, Militant Liberty did not end up sparking a crisis in civil-military relations. The drive to formalize Americanism was a top-down imposition from civilian and military leadership rather than an idea born of service culture. One staff officer scoffed at Militant Liberty's description of a struggle featuring the free world in "a consolidated position based on sensitive conscientious individuals versus the imposed class conscience of the authoritarian state." He wondered what a soldier would say to the program's stilted ideological cant if it ever reached him. "But don't worry, it won't. This is just another of those front-office boondoggles. The Admiral says we need an ideology, so they hire a guy and appoint a committee that unanimously agrees we're all for clean living and American Motherhood and the rest of it. So the fellow writes up a lot of stuff that was said better in the Boy Scout Handbook, wraps it up into a capsule, and now they think they're got something like ideological Little Liver Pills."[36]

Events proved the officer largely correct. Despite the enthusiasm of the chairman of the Joint Chiefs, the backing of the Defense Department, and the tacit approval of President Eisenhower, the services flatly refused to adopt Militant Liberty. Their sense of propriety as well as their enduring skepticism toward political indoctrination frustrated the enthusiasts' designs. The army, with its idea of itself as a school of the nation, was the most susceptible to Radford and Broger's sales pitch, if not the salesmen. Despite Radford's call for army budget reductions, the army made Militant Liberty part of the United States Military Academy's curriculum. Its information officers, however, never displayed much interest in the program. The navy and the Marine Corps scuttled the plan before it got very far, thus sparing the army and the nation's civilian schools the trouble of fending off the Department of Defense. The navy's evaluators rejected Militant Liberty as crude, propagandistic, and technically flawed. The marines argued that a concept rooted in fear and hatred was inappropriate for their affirmative training approach. Faced with this opposition, Broger had to abandon his scheme to bring formal political indoctrination to all Americans. The services had not seen the last of him, however. Broger became the Department of Defense's director of Armed Forces Information and Education in 1961.[37]

Troop Information between Two Wars

Despite the failure of the Militant Liberty plan, anticommunist propaganda made headway in the army's Troop Information program. In 1953 the army revised the program's governing language, Army Regulation 355-5. In the early 1950s 355-5 provided simply that soldiers be informed about their duties and missions. The new official regulation said explicitly that soldiers were to be indoctrinated as to the evils of communism. For the first time the program as a whole, as opposed to its individual materials, had designated the enemy.[38]

The army also abandoned the mandatory weekly Troop Information and Education session (the "TI&E Hour") in favor of the more flexible Armed Forces Talk. Commanders could hold a talk whenever they deemed necessary. They did not have to address prescribed, scheduled subjects but could discuss any topic of immediate interest to their units. What fraction of the army actually adhered to the once-a-week ritual even when it was mandatory is hard to determine, and perhaps the change to the Armed Forces Talk (later called Commander's Conference and Commander's Call) was merely OAFIE's attempt to adapt the regulations to actual practice.[39]

In any case, in 1952 OAFIE issued 138 new pamphlets to serve as the basis of Armed Forces Talks. Catalog descriptions convey a sense of their content. The wide variety of material allowed commanders to stress such diverse subjects as America's role in international affairs (no. 207, *Our Motives in Aiding Europe*), American heritage (no. 289, *The Bill of Rights—Personal Freedoms*), service life (no. 270, *Our Insignia—What Do They Mean?*), the development of atomic weapons (no. 420, *You Go to DESERT ROCK*), and, of course, anticommunism (no. 294, *The Theory of Communism*).[40]

In a study of one of these print items, OAFIE's Attitude Research Branch learned that only 11 percent of personnel who happened upon a booklet would so much as pick it up and flip through it. With such results, the organization was wise to keep a large stock of radio programs. The radio catalog of the early 1950s featured music and over three hundred transcriptions for use by the Armed Forces Radio Service's overseas stations and the AFRS short-wave stations in New York and Los Angeles. OAFIE organized the AFRS shows into twenty separate series. Five of the series (including eighty-nine programs) concerned anticommunism. Perhaps the most unusual of these was *The God that Failed* from the *This Is Russia* series. According to OAFIE's catalog it depicted "A dream of the tribunal of heaven, in which members of the Politburo were the accused," while the great democratic leaders of history sat in judgment.[41]

Five patriotic series (consisting of one hundred programs) promoted awareness of America's history and political institutions. Seven series (seventy-seven programs) covered military pride and good soldierly conduct. *The Bookshelf of the World* series featured forty-four readings of popular literary works. Other series dealt with the United Nations (thirteen programs) and character building (the thirteen-part *Brotherhood* series).[42]

The army did not force soldiers to listen to radio programs, but it did make them watch movies. In 1952 information officers could choose from nearly fifty Armed Forces Information Films (AFIFs) intended for political indoctrination, as well as a slew "service interest" films on new weapons and glamorous jobs in the military. Many of AFIFs made in the late 1940s and early 1950s covered the same topics as the Armed Forces Talks. Of Frank Capra's World War II films, only *The Negro Soldier* remained part of the catalog. Even the best-crafted, most expensive indoctrination material had a brief shelf life. Only a few films, like 1948's *Citizen in Arms* (a historical look at the American soldier) had topics static enough to avoid quick obsolescence. Others could be partially recycled. In 1952 Metro-Goldwyn-Mayer asked the army for footage of Hitler, Mussolini, and Admiral Yamamoto that appeared in *Prelude to War* for its anticommunist film *The Hoaxters*, which linked Stalin with the leaders of World War II's Axis powers as practitioners of "the big lie." The army contributed the footage, and the film went on to become one of the more enduring in the armed forces' catalog.[43]

In 1955 OAFIE cut back the number of pamphlets to seventy-five and organized the most important ones into new series: the *You and Your U.S.A.* series to foster nationalism and *Know Your Communist Enemy* to instill anticommunism. At the same time, the organization expanded its motion picture catalog with a new series of "talking heads" films. Each installment of the "Officer's Conference" series featured a discussion between a group of officers and an authority on world affairs and ranged from thirty minutes to an hour in length. Some of the better-known participants included diplomat and scholar George F. Kennan, Gen. Walter Bedell Smith, Supreme Court Justice William O. Douglas, Ambassador Henry Cabot Lodge Jr., and rocket scientist Wernher von Braun.[44]

In the late 1950s information films began appearing in color. *Tom Schuler, Cobbler-Statesman* (1958), was a twenty-five-minute animated color film. In the same year, Vice President Richard M. Nixon appeared in a forty-three-minute Officer's Conference–type film entitled *America's World Responsibilities*. Nixon was not the first politician to appear in the military's indoctrination materials, but he was certainly the most visible one ever to hold center stage in a Troop Information film.[45]

Some of the most graphically lavish items were those bearing the Code of Conduct, the army's defense against politically embarrassing prisoner-of-war behavior. In 1957 the pamphlet *Code of the U. S. Fighting Man* illustrated each article of the code with reproductions of paintings, engravings, and photographs of historical scenes. In the 1950s the Department of Defense provided information officers with two sets of posters featuring the text of the code and the executive order (10631) that prescribed it. In 1959 OAFIE added a half-hour film, *The Code*, narrated by Jack Webb of the popular television show *Dragnet*.[46]

As *Why We Fight* and *Why Korea?* summarized the cases for the last two wars, the army issued a succession of "why we serve" pamphlets during the Cold War's peaceful intervals. The booklet *Your Military Service Obligation* spent two pages describing the American tradition of the citizen-soldier and a like amount of space on the unprecedented, immediate nature of the Soviet threat. The enemy's long-range weapons could "make any American city another Pearl Harbor."[47]

Two years later, in 1955, troops received *Individual Training: Why We Serve*. In the new pamphlet, all other arguments for service were abandoned in favor of the anticommunist line. That line remained in force through the 1964 version of the pamphlet, *Why We Serve . . .*, which dramatized the message with one of the famous, frightening aerial photographs of Soviet missiles being assembled in Cuba in 1962. After 1964 military service had to be justified in terms of the Vietnam War rather than the Cold War generally. In 1968 *Freedom Is Not Free* replaced the specter of a Soviet strike with the importance of maintaining "an orderly world" as the reason soldiers were in the army.[48]

Beginning in 1962 the information agencies integrated their written and visual materials more closely by having each of the new main pamphlet series, *Alert*, directly support a film, and by issuing a host of film information guides for use with the many other films in the catalog. The early 1960s also saw the debut of the decade's mainstay anticommunist films, including *Anatomy of Aggression* (1961), *Communist Target—Youth* (1962), *Freedom and You* (1962), and *Face to Face with Communism* (1962). The latter two employed the popular motif of an America where the communists had taken over.[49]

The World War II radio program examined in chapter 2, *Life Can Be Beautiful*, used the same technique, but in general the military's anticommunist propaganda took a different approach from the antifascist campaign. The antifascist materials of World War II led with the actions of the enemies, discussing their ideological underpinnings only secondarily to explain what had motivated enemy behavior. Anticommunist materials placed their ideological arguments up front and then tried to use the actions of the Soviet Union and the People's Republic of China as evidence of the evils of the communist system.

The most obvious reason for this reversal is that when the propagandists produced the World War II materials, a war had already begun and exploitable enemy actions abounded. Nevertheless, the propagandists accorded the ideas of communism a respect that fascism never earned from them, tacitly admitting that those ideas had to be argued. The *Know Your Communist Enemy* pamphlet series was one such rebuttal.

Know Your Communist Enemy

The *Know Your Communist Enemy* series was OAFIE's main anticommunist indoctrination publication in the mid-1950s. Korean War pamphlets were "no-frills" productions; their covers featured simple block lettering on a dull beige field. The graphic presentation of the six magazine-sized *Know Your Communist Enemy* pamphlets, however, was more elaborate.

The cover of the first installment, *International Communism: Its Teachings, Aims and Methods*, featured a giant, sinister octopus squatting atop a darkened globe. *Communism in Red China* pictured Chairman Mao Zedong's face imposed on the body of a dragon whose tail blended into the Great Wall of China. On the cover of *Who Are Communists and Why?* was an evil pied piper, sporting a hat with a hammer-and-sickle insignia, and leading a parade of glassy-eyed, open-mouthed dupes. Inside, black-and-white photographs broke up text.[50]

Prelude to War opened the *Why We Fight* series with current events the soldier might have heard about, and then asked, why were these things happening? *Know Your Communist Enemy* plunged directly into "The Birth of and Growth of the Communist Idea." The first thing the soldier received was a crash course on the Industrial Revolution. The subsequent criticism of Marx was rather mild; the series portrayed him as an idealist whose ideas had been perverted by the founders of the Soviet Union.[51]

The main thrust of the series was that communism had not kept its promises to workers. Instead of liberating them from the sweatshops and factories, it had yoked them to an utterly oppressive state machinery. Instead of abolishing economic classes, it had maintained rigid class divisions. The opening *International Communism* installment explained that the leaders in communist countries thought workers were too stupid to govern themselves. Seven million party members in the Soviet Union "lorded it over" 210 million others, making the promise of a classless society a "grim joke." The authors contrasted this system to the United States's progressive trade unions and New Deal reforms. However, they also warned that any organization friendly to laborers or minorities might be a communist front.[52]

Who Are the Communists and Why? described domestic communists as dedicated, idealistic, gullible, ruthless, and lawless. However, the authors drew a distinction between members of CPUSA's relatively small hard core and the more numerous transient portion of the party. To describe these young idealists, who floated into the party's orbit and usually within a few years left, disillusioned, the authors quoted Whittaker Chambers at length. The CPUSA defector's description of life in the party evoked the reports of escapees from fringe religious cults. The party demanded that communists give over their lives and surrender their own opinions. Recruits lost touch with their friends, family, and church. The pamphlet warned that those who did not get out in time lost their sense of morality: "This hard-core Communist has almost ceased to be a human being."[53]

The pamphlet upheld OAFIE's religious frame of reference when it suggested that communism was most likely to attract "damaged souls" alienated from their own faith. There may have been a few non-churchgoers in the services who were offended by this characterization, but the authors ran a bigger risk when they described immigrants as easy marks for communist recruitment. Other recruits "belonged to minority groups who felt discriminated against." Comfortable with the state of American social justice, the authors placed the onus of feeling "discriminated against" on the wronged group rather than on the perpetrators.[54]

The appeal of communism to peoples abroad required less explanation. Even though the Soviet Union severely oppressed its people *Com-*

munism in the USSR acknowledged that it "would be a serious mistake to suppose that since 1917 all or most Soviet citizens have actively or passively resisted their bosses." Even if only 10 percent of the population benefited in some way from communist rule, that minority was sufficient to marshal the Soviet Union's immense resources for its program of aggression.[55]

The series attributed the success of communism in China to "an enormous reservoir of dissatisfaction" on the part of the "common people" ("'Common people' in China means primarily peasants—and very poor peasants at that"). Capra's World War II film *Battle of China* encouraged soldiers to regard those same people as tireless freedom fighters. It described nationalist leader Chiang Kai-shek's predecessor Sun Yat-sen as a Chinese George Washington, but *Know Your Communist Enemy* downgraded him to a befuddled figure duped by the communists.[56]

Palpable anxiety over the "loss" of China characterized the fifth installment of the series, *Communism in Red China*, written in 1955. The pamphlet charged that the Chinese communists abandoned the fight against Japan to the nationalists so they would be in a position of strength at the war's end. The leaders of the People's Republic of China, it reminded readers, "said repeatedly that they regard the United States as their main enemy in the Far East." China posed a "danger to our own peace and security . . . at least as great" as the threats America faced at the outset of World War II."[57]

Communism in Red China also indicated the information program's underestimation of Vietnamese nationalism. In Vietnam, "France had promised independence. But when it was delayed, the Communist leader Ho Chi Minh was able to take increasing control of the independence movement and eventually impose a Communist 'line' on it." At this point the information materials treated the Viet Minh leader as an agent of Beijing. By refusing to imagine how the Vietnamese might have viewed what the West considered a "delay," the authors overlooked the strength of resistors' motivation.[58]

Democracy versus Communism

The *Democracy versus Communism* series was the flagship pamphlet series in OAFIE's arsenal for four years. It replaced the *Know Your Com-*

munist Enemy series in 1959. Each of its ten pamphlets was adapted from one of the chapters of a textbook intended for high school students, also titled *Democracy versus Communism*, written by Dr. Kenneth W. Colegrove in 1957. Colegrove was a professor of political science at Northwestern University who before World War II had studied international air travel agreements and Japanese militarism. His writing on the latter topic helped vault him to a position as an advisor to Gen. Douglas MacArthur during the occupation of Japan. His political proclivities are perhaps indicated by a private letter he wrote President Truman during the Korean War, where he advocated the use of the atomic bomb and the firing of Secretary of State Dean Acheson. In 1951, before McCarran's Senate Committee on Internal Security, he testified against the editors of the journal *Amerasia*, explaining that he had left its editorial board to protest what he claimed were the procommunist activities of his former colleagues. Soon after writing *Democracy versus Communism*, he served as an editorial advisor to *American Opinion*, a journal of the John Birch Society, the ultraright organization.[59]

Trying to create a textbook that schools would adopt widely, Colegrove used arguments in *Democracy Versus Communism* that were a good deal more restrained than those of the John Birch Society. After retiring from Northwestern in 1952 Colegrove embarked on a second teaching career to combat what he saw as the leftist subversion of the nation's schools and students' ignorance of the communist threat. In 1954 the Institute of Fiscal and Political Education invited Colegrove to write an appropriate high school textbook for the anticommunist curriculum he advocated. The army's use of Colegrove's book stands in contrast to its work with Columbia's Teachers College at the beginning of the decade. The military still had close ties with universities through its funding of the sciences and its campus Reserve Officer Training Corps programs. To get material for political indoctrination, however, it went to a critic who rejected the academy.[60]

If soldiers took the time to read *Democracy versus Communism*, many would have been accustomed to its style and arguments from the approach their high schools had likely taken to world affairs. Although a "social studies" book, *Democracy versus Communism* embodied several traits that Frances FitzGerald has described as common to mid-

1950s history textbooks. As the title promised, it described the social and political systems of the Cold War adversaries by judging them against one another. The United States was admirable to the extent that it did not resemble the Soviet Union. The series exhibited anxiety about both domestic subversion and Sino-Soviet power. It treated all history as a prelude to the grand confrontation of the Cold War, and depicted the threat of communism as the greatest ever posed, greater even than that of World War II.[61]

The booklets featured primitive color graphics on the cover, black-and-white photographs, and black-and-white cartoons once every two or three pages. The first pamphlet, *Democracy Faces Communism*, stressed topical issues at the outset to establish a crisis atmosphere. In the second installment, *What Is Communism?*, Colegrove set up the struggle between the two antagonist ideologies. He located both philosophies in the earliest sources of the Western tradition, Plato and Aristotle. In his view Plato was the father of communism because the *Republic* offered a blueprint for an ideal state, and the misguided desire for a utopian community was the root of the communist philosophy. Alternatively, he saw Aristotle as the original champion of individualism.[62]

After that juxtaposition the series largely abandoned the effort to contrast the rival systems and concentrated exclusively on critiquing the communist enemy. Colegrove's book alternated pro-Western chapters with anticommunist ones, but the Department of Defense made use only of the latter. The author directed most of his argument at the Soviet Union but included a shorter section on "Red China" at the end of most of the installments.

Main themes ran throughout the series. Communism, as embodied by the Soviet Union, was by nature an oppressive and hypocritical system. At times, Colegrove's efforts to expose the hypocrisy of communist regimes made him appear nearly sympathetic to their goals of a classless society and equal rewards to all workers. Indeed, he argued that the advantages claimed by communism were better realized in the Western democracies. Colegrove identified the essential components of a free society lacking in communist countries as follows: free debate in a legislature, an opposition party, freedom of the press, freedom of speech, and free elections in which any candidate could run for office.[63]

Colegrove consistently advocated "moderation" as a key component of fair and just government. His pamphlets taught that moderates at home and abroad were men of goodwill working for the good of all people, while radicals and extremists of all stripes destabilized politics and invited communists to take over by exploiting the confusion. The message to soldiers was to distrust political activism. In this regard, his arguments were considerably different than those of the John Birch Society, whose leaders regarded moderation as at least dangerous and possibly treasonous.

Democracy versus Communism praised the moderate agendas of American unions for their moderate agendas and valiant moderates in Russian history, but was also at pains to debunk the Soviet commitment to labor, the central pillar of the regime's self-imagery. The eighth and ninth installments, *How Communism Controls Peoples' Economic Life* and *How Workers and Farmers Fare under Communism,* described the plight of workers in the USSR. Unlike laborers in the United States, their Soviet counterparts had no right to strike and no option to quit a job not to their liking. Workers in a collectivized system, Colegrove declared, were actually punished for displaying initiative.[64]

Democracy versus Communism argued that the capitalist nations satisfied workers' needs far better than the claimed dictatorships of the proletariat. In an appeal to the reader's materialism, booklet No. 2 provided a chart comparing how long a resident of New York City and a resident of Moscow would have to work to obtain basic goods. For example, a Muscovite had to toil twenty-six times as long as a New Yorker to afford a pound of sugar.[65]

Booklet No. 9 reiterated the materialist appeal with a photograph of a Russian bicycle factory. In the Soviet Union, the bicycle was an important means of getting around. In the United States, a bike was a means of conveyance only for children not yet of age to obtain a driver's license. Colegrove invited Americans to bask in the self-esteem they typically drew from their cars. The pamphlets cited an episode, likely apocryphal, in which Soviets visiting an American factory looked at the parking lot and exclaimed, "Why are so many Vice Presidents employed here?"[66]

Like *Know Your Communist Enemy, Democracy versus Commu-*

nism continued the World War II tradition of attacking the enemy as a whole instead of just lambasting its leaders. Despite the totality of Communist Party oppression Colegrove described he was reluctant to extend pure victim status to the Soviet people. In one section of *What Communists Do to Liberty*, entitled "Russians Are Used to Dictatorial Rule," a subheading proclaimed "Russians Pick Up Ideas of Rule from Mongols and Tartars." According to Colegrove, the circumstances of Russian history made them unable to sustain a democratic polity of moderation and compromise.[67]

A cartoon in booklet No. 2 displayed more palpable condescension toward the Soviet people. It depicted faceless, naked figures falling into a meat grinder and being cranked out as saluting, goose-stepping automatons. The grinder was labeled "One Party 'Democracy.' For Producing Obedient Dummies." In *Communist Party Rule of Soviet Russia*, Colegrove described the enemy's propaganda as being entirely persuasive in turning the masses behind the Iron Curtain into sheep. In discussing communist use of the "big lie," he wrote: "The Russian people apparently accepted without hesitation Stalin's claim that the Soviet Constitution was the 'most thoroughly democratic in the world.' They still seem to believe this myth, in spite of the downgrading of Stalin in 1956."[68]

Democracy versus Communism sought to direct the hostility Americans focused on the former enemy head of state into perpetual disapproval of the communist system. Colegrove stressed the continuity of violent intent from ideological forbearers Karl Marx and Friedrich Engels to every Soviet leader from Lenin to Khrushchev. Colegrove handled Marx and Engels more roughly than had *Know Your Communist Enemy*. In *How the Communist Party Operates*, he disparaged Khrushchev's criticism of his former master, Stalin, reminding the readers that the new boss was a key lieutenant in carrying out the policies of the old.[69]

In the early 1940s authors of troop indoctrination materials strove to cast the Soviets' participation in World War II in the best possible light. In the 1950s they rewrote the war record to magnify communist perfidy. During World War II, American propagandists made much of the Stalin's assertion that capitalists and communists could coexist peacefully. Colegrove characterized the statement as a transparent lie that Stalin told to cover his intellectual commitment to the inevitability of war.[70]

Similarly, in a reversal of the army's 1945 pamphlet *The USSR: Institutions & People*, *Democracy versus Communism* assailed the German-Soviet nonaggression pact and their mutual conquest of Poland in 1939, while minimizing the decisive contest on the eastern front. The readers of the series learned not that the Soviets drove the Germans back to their own territory in victorious battle in 1944–45, but merely that they occupied Poland as "German troops withdrew."[71]

With Nazi Germany established as villainous foil, the American troop indoctrination program exploited the similarities between the totalitarian and murderous aspects of the two regimes. The installment *How the Communist Party Operates* claimed that "All dictators and totalitarian forms of government put great stress on the principle of leadership by an elite. . . . [Benito] Mussolini in Italy and Hitler in Germany emphasized it constantly for years." And the communists followed suit: a few pages later the pamphlet states that Stalin tried to one up Hitler's title of "the Leader" (der Führer) by calling himself "the Great Leader."[72]

Political scientists who have stressed the similarities of Soviet and Chinese communism and the Nazi and fascist philosophies of the Axis powers have grouped the whole lot under the categorical umbrella of totalitarianism. Historians Les K. Adler and Thomas G. Paterson use the term "Red Fascism" to denote the merged images. They found that this linkage already had strong appeal to American analysts by the 1930s. The Soviets' purge trials from 1935-38 accelerated the identification. In particular, the Nazi-Soviet joint conquest of Poland in 1939 confirmed that the extreme ends of the political spectrum met in a shared disregard for individuals' freedom. The connection tended to obscure nuances and make assumptions about the behavior of "totalitarian" states. Because, as Adler and Paterson note, "The American image of 'Red Fascism' embraced emotion and simplism" the concept was useful both as a propaganda appeal and as a way of summarizing the enemy system for high school students and soldiers.[73]

Colegrove was not content with a mere linkage between the old enemy and the new, however. The author phrased most of the comparisons of the regimes so as to suggest that the Soviet and Chinese leaders had gone the Nazis one further in the refinement of tyrannical acts. For example, in the use of bogus plebiscites, the Russians had "gone far beyond the tactics of Mussolini and Hitler."[74]

Likewise, to demonstrate Soviet brutality the *What Communists Do to Liberty* installment approvingly quoted Arthur Bliss Lane, American ambassador to Poland after the war: "the Poles . . . admitted that they preferred Nazi occupation . . . there was great brutality, complete deprivation and even murders; but at least the Nazis had matters well organized. If a Pole was arrested for political reasons, his family generally knew in what town, prison and cell he was confined. Under the NKVD system, however, a person disappeared, usually clandestinely." The series tried to persuade soldiers that poor Soviet workers also favored German occupation to the rule of the Communist Party. In *How Workers and Farmers Fare under Communism*, for example, the reader learned that even having experienced the harsh reality of life under the invaders in the early 1940s, they disappointedly "considered the defeat of the Germans as proof that no power in the world could crush Communism, and consequently they felt that they must forever remain the slaves of the *kolkhoz* system."[75]

Colegrove even tried to attribute the slaughter of the Baltic's Jewish population to the Soviet Union, not the occupying Germans. In *What the Communists Do to Liberty*, he wrote, "Acting on orders from Moscow . . . Communist secret police began a systematic program to exterminate people who might stand in the way of Communist plans. There is a name for such extermination programs: *genocide*. . . . For example, the United States Information Agency reported that all but five thousand of the three hundred thousand Jewish people who lived in the Baltic countries in 1941 were gone—a result of genocide."

The author neglected to mention that the Soviets were not in authority in the Baltics after June 1941, and that it was in fact the Germans who murdered the Baltic Jews as part of their genocidal invasion of eastern Europe. Whereas Troop Information in World War II turned a blind eye to the Germans' anti-Semitism, *Democracy versus Communism* sought to make an issue of the Soviets'. It argued that both Christianity and Judaism were anathema to communists because they held the individual to be of sacred value. "Moreover, the Communist Party has long felt that Jewish family life . . . would interfere with control."[76]

The propagandist derived several advantages by identifying the Soviet Union with anti-Semitism and genocide. Before it became widely known that the Germans had murdered almost six million European Jews, American anti-Semitism was a forbidding obstacle to propagandists who might have made an issue of enemy anti-Semitism. In the postwar period, however, the weight of public opinion was hostile to the naked hatred. It was not long after the army adopted *Democracy versus Communism* that the American public began to refer to the Nazi's genocidal campaign as "the Holocaust," an event distinct from other Nazi crimes because of its scale and prioritization. As Peter Novick has demonstrated, a series of events in 1960 put Nazism back in the news, including a spate of neo-Nazi incidents, the debut of William L. Shirer's popular book *The Rise and Fall of the Third Reich*, and Israel's capture of Adolf Eichmann, one of the chief organizers of the mass murders. Colegrove's audience was more likely to be sensitized to references to the killing of the Jews than the audiences of the 1940s and even 1950s.[77]

Attributing the old enemy's most vile acts to the new enemy helped Colegrove describe the Soviet Union as an even more serious threat than the Germans posed before World War II. The transfer of the anti-Semitic trait to the Soviet Union attacked its status as Nazi Germany's greatest enemy. Simultaneously, by minimizing or ignoring Germans' crimes the pamphlets helped cultivate positive feelings toward them. As the Federal Republic of Germany was the locus of the Western military alliance's forces against the Soviet Union, Americans soldiers had to regard West Germans as allies with whom they could work without guilt, and, indeed, for whom they were willing to fight and die.

It might have been more difficult to sustain this attitude if American forces had been educated with a frank account of the war. The Soviet Union certainly earned its anti-Semitic reputation with its own lengthy list of crimes against Soviet Jews, but the soft-pedaling of Germany's record was an Orwellian reversal of emotional direction to facilitate the postwar political realignment.

Democracy versus Communism dramatized its message with sidebars, photos, and cartoons. The sidebars injected some human-interest stories into the text, such as the story of a nineteen-year-old "girl" who

Tommy-gunned her way to freedom after she simply could not take another day of communist oppression. Another one quoted a Cheka agent to the effect that all bourgeois had to be exterminated regardless of individual counterrevolutionary sentiments.[78]

The pictures and cartoons in the series pushed buttons by presenting certain images repeatedly. The pages of *Democracy versus Communism* were littered with photographs of women at work in factories and at construction sites. The unwritten subtext was that Soviet women had to perform backbreaking labor while their American counterparts were properly spared such hardships. Here, Colegrove ignored the Soviet claim of gender equity in labor, as did Vice President Nixon in his famous debate with Nikita Khrushchev at the model kitchen in the 1959 American Exhibition in Moscow. (When Khrushchev pointed with pride to Soviet women's capacity for work, Nixon insisted that women's leisure was universally desirable.)

Photos of rubble-strewn streets also appeared more than once in these pamphlets. The rubble indicated that communist countries lay in ruins and, far from building toward an idealized future, lacked the means to attain Western material standards. One caption invited the reader to compare a photo of Soviet rubble with a photograph of the Golden Gate Bridge in California, as if there were no rubble in the United States. The ninth booklet featured the quintessential *Democracy versus Communism* photo: a Russian woman working to clear a pile of rubble.[79]

The series used several other propaganda techniques, including simplification, to strengthen the writer's position. For example, in a section on the Russian revolution Colegrove wrote that Russia's "western allies" intervened against the Bolsheviks but did not mention that the United States was one such nation. Selective vocabulary reinforced the readers' contempt. The series often called Stalin "Dictator Stalin" as though that were his actual title. Lenin's failure to lead a coup in 1905 was twice described as a "miserable failure," rather than simply a failure. Unsupported allegations heightened the impression of enemy duplicity: for no particular reason, a caption beneath a picture of Lenin and Stalin suggested that the photo was faked.[80]

If the booklets were persuasive, the reader would not have questioned their introduction of blatant double standards, such as condemning communist propaganda aimed at the United States while praising Radio Free Europe, which broadcast American propaganda at nations in the enemy bloc. The series saved Colegrove's most emotionally charged chapter for the last pamphlet, *The Communist Party's Program in the United States*. The first installments established the threat of communism, and the final act brought the threat to the soldiers' home soil. Booklet No. 10 claimed that the American communists, under direction from Moscow, intended to set up a "Negro Communist state" in the American south.[81]

The Alert Series

Democracy versus Communism was the army's main political indoctrination reading material for four years. In 1962 the Directorate of Armed Forces Information and Education (DAFIE, successor to OAFIE), adopted a pamphlet series entitled *Alert: Facts for the Armed Forces* as the next chief anticommunist print weapon. The *Alert* series was formatted like a magazine and featured a slicker, brighter look than *Democracy versus Communism*. Colegrove's textbook had been chopped up to make pamphlets, but it retained the feel of a school text. With the *Alert* series, DAFIE linked each "issue" to a specific information film.

Congressional hearings on the state of the military's "Cold War Education" policies in 1962 called on the internal information program to make political indoctrination materials as "hard-hitting" as possible. The makers of *Alert* tried to heed that injunction, not always with success. Where the older series used several pamphlets to set up the general anticommunist argument (an installment on historical background, another on life under the communists, yet another on what kind of people the communists were, and so on), *Alert* sensibly condensed these themes into the first two booklets: *From Marx to Now* and *Freedom and You*. Subsequent pamphlets attacked smaller, specific issues. Another departure was that, beyond the style of their covers, the series maintained little consistency of tone or style from one pamphlet to the next. The editors drew each installment from a different source.[82]

From Marx to Now had been previously published as a "Senior Scholastic Magazine," and its prose was a dispassionate recitation of names and dates. Stephen D. Wesbrook has argued that despite the rejection of Broger's Militant Liberty program Broger implemented most of his ideas under different names when he became the Pentagon's I&E director in 1961. He cited the *Alert* series as a case in point. The series name recalled "Project Alert," a radical-right anticommunist public lecture program that enjoyed the backing of the navy in 1961. However, the actual *Alert* pamphlets were no more strident than the ones they replaced. Not since *The War in Outline* had "know your enemy" materials been so unconcerned with explaining the ideological motivations behind the opposition's actions. Unlike the previous series, *From Marx to Now* did not critique Marxism, acknowledge its good intentions, or attack its logic. It even gave soldiers a more accurate account of the Soviet victory on the eastern front in World War II.[83]

Alert's creators formatted *Freedom and You* much differently than *From Marx to Now*. Instead of lengthy paragraphs of text, *Freedom and You* consisted mostly of block quotations contrasting freedoms available to American citizens with those available to Soviet citizens. The fifth installment, *Soviet Treaty Violations*, was even sparser, simply presenting columns of Soviet promises alongside summaries of how those promises were broken.[84]

Instead of relying on an anonymous voice of authority, several of the *Alert* pamphlets were written in the first person. A former American military adviser, unidentified in the text, wrote *Lessons Learned: The Philippines 1946–1953*. The third installment, *The Truth about Our Economic System*, was a 1960 address written by former Assistant Secretary of Labor George C. Lodge. Lodge insisted that in the United States the government's regulatory role in the economy negated the Marxist criticism of capitalism. The American corporation was itself an efficient "socializing" agent that distributed wealth to millions of stockholders. The blurring of the distinction between worker and owner eliminated all vestiges of exploitative capitalism, "if in fact it ever actually existed."[85]

Alert offered the defeat of the communist insurgents in the Philippines as a blueprint for how Americans could overcome "wars of national liberation." *Lessons Learned: The Philippines* contended that firsthand knowledge of the population one was attempting to "defend" was indispensable. The unidentified author learned that Filipinos who had actually dealt with the Hukbalahop soldiers ignored atrocity propaganda emanating from the remote government in Manila. He assigned more importance to a strong civil affairs program in the Filipino armed forces, as he regarded a trusting relationship between the government's army and the people in the countryside as being essential to the suppression of a revolution.[86]

Alert's variety of topics and perspectives made it the least tedious anticommunist series yet produced by the armed forces. However, it achieved this distinction at the cost of some focus. *Alert* made no emphatic attempt to tell soldiers why they fought. *Lessons Learned: The Philippines*, for example, painted a picture of a plucky, fledgling democracy waging a heroic and intelligently fought campaign against cruel communist insurgents, but it gave no indication of what role any American under the rank of ambassador might be expected to perform in such a war.

As if aware of the slackened ideological intensity that *Alert* represented, DAFIE supplemented the anticommunist arsenal with other pamphlets and books earmarked for officers and discussion leaders. For example, a 1962 sourcebook, *Ideas in Conflict: Liberty and Communism*, redressed *Alert*'s neglect of Plato and Aristotle, described how Soviet children denounced their parents and joined the "League of the Young Militant Godless," and affirmed the wisdom of depriving American communists of their civil rights.[87]

Ideas in Conflict contained an interesting discussion of the propriety of such propaganda. Despite the admittedly negative connotation of the term *propaganda* in the United States, the editors made it a point to distinguish between dishonest propaganda, as practiced by communists, and the truth-based propaganda crafted by Americans. During the Korean War, OAFIE had insisted that information was different from propaganda; propaganda was what the enemy used. A decade later, DAFIE's source book admitted that the United States used propaganda.[88]

Though DAFIE's supplemental materials offset *Alert*'s lack of focus, they brought the program no closer to the actual needs and concerns of soldiers. Ultimately, anticommunist indoctrination did not have to prove its military worth to earn its prominent voice in the Cold War army. Nor were its practitioners required to demonstrate that they were successfully influencing soldiers. In the nation's Cold War mind-set, the value of anticommunist propaganda was self-evident. It served as a badge of right-thinking citizenship.

Cold War Americanism

Despite the deluge of anticommunist materials, patriotic citizenship training was not neglected. Americanism was the indoctrinators' second most important topic. As information officers and materials frequently intoned, it was not enough that troops know what they were against; they also had to know what they were for. The program tried to craft a positive, easily understood national identity that soldiers would value. Official Americanism did not consist solely of boasting about the greatness of the United States. Volunteers and draftees already possessed much raw nationalism. The army needed to convert such unformed sentiments into militarily useful attitudes by linking pride of country to pride of service.

Every year, the communist bloc committed fresh offenses requiring new propaganda, but the military's interpretation of American history was relatively stable. For this reason, the patriotic material enjoyed a longer shelf life than anticommunist series. For instance, while OAFIE evolved from *Know Your Communist Enemy* to *Democracy versus Communism* and then to *Alert*, *You and Your U.S.A.* remained the main American heritage series from the end of the Korean War until the beginning of the Vietnam War. Instructors used installments of the series, developed by the Ford Foundation, in conjunction with discussion sessions on various aspects of citizenship, called "Citizenship Hours." Some soldiers stated that they preferred the discussion to hearing a lecture. Still, a study of an hour on "Freedom and Responsibility" found the following: "a large majority like the hour. They said they enjoyed the discussion. However, the hour resulted in no changes in attitude toward responsibility as measured in this study. The respondents who were older, more educated, and who favored the hour were found already to have a more 'responsible' attitude than other respondents." Even when the information offices deemed the *You and Your U.S.A.* pamphlets obsolete, they adapted the text almost without alteration into issues of *Alert* devoted to Americanism.[89]

Periodically, OAFIE did update its supplement *Facts about the United*

States, which throughout the 1950s and 1960s offered soldiers a compendium of sunny statistics to describe the prosperity of their country. The 1964 edition went beyond the numbers by featuring photos of the good life. Alongside churches, majestic mountains, and the Statue of Liberty were pictures of well-stocked supermarket aisles, sprawling suburban subdivisions, and young people surfing.[90]

In the 1956 pamphlet *"We Hold These Truths . . ."* OAFIE presented the intellectual tenets supporting the prosperity. It informed troops that their ancestors founded the United States on the principles of freedom, equality, and the "dignity of man." The authors maintained that Americans' beliefs were grounded in universal religious principles, regardless of an individual citizen's particular religious practices. Specifically, it offered the Ten Commandments as a national moral guidepost to which all Americans might adhere.[91]

The argument quickly shifted from blessings to responsibilities. A democracy required virtuous citizens to survive. *"We Hold These Truths . . ."* insisted that all Americans needed to educate themselves about world affairs. Citizens not only held national truths as beliefs; they held the fate of those ideas in their hands: "Without noble truths to hold to . . . a nation breaks apart." Liberty would flourish or die depending on how Americans executed their responsibilities under siege: "In still another sense, we hold these truths as we would *hold* a fortress against assault by a tyrant's force moving on us from any direction." American society was "trying right now to treat people as free men, with mercy and justice." The communist tyrant in question promised a paradise in the future, but "then proceeds *right now* to treat human beings mercilessly."[92]

In the 1960s the *Troop Topics* issues on *Our Government* and *Our Citizenship* pressed home the connection between the enjoying the benefits of citizenship and stepping up to the responsibility of serving in the armed forces. In explaining the nation's political institutions *Our Government* gave as much attention to the Universal Military Training and Service Act as it did to Congress and the presidency. That 1948 legislation enacted the peacetime draft and was therefore responsible for the circumstances in which most Troop Information audience members found themselves.[93]

The authors of *"We Hold These Truths . . . ," Facts About the United States*, and the *Troop Topics* refrained from making arguments based on American exceptionalism. Information materials did their best to convince the troops to sympathize with European and Third World allies. A goal of the program was to inculcate a global conception of American security, a sense that the entire noncommunist "free" world was in the anticommunist struggle together. Hence, the 1964 pamphlet *How Our Foreign Policy Is Made* deemphasized America's leadership position and opted instead to portray the nation as simply an equal among allies. Neither friends nor neutrals had anything to fear from the United States. Americans' moral and political ideals meant that "this Nation—*cannot be imperialistic; cannot embark upon wars of conquest and aggression; cannot enslave peoples; cannot deceive the world as to its true intentions.*"[94]

Publications for chaplains were the most aggressive and moralistic information material produced during the Korean War. After the war, the *Duty—Honor—Country* series, used to support chaplains' "Character Guidance" talks, carried on the tradition. The creators of the Character Guidance program contended that among the American prisoners of the Korean War only one man in *twenty* resisted communist indoctrination. The chaplain was supposed to refrain from religious instruction during Character Guidance sessions because soldiers were required to attend them. Instead, the chaplain was to concentrate on patriotism and morality. Acting in this role chaplains were closer to being American "political officers" than were information officers whose responsibility, technically, was only to help the commander administer the Troop Information program.[95]

Unlike the political pamphlets the Character Guidance pamphlets did not shy away from exalting Americans above all other peoples. According to *Duty—Honor—Country* Americans' distinct virtues produced a wealth of inventions and intellectual achievements: "The American has a basic sense of decency, justice, and fair play. He wants, not only for himself but for every man, his due. He is usually for the underdog. He is basically a decent, peaceable individual, but capable of fighting fiercely to the finish once he has been aroused. This has many times been wrongly interpreted as cowardice by others, to their regret."[96]

In case this paean failed to inspire the troops to virtuous citizenship, the authors went on to nominate Abraham Lincoln as the model for American behavior. However, the military's indoctrination materials never praised Lincoln for his role in ending slavery or for his heroic defense of the nation's democratic integrity. Instead, *Duty—Honor— Country* cited his religious faith and his promise of magnanimity to the defeated Southern states after the Civil War.[97]

When information writers drew on the Civil War for examples of American heritage, they stressed episodes of reconciliation and wistful, shared memory. They celebrated a war in which everyone had followed their conscience, fought honorably, and made a civilized peace. The chaplains' material encouraged both Southern and Northern soldiers to take pride in the Civil War. One pamphlet provided a skit for troops to stage in which a Southern dentist tells his assistant and a patient about a trip to the Civil War battlefield of Bull Run:

[Assistant]: Sounds pretty much like a graveyard to me.

[Dentist]: (Getting somewhat emotionally involved.) Graveyard, my eye! Those are memorials to deserving men. Old "Stonewall" deserved all the tributes men have given him—and more. . . .

[Patient]: Ah-h-h-h-h.

[Dentist, having resumed his account of the battle]: . . . Then, just as the Yanks were really pushing them back, here comes old Jeb Stuart and his cavalry around left end (Here he moves the drill across John's mouth). . . .

[Patient]: OH-H. Doctor, you're about to murder me. Don't fight the Civil War in my mouth.

[Dentist]: I apologize. Yeah, I guess I do sorta get worked up when I talk about the Civil War. But frankly, I think Americans should show more appreciation for the history of America. We really have a wonderful heritage.

[Patient]: Yes, Sir, I guess you're about right. (Rubbing jaw.)[98]

The tacit message was that while all Americans could let bygones be bygones, active pleasure taking was reserved for the descendants of the losers. Only Northerners had to take it on the jaw. A scene in which a Northern dentist fondly reflected on a Southern defeat would have been unthinkable. Troop Information materials made little use of the Union army as a source of military pride; using the Union's cause as a source of political pride was no doubt thought needlessly divisive. The urge of many Americans' to circle intellectual wagons in the Cold War demanded that even the most divisive event in national history be made to uphold the political consensus. FitzGerald has noted that students "could not possibly infer from any text written since the thirties the passions that animated the war. Both Confederates and Unionists appear in the texts as perfectly reasonable people without strong prejudices." In this usage, the Civil War did not transform the nation or resolve a clash of opposing ideas. Instead, it just showed that Americans had always fought in a fair, honorable, above-board manner—behavior that readers could contrast to that of the underhanded communists.[99]

Those who promulgated the Cold War consensus on the Civil War within the army apparently worried little about how black soldiers regarded the endless homage to the rebels who prized slaveholding over loyalty to their country. Later, in the Vietnam War, black soldiers took note of the military's tolerance of Confederate symbols. "In the rear we saw a bunch of rebel flags," remembered Richard J. Ford III of the Twenty-fifth Division. "It was just saying we for the South. It didn't mean they hated blacks. But after you in the field, you took the flags very personally." A Marine rifleman was less sanguine. "We had already fought for the white man in Vietnam. It was clearly his war. If it wasn't, you wouldn't have seen as many Confederate flags as you saw. And the Confederate flags was an insult to any person that's of color on this planet."[100]

As in most matters of sectional or racial politics, however, the information program's first concern was to avoid offending white southerners. This was in contrast to some other government departments, such as the State Department and the United States Information Agency (USIA). Congress established the USIA in 1953 as a public relations outlet for overseas consumption. It housed, among other things, the Voice the America radio program, which broadcast propaganda beyond the Iron Curtain. These agencies were oriented outward; they were responsible for monitoring and burnishing the reputation of the United States abroad. To foreign critics, the denial of full rights to black citizens obviously contradicted the American self-image as the world's foremost democracy. Among allies and neutrals the practice of racial discrimination undercut the nation's claims to world leadership. For communist adversaries, it was a rich example of American hypocrisy.

During World War II, the Axis powers had also ridiculed American racism. Premised as their empires were on racial superiority, however, they were hardly in a position to exploit this propaganda opportunity. As usual, Cold Warriors took communist criticism more seriously. Mary L. Dudziak, in her analysis of the civil rights movement in the context of the Cold War, describes the efforts of the State Department and the USIA to dispel the bad smell of American racism. It educated embassy personnel to deal with inquiries about racial problems in the United States and coordinated overseas speaking tours by black celebrities—so long as they were willing to stress that America had made progress on race relations. The USIA issued pamphlets that tried to counter foreign criticism by revealing the country's history of slavery up front, then emphasizing the amazing progress that been achieved since slave times. In the 1950s the USIA materials unequivocally endorsed the racial integration of schools. Army materials remained silent on school desegregation, even though the government sometimes had to call on troops to enforce it.[101]

The army's information program was not as aggressive, but in another sense the army made a far greater contribution to the country's international reputation when it officially desegregated in 1948 at President Truman's order. What is surprising is how little of their catalog the information specialists devoted to facilitating this difficult process. Perhaps, initially, the program's liberals, in victory, opted to conciliate the segregationists. After the Korean War, when it had to conform more explicitly to the anticommunist line, the program had to tread more cautiously around the right-wing logic that the civil rights movement helped the communists and weakened the United States by pointing out its imperfections.

The military's slow reactions to groups of Americans asserting their equality were not simply examples of institutional stodginess. They were attempts to accommodate individual citizens who defined their creed of freedom and democracy in very different ways. Ultimately, however, it was not these fissures but the attempt to deny them that undermined

OAFIE's doctrine. Analyzing American political beliefs as if they formed a civic religion has its uses, but Americans did not organize their political culture as an actual religious faith—so the Department of Defense had discovered in its experiment with Militant Liberty in 1955–56.

The armed forces' refusal to adopt Militant Liberty coincided with academics' declaration that ideology was a spent force in the West. In his essay "The End of Ideology," sociologist Daniel Bell noted that religion, nationalism, and ideology all were forces that tapped and channeled emotional energies. An ideology that was an "all-inclusive system of comprehensive reality . . . a set of beliefs, infused with passion" and that sought to "transform the whole way of life" amounted to a civic religion. Whereas actual religions helped their adherents cope with the fear of death, he argued, the nineteenth-century ideologies of the left had lost their ability to inspire political action. Ideologists, wrote Bell, were "terrible simplifiers," whose prescriptions blunted people's understanding of any issue's individual complexities.[102]

Militant Liberty was a product of the right, but Bell's epitaph is nevertheless applicable. Broger's attempt to fashion a dynamic ideology for Americans and, less obviously, all of the patriotic and anticommunist appeals that the military offered were the ideas of "terrible simplifiers." The milder materials brushed aside the real differences between young men reared in a pluralistic society, few of whom represented an "average" or "typical" American. Those elements that did enjoy broad acceptance reflected a political consensus that, as Hartz argued, Americans interpreted as the absence of ideology. In most cases, they could not, therefore, channel emotions into military and political uses.

Those in mainstream American political life, both within the armed forces and without, may not have felt unlimited enthusiasm for civic religion, but anticommunist, self-described Americanist ideologues still flourished in ultraright organizations. Some of these groups interacted with sympathizers in the military. Whether or not ideology in the West was really exhausted by the 1950s remains debatable, but its demise in the troop indoctrination program is traceable to an episode in West Germany in the early 1960s when one such sympathizer, Maj. Gen. Edwin A. Walker of the Twenty-fourth Division, tried to give Americans more ideology than they could stomach.

5

Morale and the Muzzle

The Political Indoctrination Program Besieged

"Well," wrote sp4 Ashland P. Burchwell, "it has happened. Thursday, May 31, 1961 will go down on the calendars in Moscow as a victory for world communism. To some people it might seem a minor victory, but to those who know, the ramifications of this defeat for America may be so far reaching, so terrible, that . . . this day may be mourned by the slaves of a Communist world as the day freedom lost the war."[1]

The calamity that so anguished the Twenty-fourth Infantry Division staff member was the breakup and reassignment of the team that had operated a Troop Information program called "Pro-Blue." Though the thirty-first of May ultimately failed to live in infamy, the demise of the overzealous anticommunist information program and its patron, Maj. Gen. Edwin A. Walker, briefly captured the nation's attention. In the early 1960s, Walker used his mandate to indoctrinate his troops as a platform for attacking the country's civilian leaders as soft on communism. Although his case was the most notorious he was only the tip of a politicized iceberg. Several more ultraconservative officers took their case against government policy to the public through the medium of "Cold War seminars." When the Kennedy administration silenced the officers in question, outraged conservatives like Senator J. Strom Thurmond of South Carolina brought Troop Information under congressional scrutiny. The resulting controversy forced the army to reconcile its cherished political neutrality with the radical right's demands for strident anticommunist troop indoctrination. It became apparent that the army could not teach anticommunism as part of a national consensus while politicians like Thurmond were still using it to separate conservatives from liberals. So long as anticommunism was the grammar of

American party politics the troop indoctrination mission invited officers to violate their political neutrality.

In October 1959 the Twenty-fourth Infantry Division, stationed in Augsburg, West Germany, began work on the political indoctrination program that would become known as Pro-Blue. Major General Walker had recently assumed command of the division, and, unlike most commanders, he took a personal interest in Troop Information (TI), energizing the division's information channels. Initially, Walker's staff entitled their information plan the "Citizenship in Service Program." An April 18, 1960, Twenty-fourth Division training directive concerning "Morale and Welfare" announced that the program's purpose was to "inculcate moral and legal responsibility, to teach fundamental principles of citizenship and patriotism, and to motivate members of this command so as to reduce sociological stress in the service and generate a desire for the awards of self-discipline and public service."[2]

Citizenship in Service blended elements of typical Troop Information topics with moral instruction of the sort featured in chaplains' "Character Guidance" materials. The program trained the soldiers on democracy and anticommunism but also made a "dramatized presentation of body, mind and spirit objectives." New personnel in the "Taro Leaf" Division studied the overseas responsibilities of the United States but also learned "the importance of moral fortitude and the direct relation of spiritual fiber to theocratic doctrine." To veteran personnel, the program described "the enduring physical and social effects of incontinence, moral bankruptcy, and irresponsibility." In emphasizing "legal responsibility" the division wanted its soldiers to minimize negative incidents with their German hosts and acquaint themselves with everything from the Code of Conduct to the base's traffic regulations.[3]

Although Walker's team aimed some parts of Citizenship and Service chiefly at newly arriving personnel, they intended it for all members of the division. They repeated the program at regular intervals so that all personnel stationed in Augsburg and Munich might rotate through its course of instruction. The division devoted six hours a week to Troop Information, divided into three two-hour sessions. The sessions demonstrated that Walker's information officers approached their task with zeal and rare command support, for the army had long since abandoned the World War II–era standard of one-hour-a-week sessions as too oppressive for commanders and troops alike.[4]

In March 1960 the Twenty-fourth Division forwarded a copy of its plan to the Office of the Chief of Information. Noting that its generally patriotic, anticommunist orientation accorded with organizationwide Troop Information objectives, OCINFO found nothing objectionable in its review and signed off on Citizenship in Service. All aspects of the program, from the mundane to the spiritual, derived from the existing support material produced by OCINFO or the Department of Defense's Directorate of Armed Forces Information and Education (DAFIE). What was different about the Twenty-fourth Division was that it coordinated these materials under a single aggressive course of instruction.[5]

Citizenship in Service established a curriculum committee consisting of the information officer, the chaplain, the staff judge advocate, the surgeon, the inspector general, the provost marshal, and the assistant chiefs of staff, sections G-1 (personnel) and G-3 (operations and training). According to Maj. Archibald E. Roberts, U.S.A., a Twenty-fourth Division special projects officer, the steering committee created a troop indoctrination "traveling show." Fifteen officers and men made up this troupe. They presented the six-hour curriculum to audiences of hundreds of soldiers assembled in Augsburg theaters.[6]

The Pro-Blue Program

Less than three months later, Walker ordered the program to enlarge its anticommunist mission. The expanded effort was renamed Pro-Blue. Walker's staff prepared a large world "battle map" that depicted the communist bloc in red and the North Atlantic Treaty Organization (NATO) powers in blue. Supposedly, a staff officer said that the new program ought to be called the Twenty-fourth Division's Anti-Red Program, but Walker thought that smacked of negative thinking and, pointing to the blue countries on the map, suggested "Pro-Blue" instead.[7]

Special Plan 308–61-PRO-BLUE (U) reorganized the Twenty-fourth Infantry Division's indoctrination effort on all fronts, giving specific, coordinated instructions in three realms. The first comprised "morale, religion and education." The second included "Troop Information, Public Information and community relations." The third covered "discipline, law and order, and traffic safety." In all three, the program stressed the themes of anticommunism, the responsibilities of American citizenship, and the free world's dependence on NATO to shield western Europe from Soviet aggression.[8]

Walker's staff wanted a wide segment of the division's personnel to help administer the expanded program. OCINFO always maintained that Troop Information was a command responsibility, but it had learned to keep expectations low when it came to translating that principle into field action. The Twenty-fourth Division took the premise of command-driven information seriously, and so, according to the governing directives, information officers themselves were to have specific, limited roles. The plan called for the division's head TI officer to prepare fact sheets, find anticommunist materials to publish, make monthly presentations in support of Pro-Blue, assist the TI officers of each unit with scheduling, and report to the commanding general on the quality of TI sessions in individual units. Unit TI officers were to assist their commanders in executing Pro-Blue, develop local (unit-produced) material to support the program, and verify that at least 85 percent of the unit's present-for-duty strength attended the sessions. Though this work load was not inconsiderable, in the larger scheme of the division's ambitious campaign the IOs were practically bit players.[9]

The Citizenship in Service presentations, which by themselves constituted an unusually thorough Troop Information program, continued. Under the Pro-Blue umbrella, however, they became only one of a host of far-reaching projects. The "American Heritage Program" used a loudspeaker van to broadcast patriotic music and brief tapes promoting "Americanism." The "Freedom vs. Communism Program" and the "Commander's Notebook Program" placed anticommunist articles in the division newspaper, the *Taro Leaf*. The "Pro-Blue Fighter Program" established anticommunist libraries in each of the division's ninety-six companies and batteries. The "Freedom Speaks Program" held panel meetings with company and battery "monitors" to review the reading material made available in the new libraries.[10]

The Pro-Blue team took for granted that they had a responsibility to indoctrinate not only the servicemen of the Twenty-fourth Division but also their families, dependents, and local German friends and acquaintances. To get the division's message out to these groups, Pro-Blue established a Ladies Club and NCO Wives Club as study groups that were "organized for the discussion, evaluation and dissemination of information pertaining to the 'Communist Design for Conquest.'" To reach the children in the local military and civilian communities Pro-Blue encouraged parent-teacher associations to include the division's religious and anticommunist propaganda in the curricula of both elementary and secondary schools.[11]

Like Citizenship in Service, the expanded program was openly religious. The army provided its units with chaplains, but with the tacit acknowledgment that religious faith was a matter of individual conscience. Walker's team actively concerned itself with this presumably private matter on behalf of the division's men and their dependents. As they stated in their plan, "One of the basic areas of 'Pro-Blue' is the individual's relation to God. When the individual has the right relation with God he belongs to the family of God and as such conducts himself as a child of God." The menace of communism required their intervention in this area: "Communism is a godless ideology that is allied with the satanic forces of this world. . . . However, communism has an 'Achilles heel' when pitted against the Bible. . . . The chaplains of the division, with the help of the laymen who are dedicated to this program, as ministers and teachers of the Bible have their greatest weapon to use in helping the officers, non-commissioned officers, men, their wives and children to 'Put on the whole armor of God.' (Ephesians 6:11)."[12]

The assumption that all personnel were members of Bible-using faiths was servicewide, and does not reflect particularly on Pro-Blue (though army training circulars did not typically cite chapter and verse). What was new was the idea that chaplains needed the help of military propagandists to interpret their "greatest weapon." Pro-Blue made overt what had always been implicit about army-sanctioned religious activity: that it served the ends of military order and morale. In one sense, urging the division's chaplains to follow dictates similar to the published Character Guidance pamphlets was doing exactly what the information departments wanted. However, directly enlisting the chaplains into Pro-Blue threatened the useful illusion that the religious agents existed somehow outside the military hierarchy. Chaplains were normally adjuncts of the troop indoctrination effort. If in religious ceremonies or in individual counseling they steered men toward soldierly values, all the better for the army. They did not typically recite Troop Information's why-we-fight line of the day. Walker's plan, conversely, made no bones about the chaplain's duty, as a member of the propaganda team, to preach that the "Victory Division" was on the "Victory Side" with God.[13]

In April 1961, approximately six months after the launch of the Twenty-fourth Division's carefully planned information drive, a magazine called *Overseas Weekly* ran an exposé on the Pro-Blue program. *Overseas Weekly* catered to American servicemen in Europe. It operated on the same distribution system as the officially sanctioned *Stars and Stripes* but was not well liked by the senior command. Among its favorite subjects were corruption and inefficiency in the armed forces, instances of officers' abusing enlisted men, and the contributions of American soldiers to host nations' police blotters.[14]

Overseas Weekly questioned the propriety of the division's intensified indoctrination program and attacked Major General Walker on three counts. It accused him of forcing his personal brand of right-wing politics on his troops. It claimed that in pursuit of that goal he used materials prepared by the ultraconservative John Birch Society. Most damagingly, it charged that in a speech to about two hundred members of his division's parent-teacher association, Walker denounced former First Lady Eleanor Roosevelt and former President Harry S. Truman as communist sympathizers, calling the latter "a pinko." Walker also ranked former Secretary of State Dean Acheson, columnist Walter Lippmann, Columbia Broadcasting Service commentator Eric Severeid, and Edward R. Murrow, then director of the United States Information Agency, as either "definitely pink" or "confirmed communists."[15]

It also emerged that prior to the 1960 elections the division commander had used the *Taro Leaf* to urge his soldiers to check their candidates against a voting "index" prepared by a group known as the Americans for Constitutional Action. Walker later admitted that the organization's material had "a conservative bias."[16]

Within days, General Walker was suspended from command of his division pending investigation of the charges. Despite Walker's record of successful service in the Korean War and his command of troops protecting the 1957 integration of Arkansas's public schools, Washington evinced little skepticism about the accusations. Walker may already have been on a short leash because of his volatile personality. However, the events of April 17–18 may account for the administration's swift punitive action. The day after *Overseas Weekly* exposed Walker's redbaiting, United States–funded Cuban exiles met defeat in their attempt to invade Cuba. Though the Kennedy administration sponsored the whole affair, it supported the invasion less than half-heartedly in the futile hope it could cover its tracks. The ill-conceived assault at the Bay of Pigs was a great embarrassment and exposed the newly elected administration to charges of softness on communism. Kennedy found himself under pressure from newspaper editorials that accused him of blundering. Some called for a proper invasion of Cuba at a time when the administration was anxious to avoid further adventures. Under these circumstances, the administration must have been loath to hear from high-ranking military officers say it was not doing enough to stand up to communism.[17]

Revelations about Walker's attachment to the John Birch Society deepened his troubles. Critics claimed that the name Pro-Blue did not originate, as explained, by the benign anecdote about the general's map. Rather, it signaled Walker's allegiance to the society, whose handbook was called "the Blue Book." Major Roberts later revealed under questioning that each unit's anticommunist library featured, along with the works of J. Edgar Hoover and Eugene Kinkead, Robert H. W. Welch Jr.'s *The Life of John Birch*, a propaganda tract about the missionary written by the group's founder. Welch inhabited fringe political territory, denouncing among other things the communist underpinnings of the Eisenhower presidency and the fluoridation of drinking water. He founded the well-funded society in 1958, but it gained a national reputation as the prototypical right-wing extremist group in 1961, coinciding especially with the organization of chapters in southern California. Given that Welch was convinced that Eisenhower himself was a communist agent, he also naturally believed that the army was staffed and commanded by traitors.[18]

Now linked to the John Birch Society, the controversial Pro-Blue program afforded Roberts a second career on the anticommunist lecture circuit. In this capacity, he regularly claimed to be the primary author of Pro-Blue, despite the army's insistence that he could not even claim to be the major contributor to the curriculum. Furthermore, though Roberts never directly claimed that he had Walker's ear while he was with the Twenty-fourth Division or after the whole episode became public, he was not above permitting his listeners to form the impression that he was not only an admirer but a sort of ideological right hand to his commander. Roberts later said he joined the John Birch Society on April 10, 1961, soon after he first heard of it but after he had already left the Twenty-fourth Infantry Division. He said that he had been happy to include *The Life of John Birch* in the unit libraries, but insisted that he had not heard of the John Birch Society at the time. In any event, he claimed that the book had nothing to do with the society, despite the fact that the author, Welch, was also the society's founder.[19]

At the behest of Secretary of the Army Elvis J. Stahr, Gen. Bruce C. Clarke, the commander in chief of United States Army, Europe (USAEUR), looked into the matter of Pro-Blue. He appointed Lt. Gen. Frederic J. Brown, commander of the V Corps, as special inspector while the erstwhile commander of the Twenty-fourth Division waited at USAEUR headquarters in Heidelberg. Brown's report led to the Department of the Army's formal admonishment of General Walker on June 12 and his subsequent recall to the United States. The special inspector found that in a speech before about two hundred members and dependents of his division Walker had "made derogatory public statements about prominent Americans, the American Press, TV industry and certain commentators, which linked the persons and institutions with Communism and Communist influence." Also, he had failed to heed the warnings of superiors to refrain from embroiling himself in controversies that "were contrary to the long-standing customs of the military service and beyond the prerogative of a senior commander."[20]

In the meantime, Pro-Blue got off relatively lightly. Brown concluded that the program was not part of a larger John Birch Society conspiracy and that, despite his indiscretions, no one could doubt the sincerity of Walker's motives in instilling anticommunism in his troops. OCINFO, meanwhile, concluded that while "the program is now identified primarily with Troop Information, it is actually much broader in scope."

The army's office implied that because the Pro-Blue went so far beyond its prescribed program OCINFO was not responsible for its missteps. Still, OCINFO did not retract its earlier approval. Whatever mistakes Walker might have made, "The stated objectives of the program . . . reflect interpretation and implementation of long-standing objectives of Department of the Army in the fields of information, community relations, and other command functions."[21]

The officials who deplored Walker ultimately refused to condemn his program and limited their criticism only to his selection of materials. They made this distinction for two reasons. First, even given the zealotry evident in the Pro-Blue guidelines, it would be difficult to prove that any aspect of the program was not based on existing Troop Information materials. Second, upholding the program while denouncing its author allowed the Pentagon to insulate itself against the attacks from the anticommunist right that were sure to follow the dismissal of the talkative Walker.

Thus, the Department of Defense was not only at pains not to reproach Pro-Blue, it also insisted that the program was still in operation in the Twenty-fourth Infantry Division despite the relief of its patron. Gen. Charles H. Bonesteel III, who succeeded Walker, later remembered: "His Pro-Blue program . . . on paper, and without an overenthusiastic implementation was a sound troop education program. . . . I did not retract the Pro-Blue program, but I, of course, changed the implementation and the lesson plans very considerably and made it low-key. . . . Ted [Walker] was a grand guy, but I think he got overly excited about this thing and got out of hand a little bit."[22]

Indeed, though Pro-Blue activities really were more invasive than a typical program by themselves they would probably never have undone Walker. Rather, what proved intolerable to the government were Walker's public statements denouncing some of the nation's best-known liberals as communists. Such a gross departure from the American military's traditional political neutrality invited a severe response.

Nevertheless, what first brought Walker's conduct under scrutiny was Pro-Blue's aggressive indoctrination. The general's defenders claimed that *Overseas Weekly* sensationalized its account of the operation of the indoctrination program, and Twenty-fourth Division personnel left no record of being especially offended by the program. Still, the record of indiscretion compiled by Walker and Roberts in their affairs after April 1961 suggest that the magazine's characterization was not far off the mark. Pro-Blue would not have been possible without Walker's political extremism. Once a commander of his bent put his personality behind the program it was bound to take on his politics.

The question of the John Birch Society illustrates this influence. Whether Walker and his special projects officer were officially members of the society when they worked on Pro-Blue, or only afterward, as Roberts maintained, is of little importance. Either way, Roberts saw no problem in giving troops a book that accused former president Franklin D. Roosevelt of "making dupes of the American people . . . on behalf of Stalin" and listed famous American liberals such as Frances Perkins and Felix Frankfurter among "those who deliberately set out to make America into . . . a socialist-Marxist state."[23] Walker was not the only officer of right-wing leanings ever to command a division, but, most conspicuously, he could not compartmentalize his personal politics and his obligations as a public servant. Other commanders and information officers mastered this skill or else held uncontroversial political views.

The willingness, or perhaps the inclination, of army officers to cultivate an apolitical attitude normally rendered harmless a potentially explosive aspect of civil-military relations. The practice of political indoctrination in the armed forces invited commanders to discuss with their men what the United States ought to be doing in the world and what it meant to be an American. The more conscientiously they pursued this mission, the more likely they were to run afoul of the military's vital tradition of political neutrality.

So long as the army was content with ineffectual indoctrination programs carried on by habit or by scattered, short-lived enthusiasms, this dilemma had few consequences. But anticommunist America was not content to have uninspiring political indoctrination for its men in uniform. To much of the American public the various goals of the Troop Information program seemed like good ideas until it saw them clenched together in a single, heavy fist like Pro-Blue. Nevertheless, given the long shadow cast by the Korean War nonrepatriate scandal, neither the government nor the army took much confidence from such *New York*

Times–reading centrists and liberals. On the subject of Troop Information they dared not ignore their critics on the radical right, who were far more interested in the programs than anyone else outside the armed forces (or almost anyone in the armed forces, for that matter). Circumstances encouraged officers, some conservative, some ultraconservative, and some merely opinionated, to test the waters of political advocacy. Some became vocal opponents of the United States' posture toward the communist bloc.

Such men collided with an administration whose own plans for waging cold war made no provision for cannons careening about the deck. Nowhere was the organizational imperative as strong as in Robert S. McNamara's Department of Defense. McNamara's staff began censoring the public utterances of military officers. As the department's red pens swept through the speeches of even senior, circumspect generals and admirals, their supporters charged that Kennedy and McNamara had "muzzled" the military.[24]

Walker's case inevitably became entangled with the complaints about military censorship. Before long, conservative politicians sought to make political hay from the muzzling controversy. Foremost among them was Senator Thurmond, Democrat (once again) of South Carolina, who championed the muzzled anticommunists.

Space Age Witch Hunters

Some officials in McNamara's Pentagon saw the Walker case not as an aberration but as merely the worst example of a growing trend. Arthur Sylvester, assistant secretary of defense for public affairs, told the press that while only Walker would be punished

> It is no secret . . . that this sort of activity by representatives of the Defense Department has been a disturbing problem for us. We are trying to reach a more rational handling of this aspect of the 'cold war' effort than has been the case in the past. . . .
>
> When, as these fellows do, you change the target to looking for spies under the bed or in the PTA you divert that much energy away from the main objective of the 'cold war.' And at the same time, you instill fear and distrust of our Government and its leader.[25]

The "sort of activity" Sylvester had in mind was officers appearing at "Cold War seminars."

A spate of conferences and seminars attacking American liberalism and communist subversion sprang up across the country between 1958 and 1961. The John Birch Society was only one of many organizations to sponsor such forums. The seminar's guest speakers urged their civilian audiences to be on guard against communists infiltrating their communities and to form their own groups to educate their indifferent neighbors.[26]

The Kennedy administration speculated that more than twenty military bases had hosted such events. Less than two weeks after Walker's ouster, for example, Capt. Robert T. Kieling, commander of the naval air station at Wold-Chamberlain Field, Minneapolis, Minnesota, cosponsored "Project Action" with the Minneapolis-St. Paul Chamber of Commerce. The purpose of Project Action was to alert Twin Cities civilians to "the general degradation of morals, the complacent attitude toward patriotism and the tremendous gains the Communist conspiracy is making."[27]

Kieling, like Walker, heedlessly muddled the Troop Information and Public Information missions. Indoctrinating soldiers as anticommunists was a delicate enough business for the Troop Information program. The purpose of Public Information, on the other hand, was to explain the armed forces to the American citizenry. Not satisfied with merely representing the military to civilians, men like Kieling presumed to explain America to Americans by broadcasting the content of the Troop Information campaign to the public.

In Pittsburgh, Pennsylvania, Lt. Gen. Ridgely Gaither, commander of the Second Army, lent his support to an April 15, 1961, seminar on the "Fourth Dimension in Warfare." At the event, retired admiral and featured speaker Chester Ward lambasted George F. Kennan, then ambassador to Yugoslavia, and Adlai Stevenson, then U.S. representative to the United Nations. He warned his listeners that these top policy advisors held views so soft on communism that they "would chill the average American."[28]

Additionally, Maj. William E. Mayer continued to vex the army with his public speaking appearances. The uncertified psychiatrist argued, as he had in the 1950s, that in the Korean War one-third of the prisoners had collaborated with their captors and that their breakdown was traceable to deficiencies in American culture. Though it disavowed his views, the army permitted Mayer to air them when it could not contrive to keep him busy with his actual duties. The major received so many requests to speak (about ten a month in 1961), however, that he was compelled to turn down invitations to appear at Xavier University and Our Lady of Cincinnati College, both in Cincinnati, Ohio. Disappointed audiences accused the Pentagon of muzzling Mayer.[29]

Capt. Kenneth J. Sanger, commander of the naval air station at Sands Point, Seattle, Washington, used his position to make hundreds of "moral leadership" lecture presentations to Northwest-area high schools and colleges. These captive audiences also watched the films *Communism on the Map* and *Operation: Abolition*. *Communism on the Map*, produced by Harding College in Searcy, Arkansas, blamed Roosevelt and former Secretary of State George C. Marshall for the communists' victory in China. It also claimed that every single NATO member state was under the rule of socialists or communists, save for the United States and Portugal.[30]

Operation: Abolition was equally inflammatory. In 1960 student demonstrators in San Francisco, California, called for the dissolution of the House Committee on Un-American Activities (HUAC). The committee promptly commissioned a film portraying the student "riots" as communist directed.[31] Senator Thurmond and his supporters could rally around *Operation: Abolition* because unlike *Communism on the Map* it had Congress's semiofficial imprimatur. One could not dispute its accuracy without repudiating the committee responsible for its creation. Nevertheless, as a November 26, 1960, *Washington Post* editorial put it:

> The movie presents a mendaciously distorted view. . . . First, it suggests that the demonstrators were Communist-inspired and Communist-led. Diligent inquiry has led us to a conviction that this charge is wholly unjustified. . . . Second, the film attempts to represent the rioting . . . as resulting entirely from student violence. . . . In point of fact, the San Francisco police acted with altogether needless brutality. . . .
>
> The film edited disparate scenes together to create the impression

of mob action, and they showed out of sequence shots to make it look like the students defied police instruction when they had not. . . .

In every respect—in its distribution for private profit, in its falsification of facts, in its white-washing of the Un-American Activities Committee—this film makes a dirty joke of the congressional investigating power.[32]

The army received angry mail from soldiers and civilians when commanders used *Operation: Abolition* to indoctrinate them. However, when the army ordered these activities suspended, admirers of the programs cried "muzzle." OCINFO was loath either to shelf the film and risk offending anticommunists or to let it be shown and risk escalating the controversy. It opted for a middle course and ordered all commanders and information officers not to show the movie during official sessions, but to keep it "on call" for voluntary viewing in officers' free time. Nevertheless, the movie came back to haunt the information department when Congress held hearings on the muzzling controversy in 1962.[33]

Right-wing officers were not alone in calling for anticommunist indoctrination for the public. In the early 1960s state boards of education in several states mandated the teaching of anticommunism. Between 1961 and 1963, at least ten state legislatures enacted laws or passed resolutions encouraging anticommunist lessons in public schools. In 1961, Florida, for example, determined that all high school students would take at least thirty hours of a new course entitled, "Americanism vs. Communism." In the same year, New York authorized courses on "communism and its methods and its destructive effects." Tennessee's legislature resolved that *Communism on the Map* should be made available to all of the state's public schools. Also in 1961, the American Bar Association called on its members to support the teaching of anticommunism in schools and colleges. In 1963 the National Catholic Education Association resolved that "Students should be taught to respect the strength and cunning of their Communist opponents."[34]

Boards of education and state legislatures, however, did not have to maintain neutrality in matters of civilian politics, and the anticommunist education of the American public was anything but apolitical. Cold War seminar organizers pressured communities for shows of conformity to right-wing views. The events led to the harassment of liberal citizens and scrambled the fortunes of local liberal politicians. As Lori L. Bogle has argued, the seminars made clear "the dangers inherent in efforts to incorporate a religious mission into the nation's military policies without proper restraint." Participating in the events put the military's political neutrality at risk.[35]

The Department of Defense badly wanted to put a stop to right-wing activities in the armed forces that characterized the Kennedy administration as weak on communism. However, it could not predict who in a sea of officers might turn out to be a Kieling or a Sanger. It became tempting to lash out at archconservative senior officers who were close at hand, even if they had not violated the military's political neutrality. For instance, the Pentagon called Lt. Gen. Arthur G. Trudeau Jr. on the carpet merely for expressing some minor sarcasm over a research proposal for a military foray into space. Men like Trudeau had not achieved their high positions without accumulating a good measure of self-regard and naturally resented a close monitoring of their public utterances. Had more senior officers not taken umbrage at McNamara's censorship policy the military muzzling issue might not have gone beyond the first congressional salvos fired in protest of Walker's removal.[36]

The issue did not end with Walker. Rapid exposure of the aforementioned muzzling incidents made for mounting publicity and finally aroused the interest of liberals in Congress. Senator J. William Fulbright (Democrat, Arkansas), the chairman of the Senate Committee on Foreign Relations, sent McNamara a memorandum criticizing military participation in Cold War seminars and suggesting a review of the entire Troop Information and Education program. Military writer Brig. Gen. Samuel L. A. Marshall, U.S.A., Retired, expressed the armed forces' reaction to the inquiry. To Marshall, Fulbright's memo implied that soldiers were "stupid." He especially disliked what he took to be a "slurring tone" from a man who had "never spent a day in uniform."[37]

At the same time, Marshall blasted Walker as "scatterbrained, unofficer-like and contemptuous of the best traditions of the Army." The "self-pitying" general deserved to be punished, but Marshall thought it ridiculous to have a national debate over troop indoctrination. "One Army commander has said, 'I no longer express a political opinion in my home. I will not indoctrinate troops if ordered. It isn't safe.'" Previously, everyone had been content in the knowledge that Troop Information was "no real brain-twister of fateful consequence to the Nation." In World War II the guidance controlling indoctrination "was written in 13 ½ hours by a major and having proved suitable, lasted the war." Marshall deemed war training, not political training, as essential, and he feared that interference in the latter would destroy commanders' authority over the former.[38]

Nevertheless, on January 23, 1962, the Senate opened hearings of the Special Preparedness Subcommittee on Armed Services on "Military Cold War Education and Speech Review Policies," chaired by Senator John C. Stennis (Democrat, Mississippi). Like Thurmond, Stennis was a conservative, segregationist Democrat, but his reputation as a level-headed southern gentleman promised a stabilizing hand on his overbearing colleague. Stennis's subcommittee investigated both the muzzling of officers and the quality of the programs responsible for the ideological "preparedness" of American soldiers. Senators Stuart W. Symington (Democrat, Missouri), Henry M. Jackson (Democrat, Washington), Leverett Saltonstall (Republican, Massachusetts), Margaret Chase Smith (Republican, Maine), and E. L. Bob Bartlett (Democrat, Alaska) joined Stennis and Thurmond on the subcommittee.[39]

For his part, Thurmond promised that he would get to the bottom of why the Pentagon substituted a "namby-pamby gutless" film for *Operation: Abolition*, and why the indoctrination system that had failed in Korea had yet to be improved. The junior senator from South Carolina argued that a review of muzzling was critical to the future of free speech in the United States and dismissed the threat to civil-military relations posed by the politicization of officers. Criticisms of communism did not constitute "forays into the field of partisan politics" because Americans had surely reached a consensus on the evil nature of the enemy ideology.[40]

On the first day of the Stennis hearings, the senators heard a letter from former President Eisenhower. Eisenhower came out against the Defense Department's policy and defended the laxer rules of his own administration by distinguishing between "general" supervision of military speeches, which was all right, and "petty" censorship, which ought to be discontinued. Military men engaged in free debate posed no special danger; after all, he reminded, dictators Adolf Hitler, Benito Mussolini, and Josef Stalin were all civilians.[41]

Perhaps in thinking about the muzzling issue, Eisenhower recalled his own ability to manage vast coalitions without anyone's censoring his speeches rather than the troubles he had with overly loquacious and opinionated subordinates. In any case, conservatives applauded the letter and interpreted it as an endorsement of their position. Eisenhower's letter had another purpose, however: to deny that he had ordered the military to direct a national ideological mobilization against communism to propagandize soldier and civilian alike. The defenders of Walker, Kieling, and Sanger claimed that they were only following orders. Specifically, they pointed to a "secret cold war policy" directive written by the National Security Council (NSC) under Eisenhower in 1958 that supposedly called on all military commanders to utilize every device at their disposal to broadcast the anticommunist message. The former president denied that the NSC had given any such order and suggested that reports to the contrary resulted from material "taken out of context or general language interpreted very loosely." Thus, Eisenhower's letter helped quiet one argument in defense of the muzzled officers, even as it supported their right to make political speeches.[42]

To support its policy, in late January the administration marshaled an impressive parade of current and former service chiefs to testify, including Adm. Arleigh A. Burke, chief of naval operations; Gen. George H. Decker, army chief of staff; Gen. Thomas D. White, former air force chief of staff; Gen. David M. Shoup, commandant of the Marine Corps; and Gen. Lyman L. Lemnitzer, chairman of the Joint Chiefs of Staff. Lemnitzer said he agreed with the Pentagon's right to clear officers' speeches, and Decker disputed the idea that the army had any role in educating the public about communism. Burke leaned a bit more toward Eisenhower's position than the others. He agreed with the speech curb but argued that high-ranking officers ought to be censored only by high-ranking civilians, not by lower-rank officers as was the practice. White suggested that low-ranking censors ought not to offend the senior officers because low-ranking underlings wrote their speeches anyway.[43]

The next month, the Pentagon's muzzling policy received more good press when Rr. Adm. William C. Mott, the navy's judge advocate general, told the American Law Student Association that "amateur anti-communists," like those who had been appearing at Cold War seminars, were "about as useful as amateur brain surgeons. We don't need space age witch hunters." The phrase was widely quoted. World War II army general Omar N. Bradley and fleet admiral Chester W. Nimitz completed the rebuttal of Eisenhower's letter with their own statements to the subcommittee supporting limitations on public speaking.[44]

The chiefs' devotion to the military's subordination to civilian authority defused much of Thurmond's criticism. If they had agreed with the senator's assumption that the military ought to be ideologically committed they would have made their Troop Information and Public Information policies vulnerable to the far right. But when confronted with the principle that the armed forces should be servants rather than makers of national policy, Thurmond had little to contest. General Shoup's testimony was particularly to the point. He told the subcommittee that he did not need to be censored because he simply refrained from making political speeches. Service chiefs "ought to have enough sense to know what to say in public," he claimed. "I don't feel it's my business to get up and designate the enemy." Pressed for his opinion on the value of political indoctrination, Shoup allowed that more combat training was a better idea. "We don't teach them to hate," he said of the Marine Corps program. Hate was a "poison" that bred fear and defeatism.[45]

Thus stymied, Thurmond cast about for some ammunition with which to embarrass the armed forces. In the second week of February one of the senator's aides administered a pop quiz on communism to thirty marines at the nearby Henderson Hall Barracks. To test the effectiveness of the Troop Information program, the quiz had the marines identify such terms as *Das Kapital, Chinese commune, Presidium, brainwashing, the Daily Worker,* and *dialectical materialism,* as well as the names of various communist and socialist world leaders. It asked them: "If you were called upon to fight overseas, whom do you think we would fight?" and "Did the 'cold war' end, or is it still going on?"[46]

Thurmond secured permission to administer his quiz from a lieutenant colonel who was an io at the barracks, which struck both Shoup and the Pentagon as a duplicitous act. The Department of Defense aired the story before Thurmond had a chance to introduce the test results with his customary drama. The administration's defenders denounced the "Gestapo tactics" of Thurmond's staff. Senator Mike Mansfield, the Democratic majority leader, speculated that the Senate itself lacked the "educational ability" to pass the quiz, and in an editorial James Reston suggested that the senators be tested on such questions as "Did the Civil War end, or is it still going on?"[47]

Thurmond and other conservatives wanted the subcommittee to go after the Pentagon's individual censors and question them point by point about cuts in particular speeches. He meant to expose the country's secret "no-win" policy for the Cold War. The Kennedy administration, according to the senator, only meant to oppose actual military aggression from communist nations, not communism in general. It would not hesitate to seek accommodations and peaceful coexistence with the Soviet Union.[48]

Kennedy and McNamara resolved not to reveal the identities of the Pentagon censors. Even after the *New York Times* got hold of one of their names and published it, the administration refused to link the fourteen majors with the particular speeches they had censored. McNamara insisted that he would take responsibility for his department's actions, and the president supported the secretary's decision. Thurmond blustered that Kennedy's decision to withhold the names amounted to "one of the most dangerous acts ever committed by a president of the United States while he was president of the United States." For his part, Kennedy invoked executive privilege to protect the censors from the prospect of Thurmond badgering them, in the manner of Joseph McCarthy, over each and every censoring decision. Indeed, Thurmond cut a figure not unlike the infamous Wisconsin senator when he brandished his phonebook-sized "Victory List," a compendium of anticommunist passages deleted from military speeches.[49]

Items from his Victory List occupied over twenty pages of the *Congressional Record*. Only about a sixth of the censored items were cut from speeches to purely military audiences. Another third of the deletions were from speeches before extended military audiences of veterans, reservists, National Guard units, or academy cadets. Censors made half of their cuts in speeches to civilians. The further outside the military family the speakers ventured to make speeches, the heavier the censorship they received (allowing, of course, that Thurmond's assistants assembled and selected the evidence). The censors' main task was to police Public Information rather than Troop Information. Hence, the question of muzzling was not so much whether the Pentagon gave officers enough flexibility to indoctrinate their men, but to what degree they might try to indoctrinate the public through Cold War seminars and the like.[50]

The deleted anticommunist phrases did not reflect any lack of resolve on the part of the Kennedy administration. Most cuts merely prevented officers from saying that war with the Soviet Union was inevitable or imminent. Far from articulating a secret "no win" policy, the censors' deletions were arbitrary and dependent on the idiosyncrasies of the individual reviewing the speech. Censors frequently failed to distinguish between censorship and editing. The Department of Defense could be pleased, however, that the Stennis probe found no evidence that it had wrongfully muzzled anticommunism in the armed forces, Senator Thurmond's dissent notwithstanding. The outcome for the internal indoctrination program, however, was not as gratifying.[51]

Testimony of the Information Officers

The Stennis investigation finished with the issue of public muzzling in February and in March turned its attention to the military's internal information programs. The subcommittee heard the testimony of information chiefs from both the Department of Defense and the army, and then brought in a number of officials from the intelligence branches to comment on the programs. Thurmond was the leading questioner of each witness, as he had been in the muzzling phase of the investigation. James T. Kendall, the subcommittee's chief counsel, handled most of the questioning that Thurmond did not. Stennis was on hand for most of the testimony, and Thurmond presided when he was absent.

Thurmond argued that the offices responsible for indoctrinating soldiers, OCINFO at the army level and DAFIE at the Defense Department level, were incompetent and soft on communism. Although no others on the subcommittee were as committed to this opinion as the South Carolinian, none were willing to express any great confidence in Troop

Information. One goal that Thurmond pursued throughout the questioning was to undermine DAFIE and OCINFO's control of anticommunist indoctrination in the armed forces. Should the others have joined him in his opinion he would have been able to lead another anticommunist crusade to remake troop indoctrination. If not, he could at least take credit for forcing the existing agencies to shape up.

Thurmond was thoroughly prepared and dominated the hearings with an abrupt, bullying style of interrogation. The other subcommittee members attended the sessions sporadically and usually demanded little of the witnesses. At times they appeared confused about the proceedings. When Thurmond veered off in pursuit of some obscure detail, even senators who might have been inclined to rescue a struggling witness were struck dumb, except for chairman Stennis, who made it a habit to rein in Thurmond every so often. Stennis's intervention was necessary because Thurmond was there chiefly to attack. For instance, when he could not criticize an information film he criticized the commercial films shown on bases. When he asked Col. Alexander F. Muzyk, the chief of OCINFO's Troop Information Division, why the army disliked the film *Defense against Enemy Propaganda*, the colonel agreed that it was an excellent film that taught the soldier "how they should rely on faith and on their indoctrination not to be affected." Thurmond then charged that the army had not ordered it in sufficient quantities. On other occasions, when he could not reproach the ideological consistency of DAFIE's pamphlets, he picked items out of their bibliographies and attacked them instead. Listing a left-leaning book in a bibliography, he claimed, was tantamount to putting "enemy propaganda in the hands of our troops."[52]

Thurmond's favorite red herring was the film *Russia*, which he inaccurately characterized as the military's replacement for *Operation: Abolition*. Though DAFIE's information catalogs grouped *Russia* with films about communism and the Soviet Union, no one conceived of it as a key part of the anticommunist arsenal. The twenty-four-minute film was a historical background piece that dwelt as much on the ceremonial splendor of Czar Nicholas II's court as it did on the nature of communism. It occupied a place in the indoctrination effort little more important than the films *Brazil* or *Portugal*.[53]

Nevertheless, Thurmond railed that "a soft film on Communism has enjoyed unchallenged top billing and maximum use by the Army." He found it particularly disturbing that the film commented positively on the idea of a student exchange program between the United States and the Soviet Union. Worse, he claimed that the producers of *Russia*, the International Film Foundation, had distributed communist propaganda films in the United States.[54]

The information offices hoped that the hearings would not lead the subcommittee to call for legislation that compelled from them some minimum level of anticommunist stridency. Such a result, Stennis admitted, was not the best solution.[55] A larger threat was that the final report would recommend that the armed forces' intelligence offices, rather than their information offices, run troop indoctrination. Certainly, the subcommittee had just this idea in mind when it questioned Maj. Gen. Alva R. Fitch, the army's assistant chief of staff for intelligence, and Col. Jack L. Weigland, the chief of the Security Division of Fitch's Counterintelligence Branch.

Stennis asked Fitch directly why Intelligence was not in charge of Troop Information. Thurmond was even blunter. He announced that people who took communism seriously wanted intelligence officers to conduct troop indoctrination, and only those who did not were willing to leave it to information officers and their "public relations–type approach." Fitch showed no appetite for the role. He replied that handling Troop Information and Education would overload and dilute the intelligence mission. Invited to condemn the army's leading pamphlet series, *Democracy versus Communism*, the general declined to offer an opinion. The senator characterized the series as weaker than its predecessor, *Know Your Communist Enemy* (perhaps *Democracy versus Communism* author Kenneth Colegrove had lost some of his luster in Thurmond's mind by severing his ties with the John Birch Society in 1960). Thurmond told the witnesses about an information officer who used articles from *The Nation* in his program. To the senator's chagrin, they refused to characterize the incident as a security breach. Weigland said the Federal Bureau of Investigation, not he, had the job of determining what was and was not subversive. His office could not handle a censorship program that encompassed the whole information effort. Fitch affirmed that intelligence wanted no part of troop indoctrination.[56]

Though Thurmond failed to goad the Intelligence witnesses, he had hit upon an important point when he described the conduct of Troop Information as a public relations exercise. The thorny coupling of the army's troop indoctrination and public relations staffs in the same office was one of several organizational problems that the Stennis hearings made obvious. Another was the confusion over OCINFO and DAFIE's respective roles.

After the Korean War the Office of Armed Forces Information and Education (OAFIE) changed its name to the Directorate of Armed Forces Information and Education in part to signify that the Department of Defense's role for the services' information programs would be less to support them than to *direct* them. Simultaneously, however, the growing body of experience from the field convinced information specialists that centrally mandated sessions, topics, and materials had spawned an ineffective, slow-reacting program. The local program, they concluded, had to be autonomous if it were to work at all.

The result was that no one was exactly sure who was in charge of Troop Information. Carlisle P. Runge, the assistant secretary of defense (manpower), testified that he had named Dr. Edward L. Katzenbach Jr. as his deputy to handle military education. Katzenbach was responsible for three directorates, one of which was DAFIE. Runge and Katzenbach stressed their leadership and oversight of the services. However, when Kendall asked if an individual commander controlled his program or if the Department of Defense prescribed it, Runge said, in essence, both. His office gave "guidance" in a collaborative effort.[57]

Katzenbach argued that the Defense Department should produce most materials, but he also acknowledged that implementation had to be flexible. Good materials were those that a commander could use "for discussion in the control center of a ship or by a platoon leader at a break." A base commander who found out his men were weak on communism ought to use all his TI time at once, whereas a captain putting out to sea should probably put politics off until later.[58]

However, even DOD control over materials was a point of contention. Maj. Gen. Charles G. Dodge, the chief of information, said he was not apprehensive about McNamara's taking a greater role in directing his programs, but he and Colonel Muzyk cast doubt on the wisdom of centrally prescribed materials. According to Dodge neither the Department of Defense nor the army had enjoyed much success sending topics and materials out from a central office. The practice resulted in commands' receiving inappropriate materials: if Korean culture were scheduled for that week, then it was going to be Korean Culture Week even if you happened to be stationed in central Europe. Even prescribing general topics on a monthly basis had proved too inflexible. The army now thought of Troop Information as an ongoing process rather than a series of discrete events.[59]

It is hard to believe that Dodge really thought his program was ever so badly managed that Korean culture lessons were being taught to troops in West Germany. His comments are better understood in the light of OCINFO's ongoing struggle to fend off DAFIE's tightening control. DAFIE's expectations for the program were closer to Thurmond's than OCINFO's were. McNamara put the Department of Defense on the side of censorship and against the Cold War seminars (policies that sat well enough with the army information office). However, DAFIE itself did not reject military participation in the anticommunist indoctrination of the American public.

A case in point was the status of the infamous *Operation: Abolition*. The army and Department of Defense anticipated that Thurmond would demand to know why the film was only "on call" and were ready with their answer: it had been suspended only because a new film, *Communist Target—Youth*, was near completion and would take its place. Not so easily put off, the senator pressed Runge to admit that it had been withdrawn because of its notoriety.[60]

In contrast, DAFIE director John C. Broger gave a different reason for shelving *Operation: Abolition*: the film did not go far enough. The international communist conspiracy, according to Broger, had penetrated youth organizations much further than the filmmakers indicated. Eager to woo new patrons, Broger dazzled the subcommittee with his testimony. Whereas the other Defense Department and army witnesses would go to great lengths to avoid having to make a statement of fact or opinion, Broger teemed with information about DAFIE activities. He enthusiastically described new projects, gave details on the production process, and explained how much money he had saved by doing something one way or another.⁶¹

More than anyone else, Broger inspired DAFIE's missionary attitude toward the public. The director's background made him the consummate information man. He had specialized in psychological warfare in World War II and in its aftermath served in the politically charged campaign against the Hukbalahop in the Philippines. In the mid-1950s, he authored the Militant Liberty indoctrination campaign and never completely gave up on the idea that the program's "Battle for Liberty" kits should have been deployed in the nation's high schools. He testified that a system of five California high schools and a New York school had in fact used Militant Liberty and that he himself had spoken about it to other teachers' groups. He also pointed with pride to letters from reservists who used Troop Information material in their Sunday school classes.⁶²

Broger argued that DAFIE needed innovative, far-reaching methods of political indoctrination because existing techniques dated from the last war. He maintained that that conflict was "unlike the one in which we find ourselves today, that it was more directly confined to the military aspects of [a soldier's] motivation as well as to the ideologies in conflict between the Nazi-Fascist Axis and our own principles and values in our American heritage. What I am saying is that I don't believe it involved other nations or the world struggle in that regard. It was not nearly so sophisticated as what is required of us today."⁶³

Broger's alarm indulged a dubious presentism, one reflected in the high school texts he was eager to supplement. Cold War textbooks treated the confrontation with communism as the culmination of American history, with the struggles and upheavals of previous centuries reduced to mere prelude. Frances Fitzgerald has noted that "virtually all" of the texts described the rivalry with the Soviets in these dire terms, while "The texts of the early forties had not portrayed the Nazis as half so aggressive, or the Second World War as half such a threat to the country." Though the Cold War offered formidable challenges to American indoctrinators, it also presented advantages compared with World War II's mobilization of opinion. Because of the consensus that emerged from the last war the peacetime will to fight was better developed, the ideological contest better articulated, and isolationist sentiment far weaker in 1962 than it had been before December 7, 1941. Broger's fellow citizens largely accepted international commitments, expensive standing forces, and near-paranoiac anticommunist vigilance as the necessary costs of freedom. But Broger's insistence that the real crisis was at hand was not merely presentist; it justified his desire to thrust militarized political indoctrination into the civilian realm.[64]

OCINFO was not so grandiose. Dodge appeared defensive compared to the dynamic Broger. Having only recently arrived at his post, he professed to know little about the specifics of his programs and materials. He seemed to have little idea what had gone on in his organization before he arrived. He answered the subcommittee's questions conscientiously but gave no indication that he thought the state of Troop Information was in any way dire.[65]

Thurmond confronted Broger with a list of incidents that portrayed individual information officers as "unqualified." According to the senator, unwillingness to show *Operation: Abolition* was enough to render one unqualified. However, he also cited the inexperienced IO, the IO "so burdened down with additional duties that he has become more or less a public relations man for the Commanding General," the IO who failed to ask for guidance from his G-2 (intelligence officer), and the IO who had used *The Nation*. One medical officer had been pressed into service as an IO although it had been seven years since he had graduated from the information school. Thurmond described this officer as a needless "casualty of the cold war," given that plenty of dedicated anticommunists would "give their eye-teeth" to indoctrinate soldiers. Wasn't his assignment, Thurmond asked Dodge, "like sending him on a suicide mission in combat almost?"

"No, sir," replied the chief of information, "I would not think I would go that far."[66]

How far Dodge wanted to go was apparent from his description of what, to his mind, constituted an effective information program. He had commanded the Seventh Cavalry in Korea, and the unit possessed a high esprit de corps. The troops knew their outfit's history and were proud of it. They greeted their officers with their trademark salute, a robust, "Gary Owen, sir!" In short, unit pride was the key to good morale.[67]

Dodge seemed reluctant to affirm that the premise of Troop Information was that soldiers needed more than unit pride and service pride—that they needed to internalize a sense that their military mission was one of justice and to believe in their country's goodness and righteousness. Troop Information was all for promoting unit pride, Dodge agreed, but so was the Marine Corps, which cared little for political indoctrination.

At the same time, Dodge was not willing to say—as Marine Corps commandant Shoup had—that the troops should cultivate an apolitical professionalism. The army lacked DAFIE's confidence in the propriety of political advocacy, but it did not have the leisure to shun it completely. Thus, Dodge testified that Cold War seminars were basically good and that officers should not be prohibited from appearing at them. Wondering how officers could avoid the controversies that had sparked the hearings, Stennis put his finger on the problem: "In other words, when an Army general participates in a seminar . . . and later in that program citizen X makes a speech . . . the Army is connected with it in the public mind." The CINFO admitted that that could be a problem, but he had no solution to recommend.[68]

When Thurmond described the IO who was overburdened managing his commander's public relations he was also describing the CINFO himself. Dodge told the subcommittee that he was wearing both the hats of chief of information and chief of public information.[69] That he appeared not to have thought through the Troop Information mission's fundamental principles did not reflect badly on him in particular. No one else had challenged the hasty assumption that the same office should administer both the army's public relations and internal indoctrination.

OCINFO's confusion over where political neutrality ended and political indoctrination began made for some humiliating moments before the Stennis subcommittee. The worst came on March 9 when Thurmond delved into the alleged muzzling of Maj. William E. Mayer. Mayer had recorded some of his popular speeches on the moral delinquency of American enlisted men, and the tapes had been distributed to some information officers at various bases. When the army received some negative publicity because Mayer was unable to appear at the two Cincinnati colleges, OCINFO called in the tapes. Both Dodge and Muzyk, the TI chief, denied any knowledge of the order to recall the tapes.[70]

Thurmond had the CINFO directive, dated December 21, 1961, read into the record. After hearing it, Muzyk explained that the order was not to withdraw all the tapes but only to obtain one copy from each base to see what use was being made of them. Dodge said that the sole misunderstanding occurred at Fort Belvoir, Virginia, which sent in its only copy of Mayer's tape, only to have OCINFO return it. If Dodge and Muzyk were telling the truth then OCINFO had a fairly clumsy way of surveying the use of information materials. Thurmond blasted the officers, saying they had returned the tape to Fort Belvoir only because the subcommittee had asked about it. He demanded to know why Muzyk had recalled the tapes.[71]

Muzyk said the order had originated in his office, and he was compelled to name the subordinate who wrote it. Then, with Thurmond badgering him and cutting off his every sentence, he became flustered and reversed himself. "I don't really know where it originated but it originated in another office." There developed some confusion over whether Muzyk meant his office or Dodge's office, of which Muzyk's office was a part. Then he admitted that Dodge's deputy, Brig. Gen. George V. Underwood, had told him to get information on Mayer to see if his speeches contradicted army policy.[72]

Thurmond said there was nothing wrong with Mayer's speeches and encouraged the colonel to agree that they were "very fine material." Then Muzyk regained his composure and remembered that there was something wrong with them: they deviated from the army's official line on the nonrepatriate issue. By then, the senator was out of patience. Reminding Muzyk that Mayer was a psychiatrist, he snapped, "Are you a psychiatrist?"[73]

Finally, Stennis called a timely recess. After lunch, Thurmond ran Dodge through the catechism:

> Thurmond: The aim of Communism is to dominate the world, do you agree about that?
>
> Dodge: There is no doubt in my mind about that, sir.
>
> Thurmond: The aim of the Communists is to take the world, is it not?
>
> Dodge: Yes, sir.

Thurmond: You believe there is an international conspiracy of Communism, do you not?

Dodge: I do, yes, sir.[74]

Dodge and Muzyk could have avoided the rough handling and the indignity of being caught in a lie if either of them had been familiar with the army's objections to Mayer's views. The major's materials were not "very fine material" for use in Troop Information because they criticized American mores and institutions and leveled false charges at American prisoners of war. As General Fitch of intelligence testified, it was inappropriate for the army to endorse opinions about such matters. Such was the only course open to an organization that was determined to remain subordinate to civil authority.[75]

Against the Mattoids

The Stennis subcommittee was loath to call Maj. Gen. Edwin A. Walker. Once he resigned from the army and declared himself a candidate in Texas's governor's race he had lost his appeal as a witness. Though the senators were reluctant to provide Walker with a campaigning forum, they relented on April 4, 1962. Walker's testimony reminded a *New York Times* reporter of the Army-McCarthy hearings held in the same room eight years before. As on that occasion spectators packed the chamber; the *Times* described them as "predominantly middle-aged and elderly women." Adding to the spectacle was American Nazi party leader George Lincoln Rockwell, whom the Capitol police ejected from the hearings when he refused to remove his swastika from his lapel. Walker defended Pro-Blue, attacked civilian control of the military establishment, and reiterated his charges against some of public figures whom he had called communists in West Germany—and added, for good measure, parallel accusations against McNamara's special assistant Adam Yarmolinsky.[76]

Determined to remain on the national stage, the disgraced general later resurfaced on September 30, 1962, in Oxford, Mississippi, where African-American student James Meredith was about to integrate the all-white University of Mississippi. By urging Mississippians to resist integration as the work of the Antichrist, Walker squandered whatever laurels he had earned at Little Rock in 1957. He was arrested for attempting to incite violence against Meredith. When he learned that Walker was on the campus, John F. Kennedy remarked, "Imagine that son of a bitch having been commander of a division?" One of the president's aides compared him to the renegade right-wing general in the novel *Seven Days in May*.[77]

In John Frankenheimer's 1964 film version of that civil-military drama, Burt Lancaster's would-be man on horseback came across as a far more deliberate and charismatic character than Walker ever was (Lancaster's character bore a greater resemblance to Douglas MacArthur). It is difficult, however, not to suspect that the Walker incident contributed something to Sterling Hayden's unhinged General Ripper in Stanley Kubrick's contemporaneous film: *Dr. Strangelove or: How I Learned to Stop Worrying and Love the Bomb*. Although Kubrick's source material, a 1958 novel, also featured a general intent on nuclear war, Ripper's ranting about communist infiltration of the water supply (in order to sap Americans' precious bodily fluids) recalled Walker's association with the John Birch Society. The appearance of these films reflected an easing of ideological stridency in the popular culture of the early 1960s. In contrast to the humorless anticommunist dramas of the 1950s, these films found an American audience that feared anticommunist excess more than domestic subversion. Frankenheimer's earlier 1962 film, *The Manchurian Candidate*, had depicted Chinese brainwashing of American POWs in the Korean War with a gravity consistent with the anticommunist ethos of the prior decade while still heaping ridicule on a character based on Senator McCarthy. In Kubrick's hands, Ripper too is an object of fun, just as Walker and the John Birch Society were for the mainstream liberal press. Even for some conservatives, the Birchers, despite their prodigious funding and determined grassroots organizing, were not so much potential allies as sources of embarrassment.[78]

Like Walker, Maj. Arch E. Roberts also very much wanted to testify, but the subcommittee never invited him. Since the admonishment of his former commander Roberts had tried to drum up support for himself by writing to conservative officers and organizations. His mailings praised Pro-Blue and denounced the government's treatment of Walker, saying he detected "the whiff of treason in the affair." He began giving lectures about Pro-Blue to conservative groups and granted interviews in which he challenged the subcommittee to call him. When he talked to investigators for the Stennis probe he took the occasion to smear his superiors in the New York information office as communist sympathizers.[79]

Seeing Roberts's opposition to the government's policies as incompatible with the duties of an information officer, the army transferred him to a medical position—his original military occupational specialty. In April 1962 censors rejected a speech that Roberts intended to deliver at a meeting of the Daughters of the American Revolution (DAR). Claiming to be speaking off the cuff, he went ahead to give his remarks at the event. He complained about the Walker case and impugned the loyalty of Samuel Yorty, mayor of Los Angeles, and G. Mennen Williams, the assistant secretary of state for African affairs—politicians who according to Roberts were responsible for the distribution of *Overseas Weekly*.[80]

On April 27 the army relieved Roberts of his duties. Roberts in turn sued new Secretary of the Army Cyrus R. Vance to regain his position. The consensus of the army, the Senate, and the mainstream press was that Roberts had intentionally tried to martyr himself and was not on that basis entitled to a prominent voice in the muzzling debate. One paper suggested that the DAR speech was so devoid of reason that instead of muzzling the Pentagon ought to have every officer above the rank of lieutenant make a speech so the public could determine how many of them were as addled as Roberts.[81]

From that point on Roberts's anticommunist activities became increasingly bizarre. He wrote broadsides that denounced the United Nations and told parents "Why Your Soldier Son Serves under the Command of a Soviet Communist." The leaders of the United States, he argued, were not actually normal human beings, but "Mattoids—men of unbalanced and dangerous brilliance." "Mad as Hitler," the Mattoids (or "half-fools," as Roberts sometimes called them) were the monstrous product of a gene pool that had been in decline since its heyday in ancient Athens. Despite these ravings, Roberts prevailed in his suit against Vance in 1964, and the army had to reinstate him.[82]

The army could no more easily resolve all the issues that the Walker episode and Stennis investigation had raised about Troop Information than it could get rid of Roberts. It could salvage little good from Walker's ouster because it had made a national issue out of a program few knew anything about. The only information the public had was negative. The radical right came away from the episode convinced that a vital anticommunist force had been subverted.

The testimony of the Office of the Chief of Information also failed to inspire confidence in those concerned about the practice of Troop Information. The setback was bearable because ultimately the Stennis subcommittee's final report did not recommend that Intelligence take over the program. On the other hand, trying to implement the recommendations that the report did make helped to condemn DAFIE and OCINFO to more years of unproductive self-analysis and cosmetic reinvention, activities that had plagued the program in years past.

The return to the cycle of reinvention distracted the information chiefs from the serious problems revealed by the events of 1961 and 1962. The Department of Defense and the army still had not clearly defined their respective roles in regard to Troop Information duties. Whether the program should be centralized or decentralized was still in dispute. Decentralization in any organization works best when the autonomous members share operating assumptions. The emergence of the right-wing indoctrination mavericks seemed to indicate that commanders lacked the shared outlook needed for decentralization. Conversely, the natural response to criticism was more centralization. If Troop Information was out of control, the press, the public, the Congress, and the administration did not want to hear that commanders needed more autonomy. They wanted to hear that someone was in charge who would issue clear instructions that everyone would obey. Therein lay the danger of a return to an overly rigid program.

The marriage of Troop Information and Public Information continued to divide the attention of the CINFO and his staff, to say nothing of the budget. It also unnecessarily conflated two diverse functions. In 1961 political indoctrination, which had yet to prove definitively that it had any value to soldiers, seemed bent on escaping its military bounds and spreading to the public. The trend toward political advocacy embodied by Walker, Roberts, Mayer, and the Cold War seminar speakers exposed the lack of systemic protections against partisanship in Troop Information. Anticommunism could not, in the end, be separated from domestic partisan politics. With no way to reconcile the mission of political advocacy with the ideal of political neutrality, the programs remained an open invitation for officers to politicize themselves. Though this structural flaw went uncorrected, the problem receded of its own accord. The majority of officers had a sense of what was appropriate and avoided trouble in any case, and Walker's fate cowed the rest into silence. Ideological extremism had peaked. Indifference rather than fervor characterized the indoctrinators' approach to the new war in Vietnam.

6

Information's Impossible War

Political Indoctrination in the Vietnam War

The congressional hearings on the military's "Cold War Education" policies sent the indoctrinators into a cycle of self-analysis. They readily identified the program's deficiencies and called for a return to "hard-hitting" materials like *Why We Fight*. Despite several attempts to reconceptualize troop indoctrination, however, the process was fruitless. The Command Information program waged the Vietnam War, its most trying campaign for the hearts and minds of American soldiers, with mostly the same sort of methods and materials used throughout the Cold War. The army's office spent the war battling a shrinking budget and assertive Defense Department control. Neither office confronted the war in Vietnam with their full attention or creativity. Viewing Vietnam as almost a distraction from their basic "democracy versus communism" mission, they missed a chance to seize on "area orientation" and Troop–Community Relations as the more useful and realistic role for the programs. By the end of the war, information officers were demoralized along with the rest of the army, and in any case unable to answer the challenges that the war posed to national assumptions of righteousness.

The Information Program Critiqued

On October 19, 1962, the Senate Committee on Armed Services's Special Subcommittee on Preparedness issued its conclusions on the state of the Troop Information and Education program. Compared to the rebukes that the information officers received while testifying, the final report was sober and restrained. Nevertheless, Chairman John C. Stennis and his colleagues had little good to say about the military's political indoctrination campaign.

The Stennis report affirmed that the armed services were squarely responsible for making soldiers perceive freedom as a virtue and communism as a threat. Of the two halves of the equation, the subcommittee laid heavier emphasis on promoting the merits of the United States and its political system than on sandbagging the enemy. In this way the report failed to reflect the alarm of Senator Strom Thurmond, who throughout the hearings charged that Troop Information was soft on communism.[1]

The subcommittee found the existing programs inadequate for a variety of reasons. The senators argued that the uneven quality of the information pamphlets and films unnecessarily confused the implementation of the program. "The sheer volume of training material made available by the Department of Defense—some excellent, some mediocre, some worse—itself presents a problem since the commander may not have the qualifications or the time to select the specific materials best suited to the needs of his troops."[2]

The subcommittee addressed the issue of suitability to specific audiences by calling for a more select pool of materials. However, it did not explain why it thought that allowing the local commander fewer rather than more options would have increased the troops' odds of receiving information tailored to their specific circumstances. The report displayed little confidence that the commander was in the best position to understand the needs of his men. The urge to gain control, via centralization, of a few problematic materials undermined the premise that the local commander was responsible for implementing the program.

The senators cited the lack of self-evaluation and qualified instructors as Troop Information's most serious deficiencies. The Directorate of Armed Forces Information and Education and the army's Office of the Chief of Information did study the effectiveness of their programs, if less systematically than the Information and Education Division had during World War II. The subcommittee's investigators, however, had found several information officers who seemed confused or overwhelmed by their duties. During the hearings Thurmond had introduced these examples with dramatic flourishes that made them appear all the more pervasive and damning.[3]

Although the IOs in question did not always seem assured in the way they did their jobs, none could be deemed incompetent or even "unqualified" on the evidence that Thurmond provided. Because of the general lack of enthusiasm for Troop Information the subcommittee's assistants did not have to range far from Washington DC to find IOs who could be made to look unprepared. The subcommittee ascribed this state of affairs to the quality of the IOs, but they might also have noted the lack of support those officers received from their commanders in the field. Because the service culture rejected Troop Information, IOs could seldom popularize it with only their own enthusiasm and resourcefulness. It was true enough, however, that the armed forces did not value political indoctrination highly enough to attract the best personnel to information specialties.

To remedy the defects the Stennis report offered general and specific measures. It called for the Department of Defense to offer more guidance to commanders in selecting information materials and to produce more materials featuring America's "magnificent heritage." The senators advised the military to create a program to burnish junior officers' presentation skills. In a nod to Thurmond's yen for demonstration teams the report suggested that such troupes could be used to instruct future instructors.[4]

The report also called for IOs to make maximum use of information generated by intelligence officers, though it did not recommend that Troop Information be in any way subordinate to the intelligence branches. In total, it urged "That every effort be made to make troop information as hard-hitting, factual, interesting and inspiring as possible, particularly in view of the necessity for balancing troop information with combat, tactical, and weaponry training in an already crowded schedule."[5]

The Stennis subcommittee recognized that only a small part of training could be devoted to political indoctrination. Making this limited available time action packed and memorable was therefore all the more important. The Stennis report's call for "hard-hitting" political content became the refrain of the information specialists.

The Department of Defense tried to preempt the congressional report by setting up a blue-ribbon committee to make a parallel study of the Troop Information program. On February 2, 1962, Secretary of Defense Robert S. McNamara announced that Karl R. Bendetsen, former undersecretary of the army, would chair the Advisory Committee to the Secretary of Defense on Non-Military Instruction. The committee included such prestigious figures as former Chief of Naval Operations Arleigh A. Burke, Central Intelligence chief Allen W. Dulles, former NATO commander Alfred M. Gruenther, and former Air Force chief of staff Thomas D. White. McNamara asked the Bendetsen committee to visit various commands and units over a ninety-day investigation. The object of the investigation was to ascertain Troop Information's proper goals and subject matter and to discover the best way of measuring the program's performance.[6]

The work of the Bendetsen committee largely duplicated that of the Stennis subcommittee and reached similar conclusions. Reflecting the committee members' more articulate opinions on military organization, however, its recommendations were both more specific and more radical than those of the Senate report.

The Bendetsen committee agreed with DAFIE director John C. Broger that the world situation demanded a higher level of ideological militancy from Americans than in the past. Because the communist enemy "uses para-military, guerrilla and propaganda methods . . . our officers must be schooled in politics and economics as well." They claimed that the very terms *combat* and *readiness* had new, political meanings in the Cold War. Still, the members did not paint as pessimistic a picture of the American serviceman as did the most alarmist of the politicians on the Stennis subcommittee. "There is little evidence," it reported, "to support the view expressed in some quarters that the serviceman lacks an awareness of the communist threat."[7]

The report was not an apology for the Troop Information program. Political training in the armed forces could not be expected to correct all the defects of premilitary education, but it could exhibit a "sense of excellence" that the committee found too often lacking in the program. The main problem, as the members saw it, had never been stated in previous studies. It was simply that Troop Information had come to be considered an end unto itself rather than a part of training generally. Outside of the traditional course, the program had to compete with the training schedule, a competition that no competent commander could permit it to win.[8]

The Bendetsen committee recommended that political indoctrination abandon all titles like "Troop Information," "internal information," and "information and education" and instead rename itself "General Military Training." As it stood, commanders often failed to distinguish between Troop Information and the information resources that were devoted to communicating with the public. In other words, the armed forces had become confused by their own euphemisms. General Military Training (GMT) would not be "a needless exercise" nor "an end in itself." It would not have a status separate from regular training.[9]

Like the Stennis subcommittee, the Bendetsen committee concluded that the Department of Defense and the services produced too many materials of uneven quality. They envisioned that GMT would concentrate on only four topics: the American Political Tradition, Communism in Action, National Policies, and Area Orientation. American Political Tradition ranked first in priority because "it is more important for the serviceman to know what he is for than it is to know what he is against."[10]

In stressing "Communism in Action" rather than simply "Communism" the Bendetsen committee suggested that the enemy's military and paramilitary tactics might be of more importance to soldiers than examinations of political philosophies. In contrast, materials like *Democracy versus Communism* explained communism by way of Plato and Aristotle.[11]

Bendetsen and his colleagues no doubt recalled the persuasiveness of the *Why We Fight* films when they wrote "the committee is of the opinion that high grade, professionally prepared motion pictures constitute one of the most effective media for such instruction and particularly in the four specified subject areas." A minor office in the army or the Department of Defense could not easily procure high-grade, professionally made films. Capra's troubles with the Signal Corps during World War II suggested that Hollywood-quality troop indoctrination movies could only be supervised at a relatively high level.[12]

Consequently, the authors of the GMT plan argued for top-down direction of the indoctrination program. The Department of Defense was to have control over the content of materials produced in the four basic areas. The Bendetsen committee recommended that the Office of the

Assistant Secretary of Defense, Manpower and Personnel (ASD [MP]), take a direct hand in providing materials. As it stood in the early 1960s, the ASD (MP) controlled DAFIE through an education office, which itself was busy with two other directorates. To make troop indoctrination part of regular military training it would have to be disassociated from extramilitary education. The committee recognized the need to build command interest through decentralized control, but their recommendation to do this was less emphatic than their impulse to rationalize the program at the DOD level.[13]

The fate of the existing information bureaucracies was unclear in the future envisioned by the Bendetsen plan. Under GMT, OCINFO would certainly have been ousted from its role in the political indoctrination process. The committee allowed that the information services could continue to supply motivational materials but only in the form of supplementary radio, television, and print items to appear in *Stars and Stripes* and the like. In other words, OCINFO was welcome to try to find a voluntary audience among servicemen, but it would not have a voice in the mandatory political training.[14]

Replacing Troop Information with GMT meant that political indoctrination would have no status apart from regular war training. It also apparently meant that at the army level, it would have no office apart from regular war training either. Troop Information would have received a bureaucratic divorce from Public Information in this arrangement, but independence would have come at the expense of established roles and careers.

The military establishment ignored the committee's advice in the short term. Six years after the report the Pentagon did remove DAFIE from Office of the ASD (MP)'s education office and make it an equal office directly under the ASD (Manpower and Reserve Affairs). In the process, it changed its name to the Office of Information for the Armed Forces (OIAF). Broger remained in charge, as he would throughout the Vietnam War.[15]

The study demonstrated the military's willingness to reevaluate Troop Information even as it underwent public scrutiny. But the army's information organization, so casually cast in bureaucratic stone in the late 1940s, proved resistant to the more sweeping recommendations. The

Stennis and Bendetsen reports generated a flurry of name changes and affirmations of newly found fresh attitudes. Nevertheless, the programs continued much as before in terms of their structure, materials, and confusion of duties between the Department of Defense and the services. In early 1964 Troop Information officially became "Command Information" in order to get commanders to take it more seriously, but the ambitious GMT plan went by the wayside.[16]

Political Indoctrination as Public Relations

Brig. Gen. George V. Underwood Jr., the deputy chief of information, succeeded Maj. Gen. Charles C. Dodge as CINFO in 1963 and served in the post until 1966. Like CINFOS past, his background was on the Public Information side of the department. Underwood had attended the University of Wisconsin's course on public relations, to which he gave his enthusiastic support as chief. Starting in 1959, Wisconsin offered the Advanced Public Relations course to fill the military's need for "graduate level training" in the information specialty. In the early 1960s the classes served as the only opportunity for IOs to receive professional education after graduation from the military information schools. As Underwood told the class of 1964, "Neither the U.S. Army Information School nor the DINFOS [Defense Information School] conducted an advanced course; this is our advanced course."[17]

Advanced Public Relations ran eight weeks and each year enrolled about twenty-five officers and civilians working for the army in an information capacity. A board of officers screened potential students, and the CINFO approved the final selections. The course taught "political, sociological, and communications problems related to information duties at the policymaking level." Students attended classes similar to those at the DINFOS on practical photojournalism, radio, and television work, but they also had more theoretical fare such as the principles of communications, the analysis of public opinion, and the philosophy of public relations.[18]

The Wisconsin course used case studies to prepare information officers for problems they might encounter in the field. The syllabus of 1964's summer session offered cases such as Big Lift ("a study in the care and feeding of the press"), Swift Strike ("a step-by-step procedure in softening up a civilian community for the influx of a large maneuver element"), Recruits' Air Crash ("bad press is unavoidable sometimes"), Alaska Murder ("how to turn a bad story into a showcase for the Army's cooperation with the civilian community"), and Fort Sill Land Grab ("how an information shop organizes for a fight with a minority group").[19]

The cavalier case descriptions betrayed an adversarial attitude toward the civilian press and public. The censorship episodes of the Korean War and the muzzling controversies of the early 1960s had already done much to reinforce the army's natural suspicions toward these groups. The University of Wisconsin's instructors did little to prevent IOs from adopting the attitude, much in evidence during the Vietnam War, that the public was to be deceived and manipulated as a matter of course.

Wisconsin's approach to Public Information was not wholly constructive, but it tried to arm IOs with useful skills. It mostly ignored the troop indoctrination aspect of the job. Of twelve case studies only two concerned internal information, and only one of those exclusively. Granting that the course's subject was designated as public relations, it confirmed for the most qualified IOs at their highest level of training that Public Information rather than Command Information was their most important work.

Underwood was aware of the internal program's lesser status and tried to remind his IOs that Troop Information was as important as Public Information. "PI" got the glamour, he admitted in his many speeches, but "the money is in Troop Information." The practice of political indoctrination was "the bedrock and bugaboo" of their mission. By bugaboo, he meant "our main problem in the Troop Information area is psychological, not substantive." The Stennis and Bendetsen committees had cited lack of command interest as a critical weakness, but OCINFO's inspections convinced Underwood that it had strong support from commanders. Recent advances in technique, he argued, neutralized most of the criticisms leveled at the program. There was still room for improvement: "We need to convince some neanderthal types that the World War II program is no longer in effect."[20]

Underwood's remarks can be grouped with Broger's testimony before the Stennis subcommittee. Both trumpeted the fresh, innovative techniques in development. Both dismissed the World War II inheritance as stale, unsophisticated, and irrelevant to the problems at hand. Because of the disproportionate weight critics placed on the Korean War non-repatriate scandal, it seemed politically necessary to sever ties with the past. Despite continued reverence for the *Why We Fight* films, the Vietnam-era indoctrinators were disconnected from useful elements of the 1940s orientation campaign, such as the old Research Branch's constant study of the program's effectiveness.

Underwood was sensitive to the inferiority complex suffered by information specialists generally. IOs were sometimes unappreciated "damage control officers." The OCINFO battle cry, he said, was the less-than-inspirational "Let's not come unglued!" One may gauge some of the areas of discontent by noting what Underwood was compelled to deny. In his speeches to Army information conferences and graduating classes at DINFOS, he assured his "information warriors" that an information specialty would not hurt their chances for advancement. Further, their position in a "small family" of the army ensured them a sympathetic hearing for their service preferences.[21]

He also assured the IOs who concentrated on troop indoctrination that the army valued their contributions. Two years into his tenure the "myth" persisted that "Public Information is the name of the game and that anyone who gets caught in a Command Information assignment is clumsy, colorless and unambitious. Too many information operators set too much store by the romance and color of wheeling and dealing with the Great American Press. Well—here is my reaction to that type of information warrior. The real name of the game is public understanding. . . . You are in the game and on the team when you are carrying the Command Information ball." If the internal program could arm draftees and short-term enlistees with positive feelings about the army, Underwood argued, then those men could spread that attitude to the public at large. The best rationale the CINFO could offer for the value of Command Information was that it could produce good Public Information. In this conception, the army carried out political indoctrination not to make draftees into better soldiers but to make departing soldiers into supportive civilians.[22]

Despite his somewhat backhanded support for the Command Information mission, Underwood was optimistic about the performance of both of his branches as in 1965 the United States sent large numbers of troops to the Republic of Vietnam to prevent the collapse of the American-backed regime. He enthused that press coverage of "Vietnam" was much better than in the Korean War, and Lt. Gen. William C. Westmoreland, commander of Military Assistance Command, Vietnam (MACV), was "getting a smoother ride" than his predecessor, Lt. Gen. Paul D. Harkins. Despite the "deviant behavior of Anti-Vietnam minorities" the war was enjoying much broader public support than the unpopular conflict of the last decade. Underwood also claimed that, in contrast to the Korean War, "the American soldier is considered a highly motivated professional who understands the communist threat and the need for sacrifice."[23]

That the American soldier be "considered" a highly motivated anticommunist seemed to be of more immediate concern to the CINFO than his actual frame of mind. That commanders imbue their men with a "wholesome outlook" was "vitally important," said Underwood, if they were to transmit that attitude to their civilian communities.[24]

Of course, the light that Underwood saw at the end of the information tunnel proved illusory. One may well ask why, once American soldiers engaged the enemy, Command Information did not command more respect vis-à-vis Public Information. Public Information assumed the prominence it did in the Vietnam War for good reason. The fact that personnel rotated out of the theater of operations every thirteen months may account for Underwood's emphasis on soldiers as promoters of the army's image. The successful prosecution of a war of dubious national value depended on civilian morale as well as that of the fighting men. Indeed, the deterioration of civilian morale after the enemy's January 1968 Tet Offensive was arguably a more pressing problem than the deterioration of the army's.

The war at hand was not necessarily foremost in Underwood's mind. Like many of the army's institutions, OCINFO was prone to treating the Vietnam War not so much as a war in the immediate sense as a distraction from the preparations for possible future wars.[25] Public Information's most important campaign was to convince Americans to regard the army with the same (or preferably more) respect they accorded the navy and the air force. To help ensure that the army retained a vital, successful, and prestigious role in a possible general war with the Soviet Union, the public's perception that the army was healthy trumped in importance the cultivation of a sense of purpose in the limited war in Vietnam.

The attitude was perhaps at its most perverse in the literature on prisoner of war (POW) conduct. *The U.S. Fighting Man's Code* urged soldiers not to reveal military secrets if captured. Yet of far greater concern to the authors was that they not allow themselves to be used as enemy propaganda. The booklet contained few hints for surviving enemy camps but listed numerous scenarios in which POWs' behavior might embarrass the United States, particularly in communist indoctrination sessions like those observed in the Korean War. The army instructed its men that if their overseers tried to coerce their participation in such sessions, they should try to call the enemy's bluff. After all, many death sentences for POWs in North Korea had turned out to be empty threats. The *Code* rejected the common belief that each prisoner had a breaking point because "The man who dies resisting is not broken." The army held POWs to high standards for military and psychological reasons, not just political ones. Nevertheless, soldiers who read *The U.S. Fighting Man's Code* could be forgiven if they found the military establishment's preoccupation with adverse publicity distasteful.[26]

Command Information for Vietnam

The image of the American soldier in Vietnam is an unhappy one. It is replete with disaffection, criminality, loss of confidence in the government and its war aims and treatment of Vietnamese civilians that ranged from casual abuse to murder. In postwar recriminations over the American public's uneven support for the war it is sometimes forgotten that, by 1970, the antiwar counterculture had taken root in the service itself. Although actual antiwar demonstrations by troops took place mostly stateside, the army in Vietnam experienced passive resistance from infantrymen who shirked missions and faked patrols. In 1970 and 1971, there were ten open mutinies, some as high as the company level. The army admitted to over five hundred instances in which troops attempted to assassinate their officers (eighty-six successfully), and analysts suspected units of underreporting these attacks.[27]

Political scientist (and Vietnam veteran) Stephen D. Wesbrook has argued that the poor performance of the army's political indoctrination program contributed to these failures of morale: "Perhaps fewer television sets and a little bit of explanation as to why we were fighting would have lessened the tremendous psychological impact of the war. . . . It might also have saved a few aggressive officers later in the war from being assassinated by men who thought that these leaders might get them killed for what was perceived to be no purpose." To Wesbrook, neither the political materials nor the morale-boosting ones truly armed the soldiers with the education they needed to make sense of why they were in Vietnam. Charles C. Moskos argued in his 1971 study, *The American Enlisted Man*, that the army had taken too much to heart the findings of the World War II social scientists who had concluded that only primary group loyalties motivated men in combat, with patriotic appeals having little impact.[28]

Moskos claimed that in embracing the "primary group" theory of combat motivation the army had conceded too much in the battle for men's hearts and minds. The interests of the primary group, it emerged in Vietnam, were not always the same as those of the army. Pointed in the right direction, primary group loyalties could help carry the men forward toward military objectives. But undirected by higher loyalties, the cohesion of the primary group could reinforce the instinct for self-preservation at the expense of the mission. Soldiers need not be ideologues in order to fight effectively, but they needed at least an underlying faith in the rectitude of the society that sent them into battle.[29]

There are other possible explanations for the collapse of morale in Vietnam besides the inadequacies of the Command Information program. It could be argued that despite a prominent enough airing of the government's rationale for the war, the rebellious soldiers simply would not make their own a cause in which the United States imposed its presence upon a foreign people. Discounting the influence of antiwar arguments, political scientist Guenter Lewy attributed the "erosion of discipline" to the home front's lack of appreciation for soldiers, permissiveness in American society, the rotation of individual soldiers on short terms of duty, and a lowering of standards for officers and enlisted men.

Yet Lewy also noted that before the Tet Offensive, army morale in Vietnam had been considered superb.

The Tet Offensive of January 1968 severely diminished the United States's will to fight in Vietnam. The scale of the "General Uprising-General Offensive," carried out in every sizable city in South Vietnam, belied all prior American claims of progress being made toward controlling the countryside. Early 1968 also saw the proliferation of off-base GI coffeehouses in stateside military towns. These counterculture parlors provided a haven for antiwar soldiers to congregate and discuss their grievances, and drew the ire of the local military and civilian authorities. On their own initiative, army personnel circulated over 250 different GI newspapers and newsletters critical of the war or the military.[30]

Perhaps most dissenting soldiers did not find the war's justification wanting until after it became apparent that they were losing it. Rather than poor morale undermining American strategy, the palpable failure to fabricate an anticommunist state in South Vietnam (a failure dramatized by the Tet Offensive even as the American forces repulsed it) convinced civilians and subsequently troops to reject the war.[31]

In this sense, the loss of morale is a result of defeat rather than a cause. If indoctrination ultimately claimed little credit for the successful motivation of troops in World War II, it cannot bear a disproportionate share of blame for disaffection in the Vietnam War. The army's Command Information apparatus had never been an instrument capable of reversing such a widespread crisis in confidence, and the controversies of the early 1960s especially discouraged bold political activism on the program's part. How troops might have been made enthusiastic in the face of defeat is hard to imagine, especially after President Richard M. Nixon decided to abandon the war gradually to the forces of the Republic of Vietnam. Arguably, American society and the army's training programs produced a soldier of sufficient moral resiliency even though larger failures vitiated that quality.

Trying to inspire soldiers in spite of these larger failings of morality and policy was the most difficult task ever assigned to the army's information specialists. As in the Korean War, the Vietnam War was fought in an unfamiliar place on the other side of the globe. The nation mobilized a significant portion of its manpower, but did not become a nation-in-arms. The army annually rotated personnel out of the conflict on an individual rather than unit basis. The soldiers had to take it on faith that the war represented a vital national interest. America's allies spoke a different language and had unfamiliar customs. Unlike the war in Korea, however, the enemy enjoyed broad popular support among the allied people (the South Vietnamese), making American intervention unwelcome.

The history of the army's Command Information programs in Vietnam is one of steadily diminishing authority, budget, and morale. Although the programs tried to adapt to the war's special challenges, they failed either to generate the novel approaches demanded by alarmed Cold Warriors or to recapture the more successful aspects of the World War II programs.

The escalation of the crisis in Vietnam crept up on much of the military establishment. OCINFO never reached a point at which it made a conscious commitment to a full-blooded war effort. Throughout the 1960s the army and the Department of Defense continued to churn out general anticommunist material while gradually leavening their catalogs with items related specifically to Vietnam.

In 1962, they published *A Pocket Guide to Viet-Nam*. In some ways this early area orientation effort confronted the dimensions of the conflict more realistically than did materials created after years of fighting experience. The authors admitted, for instance, that French rule had "led to deep resentments by the Vietnamese" and that "like many other colonial people, the Vietnamese wanted national independence above all. That is why many followed [Viet Minh leader] Ho Chi Minh." They treated the nature of the allied regime gingerly: "Under this Constitution, largely the handiwork of the President, a good start was made. . . . The Viet-Nam Constitution, like ours, provides for separation of powers in national Government, but in practical application chief authority lies in the executive branch." Rarely had American propaganda described a dictatorship more politely, but at least a thorough reader could form a picture of the major players in the southeast Asian country that was not entirely fictitious.[32]

Departing from realism, however, the booklet heaped praise on the Army of the Republic of Vietnam (ARVN) and the unpopular Strategic Hamlets program, the government's rural pacification strategy. The reader would have no idea from the *Pocket Guide* that rural Vietnamese resisted removal from their lands and confinement in government-controlled camps. Strategic Hamlets deprived farmers of their homes, the fields they worked, and the ability to honor ancestors' graves with religious rites. Instead, the booklet proclaimed, falsely, that the people of South Vietnam enjoyed great religious tolerance. The authors gave no hint of the Buddhist majority's widespread discontent under the rule of Republic of Vietnam president Ngo Dinh Diem's Catholic regime. Americans were shocked when on June 11, 1963, a Buddhist monk immolated himself in protest. This unsettling event, and the other self-immolations that followed, had no context for Americans misled about the Diem regime's religious repression and nourished on assurances provided by optimistic propaganda like *A Pocket-Guide to Viet-Nam*.[33]

In 1965, the year of the United States's first large troop commitments, the Command Information catalog contained no items crafted for men headed to Vietnam save for old area orientation guides. Conflict orientation materials were soon on the way. One of the first was *Our Mission in Vietnam*. The first page of the booklet displayed a list of casualties in a number of small firefights that had taken place on the same day across Vietnam. The petty attrition, the authors suggested, added up to a noble purpose: a "Small War for Big Stakes." According to the pamphlet, American troops were in Vietnam for three reasons: first, because the Republic of Vietnam had asked for help; second, the greater the number of free nations there were in the world, the stronger the United States' security; and third, the free world had to show the communist bloc that they could not expand by sponsoring "wars of national liberation."[34]

Our Mission in Vietnam was less objective than the *Pocket Guide*. Legitimate aspirations no longer accounted for Vietnamese opposition to French rule after World War II. Anti-French agitation was the result of a communist plot carried out despite the fact that "All during those eight years the French government had looked forward to eventual independence for Vietnam." No longer did a yearning for independence animate the Vietnamese. Rather, "liberation" and "reunification" were simply the North Vietnamese communists' code words. Their real aim was to prevent the progress in the south from embarrassing world communism. *Our Mission in Vietnam* denied the possibility that the enemy's National Liberation Front fighters (the so-called Viet Cong) had any standing with the people of the south. Without the support of supply lines to the north, the authors argued, "the communist guerrilla effort in South Vietnam would long ago have 'withered on the vine.'"[35]

The information materials of the Vietnam War looked much better than those of the Korean War. The mid-1960s Vietnam materials used a lot of photographs and colorful cover art. The main pamphlet of 1966, *Know Your Enemy: The Viet Cong*, was one of the more visually striking information publications. It featured precisely drawn maps and evocative sketches. It minimized history lessons and concentrated on the dangers posed by the guerrilla foe: "A Viet Cong is a man, woman or child—a tough fighter, with words or weapons." The authors cautioned soldiers not to assume that any Vietnamese man, woman, or child they met was a member of the Viet Cong, but they buried this advice amid descriptions of the stealthy enemy's awesome capabilities. On the one hand, *Know Your Enemy* reminded the reader that "The Viet Cong fighting man is not '10 feet tall,' either figuratively or literally, being actually on the average only five feet three inches in height." On the other hand, it admitted that the enemy was "quite prepared to continue for 10 or 20 years."[36]

By 1968 the information catalog featured several items specific to Vietnam. In addition to *Know Your Enemy: The Viet Cong*, the new anticommunist pamphlets included *Aggression from the North: The Record of North Vietnam's Campaign to Conquer South Vietnam*, *The Struggle in South Vietnam: 'Liberation' or Conquest?*, and *The Evidence at Vung Ro Bay*, which described the discovery of a cache of guerrilla arms. Eight Vietnam films joined the information collection as well. Two, *Junk Navy* and *Montagnard*, were ten-minute shorts. A twenty-minute film from 1965, *The Line Is Drawn*, used the letters of a soldier killed in Vietnam to make the case for the war. Five others, *War and Advice*, *Why Vietnam*, *A Nation Builds under Fire*, *The Unique War*, and *Night of the Dragon*, were half-hour movies. The pamphlet *Theirs to Reason Why* condensed the basic instruction in the old Discussion Leaders' Course books into a short booklet for field use. It described the options for conducting the Command Information (CI) sessions, now called "Commander's Calls," and advised that guided discussions, panels, or breaking into groups were formats preferable to straight lecture.[37]

Even as the volume of pamphlets and films increased, the sophistication of the later materials failed to match the modestly nuanced *Pocket Guide*. The writing in a 1968 pamphlet, *The United States Army in South Vietnam*, was nearly rabid in its conviction that the enemy had no real support from the populace. It referred to the Viet Cong as "terrorists," "terrorist-assassins," or "guerrilla-terrorists" on almost all of its fifteen pages. It argued that the war depended on the separation of the "terrorists" from the noncombatants, but the chief impression it conveyed was how hard it was to tell the two apart. The enemy "may be the guerrilla who farms by day and fights by night. He may be the terrorist-assassin who throws a grenade into a crowded restaurant, or the innocent-looking youth who parks an explosive-laden bicycle in a market place in Saigon." One illustration showed six identical sketches of a Vietnamese man, one of which was circled. The message that the Vietnamese people all looked alike and that any one of them was likely to be an enemy terrorist spoke only to well-established American attitudes. It contributed nothing to making American soldiers appreciate the Vietnamese people as individuals who could potentially be alienated or won over.[38]

Public disclosure of the massacre at My Lai 4 threw into bold relief the information program's disregard for the alienation of the Vietnamese. On March 16, 1968, Company C of the U.S. Army's Americal Division slaughtered much of the hamlet's population. Thanks to a whistle-blowing soldier on the scene, the American public eventually learned of the incident. In 1971, the Command Information program finally addressed the controversy with a fact sheet full of nearly impenetrable legalese. It admitted, in the ninth paragraph, that murders had been committed. Despite how "tragic" the episode had been for the victims and "the Army units and men implicated in the allegations," the army prosecuted only one perpetrator, 1st Lt. William L. Calley Jr. Even though the enemy ignored the Geneva Convention, said the sheet, the United States would continue to uphold it. Neither the soldiers who were appalled by the murders nor those appalled by Calley's trial received any indication from the fact sheet that the army strongly disapproved of what had occurred.[39]

In 1968, CINFO Maj. Gen. Wendell J. Coats ordered his deputy, Brig. Gen. Robert B. Smith, to assess the department's "philosophy" and the quality of the relationship between information and command. The Smith report was the most comprehensive internal review of OCINFO's policies and procedures during the Vietnam War. Like previous studies it identified serious shortcomings in the army's political indoctrination program. "In measure the root problem is one of long duration. Primary interest of not only the present senior OCINFO but the subordinate command level information officers has been focused on the staggering demands of the external publics."[40]

Compared with the office's other divisions the Command Information Division (CID) had fewer graduates of the Command and General Staff College, fewer holders of master's degrees, and "generally less qualified personnel." Most CID offerings were simple printed material yet were routinely hampered by up to six-month production delays, making the program "a vestigial remains of the pre-electronics age explosion." The advent of the unified command system diminished the organization's authority in the field. This arrangement gave the Department of Defense more control over the elements of different services in a given region, and beginning in 1962 it rendered the CID less of a directing agency and more of an intermediary between OIAF and the IOs in the field.[41]

Smith recommended that to achieve the best results CID should essentially abandon to OIAF the ongoing indoctrination in the field and concentrate on creating a dynamic multimedia orientation package for soldiers entering the service. He wanted the package to stress army heritage and to be "hard-hitting," as the Stennis subcommittee had advocated. By the time the Smith report was finished, OCINFO's budgetary options were shrinking rather than expanding, and CID lacked the wherewithal to create such an orientation presentation.[42]

Reception in Vietnam

As in previous wars, many soldiers were oblivious to the efforts of the military's information services, either because more immediate concerns claimed their full attention or because they were stationed beyond the reach of the programs. One sergeant remembered that the army gave him "very little" information about what he could expect, explaining, "I was a ground pounder and I was told where and when to go." A Marine rifleman remembered that "The only thing they told us about the Viet Cong was they were gooks. They were to be killed. Nobody sits around and gives you their historical and cultural background." Asked about reading materials he received from the army, Capt. Albert C. Brown Jr. could recall "None except in one (!) indoctrination lecture about Vietnam."[43]

However, enough of the men who served in Vietnam recalled lectures, pamphlets, or films to suggest that the orientation system was in place and functioning. Contemplating the armed forces' multiple information channels, one sergeant recalled: "After a while, it became 'overkill.'" Since the end of the Korean War, OCINFO and DAFIE had been plying their trade in the peacetime military for more than a decade. Given that American troop strength in Vietnam climbed as high as half a million men, these offices managed to expose a large number of them to the information program.[44]

Previous indoctrination again played a major role in soldiers' beliefs about the purpose of the latest Cold War clash. Some answered the call to arms with a sense of duty that required little elaboration. As one career officer wrote: "The elected officials said I had a duty to fight. That was enough for me." Stephen A. Howard, a combat photographer, explained: "Mom is not college educated, so all she knows is what the propaganda situation is. She programmed us to be devoted to duty, God, state, and country. She said you got to do all these good things—like military service—to be a citizen here in America." Paratrooper Arthur E. "Gene" Woodley linked his certainty about his country's righteousness with the anticommunist argument: "I didn't ask no questions about the war. I thought communism was spreading, and as an American citizen, it was my part to do as much as I could to defeat the Communist from coming here. Whatever America states is correct was the tradition I was brought up in." Anticommunism was still a potent force in Americans' belief systems. Volunteer infantryman James R. Ebert noted self-consciously, "It sounds sort of weird to say it because I don't say it very often, but I was fighting communism." Describing himself as an "absolute rarity in Vietnam. A black West Pointer commanding troops," Capt. Joseph B. Anderson Jr. stated: "I was there to defend the freedom of the South Vietnamese government, stabilize the countryside, and help contain communism. The Domino Theory was dominant then, predominant as a matter of fact." Mortar man Robert L. Mountain thought the army activated his anticommunism at Fort Benning. After training he wanted "to shoot just one Communist to see how he looks when he falls. That's stupid as hell, but this is how they had me programmed. . . . The communism wants to captivate our allies. And if we're going to have allies, then we're going to have to come to their rescue."[45]

For many soldiers, patriotic and anticommunist motives informed their initial stances on the war but did not hold up over time. As Medic David Ross said, "I volunteered you know. Ever since the American Revolution, my family had people in different kinds of wars, and that was always the thing—when your country needs you, you go. You don't ask a lot of questions, because the country's always right. This time it didn't work out that way." Radio technician Jan Barry said that when rumors of rigged elections in the Republic of Vietnam spread in 1963, "many of us began to realize that something was really wrong and what our purpose there was—being a trip-wire protection of this police state." Robert T. Daniels, an artillerist, observed: "I was told they were helping the people from communism, so they could try to be a free country. The communism didn't let people control their own rights. But it looked like we were fighting 'em altogether."[46]

Ross's memory of his indoctrination in 1967 demonstrates that at least sometimes, soldiers heard the OIAF message loud and clear. "We were told not to bad mouth Ho Chi Minh, since the Vietnamese mistakenly thought he was the George Washington of their country because he had thrown out the French, but they didn't understand he was a communist and would bring them to a sticky end." But despite Broger's continued interest in this theme, by the mid-1960s, the information offices no longer pressed anticommunism with the same urgency they had in the 1950s. Perhaps as a consequence Vietnam veterans' characterizations of the programs, whether positive or negative, dwelt less on the theme of "democracy versus communism" than had their Korean

War counterparts. Sgt. Michael McGregor, an artillerist in Vietnam in 1968, remembered "Lectures on culture; orientation before going was good." Another NCO, Arthur M. Johns, described the materials as "all very informative." First Lieutenant Steve G. Lewis appreciated the army publication *Army Times* for being his only source of information: "we had no idea what was going on otherwise."[47]

Criticism, however, was more abundant than praise, especially further down in the ranks. One soldier dismissed the army's information campaign as simply "standard BS." One soldier, stationed in Korea during the Vietnam War, characterized information officers as "classic bureaucrats." The ideological orientation of the program seemed to be less irksome than its disconnection from soldiers' experiences. SP4 Peter L. Cullen described a thoroughly correct implementation of the information program at the unit level: "I recall a booklet we were given on Vietnam. We received pamphlets. Our [platoon] sergeant gave us briefings with [the platoon] leader also." Yet Cullen did not feel he had been adequately prepared to face the enemy. There is a hint of reproach in his recollection that "In training . . . we were told the VC were primitive in weapons and training."[48]

SP4 Allen Cherin remembered getting "films, briefings, and RVN training," though he would rather have had training on "more weapons." Sgt. Robert A. Macon alleged that his training in no way reflected "the actual conditions of Viet[nam]." Sgt. Marvin Mathiak, who regarded his military service as "stupid" and "brutal," recalled the "only info I ever got was in training in the States. Not much of it was useful in Vietnam." Charles L. Pettyjohn, a pilot of a reconnaissance plane, described army information as "boring briefings that had little to do with the reality I faced."[49]

To some men at least, training did convey the message that they were in for a difficult time. Sgt. George Abernathy learned that service in Vietnam would be "rough, deadly, and honorable," a prospect that made him "excited about serving my country." After seeing "lectures, films, [and] pamphlets," Corp. Gerald T. Lacomb remembered that "I was impressed with the fact that things would be rough." Sgt. Gary Martens, horrified to find himself in Vietnam, recalled of his 1968 stint, "I don't remember any real good information other than constant threats, early on, about how bad it was." The degree to which Command Information sessions, rather than just combat training, may have contributed to this impression of danger is unclear.[50]

Charles C. Moskos Jr. observed that in Vietnam new arrivals often received, right after the official orientation, "a final talk in a tone of gusto 'telling it like it is,'" which described the Vietnamese chiefly as prostitutes and thieves. Sgt. Matthew Brennan, a forward observer in Vietnam, remembered it well: "From that lecture, I learned two things—always shake out your boots before you put them on and always wear a rubber." As to the meaning of the war, however, he wrote: "I never understood why America was in Vietnam or what motivated the Viet Cong to fight so bitterly." Some of the soldiers' comments on the programs attested to the greater value they placed on informal rather than official information. Abernathy, who read information materials when he got them, still thought that "informal discussions with [Vietnam] vets gave me more insights." Sgt. Richard E. Ellis reported that he received "no prior information till I arrived in Vietnam, then learned from friends." Of course, this sort of informal orientation was often not aligned with the wishes of the government. As a new soldier in Vietnam, Stanley Goff had few defined opinions about the political dimension of the war until he met a fellow soldier named "Piper," "probably the brightest black of all the blacks I met in Vietnam, and I met a lot. He took it on himself to politically orient us about how the government was using us blacks." Through conversations with Piper, Goff realized that "all the money that was being poured into Nam could have been used to clean up a ghetto."[51]

Experiments in Troop-Community Relations

The frank advice that officers and comrades gave soldiers was not designed to convince them that the Vietnamese were a people worthy of American sacrifice. Rectifying this was a struggle for indoctrinators, but they were not entirely without options. In the mid-1960s the army experimented with a new approach to Command Information for troops stationed in the Far East. Beginning in May 1963 the American Institute for Research (AIR) designed and tested programs to ease soldiers' adjustment to service with Asian allies.[52]

In his memoir of his service in Vietnam in 1969, Michael Lee Landing noted that "In learning foreign languages the first words memorized are usually 'please,' 'thank you' and 'Where is the bathroom?' I never learned what these phrases are in Vietnamese. Every grunt did know how to say, 'Stop!' 'Come back here!' and 'Get the hell out of the way!'" The task of creating more positive interactions fell in the area of OCINFO's responsibility known as "Community Relations" or "Troop-Community Relations." Common Community Relations duties in the United States included arranging Armed Forces Day celebrations, setting up martial displays in local libraries, and the like. Because Troop-Community Relations had elements of both PI and CI, it had its own branch in OCINFO. Winning the approval of a civilian community around a base, whether on foreign or domestic soil, constituted Public Information. Convincing soldiers to respect the ways of the community was a Command Information problem. When getting along with the allies also meant working with allied soldiers, however, the Command Information aspect became more urgent.[53]

In the war zone, American soldiers harbored grave doubts about the worth of their Vietnamese allies. Loren Baritz's 1985 book *Backfire* analyzed the impact of American culture on the conduct of the war. He pinpointed soldiers' revulsion at the Vietnamese practice of handholding between male friends as emblematic of the distrust: "The custom proved to the GIs that South Vietnamese men were homosexuals, and this diagnosis explained why they were incompetent warriors, raising the question of why Americans had to die in defense of perverts." Conditioned by their culture's images of manhood, reinforced by basic training's standard threats to soldiers' masculinity, U.S. soldiers could not accept an overture of friendship proffered in this manner: "If a Vietnamese took the hand or touched the leg of an American grunt . . . the gesture, if unchallenged, would call into question the American's 'manhood.'"[54]

Standard Command Information material did not acknowledge a cultural rift of this magnitude. Numerous "area orientation" pamphlets and films had long been a part of the information arsenal, but the booklets resembled commercial travel guidebooks. They contained foldout maps, explained the local currency, and recommended the best-known tourist sites. Besides some basic etiquette, however, they made little effort to teach soldiers to live, as opposed to visit, abroad.

AIR's Troop-Community Relations Orientation Plan tried to go further. It identified the barriers to smooth working relationships between American personnel and their host nations and aggressively challenged them with specific arguments. AIR conducted one such program on a limited scale in Thailand in 1967. The planners reported that they had surveyed Americans and Thais to discover the specific sources of tension and then wrote lesson plans to address each one. They prepared six lessons in advance that they found generally applicable to troop-community issues, including "Bargaining," "Asking for PX Purchases," "Theft," and "American Wealth—A Cause of Friendship or Resentment?" The other two resembled more conventional Command Information fare, including "History, Communism, and the Belief in Equality," and "Why Am I Here?"[55]

The really innovative aspect of the program was not the preplanned lessons, but the use of the survey findings to write the other, area-specific lessons. OIAF and OCINFO gathered some field data on their programs, but bureaucratic inertia prevented drastic rethinking of their basic premises. AIR, as a contracted outside agency running a limited program, had a more efficient loop for translating field evaluation into better programs. With a fresh ear, AIR listened to how soldiers really reacted to their host communities.

The responses to the surveys indicated that the American fighting man's attitude left much to be desired. AIR's questionnaires allowed for open-ended answers to prevent the troops from simply picking the answers that they thought presented themselves in the best light. The vast majority claimed that they liked the Thai people, but when invited to talk about "what things gripe you the most about the Thai people?" the respondents revealed other feelings. According to the infantrymen, the Thais damaged troop-community relations by lying, being lazy, and purposely "using the language barrier to misunderstand." Many of the Americans expected the Thais to learn more English.[56]

Indeed, Americans expected many accommodations from their hosts. Thais, they said, could improve relations by cleaning up their country's "filth," improving sanitation, refraining from begging, and making a better attempt to understand the GIS. Some soldiers also admitted that they themselves could contribute to a better atmosphere by being more respectful, learning Thai customs, "leaving their women alone," and curtailing their "superior attitude."[57]

Having identified the GIS' prejudices AIR wrote corrective lessons. For instance, the organization's research on the troop-community relationship in the Republic of Korea found that some Americans criticized Koreans' personal hygiene. The program's discussion sessions then incorporated guidance material that pointed out to soldiers that generations of Americans had used the same agricultural techniques as the Koreans and lived with the same odors. Furthermore, it informed them that foreign women often considered American men's constant washing to be rather effeminate. The lessons asked troops offended by public spitting to be "at least tough-minded about it as our grandmothers were in America."[58]

Another commonly held belief was that Koreans had "lower sexual standards" than Americans. The lessons confronted the soldiers with the fact that their dollars often drove poor women and girls into prostitution, often provoking the abhorrence of their families, who in fact held American sexual mores in low regard. The trauma drove many of the victims to suicide. In the Thailand research, the troops recognized generally their role in driving Thais into prostitution but rarely acknowledged any personal responsibility for the situation. Only 6 percent surveyed admitted having "met" a prostitute in Thailand, a figure that AIR reported "is hard to reconcile . . . with the high VD rate." The findings in Korea and Thailand hinted at a larger problem in Vietnam, where sexual exploitation poisoned troop-community relations. One officer's memory of his encounter in a strip club reveals how oblivious some were to the damage. "The Vietnamese stripper took it all off" he wrote, "to show us what we were fighting for." Another veteran ruefully noted that "I helped spoil the Vietnamese economy by paying [a prostitute] five hundred piasters." Over the course of the war, the attempts of South Vietnam's American-sponsored government to control the population disrupted village life across southern countryside, and U.S. servicemen had the money to exploit the situation. After the war the Democratic Republic of Vietnam claimed that two hundred thousand women and girls had become prostitutes, and Vietnamese of all political alignments resented the soldiers who treated their country as if it were a vast brothel.[59]

The program sought to combat all misconceptions based on ignorance, prejudice, or culture shock. Some Eighth Army soldiers assumed that South Korea, as a less industrialized region, must have been rich in natural resources. Some assumed that the American presence provided up to 40 percent of the Republic of Korea's gross national product. Some thought that all Korean food was dangerous. Some Americans even had to be convinced that Koreans valued their own lives. AIR considered the soldiers who subscribed to such erroneous ideas as eminently redeemable. The researchers theorized that men had a native trend toward fair-mindedness but lacked "intellectual analytical tools." Another inhibiting factor was that troops who displayed a good attitude toward the foreign hosts suffered the ridicule of bigoted fellows.[60]

To supply soldiers with analytical tools, AIR's main tool was the discussion session. First, the program's operators gave hour-long briefings to the discussion-leading officers. Then enlisted men and junior officers received a series of sixteen hour-long discussion sessions. Each session had a question-and-answer format to encourage discussion. The breakdown of the sixteen hours is remarkable in light of normal Command Information priorities: AIR devoted two hours to basic orientation, two hours to basic ideology, and twelve full hours to culture shock issues.[61]

When critics admonished OIAF and OCINFO to make their message more streamlined and hard-hitting, their common assumption was that the agencies ought to retreat to their central theme, democracy versus communism. AIR deliberately minimized broad ideological questions. It promoted neither Americanism nor anticommunism, the bellwethers of the Cold War program. The designers concluded that soldiers regarded all talk of democracy and values as purely rhetorical. OCINFO staffers might have sympathized with this perception, but they were bureaucratically restrained from acting on it themselves. AIR tried to show soldiers that their "good" impulses were in fact expressions of the national ideology.[62]

The experiment was apparently a success. AIR contended that it improved the portion of soldiers who displayed positive attitudes toward South Koreans from 39 percent to 64 percent. It also reduced the portion of respondents with negative attitudes from 36 percent to 20 percent. Soldiers who underwent the training were more likely to confine their criticism of South Koreans to work-related problems, as opposed to cultural habits.[63]

Not all aspects of AIR's Troop-Community Relations program were equally well thought out, however. Had it failed to influence soldiers' attitudes for the better, it would be easy to blame the confrontational nature of the discussion materials. People do not normally react well to being told that they are prejudiced. Some ideas in the "action" portion of the program were of questionable value; suggested activities included celebratory tree plantings, for example.[64]

Whatever its flaws, the method seemed to offer promise to information officers concerned about the state of American-Vietnamese relations. First, the researchers took care to find out what the troops really cared about. Often these findings were unattractive, but they had to be discovered if they were to be rooted out. Lesson plans based on the soldiers' own concerns offered practical knowledge that could be applied in their own affairs. Even if the lessons failed to make democracy and national values "operational," some resourceful enlisted men could probably make use of such relevant information.

In the information field, the AIR's Far East Troop-Community Relations experiments sparked enthusiastic interest. In 1966 MACV's chief of Command Information, Lt. Col. Clinton D. Regelin, petitioned the Command Information chief in Washington, Col. Charles R. Thomas Jr., to implement the program in Vietnam. In the same year, Gen. Lewis W. Walt, commander of the Third Marine Amphibious Force in Vietnam, asked Gen. Charles H. Bonesteel III, commander of the Eighth Army in Korea, to loan him a specialist from the program to brief his own staff on "this vexing area of human relations." Senator Stuart W. Symington (Democrat, Missouri) also prodded the army to try the new programs in Vietnam.[65]

The army rejected all such entreaties. OCINFO drafted the following standard reply for dealing with the programs' many advocates: "after a careful study by military officials here and in Vietnam and the American

Institute for Research, all agree that this effort should not be made in South Vietnam at this time." OCINFO buttressed its position with the most durable obstructions in the bureaucratic lexicon. The program had not been fully assessed (despite the fact that AIR had been testing it for over three years). "Obvious instabilities" in Vietnam made it "ill-advised if not dangerous" to conduct the background research for the area-specific lesson plans. Lastly, perfect conditions could not be re-created in the war-torn country: "it would appear that there are a number of conditions which must be satisfied before the project can begin. Among these are a stable political environment, strong command interest and attention, and a substantial commitment of specially trained personnel to make the program effective. It is doubtful that any of these conditions exist in Vietnam."[66]

Thomas added in his note to Regelin, "I must advise you that it appears you will get no support from the Department of the Army, if not direct opposition. In summary, not-withstanding the recognized need for some effective program in Vietnam, this particular program is not suitable at this time." The fact that Regelin, the Command Information chief in Vietnam, wanted to try it casts doubt on OCINFO's assertion that "military officials in Vietnam" concurred with the army's rejection. As to the lack of command support, all of OCINFO's operations supposedly relied on strong command support, which, in turn, was rarely forthcoming. If Troop-Community Relations failed to earn such support, it would be no different from any of the other information efforts. That the plan required specially trained personnel was a problem to overcome but hardly a sufficient rationale for ignoring the potential benefits of the AIR method.

The objection that posed the most serious implications for the army was the instability of the situation in Vietnam. Using the state of crisis in Vietnam as a reason for inaction rather than action, when information officers like Thomas recognized the need for a more effective program, indicated an almost phobic aversion to innovation. The officials who evaluated the AIR program's suitability seemed to think it more important to find an environment that supported the program than to match the program to actual environments. Interestingly, however, when the AIR team in South Korea reported their excellent results they also revealed that "in no case was the program being implemented the way AIR designed it."[67]

If one were looking for reasons not to use the method, an inability to control the program even in a stable nation would clearly be a deficiency. A better interpretation was that the program's effectiveness even when it was implemented incorrectly showed its flexibility and durability—precisely the qualities that were needed in the field. Even if the specific program proved unsuitable, OCINFO might have noted how much more receptive the troops were to practical area orientation than to patriotic and anticommunist indoctrination.

It is unlikely that area orientation would have revolutionized the effectiveness of political indoctrination. Soldiers' own attitudes would continue to color their reactions to army-issue information. Allen Cherin, the SP4 who preferred more weapons training, was not the only soldier unimpressed with "RVN training." Staff Sergeant Phillip C. Zemke, who served in Vietnam in 1965, received "a pamphlet on the Viet language and phrases." His reaction was that "I wasn't there to 'Win the Hearts etc.'"[68] Even thorough area orientation along the lines of the AIR model could not have changed the minds of soldiers determined not to engage the Vietnamese on an interpersonal level. This caveat aside, the army's tendency to view the Vietnam War as an aberration from its preferred way of functioning thwarted the potentially useful Troop-Community Relations plan.

The Command Information Division, 1970

OCINFO's defensive attitude becomes more understandable when seen in the light of its relations with the Department of Defense's Office of Information for the Armed Forces. Throughout the 1960s the army information specialists saw Broger's office laying siege to every frontier of their fiefdom, from the design of materials to authority in the field. The struggle for control of the Armed Forces Radio and Television Service (AFRTS) was a case in point.[69]

In 1964 the Department of Defense transferred control of the Armed Forces Radio and Television stations in the Republic of Vietnam from the army to the local unified command on an emergency basis. Technically, the local programming was under the same local authority, but the

Pentagon rather than the Department of the Army became the overseer. The implication was that while the army might continue to provide the staff and do the routine work during uneventful periods, Broger's office would enjoy command of the military media during crises.[70]

The transfer of authority to the Unified Command angered the army, but it did little substantively to improve the DOD's grip. The American Forces Vietnam Network (AFVN) continued much as before; the measure lacked legitimacy because of its temporary "emergency" status. In 1970, the Pentagon exploited audiences' dissatisfaction with AFVN to make a fresh attempt at taking control. Roger T. Kelley, the assistant secretary of defense for manpower and reserve affairs, argued that Unified Commanders needed more direct authority over AFVN to stem charges of censorship and news management. The chief of Information, Brig. Gen. Winant Sidle, protested that the stations had been under Unified Command since 1964, and that the programs in question were ones operated by the unified, not army, command. In his view, the Pentagon sought to reward its own bungling by giving OIAF "a direct channel to the military broadcaster." The Department of Defense had tried, transparently, to use charges of news management to increase its control over the news.[71]

Emergent technology supplied weaponry for the turf battles. In 1970 Kelley reported to Secretary of Defense Melvin R. Laird that his review of AFRTS had shown its command structure to be tangled and manned by poorly trained personnel. He applied this assessment even to DINFOS graduates. He recommended that the entire system be automated so it could receive a news feed from AFRTS's Washington DC office.[72]

OCINFO had anticipated Kelley's findings. Despite continual army protests against "force feeding," the DOD had pushed ahead with automation tests throughout 1969. Sidle's predecessor, Wendell J. Coats, had argued that the new system would certainly make it appear to soldiers that the Pentagon was managing their news. Automation would ruin their ability to identify with their local stations. Broger's office denied trying to "consolidate" the news. It merely wanted to automate the flow. Individual stations could choose between the commercial feed or the AFRTS-Washington feed. In the process, the department would save two million dollars and four hundred staff spaces.[73]

The army's resistance to the consolidation of radio and television programming was no less a losing fight than it had been in the civilian world of broadcasting. More distressing for OCINFO was its waning influence over the design of materials, films in particular. In July 1970 Sidle and the other services' information chiefs laid out their grievances at a meeting with Broger and Kelley. Broger argued that his office had to move in new directions in keeping with its expanded mandate of 1961. Sidle responded that OIAF still had to support the services. Instead, it denied them a role in formulating information materials. Kelley said that he now realized that the services had legitimate reasons to be upset with his people, and tried to mollify them by promising a new committee to facilitate better relations.[74]

The cordiality was short lived. In August the Department of Defense presented the services with four new commercially produced films for the troops, three on race relations and one on antiwar demonstrations in the United States. Following standard procedure, Sidle's staff reviewed the films so the army could decide how many copies, if any, it wanted to order. OCINFO's lack of enthusiasm reflected its annoyance at not having been consulted beforehand.

First Lieutenant Eugene A. Kroupa reviewed the films for the OCINFO. The first film, *Black and White: Uptight*, sought to dispel viewers' prejudices by exploding common stereotypes. Kroupa commented, sourly, that trying to make soldiers feel guilty would simply harden their attitudes. More to the point, the film was too long to use in standard Command Information sessions. The second, *Black History: Lost, Stolen, or Strayed*, narrated by actor-comedian Bill Cosby, was a Columbia Broadcasting System (CBS) documentary devoid of military content. Not surprisingly, Kroupa deemed it unsuitable for the army. The last, *Black Soldier*, also narrated by Cosby, won grudging approval as it kept to straightforward, relevant themes: pride for the black soldier and a teamwork lesson for the white soldier.[75] Despite the nonmilitary orientation of *Black and White: Uptight*, the other services liked it best, and the army reluctantly agreed to order two hundred copies.

Race relations in the army seemed to fray throughout the Vietnam War. The disproportionate number of black soldiers killed in combat became a matter of comment as early as 1965, and though the army and marines took corrective action that evened the numbers out over the course of the war, the perception of "cannon fodder" treatment remained. Black troops increasingly voiced their dissatisfaction with the discrimination they received from white officers and comrades. In 1968, black soldiers led two large military prison uprisings in Vietnam, assumed prominent places in the GIs' antiwar movement, and engaged in several bloody brawls with white soldiers. Therefore, OCINFO considered it a top priority to deploy a film to soothe race relations in the field. However, even the compromise in favor of *Black and White: Uptight* bore disappointment when, on October 25, the Department of Defense slashed the race relations film budget and asked the services to accept "3 low budget IAF-produced films in lieu of the commercial film each service ordered."[76]

The OIAF bait-and-switch was disheartening enough. Broger's office made it especially bilious by simultaneously pressuring the services to adopt the film about the antiwar movement, entitled *In the Name of Peace*. OCINFO had already field tested *In the Name of Peace* at Fort Meade, Maryland, and rejected it based on the findings. The thirty-minute movie concerned the motives of the hundreds of the thousands of people who marched against the war in Washington DC in November 1969. These protests included a March Against Death (in memory of U.S. soldiers) from Arlington National Cemetery to the White House, and a mass rally on the mall by the Washington Monument. In the military's film of the event, members of the Communist Party U.S.A. and the Socialist Workers Party as well as pediatrician Dr. Benjamin Spock spoke in favor of the peace march. The point of the film was that the peace advocates had been duped into doing the communists' bidding.[77]

According to army surveys, 25 percent of the Fort Meade viewers disliked the movie. OCINFO asked soldiers present at the screening eleven questions about the material and compared their responses to a control group also made up of Fort Meade soldiers. The film had an impact on troops' opinions about six of the eleven questions. In three of those six, the film influenced the soldiers in an undesirable direction. Troops viewing *In the Name of Peace* were more prone to *disagree* with the statements that "There are better ways to get things changed than by marches" and, crucially, "Protests and marches have no place in the Army." They were *less* likely to agree that "If we pull out of Vietnam, the government will fall to the Communists."[78]

In the Name of Peace was a Department of Defense effort in the tradition of the House Un-American Activities Committee's film *Operation: Abolition*, though not as meanspirited.[79] It tried to shape soldiers' political opinions about civilian groups. It also reflected Broger's preoccupation with communist subversion. OCINFO, whether from army-specific concerns or from doubts about political indoctrination, focused on drug abuse and racism in the service. The Department of Defense's OIAF, however, wanted to confront the growing opposition to the war. When the United States flooded South Vietnam with troops in the 1965, domestic opposition came chiefly from a nucleus of academics and intellectuals. By 1967, the movement against the war was national in scale and included Americans from all backgrounds and economic strata. By the end of the decade, it also included a noticeable portion of the armed forces. Broger's office was willing to argue politics but could not frame its answer to the protests using anything but the "red scare" model of the 1950s. The test results in 1969 indicated that, increasingly, this approach just alienated soldiers.

Nevertheless, with the debates over *In the Name of Peace* still ongoing, OIAF began planning yet another film on domestic protests. OCINFO's Command Information Division did not hear about the project until Broger's office had already met on it four times and reached "the cost overrun stage." Col. Walter N. Moore, the CID chief, was exasperated. In a memo to Sidle, he complained: "I cite this project as an example of IAF's continuing lack of cooperation and candor with us. Requests by the Services for films on priority topics such as race relations and alcohol abuse have been either cut back or denied because IAF officials claim they lack funds, yet this unsolicited film can be funded. We suspect this film was directed by a higher authority. If so, IAF should have leveled with us." He urged the CINFO to bring it up in his next lunch with Broger and promised that his counterparts would urge the navy and air force information chiefs to do the same.[80]

The services wanted to be involved at the conceptual level so they could put forward their own particular needs. The DOD saw its role as the directing agency, not as a resource center for the individual services. To forestall petty wrangling, it tried when possible to present the services with a fait accompli. The services then received materials that they were inclined to resent, thereby increasing the bureaucratic bickering.

The army placed a token order for fifty copies of *In the Name of Peace*, though it had no serious plans to use it. What the services would rather have had, along with films on drugs and racism, was a high-quality *Why We Fight* type of film that addressed soldiers' concerns about the justice of the Vietnam War. Just as there had been a *Why Korea*, the government produced a *Why Vietnam. Why Vietnam* debuted in 1963, however, and was long outdated by 1970. No simple changes were likely to transform it into a propaganda masterpiece of the Frank Capra variety. Nevertheless, the air force asked OIAF to update what the services still considered a useful film. OIAF advised the air force to undertake the work itself, but it refused, saying that the job belonged to the Department of Defense.[81]

Before the war threw the army's racial problems into bold relief, the DOD had been in the vanguard on race relations, and it had been the army dragging its heels. In the summer of 1964 DAFIE wanted to produce a pamphlet that would give simple answers to questions about the armed forces' antidiscrimination policies, such as, "If I am subject to discrimination, who do I see about it?" and "Can I get decent off-base quarters and non-segregated schooling for my family?" OCINFO rejected the idea because, it claimed, the question-and-answer format was "inappropriate" and "confusing in the field." Its obstinacy reduced the pamphlet to a more disposable fact sheet, sans specific questions.[82]

The DOD's proposal was part of a minor but decade-long offensive against racism insofar as it affected "quality of life" issues. Its effort ran into the characteristic deficiencies of local power and higher authority. The higher authority, the Department of Defense, tried to rule by fiat and sometimes issued instructions blind to how they might by received. For example, the army rejected a 1970 DOD proposal to standardize the music played in enlisted men's and noncommissioned officers' clubs so music by both white and black artists would be heard. Instead of helping the situation, the army argued, such an intrusion into soldiers' private time might have fanned racial animosities further. Nevertheless, as the more local authority the army could find numerous such "practical" obstacles to block any proposal it did not want to implement.[83]

Black protest in the 1960s forced the information offices to rediscover some of their late 1940s liberalism. Army information planners began to take more seriously the accumulation of racism's daily outrages upon American soldiers. Whereas they had once privileged the sensitivities of racists and segregated communities, during the war they assumed a slightly more aggressive posture. Information materials became less tolerant of off-base discrimination. Still, these changes lagged far behind the pace of black soldiers' critiques, and the new materials sometimes inadvertently contained vestiges of patronizing language.[84]

If OCINFO and OIAF struggled to find the right voice to communicate with soldiers about race relations, they had an even rougher time trying to talk to the youth of America. Warnings against desertion and substance abuse had long been part of the internal indoctrination program. But at the height of the Vietnam War, the army faced rebellion on an altogether different scale. The resisters were not merely isolated malcontents but potentially a movement of epidemic proportions. Information leaders viewed the problem in generational terms. To stem antiwar dissent and drug use they searched for a vocabulary to span the age gap. General Sidle told his officers they needed "Pool Hall PR" rather than "Podium PR." Young people did not want to hear "the clichés and platitudes of yesterday." The Department of Defense issued a film on how to talk to "the so-called Now Generation." As the CINFO also advised, the film *Youth Communications* suggested that the 10s eliminate "the frills and platitudes of polite conversation" when talking to dissenting teenagers and college students. Authority figures had to admit their mistakes and deal honestly with youths to gain their trust: "Reality? Okay, let's have it. Tell it like it is? Okay, let's tell it like it is. . . . Behind all the confusion, the pills, the pot, the newspaper headlines, the draft card burning, the campus riots, the street fights, a voice is heard. It is a cry for help from many who are confused by the pressures of today's society."[85]

This passage makes evident how deeply OIAF misunderstood what it was up against. By characterizing antiwar and larger social critiques as incoherently confused, the information specialists ignored the logic and passion that informed them. Burned draft cards were hardly cries for help; they represented a more purposeful attack on military values than the makers of *Youth Communications* were ready to contemplate. The 1965 escalation of the war sparked individual draft resistance, and within two years antidraft activists not only refused to serve but had disrupted numerous induction centers. Prominent in the antidraft movement were students schooled in the civil rights movement's Student Non-Violent Coordinating Committee. They were not the aimless adolescents of *Youth Communications* but highly politicized activists whose resistance to the war drew on the same moral logic that informed their work for racial equality.[86]

Attempts to speak the language of the young were particularly disastrous in the military's antidrug materials, as the script for the (mercifully uncompleted) film "The Fruits of Marijuana" attests. In the script, the narrator sympathized with a young soldier who wanted to be part of a "grovey [sic] scene." Nonetheless, he cautioned that while marijuana could give one a "don't-give-a-damn high," it might turn out to be a harmful "high grade, indian-hemp mind bending knockout bummer." The message to the illegal drug user was: "You might think you're . . . faster than a speeding locomotive" and able to "jump tall buildings in a single bound, but you can't! Only Superman can do that!" Drugs would be of no help to the troubled Vietnam serviceman. Marijuana "sure as hell isn't a freedom bird." A soldier had better means of mental relaxation: "What is grooving? Grooving is a feeling deep inside you that calms you—a feeling of inner peace . . . so groove, man, groove, but do it the natural way, not with smoke!"[87]

Going from one extreme to the other, OCINFO eventually located a segment of American youth it could converse with. The Public Information Division planned a television event titled the *Pentagon Forum*. Four college students would ask high- ranking officers hard questions about the Vietnam War, and the military would present its case. The participating officers were Maj. Gen. John M. Wright Jr., the comptroller of the army, and Maj. Gen. Lloyd B. Ramsey, the provost marshal general. After several months of searching, OCINFO settled on the questioners: four students from Princeton University. One, an ROTC student, was the former president of the campus's Young Republicans Club. Another was its current president.[88]

Locally produced army newspapers compiled a better record in "youth communications." It turned out that the best way to create materials that spoke to the nineteen- or twenty-year-old enlistee was to follow Command Information's own cherished principle of ceding authority to the personnel on the scene. Information officers in the field were more likely to be close in age to the men they were trying to influence. They were less likely to embarrass themselves with futile efforts to employ up-to-date slang or to assume that soldiers' concerns resembled those of a Princeton ROTC cadet.

Worldwide, army units published over five hundred newspapers. As in previous wars, some IOs and other interested personnel got the chance to be journalists and editors and proved to be skillful at it. A few produced unit newspapers that were anticipated and read. IOs recognized that unit newspapers stood a higher chance of getting read than did information pamphlets. The indoctrinators were therefore tempted to insert Command Information material into papers, which OCINFO only loosely supervised.[89]

The problem with this tactic, as one IO remembered World War II cartoonist Bill Mauldin saying, was that "to gain credibility, Army newspapers have to lose legitimacy." As Charles Moskos has reported, by the time of the Vietnam War, *Stars and Stripes* had been replaced by the *Overseas Weekly* as "*the* enlisted man's newspaper"—its circulation no doubt boosted by the controversy surrounding the Walker case. Indeed, one soldier blasted *Stars and Stripes* as "a joke," claiming that "Everyone knew the paper was censored." On the other hand, SP4 Gerald F. Mazur noted that soldiers' newspapers, including *Overseas Weekly*, were "too governmental-biased and tabloid-ish."[90]

This criticism applied, for example, to *The Old Reliable*, the paper published by the information officers of the Ninth Division, from the unit's arrival in Vietnam in 1966 to its departure in 1969. The editors concentrated almost solely on the Ninth Division's various missions, leaving coverage of the larger war effort and other news to other publications. The paper was not a vehicle for official information materials, nor did it carry any announcements of orientation sessions, lectures, or films. However, its unmistakable editorial policy was to cast the activities of the division in terms of unqualified success. Few articles in *The*

Old Reliable indicate the enemy taking the initiative or mention any American setbacks or losses.

Instead, the organ was full of stories of division personnel taking the fight to the enemy and inflicting heavy (and precisely counted) losses. The editors emphasized the ingenuity and aggression of American troops rather than their firepower. Many stories reported Americans outwitting or getting the drop on enemy guerillas, perhaps reflecting an editorial attempt to undermine the Viet Cong's reputation for stealth and cleverness. Another recurrent theme in the coverage was the contributions of enemy deserters who came in under amnesty programs. Stories about these "Hoi Chanh" suggested, optimistically, that support for the communists was in decline. The paper made its most overtly political judgments in its coverage of the Tet Offensive, in which it portrayed the enemy as the sole author of the destruction in the town of My Tho, without also mentioning the impact of American shelling on the city.[91]

The *Cavalair*, official newspaper of the First Air Cavalry Division, also focused its coverage on division exploits and eschewed formal information materials, though its editors were more interested than *The Old Reliable* in larger political issues. The *Cavalair* featured a column by a chaplain addressing troop behavior as well as articles urging soldiers to respect Vietnamese traditions. A December 11, 1968, piece entitled "Gifts to Vietnamese Can Hurt Relations" offered a particularly nuanced look at the U.S. soldiers' time-honored custom of handing out candy to children. The author argued that the Vietnamese appreciated gifts to orphans but found general giveaways to children degrading and disrespectful of the elders of a community. In the coming holiday season, the piece suggested, it would be better for the Americans to support the celebration of Tet "rather than attempt to force Santa Claus and all the trappings of Christmas on them."[92]

In contrast to these papers published in the war zone, the *Monmouth Message* from Fort Monmouth, New Jersey, featured a weekly Command Information column. Most installments of "Command Information, Completely Informed" covered apolitical topics such as veterans' benefits, grievance procedure, military protocol, and the function of different units. However, interspersed with these columns were the program's familiar patriotic and anticommunist offerings. In 1968, Fort Monmouth's information office used its forum to discuss the ideas of John Locke and Immanuel Kant in a series on "The Nature of Liberty," to recommend books about Chinese and Soviet threats, and to address antiwar protests. "Nearly all" the protests, the *Message* insisted, were "led, instigated, or fostered by the Communist Party apparatus." Despite what some might have thought, it averred, "The Communist aim of world domination remains and cannot safely be ignored." Occasionally, the *Message* promoted the screening of information films with announcements or corresponding content. According to the paper, one film, called *Outlook Southeast Asia*, ran at least seven times in mid-September 1968. Normally, however, one could not learn the schedule for the fort's CI events from the *Message*.[93]

Soldiers could consider their military papers to be unreliable and appreciate them at the same time. Col. Ralph L. Godwin, for example, viewed such publications as "OK" even though they were "prejudiced in favor of the military." Sgt. Fred Waterman described *Stars and Stripes* as "purely rear echelon in nature although we always read it." Raymond R. Furnish "Enjoyed *Stars and Stripes*. Especially sports section." However, he objected to the "body counts on the last page. They made it sound like a ballgame." Readers could filter their own unit papers for the content they found congenial while draining off what they considered propaganda, just as World War II soldiers did when they listened to the entertaining enemy broadcasts of "Tokyo Rose."[94]

Still, the most popular papers were invariably the ones with the least supervision and the most adversarial attitude toward the military establishment. In September 1970 OCINFO reviewed a controversial paper, the *Joint Concern* of the Eighty-first Artillery's First Battalion. Investigation revealed that though the paper made damaging complaints against the army it contained nothing "really shocking or subversive." Furthermore, it had the support of the battalion commander. OCINFO concluded that the paper was an effective tool for the commander even though it "did not push the Command Information program in the usual manner."[95]

Some information officers theorized that unit newspapers should be a bit rebellious in order to boost their credibility with soldiers. Allowing papers to air complaints might have created a safety valve for negative attitudes before they flowered into full-fledged dereliction of duty. To work properly, the complaints would have had to have been substantial enough to connect with the troops but still fall within the accepted boundaries of military values. In this way, an "oppositional" newspaper could help foster the atmosphere of a free and open society without conveying any of the indoctrinator's explicit messages. Some analysts claimed that it was just this sort "opposition" that sustained a democracy's power elite by limiting debate to the premises of the state ideology.[96]

Whatever its efficacy in the civilian realm, a strategy of officially sanctioned criticism was too subtle and unsure a tool for most IOs, and the armed forces never consciously adopted it. As CID chief Walter N. Moore warned his boss, "You should be prepared to hear opposition to the new look in Army newspapers . . . [some IOs] feel that our move toward a more liberal editorial policy will lead to over exposure of the radical left wing view." One IO feared that, even though the policy was sound, it would bring upon them the fury of high-ranking "ultra-conservatives." OCINFO continued to steer a neutral course in supervising unit newspapers.[97]

The Vietnam-era soldier was less a newspaper reader than his predecessor and more of a television watcher. Television proliferated rapidly in the early 1950s, and by 1960 87 percent of American households had a set. Army personnel in the late 1960s and early 1970s had grown up with TV during an age of conformity. Television networks worked closely with the government and kept within the established bounds of the anticommunist paradigm, making the medium, in the words of one historian, a "custodian of the cultural Cold War." In 1960 the Kennedy administration's chairman of the Federal Communications Commission, Newton Minow, urged broadcasters to convert more of the "vast wasteland" of entertainment shows to public interest programming. As Michael Curtin has argued in his history of Cold War television documentaries, the New Frontier's definition of public interest content meant TV programs that supported an aggressive foreign policy. Network executives heeded this call and flooded the airwaves with documentaries, prominent among them anticommunist specials. Curtin revealed that from 1960 to 1963 the networks aired more documentaries in prime time than in any comparable period.[98]

By 1963, however, documentary programming began to subside. Curtin suggested that the crises over Berlin and Cuba diminished the public's appetite for confrontation with the Soviet Union, and the Kennedy administration preferred to divert attention from its increasing commitment to South Vietnam rather than try to drum up support. Furthermore, such programming "also lost much of its government patronage because, despite the hundreds of hours committed to the genre, it appeared doubtful that documentary had played a discernable role in mobilizing public support for a more aggressive foreign policy." The government embarked on the Vietnam War without its earlier hopes that television could be a potent instrument of persuasion. Curtin concluded that "Attention had shifted to television's role as witness to live events rather than as interpreter of important national issues."[99]

The use of television in troop indoctrination reflects the lowered expectations. Despite the soldiers' affinity for it, TV played only a small role in the Command Information program during the Vietnam War. The armed forces' catalog of TV shows was known collectively as "*The Big Picture.*" It included a large number of world affairs and anticommunist films and an even larger number of features about military hardware. The American Forces Radio and Television Services rarely broadcast these pieces to soldiers. Experience had shown that military audiences would not stay tuned for information and education shows, even for those as short as fifteen minutes. OCINFO concluded that Command Information's best hope was thirty- to ninety-second spots inserted where commercials appeared on civilian TV.[100]

As in previous conflicts, AFRTS was more a vehicle for troop morale and entertainment than training or political indoctrination. Its main purpose was to bring stateside programming to American troops overseas. Sometimes host nations, especially those under authoritarian regimes, feared that AFRTS, with its dazzling cop shows, Westerns, and situation comedies, would infiltrate their cultures and seduce their citizens. Libyan authorities, tired of seeing Libyans become loyal viewers of American TV, tried to cut off the AFRTS signal. Spain banned all mention of "NATO, the common market, and dictatorships" and forbid AFRTS to play the "Star Spangled Banner."[101]

While mainstream American programming fought for footholds overseas, the *Big Picture* catalog did not simply rot on the shelf. The military marketed what were ostensibly Command Information shows to civilian stations as part of its Public Information mission to burnish the armed forces' image. The army's Pictorial Center on Long Island produced *The Big Picture*, but the practice was consistent with OIAF director Broger's pattern of pushing indoctrination programs beyond their military bounds. In terms of indoctrination the program may have had its greatest impact on the men before they entered the service. Ron Kovic, a Marine who was wounded in Vietnam and later joined the antiwar movement, remembered that in his youth, "The army had a show on Channel 2 called, 'The Big Picture,' and after it was over Castiglia and I crawled all over the back yard playing guns and army, making commando raids all summer."[102]

For the civilian stations, *The Big Picture* was a relatively painless way to satisfy the laws requiring them to show a certain amount of "educational" programming each day. Senator J. William Fulbright (Democrat, Arkansas), chairman of the Senate Foreign Relations Committee, denounced the practice in a December 5, 1969, speech:

> Mr. President, to illustrate how supposedly internal Army command information programs reach the general public, consider the Army's "big picture" program. This is a 30-minute feature film supposedly produced for the command information program. . . . Some 55 segments have been produced over the past two years. I would note that 17 of these 55 deal directly with the Vietnam War. . . .
>
> According to Army sources, "The Big Picture" is currently being shown to the public regularly over 313 commercial and 53 educational stations around this country. . . .
>
> The Army stresses that it is only supplied when requested, yet anyone who has attended a broadcasters' convention has seen promotional material suggesting to television station owners that "The Big Picture" is available.[103]

Fulbright saw the dissemination of *The Big Picture* as evidence that the military's large public relations apparatus was operating "with little public or congressional knowledge or interference."[104]

More than just television, the military had at its command a variety of channels to conduct what McNamara's special assistant Adam Yarmolinsky later described as "countrywide exercise[s] in propaganda." To mobilize civilian support for its projects, the Department of Defense wined and dined columnists, staged demonstrations for reporters, and furnished officers as speakers at events sponsored by civic groups. The Public Affairs office prepared briefings for congressional representatives and provided ready-made articles for friendly publications, as well as enlisting the public relations departments of firms that held military contracts to make parallel publicity efforts. Continuing a Broger tradition, the OIAF made available to schools, veterans' groups, and civic organizations extra prints of films and copies of printed materials that had ostensibly been created for the troops. By loaning equipment and technical support, the Pentagon still had ample say over the content of war movies. It helped bring to fruition John Wayne's 1968 *The Green Berets*, which justified the Vietnam War in starkly drawn terms even more devoid of nuance than the Command Information pamphlets.[105]

Fulbright's concern over the Department of Defense's influence stemmed from his regret over his advocacy of the Gulf of Tonkin Resolution (August 7, 1964), which gave President Lyndon B. Johnson leave to escalate the war in Vietnam. That very year, the senator wrote with alarm about Americans' habit of turning a blind eye to military doings. He began working consciously against the tendency to approve plans and budgets out of a misplaced faith in technology and expertise: "A vast military establishment . . . absorbs half our federal budget . . . and exercises a gradually expanding influence on public attitudes and policies."[106]

In 1970 Fulbright published *The Pentagon Propaganda Machine* to develop these criticisms at greater length. He objected mainly to the military's propaganda, whether designed for internal or external use, promoting the war in Vietnam. Materials that may have been "appropriate for showing the soldiers as part of a training program" he deemed unsuitable for public release. For instance, he revealed that throughout the war military officers had been making the same sort of politicized public speeches that had embroiled them in controversy in the early 1960s. The senator pointed out that the Command Information unit (the staff under the direction of the CID) prepared a large number of the anticommunist speeches through their widely distributed "Speech-maker Kits."[107]

Fulbright saw the prowar speeches as a threat to civilian control of the military, and he pounced on misleading information that the Pentagon had released to the public. He did not object, however, to using the same information to build the morale of the men in uniform. The senator implied that the military's need to cultivate a fighting frame of mind superseded a citizen's need for truthful information. He insisted that showing *Why Vietnam* ("an historically false, blatant piece of propaganda") was harmful to civilians but stopped short of extending his protective argument to soldiers.[108]

Dust Catchers

Senator Fulbright became a nemesis to OCINFO. Some IOs thought they spent an almost crippling amount of time fending off his attacks. Given Fulbright's unpopularity around the office, one can imagine how low the Command Information Division's morale must have sunk when Chief Walter N. Moore wrote a memo agreeing with the senator. Despite a year of congressional criticism, the army was prepared to issue a Chief of Staff regulation locking *The Big Picture* into its current programming. Moore urged information chief Sidle to protest the measure, complaining that OCINFO used Command Information funds on the TV shows even though they were oriented to civilian viewers. It was too late; Sidle had already concurred with the plan.[109]

The Command Information Division saw the Chief of Staff regulation on *The Big Picture* as yet another triumph of the Public Information Division's interests over its own. The internal information officers smarted over one policy in particular. The army awarded credit for General Staff service to the chiefs and several other officers in each of OCINFO's other divisions. Between three and six officers in the Public Information Division; the Community Relations Division; and the Policy, Plans, and Programs Division earned the distinction. In the CID the chief alone received General Staff credit.[110]

The number of credited slots was a clearer indication of the CID's inferior status than its shrinking budget, for all information offices in the army and Department of Defense had had to cope with belt-tightening during the years of the Nixon administration. From 1968 to 1969, the number of army graduates from DINFOS decreased by 30 percent. The number of students in the Information Officer Basic Course dropped from 200 to 155. From 1969 to 1970 DINFOS graduations continued to fall, and the army reduced OCINFO's staff from 337 to 310. During this period the CID had five chiefs, a high rate of turnover even by U.S. Army standards. In 1971, OIAF downsized its entire operation by 20 percent, severely cutting funds allocated to filmmaking, radio packages, and publications.[111]

The CID's "Command Operating Budget" for fiscal year 1971 was a little over half a million dollars. It projected needs for some $69,000 beyond that amount. In previous years it had reduced the number of its projects to accommodate budget slashes. The reward for austerity was the army's assumption that CID could get along without the deprioritized projects. For 1971 the CID staff stubbornly decided to fund every project to the hilt at the outset of the year and produce the highest quality items possible. If funds ran out toward the end of the year, then the whole program would grind to a halt across the board. Given this strategy, the complaints from IOs in the field about support materials arriving late or not at all were unsurprising.[112]

What remained of the nation's determination to uphold its client in South Vietnam after Tet evaporated further after U.S. and ARVN forces invaded Cambodia in April 1970. The attack on a neutral country, and the apparent reescalation it implied, set off a fresh wave of furious protest. These demonstrations in turn provoked a violent backlash from establishment supporters, culminating in the Ohio National Guard's killing of four students at Kent State University on May 4 and the killing of two students at Mississippi's Jackson State College by police on May 14. Two days later, on Armed Forces Day, soldiers from twelve different bases took part in demonstrations, while other bases cancelled their planned Armed Forces Day activities. President Nixon tried to placate the public with troop withdrawals, but this tactic worked directly to destroy what remained of the morale of the U.S. Army in Vietnam and contributed to steadily rising rates of desertion and absenteeism. In 1971 the army recorded the highest rate of desertion it had ever suffered in the twentieth century, marking the height of what was arguably the most sustained and pervasive crisis of morale in American military history. OCINFO seemed powerless to help matters. An article in a 1971 *Commanders Call* argued that the war was not being lost:

> The statistics to date have been measuring U.S. *effort* and not U.S. *achievement*. As the U.S. effort increased, the public expected a corresponding advancement toward victory. Since there is no *measurement* of achievement the public cannot see the *progress*. As a result, the war appears to some people to be a hopeless quagmire. . . . Conversely, the enemy gets all the credit. In spite of the enormous military effort against them they continue to exist. ERGO: The Viet Cong and the North Vietnamese are victorious. Some people actually believe this fantasy.

Enough people believed it to exhaust the program's capacity for such mental gymnastics. After 1971 the editors of *Commanders Call* stopped including political articles about the Vietnam War.[113]

When the OCINFO staff prepared Sidle for questions before the Defense Appropriations Committee, they anticipated that the congressmen would ask what they were doing to sell the invasion of Cambodia to the troops. It recommended that he answer: "The Department of the Army is not making any efforts to mold opinions of Army personnel."[114] Though his staff protected its chief from advocating political positions, the answer indicated that a respect for political abstention had degenerated into an abdication of Command Information's basic function: to explain why soldiers had to fight.

Instead, the CID busied itself fielding queries on behalf of President Nixon from army dissidents, discouraging job seekers, issuing Vietnam conflict maps to soldiers' worried relatives, preparing the CINFO for meetings, and giving out "Thomas Jefferson Awards" to the hardest-working, most creative IOs. Personnel rotating out of the office also received an award, a small gift that, typifying their malaise, they promptly named the "Dust Catcher."[115]

Performance in the field mirrored the despondency in the central office. After General Westmoreland became army chief of staff, OCINFO began referring to him as "the Father of Command Information." The campaign failed to get the orphan adopted, just as changing the name of Troop Information to Command Information failed to make commanders more supportive of the program. A 1967 study found that, army wide, only 26 percent of personnel attended weekly "Commander's Call" sessions. Thirty-three percent of army personnel got Commander's Calls every two to eight weeks. Another third attended the sessions less regularly than once every eight weeks, and 8 percent had never been to a Commander's Call. Up to 40 percent of unit commanders still managed to pass off the Commander's Call chore to a subordinate, and of the officers who did run the sessions over 20 percent used none of the materials prepared by OCINFO.[116]

An OCINFO inspection of the Command Information program at Fort Knox, Kentucky, revealed a "sluggish" effort with no support from the commander. During the visit, base IOs accidentally showed a class of a hundred soldiers the wrong film. The room was "freezing," and the commander did not attend. "Fortunately," reported the inspectors, "this class wasn't followed by a re-enlistment talk." At Fort Ord in Monterey, California, despite foreknowledge of an inspection, IOs could get only 4 soldiers out of a scheduled 171 to show up for a Command Information session. The quarterly reports from the most important indoctrination front were no better. Vietnam's chief IOs claimed that "the USARV [United States Army, Vietnam] Command Information program overall is effective." He also admitted, however, that they "never" received materials on time and that commanders were too busy to schedule any sessions. Furthermore, the only materials that soldiers were likely to "read" were posters.[117]

Information specialists agreed that their films were too old, Commander's Calls were too frequent, and their support material was too drab. Troops rejected what they considered to be negative, carping messages. One IO urged that the program change its name back to Troop Information, as Command Information sounded too "stuffy." Another commented that "films like the 'Why We Fight' series of World War II would be helpful."[118]

The *Why We Fight* movies had become the lost holy relics of the political indoctrination mission. It proved far easier to recall the quality of Frank Capra's films than to reproduce them. Not even the *Why We Fight* series, however, could do what the information specialists wanted. The World War II orientation films could make some men retain their content, but they could not motivate them to fight against their wills. Even those soldiers who had been influenced by the films sometimes remained skeptical of them. The difference between *Why We Fight* and *Why Vietnam* was the difference between viewers being aware that they were being successfully manipulated and being aware that they were being unsuccessfully manipulated.

Soldiers were willing to be manipulated by Capra because he tapped into their deeper indoctrination as American citizens. In the American civic religion Capra was a true believer. The true believers of the Vietnam War found themselves not in accord with the nation's deep indoctrination but at odds with it. Wesbrook hit it on the head when he wrote that "consistent with their ideology, a large percentage of Americans have traditionally regarded wars of colonialism or economic expansion as unjust. To the extent that an American soldier perceives a war to be motivated by these factors, he will also perceive hierarchical demands to be illegitimate."[119]

That this perception attached to the Vietnam War was not, however, due to insufficient political indoctrination. Though with less insistence than in the 1950s, national opinion makers had repeatedly placed the anticommunist argument before Americans as civilians and again as soldiers. The difficulty was that Americans' underlying sense of fairness was ultimately incompatible with the comparatively superficial anticommunist indoctrination that justified the war. Only a small fraction of the public went so far as to sympathize with the enemy's goal of national autonomy under communist rule. Many more, however, concluded that the conduct of the war did not reflect their values, be it because of the class-biased draft, the strategy of attrition, the publicized war crimes, the bombing campaigns, the invasion of Cambodia, or the treatment of antiwar demonstrators in the United States.

Political indoctrination, with its meager resources, bureaucratic entanglements, and unimaginative techniques, was powerless to influence soldiers when deeper national convictions manifested themselves. Nor could it convince anyone that they were winning the war when they believed they were losing. The Vietnam War revealed that whatever utility the armed forces' political indoctrination programs had at their conception in World War II they had become useless appendages to both military training and the shaping of men's beliefs.

Epilogue

Retreat from Political Indoctrination

In 1971, *Commanders Call*, the information officers' main support journal, published an article by Brig. Gen. Theodore C. Mataxis entitled "This Far No Farther." Mataxis warned that the army had not taken antimilitary sentiment seriously enough. The "nihilists of the left," he argued, were engaged in a "carefully planned strategy" to destroy the nation's armed forces. Mataxis called for the development of new techniques to quell dissension in the ranks.[1]

New techniques were in fact forthcoming. Yet as a result of them, the thing that had come that far and would go no further was the practice of political indoctrination. Lawrence B. Radine, in his 1977 book, *The Taming of the Troops: Social Control in the United States Army*, describes the army's new means of dealing with dissenters in uniform. He argued that the army abandoned its traditional coercive and paternalistic controls in favor of a manipulative strategy of "co-optive rational control." The premise of this method was that soldiers did not resist the army out of ideological conviction, but rather used ideological rationales to justify personal complaints. The organization needed to control men's behavior, not their beliefs. Hence, because "the co-optive policy maker or leader is not committed to any 'cause,' there is nothing to be lost in ideological concessions to the resisters." Rational co-optation was "a cynical approach to political commitment and values, which controls an underclass by accepting and including the opposition. In practical terms, the task is reduced to one of assessing whatever gripes GIs have and particularizing them to peripheral issues that can be reformed."[2]

After the Korean War the military responded to a false perception of ideological weakness by intensifying its efforts to mold soldiers' political convictions. Confronting an actual morale problem in the waning of the Vietnam War, it concluded that soldiers' convictions were irrelevant. The army tried to pull the rug out from under dissenters by ameliorating living conditions in the barracks, loosening restrictions on hairstyling, and transferring would-be antimilitary organizers so they could not build networks of resistance.[3]

The support material published in the *Commanders Calls* quarterlies of the early 1970s reflected this apolitical approach. Typical articles concentrated on the army's modernization efforts and soldiers' quality-of-life issues, or combated racial discord and substance abuse. One 1972 article, "Using Your History," recommended building unit pride by using regimental traditions and symbols. It said nothing about national patriotic symbols.[4]

A 1973 *Commanders Call* explicitly repudiated the program's politicized past: "Many senior commanders—and probably some younger officers as well—have unfavorable memories about Command Information. They can't help recalling that there used to be something called Troop Information. . . . Their unpleasant memories are understandable. . . . It is enough to say now that the old program was barely effective, and that some of its worst features caused actual harm to the Army." The pamphlet cited as one the old program's main faults that "it concentrated upon broad world affairs subjects while neglecting subjects of direct interest and concern to the Army and the individual soldier." It asserted that the new program avoided this serious weakness by confining itself to "Information about the Army and the individual's relationship to it."[5]

Widespread rejection of the war in Vietnam convinced the government to end the draft, and the army converted to an all-volunteer force in 1973. Military sociologist Morris Janowitz has contended that this new force, more than the draft-era army, required political training. In language reminiscent of the interwar "Citizenship" training materials, he suggested that the all-volunteer army consisted largely of "recruits from the socially marginal and poorly educated sectors of the population" who lacked the average draftee's grasp of national institutions and goals.[6]

Well aware of the research indicating that soldiers were not motivated by highly articulated belief systems, Janowitz distinguished between "ideology" and "patriotism," the latter of which was a part of servicemen's motivations. He further distinguished between "indoctrination," used by authoritarian states to foster ideologies, and "civic education," which could properly be used on a democracy's deficient soldiers. What set proper civic education apart from political indoctrination, in Janowitz's eyes, was that it taught students to reason. To develop a civic consciousness citizens would use "alternate frames of reference" to understand "social and political reality."[7]

The army would have been hard-pressed to adopt the type of pedagogy that Janowitz advocated. Civic consciousness was one of the fundamental goals of the nation's high schools and liberal arts colleges, yet they struggled constantly to teach students the habits of self-criticism and enlightened reasoning. Though critical analysis of the nation's politics is not inimical to military service, it could not have been the armed forces' job to give soldiers a liberal arts education. The civilian institutions dedicated to that mission found it perplexing enough. How the army might have succeeded at it while simultaneously inculcating the habit of unquestioning obedience is difficult to imagine.

Expecting the army to provide liberal arts education for its troops would have been unrealistic, and there were good reasons, both practically and ethically, for rejecting the experiment in political indoctrination for citizens in uniform. Did the army then have no legitimate means of communicating to soldiers why it thought they had to fight?

On the eve of Japan's attack on the United States the nation had been divided over how ready the military needed to be. Thus, orienting draftees and volunteers to the larger purposes of the war made a certain amount of sense. In World War II, nothing less than the survival of progressive Western civilization hinged on the antifascist coalition's force of arms. Such a crisis justified the expediency of political indoctrination in the U.S. Army. Even in this case, however, it is worth considering the contention of the World War II program's Research Branch that overexposure to propaganda in the first place partially explained Americans' recalcitrant attitudes before Japan's attack on Pearl Harbor. The researchers theorized that the barrage of propaganda visited upon the country in 1917–18 made its task more difficult in the 1940s:

In the course of the re-evaluation which followed the First World War, many Americans were exposed to a debunking process which challenged the worth-whileness of the most recent major cause to which they had given their allegiance. The moral drawn from this was that people became converted to supporting causes by a kind of trickery— 'propaganda'—and that it was, therefore, wise to be on one's guard against being taken in by propaganda. As a result, the very discussion of abstract ideas, especially where they concerned themselves with values, was suspect.[8]

Two thoughtful students of the army's information programs faulted them for their lack of institutional stability. Stephen D. Wesbrook argued that political training "has largely been imposed on the Army—by morale crises, wars, and domestic politics." Thomas A. Palmer has written that "Troop Information is crisis-oriented. The program was conceived in crisis, grew in crisis, and was legitimized in crisis." The broadly political orientation of soldiers in World War II was indeed a response to a crisis, but perhaps the programs' subsequent difficulties stemmed more from their institutional entrenchment than a lack thereof. The demands of the crisis of the 1940s served as a justification for permanent political indoctrination in the army. It set up a contest between the army and the Department of Defense for control of indoctrination in which the latter tried to prefabricate citizen-soldiers' political viewpoints. As both sides negotiated within this framework, they neglected orientation that was area and conflict specific, the type that was potentially the most valuable.[9]

When the nation's postwar commitments sent troops to garrisons and battlefields that, as the cliché had it, most Americans could not find on maps, the army offered uneven "area orientation" to acquaint troops with local customs. To know how their behavior affected their mission soldiers in foreign countries needed more than travel guides. They needed to know about the contending factions and how these factions perceived American soldiers. The 1960s troop-community experiment in the Republic of Korea discovered that American troops needed to be taught that Koreans valued their own lives. Yet the military abandoned a successful program that taught these lessons without trying it on a larger scale. Indeed, as Charles C. Moskos Jr. found, in Vietnam the unofficial orientation talk directly undermined the official one. As the Vietnam War could scarcely be framed as a Capraesque affirmation of community values, the soldiers sent to fight in Vietnam received neither a credible "war aims orientation" nor an "area orientation" that drew realistically on local input.[10]

In short, by concentrating on anticommunist indoctrination during the Cold War, the military tried to tell its soldiers quite a bit about where they had come from but comparatively little about where they were going. The neglected field of "area orientation" offered no explicit rationale for the purposes underlying fighting and obedience, but it sometimes gave soldiers knowledge that they could employ in their own interests or the interests of their country. It avoided the critical problem created by political indoctrination, namely, that it thrust the military into civilian politics.

Political indoctrination weakened civilian control of the military by offering the armed forces a voice of political advocacy. In particular, the linkage of the internal indoctrination program and the external public relations program clouded the distinction between what was necessary for military training and the image the army wanted to craft for itself with civilian constituencies.

Certainly, not many officers were eager to assume the role of domestic opinion makers. Officers' sense of professionalism might even be described as a key impediment to the establishment of more pervasive indoctrination programs. Yet it took only a few unprofessional officers like Maj. Gen. Edwin A. Walker and his Pro-Blue staff to subject some soldiers to partisan demagoguery and a few ambitious officials like John C. Broger to menace the country with the specter of militant political indoctrination.

The problem with political advocacy was not limited to the actions of a few zealots, however. The very attempt to define what it meant to be an American inevitably forced the army's information programs to take sides on issues that divided the nation's citizens. In a search for an elusive consensus it exalted the national values cherished by some at the expense of others' fiercely held beliefs. Even a seemingly agreed-upon topic, like anticommunism, caused divisions over matters of degree and interpretation.

The nation's impulse to explain to soldiers why they had to fight was understandable and perhaps on some occasions even necessary. But events also showed that Americans did not misplace the trust they invested in their national institutions, their educators, their young people, and their unfinished political dialogues to produce responsible citizens and thereby responsible citizen-soldiers. When what the nation asks of its soldiers accords with the best of its peoples' ideals, their commitment has been forthcoming. When it does not accord with those ideals it behooves not just soldiers but all Americans to ask why we fight.

NOTES

Introduction

1. Maj. Gen. Gilman C. Mudgett, Chief of Information (hereafter CINFO), "CINFO Remarks on PI and TI&E," n.d. (1954), file: CINFO Remarks on PI and TI&E, Ralph E. Pearson Papers, United States Army Military History Institute, Carlisle Barracks, Carlisle, Pennsylvania (hereafter USAMHI), 13; Jordan, "Troop Information and Indoctrination," 360; Janowitz, *The Professional Soldier*, 408–9.

1. Anxious to Work Bodily Destruction

1. Wesbrook, *Political Training in the United States Army*, 17, 19.

2. Foner, *Morale Education in the American Army*, 12–15.

3. Lynn, *Bayonets of the Republic*, 119, 138–39 [journals], 141 [songs], 151 [ceremonies].

4. Union Executive Congressional Committee, *A Few Plain Words with the Rank and File of the Union Armies*, no. 6 (Washington DC, 1864); reprinted in Freidel, *Union Pamphlets of the Civil War*, 2:1029–30.

5. Creel, *How We Advertised America*, 86, 91 [talks], 121 [films].

6. Bristow, *Making Men Moral*, 8–11.

7. Bristow, *Making Men Moral*, 31–34 [VD films], 80–83 [dancing], 132–34 [drinking], 43–45 [censorship], chapter 5 [race]. *Fit to Fight* (War Department Commission on Training Camp Activities, 1919) was also known as *Fit to Win*.

8. Chambers, *To Raise an Army*, 89, 96.

9. Dewey, *Democracy and Education*.

10. Munson, *The Management of Men*, 5.

11. Munson, *The Management of Men*, 389 [local problems], 580 [intelligence of soldiers], 511 [reading material], 198 [sexual repression].

12. Munson, *The Management of Men*, 480–81, vi ["industrial morale"].

13. War Department, *Citizenship*, 6–7.

14. War Department, *Citizenship*, 3 [census], 23 [immigration].

15. On foreign-born soldiers in World War I, see Ford, *Americans All!*; War Department, *Citizenship*, 23 [class], 67 [socialism].

16. War Department, *Citizenship*, 7, 91 [democracy], 79 [free speech].

17. Bendersky, *The "Jewish Threat,"* see chapter 4 on immigration and chapter 5 on the War College; Wesbrook, *Political Training in the United States Army*, 16 [pay, leave, and promotion].

18. War Department, *The War in Outline*.

19. War Department, *The War in Outline*, i, 4.

20. Stouffer, *The American Soldier*, 2:150, 169; Ellis, *The Sharp End*, 315. Three hundred of the men who went to Spain formed the sample for John Dollard's study *Fear in Battle*. Dollard found that more of these highly motivated volunteers (77%) cited "belief in war aims" as among "the most important things that help a man overcome fear in battle" than any other factor (41–42). Dollard's respondents indicated that men who discussed war aims and were kept abreast of "straight" war news made better soldiers. "Victory, they say, is won day-by-day by the informed soldier" (52).

21. Marshall, *Men against Fire*, 153–54; Maudlin, *Up Front*, 60; Little, "Buddy Relations and Combat Performance," 195–224; Fussell, *Wartime*, 4.

22. Wiley, *The Life of Johnny Reb* and *The Life of Billy Yank*; Lender, *The New Jersey Soldier*.

23. Moskos, *The American Enlisted Man*, 147–48.

24. Royster, *A Revolutionary People at War*; McPherson, *For Cause and Comrades*; Frank, *With Ballot and Bayonet*; Linderman, *The World within War*, 65 [prayer], 266–68 [comradeship].

25. Osborn, *Preface to Eugenics*, 295–96; Foner, *The Story of American Freedom*, 237; on OWI's liberalism, see Winkler, *The Politics of Propaganda*.

26. *The Information and Education Division*, privately printed limited edition yearbook, 1945, Library Collection, USAMHI, 17–22; Arbogast, "Issues and Answers," 5–6.

27. "Samuel Stouffer, Sociologist, Dead," *New York Times*, 25 August 1960, 29; Samuel A. Stouffer to Gen. Frederick Osborn, "Some Reflections on the Program of the Research Division," 9 June 1942 [free-flowing, key men], file: History of the Research Branch to 1946, box: 969, RG 330 (89), United States National Archives (hereafter NA); Stouffer to Lt. Colonel Branch, 16 October 1942, file: History of the Research Branch to 1946, box: 969, RG 330 (89), NA.

28. Griese, *Arthur W. Page*, 241, 245.

29. *The Information and Education Division*; Geisel created the popular cartoon character "Private Snafu." On Geisel's prewar and wartime antifascist cartoons see Art Spiegelman, "Horton Hears a Heil," *New Yorker*, 12 July, 1999, 62–63.

30. War Department, *Guide to the Use of Information Materials*, 1. Subsequent page references from this source appear parenthetically in the text.

31. Stouffer, *The American Soldier*, 2:157, 164–65. Vindictiveness was in greater supply where Japan was concerned. Racism probably explained a larger part of the difference than personal experience in the Pacific theater or the fact that Japan had attacked the United States (160–62).

32. Stouffer, *The American Soldier*, 1:449–451.

33. Stouffer, *The American Soldier*, 1:472 [contradiction], 468–69 [frequency of meetings]; Griese, *Arthur W. Page*, 243, 247.

34. Stouffer, *The American Soldier*, 1:470 [reading every word]. One enlisted man charged with discussion-leader duty read not only every word in an information pamphlet, but also the boxed instructions to the presenter, and the portion entitled "Special to the Information Officer." Brig. Gen. Charles T. Lanham, "Address to AIS Course I," 13 March 1946, folder: Speeches 1945–47, box: 12, Charles T. Lanham Papers, 7.

35. War Department, *You Don't Think . . .* , 1–5; War Department, *Invisible Weapon*, 1–5.

36. Capra, *The Name above the Title*, 326–28.

37. Capra, *The Name above the Title*, 330.

38. "Chronicle of the Research Division Special Services Branch," n.d., 1942, 12, file: History of the Research Branch to 1946, box: 969, RG 330 (89), NA; Arthur W. Page, "Notes on Informal Talk by Arthur W. Page to Members of Information Dept. on his return from London," 19 July 1944, quoted in Griese, *Arthur W. Page*, 244; Capra, *The Name above the Title*, 331, 334–35.

39. *Mr. Smith Goes to Washington* (dir. Frank Capra, b. & w., 125 min., Columbia, 1939); *Meet John Doe* (dir. Frank Capra, b. & w., 123 min., Warner Bros., 1941).

40. Capra, *The Name above the Title*, 335.

41. Winkler, *The Politics of Propaganda*. The most comprehensive thematic study of the *Why We Fight* series is Bohn, "An Historical and Descriptive Analysis of the 'Why We Fight' Series." For a discussion of Capra's technique, see Murphy, "The Methods of Why We Fight," and on the making of *The Negro Soldier* specifically, see Cripps and Culbert, "*The Negro Soldier*." Wolfe (*Frank Capra*) provides a detailed, annotated list of writings on Capra's films.

42. All observations about the film are based on the edition: War Department, *Prelude to War* (Piscataway NJ: Alpha Video Distributors, 1942). The Americans were not chiefly to blame for distorting the January 26, 1941, letter in which Yamamoto expressed pessimism about a war with the United States, as Japan's prowar faction made the same use of it (Prange, *At Dawn We Slept*, 11).

43. Dower, *War without Mercy*.

44. Bendersky, *The "Jewish Threat,"* 345–46; Stouffer, *The American Soldier*, 2:571.

45. Novick, *The Holocaust in American Life*. See especially chapter 3 on American perceptions of the Holocaust during wartime and chapter 7 on the impact of the Eichmann trial.

46. Capra, *The Name above the Title*, 328–29.

47. War Department, *Divide and Conquer*.

48. On the debate over the number of victims, see Yang, "Convergence or Divergence?," 849–53.

49. War Department, *The Battle of China*. Other efforts from the film branch included *The Negro Soldier*, an attempt to instill pride in black troops and educate white troops as to their value, and the *Know Your Enemy, Know Your Ally* series (Wolfe, *Frank Capra: A Guide*, 147, 144, 152–54). The pervasive racism of *Know Your Enemy: Japan* is described in detail in John Dower's *War without Mercy*, 18–23. It stands as another example of the policy of demonizing the enemy population rather than distinguishing between innocent civilians and supporters of a war faction.

50. Dale Leroy Hall survey, box: Second Armored Division, Sixty-sixth Armored Regiment, World War II Veterans Survey (hereafter WWII VS); USAMHI; James M. Thomson survey, box: First Infantry Division, Twenty-sixth Infantry Regiment, WWII VS, USAMHI; Edwin H. J. Cornell survey, box: Twenty-eighth Infantry Division, 110th Infantry Regiment, WWII VS, USAMHI; Reynold W. Ross survey, box: 28th Infantry Division, 110th Infantry Regiment, WWII VsS, USAMHI; Thomas Molle survey, box: First Armored Division, WWII VS, USAMHI.

51. Edmond L. Morris survey, box: Anti-Aircraft Artillery Battalions Including AAA-AW 478–557, WWII VS, USAMHI; Hill C. Higdon survey, box: Anti-Aircraft Artillery Battal-

ions Including AAA-AW 478–557, WWII VS, Stouffer, *The American Soldier*, 1:88; USAMHI; Hervey Painter survey, box: Army Air Forces Bases, WWII VS, USAMHI; John Schell survey, box: Twenty-sixth Infantry Division, WWII VS, USAMHI; Roger Lee Farrand Twenty-eighth Infantry Division, 110th Infantry Regiment, WWII VS, USAMHI.

52. George P. Nestor survey, box: First Infantry Division, Twenty-sixth Infantry Regiment, WWII VS, USAMHI; Francis H. Strickler survey, box: First Infantry Division, Twenty-sixth Infantry Regiment, WWII VS, USAMHI; Russell Davidson survey, box: Anti-Aircraft Artillery Battalions Including AAA-AW 478–557, WWII VS, USAMHI; Wilbur D. Cook survey, box: First Armored Division, WWII VS, USAMHI.

53. Rufus Winfield Johnson survey, box: Ninety-second Division, WWII VS, USAMHI; Edgar Piggott survey, box: Ninety-second Division, WWII VS, USAMHI; Emeral E. Hayden survey, box: Ninety-second Division, WWII VS, USAMHI; Willard F. Harper survey, box: Ninety-second Division, WWII VS, USAMHI.

54. "AFRS Fact Sheet," 1970, file: [precedes files], United States Army Chief of Information Papers (hereafter CINFO Papers), USAMHI; Griese, *Arthur W. Page*, 234, 241.

55. Hovland, Lumsdaine, Sheffield, *Experiments in Mass Communication*, 131.

56. The United States (mostly with Voice of America and Radio Free Europe), the Soviet Union (with Radio Moscow), and the People's Republic of China (with Radio Beijing) made extensive use of radio propaganda throughout the Cold War. For instance, America's Radio Swan and Radio Martí broadcast a steady stream of propaganda to Cuba in a failed attempt to foment counterrevolution. The Soviet invasion of Afghanistan in 1979 was accompanied by a barrage of radio justifications and misinformation. The basic strategy remained unchanged across the decades: programmers inserted political material between the popular music that kept listeners listening, the same method by which advertisers sell products over commercial radio (Jowett and O'Donnell, *Propaganda and Persuasion*, 87–90, 17–18).

57. *Life Can Be Beautiful*, part of the series *The Victory Front* (Armed Forces Radio Service, 1942). R:15522–R:15523, Library of the Museum of Television and Radio, New York.

58. For some examples of "sexual threat" posters, see Paret, Lewis, Paret, *Persuasive Images*, 21, 25, 54.

59. Westbrook, "Fighting for the American Family," 198.

60. Ben L. Rose survey, box: Chaplain Corps, WWII VS, USAMHI; Thomas Joseph Deming survey, box: Tenth Infantry Division Mountain, WWII VS, USAMHI; Joseph M. Green survey, box: Tenth Infantry Division Mountain, WWII VS, USAMHI.

61. Griese, *Arthur W. Page*, 243.

62. Jesse A. Brewer survey, box: Ninety-second Division, WWII VS, USAMHI; James G. O'Brien survey, box: Twenty-sixth Infantry Division, WWII VS, USAMHI; Frank P. Sawicki survey, box: First Infantry Division, Twenty-sixth Infantry Regiment, WWII VS, USAMHI; Raymond C. Chariton survey, box: Army Air Forces Bases, WWII VS, USAMHI; Arthur Fikentscher survey, box: Anti-Aircraft Artillery Battalions Including AAA-AW 478–557, WWII VS, USAMHI; Northham H. Stolp survey, box: Eighty-second Airborne Division 505th PIR 1, WWII VS, USAMHI.

63. Mark J. Alexander survey, box: Eighty-second Airborne Division 505th PIR 1, WWII VS, USAMHI; Attil A. Pasquini survey, box: Twenty-seventh Division, 106th Infantry Regiment, WWII VS, USAMHI; Leroy A. Lewis survey, box: Tenth Infantry Division Mountain, WWII VS, USAMHI.

64. Norris H. Perkins, Second Armored Division, Sixty-sixth Armored Regiment, WWII vs, USAMHI; Hoffman and Hoffman, *Archives of Memory*, 157; George P. Nestor survey; Edgar Piggott survey; William J. Allison survey, Twenty-seventh Division, 106th Infantry Regiment, WWII vs, USAMHI; Marshall, *Men against Fire*, 92.

65. Linderman, *The World within War*, 306–9; Ellis, *The Sharp End*, 316.

66. Albert C. Zerr survey, box: First Infantry Division, Twenty-sixth Infantry Regiment, WWII vs, USAMHI; Merritt Bragdon survey, box: Second Armored Division, Sixty-sixth Armored Regiment, WWII vs, USAMHI; Joseph P. Ghilardi survey, box: Anti-Aircraft Artillery Battalions Including AAA-AW 478–557, WWII vs, USAMHI; Francis J. Hanrahan survey, box: Anti-Aircraft Artillery Battalions Including AAA-AW 478–557, WWII vs, USAMHI.

67. William F. Houser survey, box: First Armored Division, WWII vs, USAMHI; Russell Davidson survey, box: Anti-Aircraft Artillery Battalions Including AAA-AW 478–557, WWII vs, USAMHI; Leopold J. Arthold Twenty-seventh Division, 106th Infantry Regiment, WWII vs, USAMHI.

68. Atwell, *Private*, 13–14.

69. Interview with Irving E. Pape, Rutgers Oral History Archives of World War II, Department of History, Rutgers University, New Brunswick NJ.

70. Interview with Franklyn A. Johnson, Rutgers Oral History Archives.

71. Becker and Theobaben, *Common Warfare*, 119–20.

72. MacDonald, *Company Commander*, 25, 273–74.

73. James Ritchey survey, box: Twenty-eighth Infantry Division, 110th Infantry Regiment, WWII vs, USAMHI; Alfred E. Grossenbacher survey, box: Twenty-eighth Infantry Division, 110th Infantry Regiment, WWII vs, USAMHI; Loren Randall Tinker survey, box: Twenty-eighth Infantry Division, 110th Infantry Regiment, WWII vs, USAMHI; Stephen B. Morrissey survey, box: First Infantry Division, Twenty-sixth Infantry Regiment, WWII vs, USAMHI.

74. McPherson, *For Cause and Comrades*, 92.

75. Northham H. Stolp survey; Carl Joseph Morano survey, box: Twenty-sixth Infantry Division, WWII vs, USAMHI; Benjamin H. Feldman survey, box: Tenth Infantry Division Mountain, WWII vs, USAMHI; Charles F. Stewart Jr. survey, box: Twenty-seventh Division, 106th Infantry Regiment, WWII vs, USAMHI; Cawthon, *Other Clay*, 16.

76. Becker and Theobaben, *Common Warfare*, 6–7; Joseph S. Sykes survey, box: Twenty-seventh Division, 106th Infantry Regiment, WWII vs, USAMHI; Richard W. Mote survey, box: Eighty-second Airborne Division 505th PIR 1, WWII vs, USAMHI.

77. Stouffer, *The American Soldier*, 1:441.

78. Melzer, *Coming of Age in the Great Depression*, 101 [patriotic rituals], 110 [camp papers], 126–27 [instructors].

79. Frederick Edward Getler survey, box: Twenty-seventh Division, 106th Infantry Regiment, WWII vs, USAMHI; Dennis, "Major Problems of Political Socialization Research," 5 [diffuse support]; Sam S. Ozaki survey, box: 442nd Regimental Combat Team (Separate), WWII vs, USAMHI; Shukichi Yoshino survey, box: 442nd Regimental Combat Team (Separate), WWII vs, USAMHI.

80. Central Pacific Base Command, *A Pocket Guide to Hawaii*, 7–8.

81. Bert N. Nishimura survey, box: 442nd Regimental Combat Team (Separate), WWII vs, USAMHI; Roger Hiraoka Yoshimi survey, box: 442nd Regimental Combat Team (Sepa-

rate), WWII VS, USAMHI; Shuji Akiyama survey, box: 442nd Regimental Combat Team (Separate), WWII VS, USAMHI; Katsuki Tanigawa survey, box: 442nd Regimental Combat Team (Separate), WWII VS, USAMHI.

82. Stouffer, *The American Soldier*, 2:551–60.

83. Gray, *The Warriors*, 156.

84. Hovland, Lumsdaine, and Sheffield, *Experiments on Mass Communication*, 136.

85. Hovland, Lumsdaine, and Sheffield, *Experiments on Mass Communication*, 213–16.

86. Hovland, Lumsdaine, and Sheffield, *Experiments on Mass Communication*, 106.

87. Hovland, Lumsdaine, and Sheffield, *Experiments on Mass Communication*, 111, 114 [polygraph results], 86 [*Why We Fight*], 81 [entertaining]. Following the dictates of the audience polygraph did not necessarily produce a more palatable film. For example, the 1958 information film *The History of the Korean War* was composed almost entirely of "like button" scenes (mostly incessant artillery fire, but also some aerial combat footage). Yet its monotonous narration and lack of dramatic timing made it a far less entertaining movie than any of the *Why We Fight* installments.

88. Hovland, Lumsdaine, and Sheffield, *Experiments on Mass Communication*, 165.

89. Hovland, Lumsdaine, and Sheffield, *Experiments on Mass Communication*, 46.

90. Hovland, Lumsdaine, and Sheffield, *Experiments on Mass Communication*, 24.

91. Special Services Division, Research Branch, "What the Solider Thinks," no. 2, Quarterly Report, 1943, file: AGF 461/2, box 965, RG 337 (Headquarters, Army Ground Forces), NA.

92. Hovland, Lumsdaine, and Sheffield, *Experiments on Mass Communication*, 34, 58.

93. Hovland, Lumsdaine, and Sheffield, *Experiments on Mass Communication*, 44–45; Research Branch, Information and Education, Headquarters, Theater Service Forces, European Theater, "A Study of the Effectiveness of Unit Orientation Programs," September, 1945, file: ETO 101 Effen. In Unit Orie. Program, box: 1017, RG 330 (94), NA.

94. Stouffer, *The American Soldier*, I:441; Jowett and O'Donnell, *Propaganda and Persuasion*, 129, 134.

95. Jowett and O'Donnell, *Propaganda and Persuasion*, 65 ["previous"], 88 [motivational purpose]. Soldiers who objected to the films often cited scenes they thought were "faked," including footage of aerial combat and scenes taking place inside enemy territory, such as Hitler at work in his office. Plane-mounted cameras captured most of the combat footage, but a few soldiers correctly pinpointed staged reaction shots of "German" pilots. The pictures of the Axis leaders were authentic; after the study the *Why We Fight* films were amended to state explicitly that the filmmakers took such footage from enemy newsreels (90–92).

96. Jowett and O'Donnell, *Propaganda and Persuasion*, 69–70.

97. Jowett and O'Donnell, *Propaganda and Persuasion*, 67–68.

98. Heller, *Catch-22*, 102.

99. Stouffer, *The American Soldier*, 2:150–52.

100. Jowett and O'Donnell, *Propaganda and Persuasion*, 106–9; Lasswell, *Propaganda Technique in the World War*, 220–21, as cited by Jowett and O'Donnell, *Propaganda and Persuasion*, 99.

2. The Morale and Whatnot of the Army

1. Scholars from different fields have disputed the effectiveness of the army's political indoctrination programs. They include Edward Stuart Wells, "A Study of the United States Army's Internal Information Program"; Arthur George Haggis Jr., "An Appraisal of the Administration, Scope, Concept, and Function of the United States Army Troop Information Program"; and William R. Arbogast, "Issues and Answers: The U. S. Army Command Information Program" and "An Analysis of Modernization in Army Newspapers"; and Stephen D. Wesbrook, *Political Training in the United States Army*.

2. Kellet, *Combat Motivation*.

3. Stouffer, *The American Soldier*, 1:480 ["liked"], 432 [idealism and cynicism].

4. Lynn, *Bayonets of the Republic*, 28.

5. Goldhamer, *The Soviet Soldier*, 242; Janowitz, *The Professional Soldier*, 401, 403.

6. Palmer, "'Why We Fight,' A Study of Indoctrination Activities in the Armed Forces," 126 [AFRTS], 187 [Berlin].

7. Wesbrook, *Political Training in the United States Army*, 49.

8. Bogle, *The Pentagon's Battle for the American Mind*; Alpers, "This Is the Army," 131, 163 ["Fears"]. For a skeptical view of the strength of traditional American antimilitary sentiment, see Lane, "Ideology and the American Military Experience," 15–26.

9. Jane Temple, *WACs on Parade*, radio script, Columbia Broadcasting System, 7 March 1945, file: Radio Scripts—P.R.O. Battery General Hospital, Rome, Georgia, 13 August 1944–27 September 1945, Jane Temple Papers, USAMHI; Blum, *V Was for Victory*; Westbrook, "Fighting for the American Family."

10. Manchester, *Goodbye, Darkness*, 100.

11. Bennett, *When Dreams Came True*, 194 [likelihood of depression]; May, *Homeward Bound*, 56, 59 [gender roles].

12. Temple, *WACs on Parade*, 6 September 1945.

13. Wolfe, *Frank Capra*, 157–58.

14. "Information Control in Germany," 1945 booklet, file: Booklet, "Information Control in Germany," James Bruce McWilliams Papers, USAMHI; "The Generals Speak for OWI," *New York Times*, 16 June 1945, 12.

15. William H. Webber, Deputy Director, Operations, to the American Staff, OWI, "Comments on Work of the Office of War Information," 5 July 1945, file: Office of War Information, Outpost Reports, June, July–August, James Bruce McWilliams Papers, USAMHI.

Information and Education writer William L. Shirer retorted, in his June 17, 1945 *New York Herald Tribune* column, "that sound and clear-thinking though we Americans admit ourselves to be, few of us speak and write the 27 foreign languages with which OWI operates. Representative Gavin did not touch on this point. 'To me,' he said, 'OWI is a great mental disturbance.' That is too bad. No upright citizen could like to inflict a mental disturbance on the gentleman from Pennsylvania. But is it a legitimate reason to still the voice of America in this world?"

16. Headquarters, Third United States Army, *Occupational Handbook: Questions and Answers for the Enlisted Man*, December 1945, file: Office of War Information, Outpost Reports, June, July–August, James Bruce McWilliams Papers, USAMHI.

17. Wolfe, *Frank Capra*, 156–57.

18. Scherle and Levy, *The Films of Frank Capra*, 220.

19. American Historical Association, *G.I. Roundtable: What Shall Be Done about Germany after the War?*, 4–5, 12–13, 19. In the notes to the discussion leader, the unidentified historian-authors wrote confidently, "Here is stuff for lively and useful discussion. . . . You have in this pamphlet material which is superbly organized for practical use by a discussion or forum leader" (21).

20. American Historical Association, *G.I. Roundtable: What Shall Be Done about Germany after the War?*, 14, 7; *G.I. Roundtable: What Shall Be Done with the War Criminals?*, 32, 10 (quotation).

Despite the acknowledgment of Russian losses, the authors suggested that the lead prosecutor in the upcoming war crimes trials would be the state that "had suffered the greatest injury from the crime. . . . The case might well be entitled *The United Nations ex rel. The United Kingdom* v. *Adolf Hitler*" (*G.I. Roundtable: What Shall Be Done with the War Criminals?*, 25).

21. Ellis, *The Sharp End*, 320; Atwell, *Private*, 367–68.

22. Atwell, *Private*, 346–48 [German woman], 368 ["The fact remains . . . "].

23. Research Branch, I&E Division, "What the Soldier Thinks about Germany and the Germans," June 1946, file: 7–302, box 1005, RG 330 (93), NA, 2–3.

24. Borowski, *This Way to the Gas, Ladies and Gentlemen*, 164–65; Goedde, *GIs and Germans*; Bendersky, *The "Jewish Threat,"* 353 [displaced persons]; Stouffer, *The American Soldier*, 2:551, 557, 564 [French].

25. Stouffer, *The American Soldier*, 2:572 [positive terms], 573 [tough policy].

26. Dower, *Embracing Defeat*, 129 [prostitution], 206–7 [arrogance], 211 ["were empowered"].

27. Dower, *Embracing Defeat*, 214 [Civil Affairs], 215–17 [*Your Job in Japan*].

28. Ross, *Preparing for Ulysses*, 169–72 [points system], 182–83 [demonstrations].

29. Gen. J. Lawton Collins, USA (ret.), interview by Lt. Col. Charles C. Sperow, Project 72–1, Vol. II, United States Army Military History Institute Senior Officers Oral History Program, 1972, J. Lawton Collins Papers, USAMHI, 274–75.

30. Edward S. Sullivan to unidentified superior, 27 March 1945, file: Office of War Information—Memoranda, Intra-Office Memos, Edward S. Sullivan Papers, USAMHI (original punctuation and spelling retained).

31. Edward S. Sullivan to unidentified superior, 27 March 1945, file: Office of War Information—Memoranda, Intra-Office Memos, Edward S. Sullivan Papers, USAMHI. The identity of the author to whom he referred is unclear.

32. Felix Johnson, Director of Public Information, USN, to Office of Assistant Secretary of Defense, January 1948; file: Battle of Russia, box: 663, RG 330 (140), NA; Fitzgerald, *America Revised*, 116–17.

33. War Department, *Your Red Army Ally*, 1.

34. War Department, *Your Red Army Ally*, 3.

35. War Department, *Your Red Army Ally*, 20–22.

36. *The USSR: Institutions & People*, 5.

37. *The USSR: Institutions & People*, 63–64.

38. See for example, Williams, *The Tragedy of American Diplomacy*.

39. *The USSR: Institutions & People*, 65.

40. *The USSR: Institutions & People*, 27, 30.

41. *The USSR: Institutions & People*, 41–43.

42. *The USSR: Institutions & People*, 65.

43. J. Lawton Collins, USMHI Oral History, 288.

44. Bendersky, *The "Jewish Threat,"* 400 [Willoughby]; Schrecker, *Many Are the Crimes*, 276 ["A liberal is . . . "].

45. Ellis, *The Sharp End*, 321–22 [Army Education Corps].

46. J. Lawton Collins, USMHI Oral History, 271–72; Griese, *Arthur W. Page*, 255.

47. Griese, *Arthur W. Page*, 254–55.

48. Marchand, *Creating the Corporate Soul*, 101.

49. Marchand, *Creating the Corporate Soul*, 103–5 [corporation as an army and family], 108–14 [employee magazines].

50. Janowitz, *The Professional Soldier*, 12; Marchand, *Creating the Corporate Soul*, 4.

51. Richard P. Taffe survey, continuation sheet 59c, box: Twenty-sixth Infantry Division, WWII VS, USAMHI; continuation sheet 49c: Capt. Richard P. Taffe, "I'm Not Afraid of the A-Bomb," *Collier's*, 26 January 1952, 14–15, 41.

52. Jordan, "Troop Information and Indoctrination," 359–60.

53. J. Lawton Collins, USMHI Oral History, 271–72.

54. J. Lawton Collins, USMHI Oral History, 271, 295.

55. Collins, *Lightning Joe*, 344.

56. J. Lawton Collins, USMHI Oral History, 277, 279.

57. J. Lawton Collins, USMHI Oral History, 288.

58. Brig. Gen. H. I. Hodes, Assistant Deputy Chief of Staff, memorandum for Chief, Information and Education Division, 17 January 1947, file: Justifications for Existence of Res. Div., box: 970, RG 330 (89), NA; Charles T. Lanham to J. Lawton Collins, 10 September 1946, file: Justifications for Existence of Res. Div., box: 970, RG 330 (89), NA; Attitude Research Section, 7700th Information and Education Group, "Attitudes of Officers and Enlisted Men Concerning the Troop Information Program in the European Theater," 1 May 1947, file: E-6-88 "Att of O&Em Toward Tip," box: 1020, RG 330 (94), NA, 1.

59. "Army Chief Backs 'All-Out' War of Ideas on Soviet Propaganda," *Washington Evening Star*, 26 March 1952, file: Gen. J. Lawton Collins, Chief of Staff, USA, Press Clippings for the Period August 1951–July 1952, J. Lawton Collins Papers, USAMHI, 274.

60. Larry Lesueur, radio transcript, Columbia Broadcasting System, 26 March 1952, file: Gen. J. Lawton Collins, Chief of Staff, USA, Press Clippings for the Period August 1951–July 1952, J. Lawton Collins Papers, USAMHI, 274.

61. "Collins Orders Army to Study Its History," *Washington Post*, 27 November 1952, file: Gen. J. Lawton Collins, Chief of Staff, USA, Press Clippings for the Period August 1952–August 1953, J. Lawton Collins Papers, USAMHI, 73.

Later, in 1971, Collins used the information officer's favorite bromide during an "Elements of Command" speech to the Army War College on the subject of officer integrity. He described Baron Friedrich Wilhelm August von Steuben's purported letter to a Prussian friend saying that American soldiers had to be given a reason before they would follow orders. "Now I would say that the old Heinie . . . put his finger on the essence of American discipline. . . . If you explain the reason why, the American soldier will follow you anywhere, under any conditions. But unless you explain to him what's going on, what in the hell you're driving at, then you're going to have trouble" (Collins address to the Army War College, file: "Elements of Command" Speech at the Army War College, J. Lawton Collins Papers, USAMHI, 19).

62. Public Information Office, Army Information School, *1946–1956 Army Information School*, pamphlet, February 1956, file: The Army Information School and Armed Forces Information School, the Carlisle Barracks Collection, USAMHI; Griese, *Arthur W. Page*, 256.

63. Col. H. L. Hunter Jr., "Report of Interviews with Williston B. Palmer, General, U.S.A. (Retired)," Senior Officer Debriefing Program, 1972, Williston B. Palmer Papers, USAMHI, 8.

64. Gen. Williston Birkhimer Palmer, USA (ret.), interview by Lt. Col. H. L. Hunter, United States Army Military History Institute Senior Officers Oral History Program, 1971–72, Williston B. Palmer Papers, USAMHI, 40.

65. Gen. Williston Birkhimer Palmer, USA (ret.), interviewed by Lt. Col. H. L. Hunter, United States Army Military History Institute Senior Officers Oral History Program, 1971–72, Williston B. Palmer Papers, USAMHI, 40. Discussing the Crusades, Palmer commented skeptically on the motivational value of great causes: "No battles, no objectives, nothing ever won, nothing ever accomplished. Some people went along just for the Jesus of it" (Col. Grover Asmus, "General W. Palmer Anecdotes," file: Anecdotes—Undated, Williston B. Palmer Papers, USAMHI).

66. *1956 Army Information School.*

67. Hunter, "Report of Interviews," 40; Asmus, 2; Griese, *Arthur W. Page*, 256.

68. Charles T. Lanham, "Address to AIS Course I," 13 March 1946, folder: Speeches 1945–47, box: 12, Charles T. Lanham Papers, 17 [orientation], 1 [Slings and Arrows], 2 [aristocracy], 3, 12 [chain of command], 22 ["little bundle"].

   Three years later Lanham was even more vocal in supporting integration, writing in a report about the injustice of black soldiers in World War II having to fight against the "vicious fantasy" of "Aryan supremacy" abroad and simultaneously "for 'white supremacy' at home." (Lanham to James King, Office of the Secretary of the Army, "Equality of Opportunity and Treatment in the U.S. Army," 3 August 1949, folder: Report by CTL: Equality Report to Jim King, box: 9, Charles T. Lanham Papers.

69. *1956 Army Information School.*

70. Bendersky, *The "Jewish Threat,"* 389–91; George W. Bernard, John Beumer III, Andrea Herzberg-Morrison, and Bernard G. Sarnat, "Fred Herzberg, Oral Biology: Los Angeles, 1994, University of California: In Memoriam," *University of California History Digital Archives Collection*, http://sunsite.berkeley.edu/uchistory.

71. Millett and Maslowski, *For the Common Defense*, 483; Weigley, *History of the United States Army*, 486.

72. Alpers, "This Is the Army" [promoting army as democratic]; Millett and Maslowski, *For the Common Defense*, 482 [military justice].

73. *Armed Forces Information School Bulletin* 2, no. 4 (February 1951), file: The Army Information School and Armed Forces Information School, the Carlisle Barracks Collection, USAMHI, 7.

74. *Armed Forces Information School Bulletin* 2, no. 2 (August 1950):3, and no. 4 (February 1951):5–6.

75. *Armed Forces Information School Bulletin* 2, no. 2 (August 1950):3–4, and *Armed Forces Information School Bulletin* 2, no. 4 (February 1951):6.

76. *Armed Forces Information School Bulletin* 2, no. 1 (April 1950):3–6.

77. *Armed Forces Information School Bulletin* 2, no. 2 (August 1950):3–4.

78. *Armed Forces Information School Bulletin* 2, no. 1 (April 1950):3.

79. *Armed Forces Information School Bulletin* 2, no. 2 (August 1950):3, and no. 4 (February 1951):4–5. On the *Hours of Freedom* series, see chapter 3.

80. *1956 Army Information School.*

81. *1956 Army Information School* and *Armed Forces Information School Bulletin* 2, no. 3 (December 1950):3–4.

82. Armed Forces Information School, "Armed Forces Information School Graduation Exercises," program, 9 August 1950, file: The Army Information School and Armed Forces Information School, the Carlisle Barracks Collection, USAMHI.

83. *1956 Army Information School.*

84. *Armed Forces Information School Bulletin* 2, no. 3 (December 1950):5–6.

85. Attitude Research Branch, Armed Forces Information and Education Division, "Morale Attitudes of Enlisted Men: IV. Soldiers' Reactions to the Troop Information Program Talks," May–June 1949, file: E-6-88 "Att of O&Em Toward Tip," box: 1020, RG 330 (94), NA, 1.

3. OAFIE's Voice

1. *United States Government Organizational Manual, 1950–51*, 113.

2. Whitfield, *The Culture of the Cold War*, 10.

3. Paragraph summarizes Department of the Army, *Catalog of Armed Forces Information Materials*, 3–66.

4. "Loyalty Investigations for Prospective Members of the Civilian Committee on the Armed Forces Education Program," 7 May 1952, file: Section I, box: 946, RG 330 (88), NA.

5. Lt. Col. Narwrocky, Department of the Army Office of the Chief of Information (hereafter OCINFO), "Report on Citizenship Training in the Army," 22 July 1952, file: Section XVIII, case 351, box 272, RG 319 (G-3), NA.

On the embarrassment of the World War I academics, see Blakey, *Historians on the Home Front.*

6. Training Branch, Organization and Training Division memo to OCINFO, 25 July 1952, file: Section XVIII, case 351, box: 272, RG 319 (G-3) 353, NA; Army Field Forces, Fort Monroe, Veterans Administration (VA) memo to Troop Information Division, OCINFO, "Report of Columbia 'Hours' Testing in Six Continental Armies," 4 June 1952, file: Section XVIII, case 351, box: 272, RG 319 (G-3), NA.

7. "Report of Columbia 'Hours' Testing."

8. Bogle, "Creating an American Will," 229.

9. Department of the Army, *Army Four-Hour Pre-Combat Orientation Course (Korea)*, 4–8. Subsequent page references from this source appear parenthetically in the text.

The *Pre-Combat* course did not address the experience of combat specifically. The army dealt with that subject in a 1951 pamphlet entitled *The Soldier in Combat*, which attempted to describe the "face of battle" to green troops. It assured them that their fear was natural (5), that their chance of survival was "*not solely* a matter of luck" (9), and that they could improve their odds by firing their weapons (8).

10. Ridgway, *The Korean War*, 264–65; Harry G. Summers Jr., interview in Tomedi, *No Bugles, No Drums*, 106; Summers, *On Strategy.*

11. Citizens Advisory Committee on Armed Forces Training Installations, "Third Report," n.d. (1951), file: Section I, box 926, RG 330 (88), NA.

12. Charles O. Porter to George C. Marshall, Secretary of Defense, 28 January 1951, file: [correspondence], box 945, RG 330 (88), NA.

13. Porter to Marx Leva, Assistant Secretary of Defense (Legal and Legislative Affairs), 14 February 1951, file: [correspondence], box 945, RG 330 (88), NA; Leva to Porter, 20 February 1951, file: [correspondence], box 945, RG 330 (88), NA.

14. Orwell, *1984*; Koestler, *Darkness at Noon*; Joe Michaels to Devine, n.d., file: [correspondence], box 945, RG 330 (88), NA.

15. Lt. Gen. LeRoy Lutes, Fourth U.S. Army Commanding, to Maj. Gen. Floyd L. Parks, CINFO, 18 September 1951, file: [correspondence], box 945, RG 330 (88), NA.

16. Corwin Hoyt Barnett to Louis Johnson, Secretary of Defense, 27 July 1950, file: [correspondence], box 945, RG 330 (88), NA.

17. Col. Harrod G. Miller, Signal Corps Deputy Training Commander, to Chief Signal Officer, Department of the Army, 27 February 1950, file: [correspondence], box 945, RG 330 (88), NA.

18. F. A. Rohrman, chairman, Committee for University Research, University of Colorado, Boulder, "Formulation of an Improved Information Program for the Armed Forces," 9 July 1951, file: [precedes files], box: 971, RG 330 (89), NA; Memorandum, "Conference with Dr. Robert H. Connery, Professor of Foreign Relations, Duke University, 31 March 1951, file: [precedes files], box: 971, RG 330 (89); George C. Marshall, Secretary of Defense, to Dean Paul Gross, Duke University, 13 March 1951, file: [precedes files], box: 971, RG 330 (89).

19. Devine, memorandum, 13 March 1951, file: [correspondence], box 945, RG 330 (88), NA.

20. George, *The Chinese Communist Army in Action*, 95–108; Goldhamer, *The Soviet Soldier*, 248. The Chinese political indoctrination specialists also forced their American POWs to criticize one another or to participate in "self-criticism," most likely to develop confessional habits and to break down prisoners' group cohesion. POWs were not invited to criticize their captors (Biderman, *March to Calumny*, 57–58).

21. Maj. Gen. Gilman C. Mudgett, CINFO, "CINFO Remarks on PI and TI&E," n.d. (1954), file: CINFO Remarks on PI and TI&E, Ralph E. Pearson Papers, USAMHI, 3, 9, 12.

22. TI&E, Ralph E. Pearson Papers, USAMHI, 13.

23. During the Berlin airlift in 1948, for example, a former internal information director notified his old department when he saw a story about a soldier asking for a schedule to catch a train to Berlin, then under blockade (Brig. Gen. Charles T. Latham, Office of the Secretary of Defense to Chief, Troop Information Division, 15 February 1949, file: Section I, box: 828, RG 330 (88), NA).

24. Office of the Adjutant General memorandum, "Phased Minimum Standards for Troop Information," 12 May 1952, file: [correspondence], box 945, RG 330 (88), NA.

25. Col. James T. Sheridan, USAF, Chief Censor, to Colonel Richard H. Merrick, Chief Policy and Plans Division, OCINFO, 19 November 1953, file: Correspondence of Richard H. Merrick, 1942–63, 1976, Richard H. Merrick Papers, USAMHI; Vorhees, *Korean Tales*, 101, 111, 115.

26. "Army Objected to Comment on M'Arthur," *Washington Post*, 13 February 1953.

27. Department of the Army, *Army Forty-Hour Discussion Leader's Course*, 9, 14 ["frill"], 12 ["haze"]. Subsequent page references from this source appear parenthetically in the text.

28. Burstyn, *The Rites of Men*, 182–85.

29. Department of the Army, *Duty, Honor, Country*, Series IV, Pamphlet 16–8 (Washington DC: U.S. Government Printing Office, 1951), 66.

30. Chomsky, *The Chomsky Reader*, 33. The literature on sport and society is extensive. For a relevant analysis, see Coakley, "Sport as Opiate," 250–54.

31. Department of the Army, *Armed Forces Newspaper Editors Guide*, 32.

32. Office of Armed Forces Information and Education (hereafter OAFIE) memorandum, "AFRS—Short-wave Master Schedule," 1 July 1952, file: Section I, box: 926, RG 330 (88), NA.

33. Ephram S. Glasser survey, box: Field Artillery, KWVC (KWVC), USAMHI; Morton Wood Jr. survey, box: First Cavalry Division, KWVC, USAMHI; Robert J. Weeks survey, box: Ordnance Battalions and Companies, KWVC, USAMHI.

34. Venico C. Gacono survey, box: Outside the Theater of Operations, KWVC, USAMHI; Arthur Brown survey, box: Transportation, KWVC, USAMHI.

35. Jack R. Dillon survey, box: Engineer Battalions and Companies, KWVC, USAMHI.

36. Gerald L. Trett, "Remembering the Forgotten War," post to *Korean War Project*, 2 October 2000, http://www.koreanwar.org/html/units/98en_photo.htm.

37. Gerald L. Trett, "Remembering the Forgotten War," post to *Korean War Project*, 2 October 2000, http://www.koreanwar.org/html/units/98en_photo.htm; John E. McGregor survey, box: Medical, KWVC, USAMHI.

38. Whitfield, *The Culture of the Cold War*, 196.

39. Exoo, "Cultural Hegemony in the United States," *Democracy Upside Down: Public Opinion and Cultural Hegemony in the United States*, 5–6.

40. Department of the Army, *Overseas Orientation Course*.

41. Department of the Army, *Truth Is Our Defense*, 2–3.

42. Department of the Army, *Separation Series*, 11. Other examples of the rational argumentative style include *Troop Topics: Discipline* (1953), *Troop Topics: Information and You* (1953), and *Troop Topics: Why Training Is Tough* (1953).

43. In reviewing its films for officers, an OAFIE study stated: "It has been customary, heretofore, to simplify the language used and the topics discussed in information films in order that they might be easily understood by the least well informed enlisted man who might view them" (Thomas C. Erdington, OAFIE Research Division, "Service and Acceptance of 'Officers Conference' Films," Research Report 143–358, December 1954, Library Collection, USAMHI, 7).

44. *Armed Forces Newspaper Editors Guide*, 1952, 26 ["editorial comment"]; Capt. William J. Strachan, USN, "Report on the Coverage of 1952 Political Campaign over AFRS," 28 November 1952, file: Section I, box: 926, RG 330 (88), NA [monitoring]; Department of the Army, *Voting Information 1952*.

45. Department of the Army, *The Soldier and the Community*, 10–11.

46. See, for example, Department of the Army, *Travel Talks*, Pamphlet 20–107.

47. Whitfield, *The Culture of the Cold War*, 83–84 [religion in the Cold War], 94 [Spellman].

48. Nash, *The Conservative Intellectual Movement in America Since 1945*, 60.

49. Department of the Army, *Duty, Honor, Country*, Series I, Pamphlet 16–5, 34, 62, 77.

50. Department of the Army, *Duty, Honor, Country*, Series III, Pamphlet 16–7, 80–81.

51. OAFIE memorandum, "Short-wave Quarterly Reports," 1951–52, file: Section II, box: 926, RG 330 (88), NA.

52. *Catalog of Armed Forces Information Materials*, 1952, 56; on *Life Can Be Beautiful*, see chapter 1.

53. *Catalog of Armed Forces Information Materials*, 1952, 58–59; Ayn Rand, "Hearings Regarding Communist Infiltration of the Motion Picture Industry," 20 October 1947, testimony before the House Committee on Un-American Activities, quoted in Bentley, *Thirty Years of Treason*, 118.

54. "Short-wave Quarterly Reports," 1951–52. The show *Juke Box U.S.A.* had the most mail: 1,187 letters.

55. *Catalog of Armed Forces Informational Material*, 1952, 26–27.

56. M. Weidenhamer and Reuben Cohen, Department of Defense, OAFIE, Research Division, "Research Report: How Soldiers React to the Troop Information Program," 145–357, April 1955, file: [precedes files], CINFO Papers, USAMHI, 1–2, 14, 16–17, 20–23.

57. Weidenhamer and Cohen, 25, 32.

58. Weidenhamer and Cohen, 40–46 [quiz questions], 114.

59. "Attitude Research Branch, Armed Forces Information and Education Division, Reaction to the Film: 'Face to Face with Communism,'" August 1951, file: Special Memorandum No. 53, box: 1010, RG 330 (93), NA, 1, 3; "New Soldiers' Attitudes—After Six Weeks of Training," March 1951, file: Report No. 114–338, I, II, box: 1008, RG 330 (93), NA, 14–15, 17.

60. Stanley Weintraub interview in Tomedi, *No Bugles, No Drums*, 191.

61. Matthew R. Thome survey, box: 24th Division 34th Regiment, KWVC, USAMHI; George E. Sites Jr. survey, box: Field Artillery, KWVC, USAMHI; Allan D. Carlson, survey, box: Military Police, KWVC, USAMHI; James O. Christensen survey, box: Engineer Battalions and Companies, KWVC, USAMHI.

62. First Cavalry Division, KWVC, USAMHI; Michael Billig survey, box: Field Artillery, KWVC, USAMHI; Robert J. Barnes survey, box: Signal, KWVC, USAMHI; Lewis Sanders survey, box: Ordnance Battalions and Companies, KWVC, USAMHI.

63. Herbert H. Braden survey, box: Outside the Theater of Operations, KWVC, USAMHI; Arnold Tiscarino survey, box: Outside the Theater of Operations, KWVC, USAMHI; Henry A. Pernicko survey, Field Artillery, KWVC, USAMHI; Uzal Ent interview in Tomedi, *No Bugles, No Drums*, 22; Francisco Talavera survey, Twenty-fourth Division, Thirty-fourth Regiment, KWVC, USAMHI; Robert P. Hatch survey, box: Field Artillery Alphabetical Boxes, KWVC, USAMHI.

64. Joseph C. Bracale Jr. survey, box: Engineer Battalions, Companies, KWVC, USAMHI.

65. William Love survey, box: First Cavalry Division, KWVC, USAMHI; Thomas G. Hannon survey, box: Field Artillery, KWVC, USAMHI; Richard E. Donaldson survey, box: Outside the Theater of Operations, KWVC, USAMHI; Chester Savory survey, box: Outside the Theater of Operations, KWVC, USAMHI.

66. George G. Berhard survey, box: Outside the Theater of Operations, KWVC, USAMHI; William J. Wehman survey, box: Engineer Battalions and Companies, KWVC, USAMHI.

67. Rishell, *With a Black Platoon in Combat*, 7; James D. Stone survey, box: Field Artillery, KWVC, USAMHI; Donald F. Paul survey, box: Signal, KWVC, USAMHI; James H. Clutch survey, box: Outside the Theater of Operations, KWVC, USAMHI; James L. Wasson survey, box: Engineer Battalions, Companies, KWVC, USAMHI; Wayne H. Finley survey, box: Outside the Theater of Operations, KWVC, USAMHI.

68. Robert F. Roser survey, box: Outside of Theater of Operations, KWVC, USAMHI; Robert R. Bayless survey, box: Twenty-fourth Division, Thirty-fourth Regiment, KWVC, USAMHI; Richard P. Shane survey, box: Twenty-fourth Division, Thirty-fourth Regiment, KWVC, USAMHI; Viktor Tkaczenko survey, box: Outside the Theater of Operations, KWVC, USAMHI.

69. Leslie R. Davis survey, box: Engineer Battalions and Companies, KWVC, USAMHI; Robert J. Wienhold survey, box: Outside the Theater of Operations, KWVC, USAMHI.

70. William G. Cave survey, box: Signal, KWVC, USAMHI; Thomas Beck survey, box: Engineer Battalions and Companies, KWVC, USAMHI; Herbert C. Weaver survey, box: Outside the Theater of Operations, KWVC, USAMHI; Jacob J. Huffacker survey, box: Signal, KWVC, USAMHI.

71. Herbert J. Lakebrink survey, box: Engineer Battalions and Companies, KWVC, USAMHI; John L. Yack survey, box: Ordnance Battalions and Companies, KWVC, USAMHI; Robert D. Mitzel survey, box: Outside the Theater of Operations, KWVC, USAMHI; Charles H. Rose survey, box: Field Artillery, KWVC, USAMHI; Leon O. Anderson Jr. survey, box: Outside the Theater of Operations, KWVC, USAMHI; Edward G. Abraham survey, box: Twenty-fourth Division, Thirty-fourth Regiment, KWVC, USAMHI.

72. Morrow, *What's a Commie Ever Done to Black People?*, 8–9, 34.

73. United Nations Repatriation Group (hereafter UNREG) memorandum: "Verbal, non-attributable, statement to be made to press (nothing to be given out in writing!)," n.d., File: Official Papers, Diaries and Clippings. Letters Concerning Repatriation of Korean War Prisoners, Especially Those Not Choosing Repatriation, 30 October–2 December 1953, Ralph E. Pearson Papers, USAMHI.

74. UNREG press release, "Neutral Nations Repatriation Commission: Full Text of the Representation from PsOW of the North Camp and NNRC's Reply Thereto," 29 November 1953, file: Daily Journals, papers, etc. concerning the Repatriation of Korean War Prisoners, PIO Journal, UNCREG, 30 October 1953–18 January 1954, Ralph E. Pearson Papers, USAMHI, 12.

75. "Neutral Nations Repatriation Commission," 15, 18.

76. "Neutral Nations Repatriation Commission," 13–14.

77. "Neutral Nations Repatriation Commission," 19.

78. "Neutral Nations Repatriation Commission," 1–3, 6–7.

79. Maj. Gen. Gilman C. Mudgett, USA, CINFO, "DA Information Objectives and Plans: Background Reading for AWRC," Lecture 4–11, AWC2–D4, 23 November 1954, Special Services Section, Army War College, USAMHI, inclusion no. 3, 3–4.

80. Col. Harold C. Lyon, USA; Lt. Col. William A. McKee, USA; and Lt. Col. John B. Blair, USA, "Ad Hoc Committee Report on Troop Information and Education," 31 January 1955, Library Collection, USAMHI, 1–3, 8.

81. OCINFO memorandum, "Summary of Major William E. Mayer's Activities and

Department of the Army Position Concerning These Activities," n.d., 1962, file: Report on "Maj. Mayer, Maj. A. E. Roberts," Archibald E. Roberts Papers, USAMHI, 1.

The actual number of serious offenders was probably far lower. Of the 192 "cases" only 47 were approved for court martial, and 35 of those never came to trial (Kinkead, *In Every War But One*, 65, 73).

82. "Summary of Major William E. Mayer's Activities," 3.

83. "Summary of Major William E. Mayer's Activities," 4.

84. Kinkead, "Reporter at Large," *New Yorker*, 26 October 1957, 102–53; *In Every War But One*, 31. Subsequent page references from this source appear parenthetically in the text.

85. Department of Army, *Behind Enemy Lines*, 7.

86. Department of Army, *Behind Enemy Lines*, 9–10.

87. Biderman, *March to Calumny*. Subsequent page references from this source appear parenthetically in the text.

88. Huntington, *American Politics*, 15; Hartz, *The Liberal Tradition in America*, 9 [Supreme Court], 11 "The American Way . . ."], 276 [New Deal].

4. An Arsenal of Democracy

1. Foner, *The Story of American Freedom*, 254–55, 256 [quotation].

2. Joseph V. Wittmann Jr. survey, box: Cold War Veterans Collection, USAMHI.

3. Attitude Research Branch, "New Soldiers' Attitudes: 2. Information about World Affairs," March 1951, file: Report No. 113–338–I, box: 1008, RG 330 (93), NA, 2; Colegrove, *Democracy versus Communism*.

4. Rumer, *The American Legion*, 306; Chambers, *Witness*; Hoover, *Masters of Deceit*; Spillane, *One Lonely Night*; *Big Jim McLain*, dir. by Edward Ludwig (90 min., b & w, Warner Bros., 1952); *My Son John*, dir. by Leo McCarey (122 min., b & w, Paramount, 1952); *I Led Three Lives* (syndicated, 117 episodes x 30 min., b & w, ZIV Television Programs, 1953–56); Barson and Heller, *Red Scared!*, 60–73 [magazines], 110–11 [cards].

5. Doob, *Patriotism and Nationalism*, 42 [" . . . so keen"], 43 [parents]; see also Katz and Lazarsfeld, *Personal Influence*.

6. Wesbrook, *Political Training in the United States Army*, 6–7.

7. Langton and Jennings, "Political Socialization and the High School Civics Curriculum in the United States," 388, 390.

8. Easton and Dennis, "A Political Theory of Political Socialization," and "The Child's Image of Government," in Dennis, *Socialization to Politics*, 50, 61, 73–74; Biderman, *March to Calumny*, 258.

9. Goldhamer, *The Soviet Soldier*, 206–7, 249–54.

10. Moskos, *The American Enlisted Man*, 152–54; Westbrook, "Fighting for the American Family," 198.

11. *A Public Trust*, Troop Information Fact Sheet no. 22, 21 June 1962, file: 103–01 Reference Publication Files, Soldier Voting, CINFO Papers, USAMHI, 2; Capt. C. J. Rittman, Adjutant General Corps, Plans and Services Officer, memo for the record, 17 July 1967, file: 718–10 Soldier Voting Files (67), CINFO Papers, USAMHI, 1. *A Public Trust* also bemoaned the fact that naturalized citizens voted more regularly than native-born citizens (3).

12. Lt. Col. Thomas Watt, United States Army Reserves, "Report of MOBDES Training for 1967," 25 August 1967, file: 718–10 Soldier Voting Files (67), CINFO Papers, USAMHI, 4–8; Department of Defense, *Ballots That Fly*, 9 min., Armed Forces Information Film 129, 1964); Army Voting Award [copy of certificate], file: 103–01 Reference Publication Files, Soldier Voting, CINFO Papers, USAMHI; Department of Defense, *Your Vote*, Pamphlet 5–10, 11; "Beautiful Delivery" [photo of Gen. William C. Westmoreland, Army Chief of Staff, and Sp5 Brenda Davis, "the Army's Miss Military Voter"], Army News Photo Features, 21 September 1970, file: Soldier Voting Files, CINFO Papers, USAMHI.

Your Vote chided that "Freedom, like a receding hairline, isn't lost all at once. It goes gradually. If you can spare a few minutes each day using hair tonic to save your hair, can't you spend a few minutes at the polls to save your scalp?" (11). Presumably the author did not really intend to suggest that the effective impact of voting on the nation's government was as minimal as that of hair tonic on one's head.

13. Department of Defense, *The Office of Civil Defense*, Information Bulletin no. 129, 19 February 1965, file: 404–12 Command Information Reference Papers File "Civil Defense," CINFO Papers, USAMHI.

14. Whitfield, *The Culture of the Cold War*, 87; Bogle, *The Pentagon's Battle for the American Mind*, 72.

15. On the conservatism of the army, see Janowitz, *The Professional Soldier*, 248; Lovell, "The Professional Socialization of the West Point Cadet," 129, 152–53. On the political orientation of veterans, see Karsten, *Soldiers and Society*, 318.

16. Attitude Research Branch, "Reactions of Enlisted Men in the Armed Forces to the Film: LETTER TO A REBEL," January 1951, file: Special Memorandum No. 48, box: 1010, RG 330 (93), NA, 1.

17. Myrdal, *An American Dilemma*, 3–25; Hartz, *The Liberal Tradition in America*, 10–11; Whitfield, *The Culture of the Cold War*, 55.

18. Department of the Army, *Duty Honor Country*, Pamphlet 16–13, 38–39.

19. Army, *Duty Honor Country*, 37 [synopsis of *The Lady in the Military Service, Training Film 16–3415* (n.d.)]; Department of the Army, *Human Self Development*, I-B-3.

20. *Mission to Moscow*, 123 min., dir. Michael Curtiz, Warner Brothers, 1943; *The North Star*, dir. Lewis Milestone, 108 min., Metro-Goldwyn-Mayer, 1943.

21. Caute, *The Great Fear*, 296.

22. On the 1962 hearings, see chapter 5.

23. On the Monmouth hearings, see Oshinsky, *A Conspiracy So Immense*, 330–44.

24. Griffith, *The Politics of Fear*, 209–11; Caute, *The Great Fear*, 105.

25. Wesbrook, *Political Training in the United States Army*; Palmer, "'Why We Fight,'" 96–97 [*Stars and Stripes*]; Testimony of Dr. Bella V. Dodd, U.S. Congress, Senate, Committee of the Judiciary, Subcommittee on Internal Security, *Interlocking Subversion in Government Departments—Army Information and Education*, 83rd Cong., 2d Sess., Part 20, 1954, 1461–1462.

26. Caute, *The Great Fear*, 406. The Yale University Press's "Annals of Communism" series published after the fall of the Soviet Union makes the case for Soviet influence over CPUSA. The best-known volume of the series is Klehr, Haynes, and Firsov, *The Secret World of American Communism*.

27. FitzGerald, *America Revised*, 10, 121 [informing], 37 [quotation].

28. Bendersky, *The "Jewish Threat"*, 403–4.

29. Department of the Army, *Foundations of American Democracy*, 3, 133–34.

30. Palmer, "'Why We Fight,'" 46–48. On the religious alliance between Broger and Radford, see Loveland, *American Evangelicals and the U.S. Military 1942–1993*, 61.

31. Hale, "'Militant Liberty' and the Pentagon," 30.

32. Wesbrook, *Political Training in the United States Army*, 26; Palmer, "'Why We Fight,'" 49; Hale, "'Militant Liberty' and the Pentagon," 32. The National Security Council also considered using "Militant Liberty" overseas to inspire, for one, the Republic of Vietnam's government forces to the same dedication displayed by the communist insurgents (Chomsky, *For Reasons of State*, 97).

33. Palmer, "'Why We Fight,'" 52–53, 55.

34. On the military's influence over scripts, see Suid, *Guts and Glory*; Huntington, *The Soldier and the State*, 397.

35. Hale, "'Militant Liberty' and the Pentagon," 32–33.

36. Hale, "'Militant Liberty' and the Pentagon," 31.

37. Palmer, "'Why We Fight,'" 51 [Eisenhower], 54 [Military Academy], 59 [services' objections].

38. Wesbrook, *Political Training in the United States Army*, 24, citing Department of the Army, Army Regulation 355-5, Troop Information and Education, 12 March 1953, 2.

39. Department of the Army, "This Is TI&E," 47.

40. Department of the Army, *Catalog of Armed Forces Information Materials*, 3–21 [complete listing of Armed Forces Talks], 3 [no. 207], 7 [nos. 289, 294], 6 [no. 270], 19 [nos. 420, 408].

41. Attitude Research Branch, "Preliminary Report on a Study of the Comic Book Entitled STRONG FOR THE PEOPLE," March 1952, file: Special Memorandum No. 54–346, box: 1010, RG 330 (93), NA; *Catalog of Armed Forces Information Materials*, 1952, 45–66 [data on series], 55 [description of *The God that Failed*, IE-96-15].

42. *Catalog of Armed Forces Information Materials*, 45–66. For an account of the operation of an AFRS overseas station in this period, see Priscaro, "An Historical Study of the American Forces Korea Network and Its Broadcast Programming, 1957–1962."

43. *Catalog of Armed Forces Information Materials* (1952), 22–27; Department of Defense, *Catalog of Information Materials*, 51; War Department, *The Negro Soldier*, 41 min., Orientation Film 51, 1944; Department of the Army, *Citizens in Arms*, 15 min., Orientation Film 48, 1948; Lt. Col. Clair E. Towne, Motion Picture Section, Pictorial Branch, to Orville Crouch, Metro-Goldwyn-Mayer Pictures, 21 July 1952, file: The Hoaxters, box: 689, RG 330 (140), NA, *The Hoaxters*, 38 min., Armed Forces Information Film 46, 1953 (descriptions based on catalog entries).

44. Department of the Army, *Armed Forces Information Materials*, 9–17, 24; Department of Defense, *Catalog of Information Materials*, 24; *Soviet Objectives*, 52 min., Officer's Conference 1, 1955 [Kennan]; *Which Way for the Germans?*, 42 min., Officer's Conference 2, 1955 [Smith]; *What We Face in Southern Asia*, 61 min., Officer's Conference 3, 1955 [Douglas]; *Red China and the United Nations*, 30 min., Officer's Conference 4, 1955 [Lodge]; *The Challenge of Outer Space*, 61 min., Officer's Conference 8, 1956 [von Braun] (descriptions based on catalog entries).

45. Department of Defense, *Catalog of Information Materials*, 21, 24; *Tom Schuler,*

Cobbler-Statesman, 25 min., Armed Forces Information Film 73, 1958; *America's World Responsibilities,* 43 min., WA-6, 1958 (descriptions based on catalog entries).

46. *Catalog of Information Materials,* 1959, 8; Department of Defense, *Armed Forces Information and Education Catalog of Current Information Materials,* 17, 22 (descriptions based on catalog entries).

47. Department of the Army, *Your Military Service Obligation,* 2–3, 5 [quotation].

48. Department of the Army, *Troop Topics: Individual Training: Why We Serve,* Pamphlet 355–2; Department of the Army, *Troop Topics: Why We Serve . . .,* Pamphlet 360–206, [unpaginated]; Department of the Army, *Freedom Is Not Free,* Pamphlet 360–236, 4.

49. Department of Defense, *Catalog of Information Materials,* 22, 26; *Anatomy of Aggression,* 28 min., Armed Forces Information Film 108, 1961; *Communist Target Youth,* 31 min., Armed Forces Information Film 116, 1962; *Freedom and You,* 60 min., Armed Forces Information Film 120, 1962; *Face to Face with Communism,* 26 min., Armed Forces Information Film 21, 1962.

50. Department of the Army, *International Communism: Its Teachings, Aims, and Methods, Know Your Communist Enemy* no. 1; *Communism in Red China, Know your Communist Enemy* no. 5; *Who Are the Communists and Why?, Know Your Communist Enemy* no. 6.

51. *International Communism,* 1–4.

52. *International Communism,* 8–9, 14.

53. *International Communism,* 5.

54. *International Communism,* 7.

55. Department of the Army, *Communism in the U.S.S.R., Know Your Communist Enemy* no. 3, 11–12.

56. *Communism in Red China,* 4 ["Common people"], 5–6 [Sun Yat-sen]. Just as Capra's China installment used the harshest atrocity footage in the *Why We Fight* series, so *Know Your Communist Enemy*'s China pamphlet featured the series' most potent images: photos of helpless, bound prisoners on trial and about to be executed by gunshot to the back of the head (13). *Communism in Red China* also contained a cartoon of a Soviet and a Chinese officer squeezing the globe with a "'Commie' Pincer Movement" (back page, unpaginated). The drawing of the Chinese character was a throwback to racist depictions of the enemy more typical of the poster art of the World Wars.

57. *Communism in Red China,* 4, 11, 7.

58. *Communism in Red China,* 12–13.

59. Colegrove, *Democracy versus Communism, International Control of Aviation,* and *Militarism in Japan;* Colegrove to Truman [private letter], 30 November 1950, published in Giangreco and Moore, *Dear Harry . . . Truman's Mailroom, 1945–1953,* 321; "Scope and Content Note," Kenneth W. Colegrove Papers, *Herbert Hoover Presidential Library and Museum* Web site, www.hoover.archives.gov./index.html.

60. "Scope and Content Note," Kenneth W. Colegrove Papers; on the relationship between the military and the academic community see Yarmolinsky, *The Military Establishment,* 232–33, 304–7, 335.

61. FitzGerald, *America Revised,* 118–21.

62. Colegrove, *What Is Communism?,* 2–4.

63. Colegrove, *What Is Communism?,* 19.

64. Colegrove, *What Is Communism?*, 12; Colegrove, *How Communism Controls Peoples' Economic Life, Democracy Versus Communism*, no. 8, 7; *How Workers and Farmers Fare under Communism, Democracy Versus Communism*, no. 9, 2–3.

65. Colegrove, *What Is Communism?*, 16.

66. Colegrove, *How Workers and Farmers Fare under Communism*, 9.

67. Colegrove, *What Communists Do to Liberty, Democracy versus Communism*, no. 3, 3.

68. Colegrove, *What Is Communism?*, 21; Colegrove, *Communist Party Rule of Soviet Russia, Democracy versus Communism*, no. 7, 2.

69. *What Is Communism?*, 8; Colegrove, *How the Communist Party Operates, Democracy versus Communism*, no. 5, 14–15.

70. Colegrove, *Communist Conquest and Colonization, Democracy versus Communism*, no. 10, 1–2.

71. War Department, *The USSR: Institutions & People*; *What Communists Do to Liberty*, 23.

72. *How the Communist Party Operates*, 1–2, 12.

73. Adler and Paterson, "Red Fascism," 1048 [1930s], 1063 [quotation].

74. Colegrove, *Communist Party Rule of Soviet Russia*, 4.

75. Colegrove, *What Communists Do to Liberty*, 25; Colegrove, *How Workers and Farmers Fare under Communism*, 10.

76. Colegrove, *What Communists Do to Liberty*, 22 [genocide], 11–12 ["Moreover"].

77. Novick, *The Holocaust in American Life*, 128; Shirer, *The Rise and Fall of the Third Reich*.

78. Colegrove, *What Communists Do to Liberty*, 27; Colegrove, *How Communists Gain and Keep Power, Democracy versus Communism*, no. 6, 16.

79. Colegrove, *Democracy Faces Communism, Democracy versus Communism*, no. 1, 15; Colegrove, *How Communism Controls Peoples' Economic Life*, 6, 11; Colegrove, *How Workers and Farmers Fare Under Communism*, 5, 11; May, *Homeward Bound*, 12.

80. Colegrove, *How Communists Gain and Keep Power*, 14; Colegrove, *What Is Communism?*, 20; Colegrove, *What Communists Do to Liberty*, 9.

81. Colegrove, *What Communists Do to Liberty*, 10; Colegrove, *The Communist Party's Program in the United States, Democracy versus Communism*, no. 11; *Communist Conquest and Colonization*, 4 ["Negro Communist state"].

82. Department of the Army, *From Marx to Now*; *Freedom and You*. On the Cold War Education hearings, see chapter 5.

83. *From Marx to Now*, 4, 11–12, 17; Wesbrook, *Political Training in the United States Army*, 26; Bogle, "Creating an American Will," 333–35 [Project Alert].

84. Department of the Army, *Soviet Treaty Violations*.

85. Department of the Army, *The Truth about Our Economic System*, 3, 5, 2.

86. Department of the Army, *Lessons Learned: The Philippines 1946–1953*, 3–4.

87. Department of Defense, *Ideas in Conflict: Liberty and Communism*, 6, 97, 140, 15, 5. Two years later DAFIE adopted William Ebenstein's political science textbook, *Two Ways of Life: The Communist Challenge to Democracy*, as an additional sourcebook. The first cover featured sketches of Lenin and Thomas Jefferson (usually Troop Information's

favorite founding father) facing off against each other. Subsequent editions dropped Lenin from the cover. *Two Ways of Life* resembled Colegrove's *Democracy versus Communism* in its comprehensive treatment. It described the Soviet Union as "one vast prison" populated by millions of slave laborers (126, 175).

88. Department of Defense, *Ideas in Conflict*, 89–90.

89. *Catalog of Information Materials*, 1963, 17; John W. French, OAFIE Research Division, "How Service Personnel Reacted to 'Freedom and Responsibility,': A Citizenship Hour from the Series 'You and Your U.S.A.," Research Report 141–355, OAFIE Research Division, August 1954, file: Report 141–355, box 1009, RG 330 (93), NA, i, 10–11.

90. Department of Defense, *Facts about the United States*, 23.

91. Department of Defense, "*We Hold These Truths* . . . ," 3, 8.

92. Department of Defense, "*We Hold These Truths* . . . ," 7, 9, 11, 13 (italics retained from original source).

93. Department of the Army, *Troop Topics: Our Government*, 4; *Troop Topics: Our Citizenship*, 7.

94. Department of Defense, *How Our Foreign Policy Is Made*, 4 (italics retained from original source). DAFIE devoted an entire pamphlet, *The Future Belongs to Freedom*, to refute charges of imperialism. It presented the Monroe Doctrine, the nation's conquest of Hawaii and the Philippines, and its domination of Cuba as examples of American-sponsored "training for freedom" (14). The strange cover art featured two identical photos of an Asian man reading a book against a washed-out yellow background.

95. Griffith, "Army Chaplains and the Program for Moral Build-Up," 183–85.

96. The title of the series was taken from the motto of the United States Military Academy; it also appeared in an address by Gen. Douglas MacArthur. Department of the Army, *Duty—Honor—Country*, Pamphlet 16–12, 14, 16–17, 25.

97. Department of the Army, *Duty—Honor—Country*, Pamphlet 16–12, 25–26. The best example of Lincoln's greatness that the authors could muster was an exchange in which Lt. Gen. Ulysses S. Grant purportedly asked Lincoln if Gen. Robert E. Lee ought to be shot. The president supposedly replied, "Shoot Lee! If they do, they better shoot Abe Lincoln as well" (26).

The information offices eventually found use for another aspect of the sixteenth president's legacy. In 1968 the stern but forbearing visage from the Lincoln Memorial was reproduced on the cover of *To Insure Domestic Tranquility* (Department of the Army Pamphlet 360–81). The pamphlet was intended to prepare troops to control antiwar protesters and so, on the front cover, invoked the words of a Lincoln speech: "There is no grievance that is a fit object of redress by mob law" (Lincoln, "Address to the Young Men's Lyceum of Springfield, Illinois," 27 January 1838, reprinted in *Selected Speeches and Writings*, compiled by Don E. Fehrenbacher [New York: Vintage Books/Library of America, 1992], 18).

98. Department of the Army, *Duty—Honor—Country*, Pamphlet 16–12, 10–11.

99. FitzGerald, *America Revised*, 156.

100. Richard J. Ford III and Malik Edwards interviews in Terry, *Bloods*, 14, 40.

101. Dudziak, *Cold War Civil Rights*, 58 [State Department], 49 [USIA].

102. Bell, *The End of Ideology*, 400 ["all-inclusive . . . "], 405 ["terrible simplifiers"].

5. Morale and the Muzzle

1. Ashland P. Burchwell, SP4, USA, in a letter quoted by Maj. Archibald E. Roberts, USA, "Comments on 'Summary of Interview,'" Report of Interview with Investigators, Special Subcommittee Senate Armed Services Committee, 13 December 1961, tab A, file: Speeches and Related Papers, Archibald E. Roberts Papers, USAMHI, 22.

2. Col. James H. Skeldon, General Staff (GS), Chief of Staff, "Morale and Welfare: Citizenship in Service program," Training Directive 3, Headquarters, Twenty-fourth Infantry Division, 18 April 1960, tab B, file: Speeches and Related Papers, tab B, Archibald E. Roberts Papers, USAMHI, 1.

3. Skeldon, "Morale and Welfare," 1–2, Annex A.

4. Skeldon, "Morale and Welfare," Annex A.

5. Skeldon, "Morale and Welfare," 3, and OCINFO inclusion item 2 in Roberts, "Comments on 'Summary of Interview.'"

6. Roberts, "Comments on 'Summary of Interview,'" 7.

7. Roberts, "Comments on 'Summary of Interview,'" 10.

8. Col. James H. Skeldon, GS, Chief of Staff, "Education and Training: 24th Infantry Division Pro-Blue Program," Circular Number 350–20, Headquarters, Twenty-fourth Division, 4 January 1961, file: Vol. I, Section 1, Archibald E. Roberts Papers, USAMHI, 1.

9. Skeldon, "Education and Training," 3–4.

10. Skeldon, "Education and Training," 5–6.

11. Skeldon, "Education and Training," 6.

12. Skeldon, "Education and Training," 2.

13. Skeldon, "Education and Training," 2.

14. Although the *Overseas Weekly* broke the story in their April 16 issue, it must have hit the newsstands several days before that date because the *New York Times* carried the story on the 14th (Sydney Gruson, "Birch Unit Ideas Put to U.S. Troops," *New York Times*, 14 April 1961, 1, 19; "Walker Is Relieved of Command While Army Checks Birch Ties," *New York Times*, 18 April 1961, 1, 24; and "Army's Handling of General Walker's Case Disturbs Troops in Europe," *New York Times*, 21 September 1961, 20).

15. Gruson, Birch Unit Ideas Put to U.S. Troops," 19; "Army's Handling of General Walker's Case," 24.

16. John W. Finney, "Walker Asserts He Is Scapegoat of 'No-Win' Policy," *New York Times*, 5 April 1962, 17.

17. Reeves, *President Kennedy*, 108.

18. Roberts, "Comments on 'Summary of Interview'," 11–12. The anticommunist libraries were to include: Hoover, *Masters of Deceit*; Kinkead, *In Every War But One*; Welch, *The Life of John Birch*; Fox, *The Pentagon Case*; and several other tracts on Soviet propaganda and communist subversion in the United States.

On the growth of the John Birch Society, see McGirr, *Suburban Warriors*, 75–76, 78. On Welch's theories, see Westin, "The John Birch Society," 206–7.

19. Roberts, "Comments on 'Summary of Interview'," 11–12, OCINFO inclusion item 8 [claim of authorship], 13 [joined JBS].

A month after the story first broke, Gene Grove of the *New York Post* infiltrated a meeting of the John Birch Society in New York, where, he reported, a member confided to the group that Roberts was secretly working with the society (Gene Grove, "Inside the John Birch Society," *New York Post*, 23 May 1961, 1 [daily magazine]).

20. Admonishment, which can be administered orally, is a lighter form of punishment than a reprimand, though Walker was through in any case (Department of the Army statement, 12 June 1961, tab A, file: [untitled], Archibald E. Roberts Papers, USAMHI).

21. Department of the Army statement, 12 June 1961, and "Evaluation of 24th Infantry Division 'Pro-Blue' Program," included in OCINFO fact sheet on Maj. Archibald E. Roberts, file: Report on Major William E. Mayer and Major A. E. Roberts, Archibald E. Roberts Papers, USAMHI.

22. Gen. Charles H. Bonesteel III, USA (ret.), interview by Lt. Col. Robert St. Louis, Project 73-2, Vol. II, United States Army Military History Institute Senior Officers Oral History Program, 1973, Charles H. Bonesteel Papers, USAMHI, 274–75. On the other hand, Roberts, as well as team member Ashland P. Burchwell, SP4, claimed that reassignments gutted the program.

23. Welch, *The Life of John Birch*, 71, 90.

24. Use of the term *muzzle* to mean curtailing an officer's public speech predated the Kennedy administration, as did the practice itself. During the administration of President Eisenhower, the *Army Times* complained that the Department of Defense had illogically diminished the OCINFO public information staff in order to "muzzle" defiant admirals ("Odd Way to Kill a Cat," *Army Times*, 9 April 1955, 1, file: Clippings of Eisenhower's Censorship Policies 1955, Richard H. Merrick Papers, USAMHI).

25. Cabell Phillips, "Right-Wing Officers Worrying Pentagon," *New York Times*, 18 June 1961, 56.

26. For a comprehensive analysis of the Cold War seminars, see Bogle, *The Pentagon's Battle for the American Mind*, chap. 5.

27. Phillips, "Right-Wing Officers Worrying Pentagon."

28. Phillips, "Right-Wing Officers Worrying Pentagon."

29. "Summary of Major William E. Mayer's Activities and Department of the Army Position Concerning These Activities," file: Report on Major William E. Mayer and Major A. E. Roberts, Archibald E. Roberts Papers, USAMHI, 5–6.

30. The title of the second film referred to student demonstrators' goal of abolishing the House Committee on Un-American Activities (Phillips, "Right-Wing Officers Worrying Pentagon," 56).

31. Phillips, "Right-Wing Officers Worrying Pentagon"; *Operation: Abolition*, 45 min. (San Francisco: House Un-American Activities Committee, 1960).

32. "Forgery by Film," *Washington Post*, 26 November 1960, A8; Maj. Gen. William W. Quinn, GS, CINFO, memo re: status of "Operation: Abolition" to Information Officers, major commands, 19 May 1961, file 404-12 Command Information Papers, "Operation: Abolition," CINFO Papers, USAMHI.

33. As late as 1965 OCINFO was still receiving complaints that *Operation: Abolition* was either being shown or restricted from being shown. For example, SP4 Richard D. Kennedy prompted a congressional inquiry when he wrote to Representative James Roosevelt (Democrat, California) that he had seen the film at Fort Eustis, Virginia, and that "there are two uncomplimentary references to you in this picture . . . I wonder what you think of this film and if you are aware that it is obviously part of the Troop Information program" (SP 4 Richard D. Kennedy, Fort Eustis, Virginia, to the Honorable James Roosevelt, U.S. Congressman, California, 18 November 1963; see also George D. Barker, East Point, Georgia, to Richard B. Russell, U.S. Senate, 7 September 1964; Charles Lan-

dau, Antioch College Union, Yellow Springs, Ohio, to Robert S. McNamara, Secretary of Defense, 21 February 1965, file: 404–12 Command Information Papers "Operation: Abolition," CINFO Papers, USAMHI).

34. Miller, *Teaching about Communism*, 251–54, 261 [Florida]; 263 [New York], 274 [Tennessee], 276 [American Bar Association], 278 [National Catholic Education Association].

35. Bogle, *The Pentagon's Battle for the American Mind*, 186.

36. "Army R&D Chief Trudeau Testifies on Space Directive, Then Writes a Letter," *Army-Navy-Air Force Journal*, 25 March 1961, 3; U.S. Congress, Representative O. C. Fisher of Texas, "Notorious *Overseas Weekly* Attacks Anticommunist Pro-Blue Americanism Program of Gen. Edwin A. Walker," *Congressional Record*, 87th Cong., 2d sess. (24 May 1961), 8849–51. Fisher, a Democrat, was Walker's congressman.

37. Marshall, "Walker Miscast Catalyst in 'Muzzling' Controversy," *Washington Post*, 11 February 1962, E2.

38. Marshall, "Walker Miscast Catalyst in 'Muzzling' Controversy," E2. The major to whom Marshall refers is probably himself, though it would not be accurate to say that his guidance material was all that was needed to direct TI policy throughout the war; see chapter 1 (Special Services Division, *The War in Outline*).

39. "Decorous Inquisitor: John Cornelius Stennis," *New York Times*, 24 January 1962, 14.

40. J. Strom Thurmond, "The Walker Case Issue," *New York Times*, 14 January 1962, 78–79 (magazine); Jack Raymond, "Pentagon to Back Censorship Role," *New York Times*, 14 January 1962, 42.

41. "Eisenhower Backs Speeches on Reds by Military Men," *New York Times*, 24 January 1962, 14.

42. "Eisenhower Backs Speeches on Reds by Military Men," 14.

43. Jack Raymond, "Burke and White for Speech Curb," *New York Times*, 26 January 1962, 8; "Pentagon Uneasy over Issue of Political Role of the Military," *New York Times*, 28 January 1962, 1, 58.

44. "Bradley and Nimitz Back Limitations on Speeches, *New York Times*, 30 February 1962, 2; "Navy's Law Chief Assails Speeches," *New York Times*, 26 February 1962, 10.

45. "'Hate Enemy' Idea Opposed by Shoup," *New York Times*, 31 January 1962, 11; Tom Scanlan, "Probe Pace Is Pedestrian," *Army Times*, 3 February 1962, 1.

46. "Quiz of Marines Angers Senators," *New York Times*, 9 February 1962, 10.

47. "Quiz of Marines Angers Senators," *New York Times*; James Reston, "What If Intelligence Tests Spread to Congress?" *New York Times*, 9 February 1962, 28.

48. Jack Raymond, "President Wary on Censor Issue," *New York Times*, 4 February 1962, 34.

49. "Wielder of a Red Pencil," *New York Times*, 9 February 1962, 10; "Kennedy Invokes Executive Privilege," *New York Times*, 9 February 1962, 1, 10. Despite the effort to shield the censors, they were still subjected to a smear campaign by radical rightists. According to a newsletter circulated by Arch E. Roberts, all fourteen were either communists, alcoholics, or "perverts" (excerpt from Edward Hunter, *Tactics* 1, no. 12, December 1964, that Roberts sent to OCINFO, tab B, file: [untitled], Archibald E. Roberts Papers, USAMHI).

50. U.S. Congress, Senator Strom Thurmond of South Carolina, "Senator Thurmond

Presents Anti-Communist Items Censored from Military Statements," *Congressional Record*, 87th Cong., 2d sess. (19 February 1962), 2471-91.

51. Senator Bartlett alone added the caveat that officers ought not participate in Cold War seminars at all since they were a distraction from the military mission (Cabell Phillips, "Panel Discounts 'Gag' on Military," *New York Times*, 26 October 1962, 7).

52. U.S. Congress, Committee on Armed Services, *Military Cold War Education and Speech Review Policies*, pt. 3, 1086 [Muzyk testimony]; pt. 4, 1878 [bibliography items].

53. Department of Defense, *Catalog of Information Materials*, 48, 50; *Russia*, 24 min., Armed Forces Information Film 87, 1958; *Brazil*, 15 min., Armed Forces Information Film 33, 1953; *Portugal*, 18 min., Armed Forces Information Film 29, 18 min., 1952.

54. U.S. Congress, *Military Cold War Education and Speech Review Policies*, pt. 3, 1090.

55. U.S. Congress, *Military Cold War Education and Speech Review Policies*, pt. 3, 973.

56. U.S. Congress, *Military Cold War Education and Speech Review Policies*, pt. 4, 1552 [Stennis questions Fitch], 1584 ["public relations"], 1570 [Fitch on *Democracy versus Communism*], 1592-95 [*The Nation*], 1862, 1873 [Weigland testimony], 1569 [Fitch testimony]; Colegrove, *Democracy versus Communism* series, nos. 1-11; "Scope and Content Note," Kenneth W. Colegrove Papers, Herbert Hoover Presidential Library and Museum Web site, www.hoover.archives.gov./index.html (accessed 1 January 2005).

57. U.S. Congress, *Military Cold War Education and Speech Review Policies*, pt. 3, 906 [Runge testimony], 912 [Katzenbach testimony], 919 ["guidance"], 921.

58. U.S. Congress, *Military Cold War Education and Speech Review Policies*, pt. 3, 926.

59. U.S. Congress, *Military Cold War Education and Speech Review Policies*, pt. 3, 1072 [Dodge not apprehensive], 1075 [centralization], 1064 [Korean culture lessons].

60. U.S. Congress, *Military Cold War Education and Speech Review Policies*, pt. 3, 1089 [*Communist Target—Youth*], 968, 970 [Runge on controversy]; Department of Defense, *Communist Target—Youth*, 31 min., Armed Forces Information Film 116, 1962.

61. U.S. Congress, *Military Cold War Education and Speech Review Policies*, pt. 3, 992-99.

62. On Militant Liberty, see chapter 4. U.S. Congress, *Military Cold War Education and Speech Review Policies*, pt. 3, 989-90 [Broger's background], 1033-35 [Broger on Militant Liberty].

63. U.S. Congress, *Military Cold War Education and Speech Review Policies*, pt. 3, 1029.

64. FitzGerald, *America Revised*, 121.

65. U.S. Congress, *Military Cold War Education and Speech Review Policies*, pt. 3, 1077.

66. U.S. Congress, *Military Cold War Education and Speech Review Policies*, pt. 3, 1111.

67. U.S. Congress, *Military Cold War Education and Speech Review Policies*, pt. 3, 1082.

68. U.S. Congress, *Military Cold War Education and Speech Review Policies*, pt. 3, 1097.

69. U.S. Congress, *Military Cold War Education and Speech Review Policies*, pt. 3, 1063.

70. U.S. Congress, *Military Cold War Education and Speech Review Policies*, pt. 3, 1119–20.

71. U.S. Congress, *Military Cold War Education and Speech Review Policies*, pt. 3, 1121–22.

72. U.S. Congress, *Military Cold War Education and Speech Review Policies*, pt. 3, 1123.

73. U.S. Congress, *Military Cold War Education and Speech Review Policies*, pt. 3, 1124–25.

74. U.S. Congress, *Military Cold War Education and Speech Review Policies*, pt. 3, 1137.

75. U.S. Congress, *Military Cold War Education and Speech Review Policies*, pt. 4, 1548.

76. U.S. Congress, *Military Cold War Education and Speech Review Policies*, pt. 4, 1447 [Walker on Yarmolinsky]; John W. Finney, "Walker Asserts He Is Scapegoat of 'No-Win' Policy," 1, 17.

77. Reeves, *President Kennedy*, 360, 364; Knebel and Bailey, *Seven Days in May*. Grimly, the antagonists were linked one more time when seven months before he assassinated Kennedy, Lee Harvey Oswald attempted to kill Edwin A. Walker. On April 10, 1963, with the same rifle he used to shoot the president, Oswald fired at Walker through a window in the general's Texas home but only grazed him.

78. John Frankenheimer, dir., *Seven Days in May* (b & w, 118 min., Paramount and Warner Bros., 1964); Stanley Kubrick, dir., *Dr. Strangelove or: How I Stopped Worrying and Learned to Love the Bomb* (b & w, 94 min., Columbia Pictures, 1964); George, *Red Alert* (published in Britain under the pseudonym Peter Bryant as *Two Hours to Doom*); John Frankenheimer, *The Manchurian Candidate* (b & w, 126 min., United Artists, 1962); Nash, *The Conservative Intellectual Movement in America since 1945*, 293.

79. Roberts, "Comments on 'Summary of Interview'," 25, and "In Defense of General Walker" [copy of undated mailing Roberts sent to numerous recipients in 1961 and 1962], tab B, file: [untitled], Archibald E. Roberts Papers, USAMHI.

80. Roberts, "Address of Major Arch E. Roberts, MSC, United States Army" [transcript of speech to Daughters of the American Revolution chapter in Washington, DC, 19 April 1962], file: Section 3, Vol. IV, Archibald E. Roberts Papers, USAMHI, 1–5.

81. Col. Robert B. Smith, Chief, Troop Information Division, [memo re: Roberts' suit] to Deputy CINFO, 26 September 1962, tab B, file: [untitled], Archibald E. Roberts Papers, USAMHI; "How Many More Are There?" *Washington Post*, 22 April 1962, E4.

82. Roberts, "Why Your Soldier Son Serves under the Command of a Soviet Communist," self-published newsletter, May 1965, tab B, file: [untitled], Archibald E. Roberts Papers, USAMHI and "The Anatomy of a Revolution," *The Woman Constitutionalist*, 3 August 1968, 1; Jack Raymond, "Army Is Ordered to Reinstate Major Allied with Gen. Walker," *New York Times*, 19 June 1964, 11.

6. Information's Impossible War

1. U.S. Congress, *Report of Senate Special Preparedness Subcommittee*, 87th Cong., 2d sess. (19 October 1962), 2–3.

2. U.S. Congress, *Report of Senate Special Preparedness Subcommittee*, 4.

3. U.S. Congress, *Report of Senate Special Preparedness Subcommittee*, 7.

4. U.S. Congress, *Report of Senate Special Preparedness Subcommittee*, 2 ["heritage"], 5–6.

5. U.S. Congress, *Report of Senate Special Preparedness Subcommittee*, 7.

6. Robert S. McNamara, Secretary of Defense, "Advisory Committee to the Secretary of Defense on non-Military Instruction," 2 February 1962, file: [untitled], tab A, Archibald E. Roberts Papers, USAMHI.

7. "Bendetsen Report," draft, file: 404–12 Command Information Reference Papers, CINFO Papers, USAMHI, 2, 4.

8. "Bendetsen Report," 50.

9. "Bendetsen Report," 7.

10. "Bendetsen Report," 6–7, 13 [quotation].

11. Colegrove, *What Is Communism?*

12. "Bendetsen Report," 14. On Capra and the Signal Corps, see chapter 1.

13. "Bendetsen Report," 15–17.

14. "Bendetsen Report," 8, 19.

15. *United States Government Organizational Manual 1968–69*, 129.

16. Department of the Army, Army Regulation 360–81, Command Information, 20 April 1964.

17. Despite the creation of DINFOS, the Army Information School remained in operation under the Continental Army Command (hereafter CONARC). OCINFO Memorandum, "Input for CINFO's Speech to the Advanced Public Relations Course at Wisconsin," 17 June 1964, tab C, file: Advanced Public Relations Course, University of Wisconsin, file: Speeches, 1963–1968, George V. Underwood Papers, USAMHI, 1.

18. "Input for CINFO's Speech to the Advanced Public Relations Course at Wisconsin," 2.

19. OCINFO Memorandum, "University of Wisconsin Summer Session, June 19, 1964," tab B, file: Advanced Public Relations Course, University of Wisconsin, George V. Underwood Papers, USAMHI.

20. Maj. Gen. George V. Underwood Jr., USA, "Remarks at the Army Commanders' Conference," 1 May 1963, tab D, file: Speeches, 1 March 1963–1 December 1965, George V. Underwood Papers, USAMHI, 11–12, 15.

21. Underwood, "Statement to 6th Army information Conference," 1 March 1963, tab B, file: Speeches 1 March 1963–1 December 1965, George V. Underwood Papers, USAMHI, 1–2; "Input for CINFO's Speech to the Advanced Course at Wisconsin," 3.

22. Underwood, "Problems and Prospects for Information Personnel" (graduation address to DINFOS, 30 April 1965), tab AC, file: Speeches 1 March 1963–1 December 1965, George V. Underwood Papers, USAMHI, 12–13.

23. Underwood, "Remarks to the Army Commanders' Conference," 1 December 1965, tab AJ, file: Speeches 1 March 1963–1 December 1965, George V. Underwood Papers, USAMHI, 7–8.

24. Underwood, "Remarks to the Army Commanders' Conference," 11.

25. See in particular Krepinevich, *The Army and Vietnam*.

26. Department of Defense, *The U.S. Fighting Man's Code*, Pamphlet Gen-28 (Washington DC: U.S. Government Printing Office, 1967), 42, 44, 86. Another POW pamphlet,

Barbed Wire Command, was even less useful, featuring as it did optimistic drawings of prisoners playing basketball, woodworking, and teaching their own classes (Department of the Army, *Troop Topics: Barbed Wire Command*, 8).

27. Cortright, *Soldiers in Revolt*, 35–39 [open mutinies], 44 [assassinations]; Lewy, "The American Experience in Vietnam," 96–97 [assassinations]; Hersh, *My Lai 4*, [civilians murdered].

28. Wesbrook, *Political Training in the United States Army*, 6–7, 48 [quotation]; Moskos, *The American Enlisted Man*; Stouffer, *The American Soldier*, vol. 2, *Combat and Its Aftermath*.

29. Moskos, *The American Enlisted Man*, 146–48.

30. Cortright, *Soldiers in Revolt*, 53–54 [coffee houses], 55 [newspapers].

31. Lewy, "The American Experience in Vietnam," 94, 101–3.

32. Department of Defense, *A Pocket Guide to Viet-Nam*, 19–20 [Ho Chi Minh], 63 ["Under this Constitution . . . "].

33. Department of Defense, *A Pocket Guide to Viet-Nam*, 31–32; Gibson, *The Perfect War*, 82–83; Young, *The Vietnam Wars 1945–1990*, 96.

34. Department of Defense, *Armed Forces Information and Education Catalog of Current Information Materials*; Department of the Army, *Troop Topics: Our Mission in Vietnam*, 2–3.

35. Department of the Army, *Troop Topics: Our Mission in Vietnam*, 7, 9.

36. Department of Defense, *Know Your Enemy: The Viet Cong*, 2, 7, 22.

37. Department of the Army, *Current Information Materials Catalog*, 20–21, 28–29; Department of the Army, *Officer's Call: Theirs to Reason Why*. To persuade officers to hold Commander's Calls, the authors invented a prestigious history of the practice: "On July 9, 1776, General George Washington had called his troops together to hear that the Continental Congress had declared independence from Great Britain. This announcement was 'the first formal Commander's Call,'" (6–7).

38. Department of the Army, *Troop Topics: The United States Army in South Vietnam*, 7, 10.

39. Department of the Army, "Incident at Son My," 57–59.

40. Brig. Gen. Robert B. Smith, USA, Deputy CINFO, "A New Direction in Army Information," 24 July 1968, file 404–12 Reorganization, Smith Committee, CINFO Papers, USAMHI, sec. F, 1, 4.

41. Smith, "A New Direction in Army Information," 5, 7 [quotation], 10.

42. Smith, "A New Direction in Army Information," 11.

43. John E. Valasquez, VN 023–03–11, Vietnam Veterans Surveys (hereafter VVS), USAMHI; Malik Edwards, interview in Terry, *Bloods*, 7–8; and Albert C. Brown Jr., VN 330–02–03, VVS, USAMHI.

44. Robert Rizzardi VN 168–02–6, VVS, USAMHI.

45. Landing, *The Only War We Had*, 1; Stephen A. Howard, Arthur E. "Gene" Woodley Jr., Joseph B. Anderson Jr., and Robert L. Mountain interviews in Terry, *Bloods*, 123, 245, 226, 180; Ebert, *A Life in a Year*, 11.

46. David Ross and Jan Barry interviews in Santoli, *Everything We Had*, 44, 8; Robert T. Daniels interview in Terry, *Bloods*, 237.

47. Ross interview in Santoli, *Everything We Had*, 38; Michael McGregor, VN 035–03–09; Arthur M. Johns, VN 212–02–6; Steve G. Lewis VN 023–03–10, VVS, USAMHI.

48. Frederick J. Carll, VN 296–02–06; James Larose, VN 0350–03–12, Peter L. Cullen, VN 294–02–03, VVS, USAMHI.

49. Allen Cherin VN 056–03–01, Robert A. Macon VN 056–03–02, Marvin Mathiak VN 006–03–01, Charles L. Pettyjohn VN 037–03–03, VVS, USAMHI.

50. George Abernathy VN 330–02–03, George T. Lacomb VN 016–03–07, Gary Martens VN 212–2–02, VVS, USAMHI.

51. Moskos, *The American Enlisted Man*, 97; Brennan, *Brennan's War*, 5 [From that lecture . . .], 2 [I never . . .]; Abernathy VN 330–02–03, Richard E. Ellis VN 330–02–05, VVS, USAMHI.

52. Col. Charles R. Thomas Jr., USA, Chief, Command Information Division (hereafter CID), "Troop-Community Relations Orientation Program," 5 January 1968, file: 404–03 Troop-Community Relations Orientation Plan, CINFO Papers, USAMHI.

53. Landing, *The Only War We Had*, 68.

54. Baritz, *Backfire*, 7.

55. John M. Mobius, "Troop Community Relations in Thailand," Second Quarterly Progress Report, 1 December 1967, file: 404–03 Troop-Community Relations Orientation Plan, CINFO Papers, USAMHI, 1–2.

56. Mobius, "Troop Community Relations in Thailand," 28, 51.

57. Mobius, "Troop Community Relations in Thailand," 31 ["filth," "understand"], 35 ["leaving," "superior attitude"].

58. Eighth U.S. Army, *Eighth U.S. Army Cold War Education and Action Program*, Pamphlet 600–205, 1970, file: 413–02 Information for the Armed Forces 1970 Planning File, CINFO Papers, USAMHI, 16–17, 21, 24.

59. Paul Spector, Troy C. Paris, Robert L. Humphrey, Joel B. Aronson, and Charles F. Williams, "Troop-Community Relations Research in Korea: Technical Report," International Research Institute, April, 1969, file: "TDA," CINFO Papers, USAMHI, 4–5, 12; Mobius, "Troop Community Relations in Thailand," 16; Gibson, *The Perfect War*, 262; Landing, *The Only War We Had*, 111; Yezzo, *A G.I.'s Vietnam War Diary*, 21 April 1969 entry.

60. Spector et al., "Troop-Community Relations Research in Korea," 4–8.

61. Spector et al., "Troop-Community Relations Research in Korea, 14.

62. Spector et al., "Troop-Community Relations Research in Korea, 10–12. One way to activate values was by appealing to popular culture. In one session, troops heard a soldier tell an affecting story about the guilt he felt for not defending South Korean allies from bullies in his unit. He compared his situation to one that typically arose in John Wayne movies. He lamented that as a viewer he had identified with the hero who stood up to the small-minded townspeople, but in real life, "Suddenly no longer is any one Big John, the rugged defender of the down-and-outers. We're all just like the disgusting crowd back in the picture" (*Eighth U.S. Army Cold War Education and Action Program*, 48).

63. Spector et al., "Troop-Community Relations Research in Korea," v, 29–31.

64. Spector et al., "Troop-Community Relations Research in Korea," 16.

65. Thomas to Lt. Col. Clinton D. Regelin, USA, Chief, CID, HQ, US MACV, 5 May 1966, file: 404–03 Troop-Community Relations Orientation Plan, CINFO Papers, USAMHI; Maj. Gen. F. W. Boye, USA, Chief Legislative Liaison, to the Honorable Stuart Symington, United States Senate, 24 May 1966, file: 404–03 Troop-Community Relations Orientation Plan, CINFO Papers, USAMHI; Lewis W. Walt, USMC, Commanding General, III Ma-

rine Amphibious Force, Military Assistance Command, Vietnam (MACV) to Charles H. Bonesteel III, USA, Commanding General, Eighth Army and United States Forces, Korea, file: 404–03 Troop-Community Relations Orientation Plan, CINFO Papers, USAMHI.

66. Thomas to Regelin, 5 May 1966.

67. Spector et al., "Troop-Community Relations Research in Korea," 23.

68. Allen Cherin VN 056–03–01, and Phillip C. Zemke VN 297–02–02, VVS, USAMHI.

69. The official name was Armed Forces Radio and Television until June 1969, when it became American Forces Radio and Television, apparently because that is how operators in the field had always referred to it (Col. Lane Carlson, USA, acting Chief, CID, "Memo for the Record," 10 June 1969, file: U.S. Army CINFO Reading File Plans Branch, Radio and Television, 1 January 1964–30 June 1969, CINFO Papers, USAMHI).

70. Brig. Gen. Winant Sidle, USA, CINFO, "Draft DOD Instructions 5120.20 American Forces Radio and Television," 22 June 1970, tab: 1–9 Apr, file: 2, CINFO Papers, USAMHI.

71. Sidle, "Draft DOD Instructions 5120.20 American Forces Radio and Television."

72. Roger T. Kelley, Assistant Secretary of Defense, Manpower and Reserve Affairs, to Melvin R. Laird, Secretary of Defense, 26 April 1970, file 401–70 Information for the Armed Forces 70, CINFO Papers, USAMHI.

73. Maj. Gen. Wendell J. Coats, CINFO, to Kelley, 15 April 1969; Memorandum, Office of Information for the Armed Forces to American Forces Radio and Television Stations, 29 February 1969, file: U.S. Army CINFO Reading File Plans Branch, Radio and Television, 1 January 1964–30 June 1969, CINFO Papers, USAMHI.

74. Sidle, "22 July Meeting of Armed Forces Advisory Council," 22 July 1970, file: 103–03 Reading File—July–August–September 1970, CINFO Papers, USAMHI.

75. 1st Lt. Eugene A. Kroupa, USA, CID, "Review of the films BLACK AND WHITE: UPTIGHT; BLACK SOLDIER; AND BLACK HISTORY: LOST, STOLEN OR STRAYED," 27 August 1970, file: 103–03 Reading File—July–August–September 1970, CINFO Papers, USAMHI.

76. Coffey, "African American Personnel in U.S. Forces in Vietnam," 5; Cortright, *Soldiers in Revolt*, 39–42; Sidle to Gen. William C. Westmoreland, USA, Chief of Staff, 4 November 1970, file: 103–3 Reading File October–November–December, CINFO Papers, USAMHI.

77. Col. Lane Carlson, USA, Chief, CID, "Field Evaluation on 'In the Name of Peace,'" 28 August 1970, file: 103–03 Reading File—Jul–Aug–Sep 1970, CINFO Papers, USAMHI.

78. Carlson, "Field Evaluation on 'In the Name of Peace,'".

79. On the controversy surrounding *Operation: Abolition*, see chapter 5.

80. Col. Walter N. Moore, USA, Chief, CID, to Sidle, "IAF Use of CI Funds," 28 September 1970, file: 103–03 Reading File—July–August–September 1970, CINFO Papers, USAMHI.

81. Lt. Col. Robert L. Chick, OCINFO Program Support Branch, "Minutes of Inter-Service Meeting," 3 September 1970, file 413–02 Information for the Armed Forces—Meetings 70, CINFO Papers, USAMHI.

82. Col. Bennett L. Jackson, USA, Chief, CID, "AFIE Conference on Civil Rights Materials," file: 404–12 Command Information Reference Papers File: Civil Rights Materials—Miscellaneous, CINFO Papers, USAMHI.

83. Moore to John C. Broger, Director, OIAF, 7 December 1970, file 103–3 Reading File October–November–December 70, CINFO Papers, USAMHI.

84. Jackson, "Information Plan—Equality of Treatment and Opportunity for Military Personnel," 16 July 1964, file: 404–12 Command Information Papers File: Civil Rights Materials—Miscellaneous, CINFO Papers, USAMHI, 3; CONARC Command Information Branch, "The Black Soldier in History," news release, 13 July 1970, file: CONARC, CINFO Papers, USAMHI [patronizing language].

85. OCINFO Memorandum, "Command Information Division Notes on the Film: 'Youth Communications,'" 27 November 1970, file: 103–3 Reading File Oct–Nov–Dec 70, CINFO Papers, USAMHI. The armed forces were not the only ones grasping for means to talk to the so-called Now Generation. The DOD managed to sell several copies of *Youth Communications* to churches and civic groups.

86. Young, *The Vietnam Wars*, 197–98.

87. "The Fruits of Marijuana," draft script, 1970, file: CONARC, CINFO Papers, USAMHI, 2, 4, 17, 13, 15, 19.

88. Carlson, "Students for Pentagon Forum," 20 July 1970, file: Reading File July–August–September 1970, CINFO Papers, USAMHI. Despite being handpicked to lob batting-practice questions, the Princeton students rose to the occasion and pressed the generals about war crimes, detention camps, and news censorship (Brig. Gen. Bertram Gorwitz, acting CINFO, to Westmoreland, "Evaluation of Pentagon Forum," 3 August 1970, file: Reading File July–August–September 1970, CINFO Papers, USAMHI).

89. "Army Newspapers," CINFO Fact Sheet, 1970, file: Table of Distribution, 1970, CINFO Papers, USAMHI.

90. Moskos, *The American Enlisted Man*, 102–3; John E. Flanagan VN 197–02–01, Gerald F. Mazur VN 219–02–06.

91. Many issues of *The Old Reliable* are available on line at the "2nd Battalion, 60th Infantry" Web site, www.2–60Inf.com/ornews.htm. For examples of pieces that emphasize American ingenuity and aggression, see "R&R Proves Fatal to Five Viet Cong," 6 March 1968: 2; or "Viet Cong Nabbed in ID Switch," 8 January 1969: 3; for a piece on deserters, "Hoi Chanh Escapes Enemy Ahead of Death Sentence," 1 January 1969, 8; and for an example of the Tet Offensive coverage, "My Tho Hospital Overflows with VC Victims," 21 February 1968: 6.

92. "Pot Smokers Are Undependable People," and "Know and Respect Vietnamese Culture, Customs, and Tradition," *The Cavalair*, 8 December 1968: 2; "Gifts to the Vietnamese Can Hurt Relations," *The Cavalair*, 11 December 1968: 3, from the collection of the Vietnam Era Educational Center of the New Jersey Vietnam Veterans' Memorial Foundation, Holmdel NJ (hereafter, VVNJMF Collection).

This warning notwithstanding, the December 25, 1968, issue of the *Cavalair* featured a photo spread of an American soldier in a frightening plastic Santa Claus mask distributing presents to Vietnamese children (*The Cavalair*, 25 December 1968, VVNJMF Collection).

93. "The Nature of Liberty," *Monmouth Message* (11 January 1968): 13; "Recommended Reading," *Monmouth Message* (22 August 1968): 13; ["Nearly all"] *Monmouth Message* (25 July 1968): 13; ["domination"], *Monmouth Message* (5 December 1968): 13; [film schedule] *Monmouth Message* (19 September 1968): 1, Communications-Electronics Command and Fort Monmouth Historical Archives, Fort Monmouth NJ.

94. Ralph L. Godwin VN 352–02–02, Fred Waterman VN 176–02–11, Raymond R. Furnish VN 301–02–04, VVS, USAMHI.

95. Maj. Joseph E. Burlas Jr., USA, Army Newspapers Branch, CID, to Sidle, 15 Sep-

tember 1970, file: 103–03 Reading File—July–August–September 1970, CINFO Papers, USAMHI.

96. Noam Chomsky, "The Manufacture of Consent," an address given at the Community Church of Boston, December 9, 1984, excerpted in *The Chomsky Reader*, 131–32.

97. Moore to Sidle, "Items for your round table discussion with IOs, 3 December," 2 December 1970, file: 401–07 Conference Reference Papers 1970, CINFO Papers, USAMHI.

98. Whitfield, *The Culture of the Cold War*, 154–55 ["custodian"]; Curtin, *Redeeming the Wasteland*, 18.

99. Curtin, *Redeeming the Wasteland*, 254.

100. Maj. Bradley S. Greenberg, Plans Branch, CID, "Study Findings," 29 July 1970, file: 103–03 Reading File—July–August–September 1970, CINFO Papers, USAMHI.

101. Col. Earl S. Browning Jr., USA, to Broger, "Report on Trip to Europe, Africa, and Middle East," 30 June 1969, file: 401–06, Staff Visits and Reports, 1970, CINFO Papers, USAMHI, 11, 15, 20. The AFRTS manager in Libya was nothing compared to its crew in Iran: "The station manager arrived with a record of suicidal tendencies and lost little time before making another attempt. . . . One of the announcers has been charged with desertion after creating many problems by his insistence on associating with drug addicts and other disreputable elements in Tehran" (p. 22).

102. Kovic, *Born on the Fourth of July*, 44.

103. U.S. Congress, Senate, Senator J. William Fulbright of Arkansas, *Congressional Record*, 92d Cong., 1st sess. (5 December 1969), S15807.

104. U.S. Congress, *Congressional Record*, S158011. On the government's use of the Gulf of Tonkin incident to escalate the war, see Moïse, *Tonkin Gulf and the Escalation of the Vietnam War*.

105. Yarmolinsky, *The Military Establishment*, 195–96; *The Green Berets*, dir. John Wayne, color, 141 min., Warner Bros., 1968.

106. Fulbright, *Old Myths and New Realities*, 116. For a detailed examination of Fulbright's many skirmishes with the military establishment, see Woods, *Fulbright*.

107. Fulbright, *The Pentagon Propaganda Machine*, 71, 73–74 [Speechmaker Kits].

108. Fulbright, *The Pentagon Propaganda Machine*, 62.

109. Moore to Sidle, "Staff Study on Audio-Visual Support for CID," 10 November 1970, file: 103–03 Reading File October–November–December 1970, CINFO Papers, USAMHI.

110. Col. Pershing Tousley, USA, Chief, CID, to Sidle and Gorwitz, 26 February 1970, file: Reading File: January–March, 1970, CINFO Papers, USAMHI.

111. "Annual Historical Summary, Office of the Chief of Information, 1 July 1968–30 June 1969," file: Historical Summary, CINFO Papers, USAMHI, 9; "Annual Historical Summary, OCINFO, 1 July 1969–30 June 1970," file: Historical Summary, CINFO Papers, USAMHI, 6–7, 52; Moore to Sidle, "IAF Reductions," 6 October 1970, file: 401–70 Information for the Armed Forces 1970, CINFO Papers, USAMHI.

112. Tousley, "FY 1971 Command Operating Budget," file: Reading File: January–March, 1970, CINFO Papers, USAMHI.

113. Cortright, *Soldiers in Revolt*, 67–68 [Armed Forces Day], 11–13 [desertion and absenteeism]; Lt. Col. Vincent R. Tocci, USAF, "Understanding the War in Southeast Asia, *Commanders Call*, 58–65 [quotation, 59].

114. OCINFO Memorandum, "Questions for BG Sidle, CINFO, Before the Defense Appropriations Committee," 11 June 1970, file: Reading File April–May–June, 1970, CINFO Papers, USAMHI.

115. One chief wrote: "The memento, commonly referred to as 'the Dust Catcher,' which is presented to departing members of OCINFO, lacks most of the qualities which might make it cherished by its recipients" (Col. John A. Stewart, USA, Chief, Policy, Plans, Programs Division, to Tousley, 6 February 1970, file: Reading File: January–March, 1970, CINFO Papers, USAMHI.

116. "Sample Survey of Military Personnel," Office of Personnel Operations and Personnel Management Report No. 69–67–E, 31 May 1967, [precedes files], CINFO Papers, USAMHI, 4, 9, 16.

117. "Liaison Visit After-Action Report—Forts Knox and Campbell," 31 March 1970, file: 401–06 Staff Visits and Reports, 1970, CINFO Papers, USAMHI; Arthur T. Carey, Major, USA, Chief, Plans Branch, CID, "Report on Liaison Trip to Sixth Army Area (23 August–4 September), Ft. Lewis, AFRTS-LA, Sacramento Army Depot, Presidio, Ft. Ord," 10 September 1970, file: 103–03 Reading File July–August–September 1970, CINFO Papers, USAMHI; "510 Quarterly Report from USARV to CINFO," 15 January 1968, file: 510 reports, CINFO Papers, USAMHI.

118. "Liaison Visit Report on 15–17 September Trip to Forts Lee, Eustis, Monroe, & HQ CONARC," 26 September 1970, file: CONARC, CINFO Papers, USAMHI; "510 Quarterly Report from USARPAC to CINFO," 26 October 1970, file: 510 Reports, CINFO Papers, USAMHI.

119. Wesbrook, "The Potential for Military Disintegration," 270–71.

Epilogue

1. Mataxis, "This Far No Farther," 52–57, 52 [quotation], 57 [new techniques].

2. Radine, *The Taming of the Troops*, 115, 89 [quotations].

3. Radine, *The Taming of the Troops*, 88–89. Radine reported that sometimes the army sent soldiers whom it identified as "GI organizers" to Vietnam (12). Punishing a soldier bent on undermining discipline by sending him to the war zone is yet another example of how the army viewed the Vietnam War as a distraction from its normal operations.

4. Department of the Army, *Commanders Call*, Pamphlet 360–805 (1971); Department of the Army, *Commanders Call*, Pamphlet 360–808 (1971), 51–56 ["Using Your History"].

5. Department of the Army, "Commander's Guide to Command Information," *Commanders Call*, Pamphlet 360–810 (1971), 7.

Some of the old language died hard. One *Commanders Call* featured the Second Infantry Division's so-called PRO-LIFE program for its troops stationed in the Republic of Korea. It was reminiscent of the Twenty-fourth Infantry Division's Pro-Blue program both in name and in its "spiritual dimensions." It differed in its politics and in its dedication to making soldiers "fit to fight," recalling the World War I film of that name (Department of the Army, "'PRO-LIFE' Program," 2–5, 2 ["fit to fight"], 4 [Spiritual Dimensions]).

6. Janowitz, "Civic Consciousness and Military Performance," 57. On the interwar citizenship program, see chapter 1.

7. Janowitz, "Civic Consciousness and Military Performance," 60.

8. Stouffer, *The American Soldier*, 1:437.

9. Wesbrook, *Political Training in the United States Army*, 35; Palmer, "'Why We Fight,' A Study of Indoctrination Activities in the Armed Forces," 185.

10. Moskos, *The American Enlisted Man*, 97.

BIBLIOGRAPHY

Primary Sources

Collected Papers

Carlisle Barracks Collection. United States Army Military History Institute at
Carlisle Barracks, Carlisle, Pennsylvania (hereafter cited as USAMHI).
Cold War Veterans Collection. USAMHI.
Collins, J. Lawton, Papers. USAMHI.
Korean War Veterans Collection (KWVC). USAMHI.
Lanham, Charles T., Papers. Seeley G. Mudd Manuscript Library. Princeton
University.
Library Collection. USAMHI.
McWilliams, James Bruce, Papers. USAMHI.
Merrick, Richard H., Papers. USAMHI.
Palmer, Williston B., Papers. USAMHI.
Pearson, Ralph E., Papers. USAMHI.
Roberts, Archibald E., Papers. USAMHI.
Records of the Army Staff. RG 319. National Archives (NA).
Records of the Headquarters, Army Ground Forces. RG 337. National Ar-
chives.
Records of the Office of the Secretary of Defense. RG 330. National Archives.
Special Services Section, Army War College. USAMHI.
Sullivan, Edward S., Papers. USAMHI.
Temple, Jane., Papers. USAMHI.
Underwood, George V., Papers. USAMHI.
United States Army Chief of Information. Papers (CINFO Papers). USAMHI.
Vietnam Veterans Surveys (VVS). USAMHI.
World War II Veterans Survey (WWII VS). USAMHI.

Films

Department of Defense. *Ballots That Fly.* 9 min. Armed Forces Information
Film 129, 1964.
———. *Communist Target Youth.* 31 min. Armed Forces Information Film
116, 1962.

————. *The History of the Korean War.* 58 min. Armed Forces Information Film 85, 1958. Piscataway NJ: Alpha Video Distributors, copyright 1955, 1995.

————. *Russia.* 24 min. Armed Forces Information Film 87, 1958.

Operation: Abolition. 45 min. San Francisco: House Un-American Activities Committee, 1960.

War Department. *The Battle of Britain.* 54 min. Fourth film in the *Why We Fight* series. Piscataway NJ: Alpha Video Distributors, copyright 1943, 1994.

————. *The Battle of China.* 64 min. Sixth film in the *Why We Fight* series. Piscataway NJ: Alpha Video Distributors, copyright 1945, 1994.

————. *The Battle of Russia.* 83 min. Fifth film in the *Why We Fight* series. Piscataway NJ: Alpha Video Distributors, copyright 1944, 1994.

————. *Divide and Conquer.* 57 min. Third film in the *Why We Fight* series. Piscataway NJ: Alpha Video Distributors, copyright 1943, 1994.

————. *The Nazis Strike.* 42 min. Second film in the *Why We Fight* series. Piscataway NJ: Alpha Video Distributors, copyright 1943, 1994.

————. *Prelude to War.* 53 min. First film in the *Why We Fight* series. Piscataway NJ: Alpha Video Distributors, copyright 1942, 1994.

————. *The War Comes to America.* 65 min. Seventh film in the *Why We Fight* series. Piscataway NJ: Alpha Video Distributors, copyright 1945, 1994.

Government Documents

American Historical Association. *G.I. Roundtable: What Shall Be Done about Germany after the War?* War Department Educational Manual 10. Washington DC: U.S. Government Printing Office, 1944.

————. *G.I. Roundtable: What Shall Be Done with the War Criminals?* War Department Educational Manual 11. Washington DC: U.S. Government Printing Office, 1944.

Central Pacific Base Command. *A Pocket Guide to Hawaii.* Washington DC: U.S. Government Printing Office, 1944.

Colegrove, Kenneth W. *Communist Conquest and Colonization.* Democracy versus Communism, no. 10. Princeton NJ: Institute of Fiscal & Political Education, 1959.

————. *Communist Party Rule of Soviet Russia.* Democracy versus Communism, no. 7. Institute of Fiscal & Political Education, 1959.

————. *The Communist Party's Program in the United States.* Democracy versus Communism, no. 11. Institute of Fiscal & Political Education, 1959.

————. *Democracy Faces Communism.* Democracy versus Communism, no. 1. Institute of Fiscal & Political Education, 1959.

————. *How Communism Controls Peoples' Economic Life.* Democracy versus Communism, no. 8. Institute of Fiscal & Political Education, 1959.

———. *How Communists Gain and Keep Power*. Democracy versus Communism, no. 6. Institute of Fiscal & Political Education, 1959.

———. *How the Communist Party Operates*. Democracy versus Communism, no. 5. Institute of Fiscal & Political Education, 1959.

———. *How Workers and Farmers Fare under Communism*. Democracy versus Communism, no. 9. Institute of Fiscal & Political Education, 1959.

———. *What Communists Do to Liberty*. Democracy versus Communism, no. 3. Institute of Fiscal & Political Education, 1959.

———. *What Is Communism?* Democracy versus Communism, no. 2. Institute of Fiscal & Political Education, 1959.

Committee on Public Information. *How the War Came to America*. N. p., 1917.

Department of the Army. *Armed Forces Information Materials: A Catalog of Publications, Films, Posters, and Maps Supplied by the Office of Armed Forces Information & Education, Department of Defense*. Pamphlet 355–50. Washington DC: U.S. Government Printing Office, 1955.

———. *Armed Forces Newspaper Editors Guide*. Pamphlet 20–23. Washington DC: U.S. Government Printing Office, 1952.

———. *Army Forty-Hour Discussion Leader's Course*. Pamphlet 20–105. Washington DC: U.S. Government Printing Office, 1951.

———. *Army Four-Hour Pre-Combat Orientation Course (Korea)*. Army Pamphlet 20–105. Washington DC: U.S. Government Printing Office, 1950.

———. Army Regulation 355–5. Troop Information and Education. 12 March 1953.

———. Army Regulation 360–81. Command Information. 20 April 1964.

———. *Behind Enemy Lines*. Pamphlet 21–46. Washington DC: U.S. Government Printing Office, 1951.

———. *Catalog of Armed Forces Information Materials*. Pamphlet 20–170. Washington DC: U.S. Government Printing Office, 1952.

———. *Commanders Call*. Pamphlet 360–805. Washington DC: U.S. Government Printing Office, 1971.

———. *Commanders Call*. Pamphlet 360–808. Washington DC: U.S. Government Printing Office, 1971.

———. "Commander's Guide to Army Information." *Commanders Call*. Pamphlet 360–810. Washington DC: U.S. Government Printing Office, 1973.

———. "Commander's Guide to Command Information." *Commanders Call*. Pamphlet 360–810. Washington DC: U.S. Government Printing Office, 1973.

———. *Communism in Red China*. Know Your Communist Enemy, no. 5. Pamphlet 21–79. Washington DC: U.S. Government Printing Office, 1955.

———. *Communism in the USSR*. Know Your Communist Enemy, no. 3. Pamphlet 21–78. Washington DC: U.S. Government Printing Office, 1955.

———. *Current Information Materials Catalog*. Pamphlet 360–508. Washington DC: U.S. Government Printing Office, 1968.

———. *Defense against Enemy Propaganda*. Pamphlet 20–79. Washington DC: U.S. Government Printing Office, 1954.

———. *Duty, Honor, Country*. Series I. Pamphlet 16–5. Washington DC: U.S. Government Printing Office, 1951.

———. *Duty, Honor, Country*. Series III. Pamphlet 16–7. Washington DC: U.S. Government Printing Office, 1951.

———. *Duty, Honor, Country*. Series IV. Pamphlet 16–8. Washington DC: U.S. Government Printing Office, 1951.

———. *Duty, Honor, Country*. Pamphlet 16–12. Washington DC: U.S. Government Printing Office, 1960.

———. *Duty Honor Country*. Pamphlet 16–13. Washington DC: U.S. Government Printing Office, 1968.

———. *Foundations of American Democracy*, draft. Pamphlet 16–(—). Washington DC: U.S. Government Printing Office, 1958.

———. *Freedom and You*. Alert: Facts for the Armed Forces no. 2. Pamphlet 355–132. Washington DC: U.S. Government Printing Office, 1962.

———. *Freedom Is Not Free*. Pamphlet 360–236. Washington DC: U.S. Government Printing Office, 1968.

———. *From Marx to Now*. Alert: Facts for the Armed Forces no. 1. Pamphlet 355–136. Washington DC: U.S. Government Printing Office, 1962.

———. *Human Self Development: Our Moral Heritage*. Pamphlet 165–10. Washington DC: U.S. Government Printing Office, 1972.

———. "Incident at Son My." *Commanders Call*. Pamphlet 360–806. Washington DC: U.S. Government Printing Office, 1972.

———. *International Communism*. Pamphlet 360–219. Washington DC: U.S. Government Printing Office, 1965.

———. *International Communism: Its Teachings, Aims, and Methods*. Know Your Communist Enemy, no. 1. Pamphlet 21–77. Washington DC: U.S. Government Printing Office, 1954.

———. *Lessons Learned: The Philippines 1946–1953*. Alert: Facts for the Armed Forces no. 6A. Pamphlet 355–139. Washington DC: U.S. Government Printing Office, 1962.

———. *Officers' Call*. Pamphlet 21–65. Washington DC: U.S. Government Printing Office, June 1954.

———. *Officer's Call: Theirs to Reason Why*. Pamphlet 360–300. Washington DC: U.S. Government Printing Office, 1967.

———. *Overseas Orientation Course*. Pamphlet 20–105. Washington DC: U.S. Government Printing Office, 1952.

———. "'PRO-LIFE' Program." *Commanders Call*. Pamphlet 360–820. Washington DC: U.S. Government Printing Office, 1974.

———. *Separation Series*. Pamphlet 20–139. Washington DC: U.S. Government Printing Office, 1952.

———. *The Soldier and the Community*. Pamphlet 20–142. Washington DC: U.S. Government Printing Office, 1952.

———. *The Soldier in Combat*. Pamphlet 20–135. Washington DC: U.S. Government Printing Office, 1951.

———. "The Soviet Armed Forces." *Officers' Call*. Pamphlet 355–22. Washington DC: U.S. Government Printing Office, January 1956.

———. *Soviet Treaty Violations*. *Alert: Facts for the Armed Forces* no. 5. Pamphlet 355–138. Washington DC: U.S. Government Printing Office, 1962.

———. "This Is TI & E." *Officers' Call*. Pamphlet 21–49. Washington DC: U.S. Government Printing Office, April 1952.

———. *To Insure Domestic Tranquillity*. Pamphlet 360–81. Washington DC: U.S. Government Printing Office, 1968.

———. *Travel Talks*. Pamphlet 20–107. Washington DC: U.S. Government Printing Office, 1951.

———. *Troop Topics: Barbed Wire Command*. Pamphlet 360–229. Washington DC: U.S. Government Printing Office, 1967.

———. *Troop Topics: Discipline*. Pamphlet 20–165. Washington DC: U.S. Government Printing Office, 1953.

———. *Troop Topics: Individual Training: Why We Serve*. Pamphlet 355–2. Washington DC: U.S. Government Printing Office, 1955.

———. *Troop Topics: Information and You*. Pamphlet 20–160. Washington DC: U.S. Government Printing Office, 1953.

———. *Troop Topics: International Communism*. Pamphlet 360–219. Washington DC: U.S. Government Printing Office, 1965.

———. *Troop Topics: Our Citizenship*. Pamphlet 360–212. Washington DC: U.S. Government Printing Office, 1964.

———. *Troop Topics: Our Government*. Pamphlet 360–204. Washington DC: U.S. Government Printing Office, 1964.

———. *Troop Topics: Our Mission in Vietnam*. Pamphlet 360–214. Washington DC: U.S. Government Printing Office, 1964.

———. *Troop Topics: The United States Army in South Vietnam*. Pamphlet 360–234. Washington DC: U.S. Government Printing Office, 1968.

———. *Troop Topics: Why Training Is Tough*. Pamphlet 20–163. Washington DC: U.S. Government Printing Office, 1953.

———. *Troop Topics: Why We Serve* . . . . Pamphlet 360–206. Washington DC: U.S. Government Printing Office, 1964.

———. *Trouble in the Satellites*. Pamphlet 355–110. Washington DC: U.S. Government Printing Office, 1957.

———. *The Truth about Our Economic System*. *Alert: Facts for the Armed Forces* no. 3. Pamphlet 355–136. Washington DC: U.S. Government Printing Office, 1962.

———. *Truth Is Our Defense.* Pamphlet 20–146. Washington DC: U.S. Government Printing Office, 1952.

———. *Voting Information 1952.* Pamphlet 21–50. Washington DC: U.S. Government Printing Office, 1952.

———. *Who Are the Communists and Why? Know Your Communist Enemy,* no. 6. Pamphlet 21–72. Washington DC: U.S. Government Printing Office, 1955.

———. "Your Command Information Program." *Officers' Call.* Pamphlet 360–300. Washington DC: U.S. Government Printing Office, August 1964.

———. *Your Military Service Obligation.* Pamphlet 20–166. Washington DC: U.S. Government Printing Office, 1953.

Department of Defense. *Armed Forces Information and Education Catalog of Current Information Materials.* Pamphlet Gen-3A. Washington DC: U.S. Government Printing Office, 1965.

———. *Catalog of Information Materials.* Pamphlet 8–4. Washington DC: U.S. Government Printing Office, 1957.

———. *Catalog of Information Materials.* Pamphlet 8–5. Washington DC: U.S. Government Printing Office, 1959.

———. *Catalog of Information Materials.* Pamphlet 8–5A. Washington DC: U.S. Government Printing Office, 1961.

———. *Catalog of Information Materials.* Pamphlet Gen-3. Washington DC: U.S. Government Printing Office, 1963.

———. *Facts about the United States.* Pamphlet Gen-13. Washington DC: U.S. Government Printing Office, 1964.

———. *The Future Belongs to Freedom.* Pamphlet 3–3. Washington DC: U.S. Government Printing Office, 1957.

———. *How Our Foreign Policy Is Made.* Pamphlet 3–11. Washington DC: U.S. Government Printing Office, 1957.

———. *Ideas in Conflict: Liberty and Communism.* Pamphlet Gen-27. Washington DC: U.S. Government Printing Office, 1962.

———. *Know Your Enemy: The Viet Cong.* Pamphlet Gen-20. Washington DC: U.S. Government Printing Office, 1966.

———. *A Pocket Guide to Viet-Nam.* Pamphlet PG-21. Washington DC: U.S. Government Printing Office, 1962.

———. *The U.S. Fighting Man's Code.* Pamphlet Gen-28. Washington DC: U.S. Government Printing Office, 1967.

———. *Your Vote.* Pamphlet 5–10. Washington DC: U.S. Government Printing Office, 1960.

Mataxis, Theodore C. "This Far No Farther." *Commanders Call.* Department of the Army Pamphlet 360–803. Washington DC: U.S. Government Printing Office, 1971.

Tocci, Lt. Col. Vincent R. "Understanding the War in Southeast Asia." *Com-*

manders Call. Department of the Army Pamphlet 360–803. Washington DC: U.S. Government Printing Office, 1971.

U.S. Congress. Committee on Armed Services. Hearings before Special Preparedness Subcommittee. *Military Cold War Education and Speech Review Policies.* 87th Cong., 2d sess., parts 1–8, 1962.

———. Committee on Armed Services. Special Preparedness Subcommittee. *Military Cold War Education and Speech Review Policies.* 87th Cong., 2d sess. Report of Proceedings. 8 parts. Washington DC: Ward & Paul, 1962.

———. House. Representative O. C. Fisher of Texas. "Notorious *Overseas Weekly* Attacks Anticommunist Pro-Blue Americanism Program of Gen. Edwin A. Walker." *Congressional Record.* 87th Cong., 2d sess., 24 May 1961.

———. Senate. Committee on Armed Services. *Report of Senate Special Preparedness Subcommittee.* 87th Cong., 2d sess., 19 October 1962.

———. Senate. Committee of the Judiciary. Hearings before the Subcommittee on Internal Security. *Interlocking Subversion in Government Departments—Army Information and Education.* 83rd Cong., 2d sess., 1954.

———. Senator J. William Fulbright of Arkansas speaking on "The Big Picture." *Congressional Record,* 92nd Cong., 1st sess., 5 December 1969.

———. Senator Strom Thurmond of South Carolina. "Senator Thurmond Presents Anti-Communist Items Censored from Military Statements." *Congressional Record.* 87th Cong., 2d sess., 19 February 1962.

United States Government Organizational Manual, 1950–51. Washington DC: U.S. Government Printing Office, 1950.

United States Government Organizational Manual 1968–69. Washington DC: U.S. Government Printing Office, 1968.

War Department. *Citizenship.* Training Manual 2000–25. Washington DC: U.S. Government Printing Office, 1928.

———. *Guide to the Use of Information Materials.* Pamphlet 20–3. Washington DC: U.S. Government Printing Office, 1944.

———. *Invisible Weapon.* Pamphlet 20–13. Washington DC: U.S. Government Printing Office, 1944.

———. *The USSR: Institutions & People: A Brief Handbook for the Use of Officers of the Armed Forces of the United States.* Washington DC: U.S. Government Printing Office, 1945.

———. *The War in Outline: Materials for the Use of Army Orientation Course.* Washington DC: U.S. Government Printing Office, 1942.

———. *You Don't Think. . . .* Pamphlet 20–15. Washington DC: U.S. Government Printing Office, 1944.

———. *Your Red Army Ally.* Washington DC: U.S. Government Printing Office, 1945.

Secondary Sources

Adler, Les K., and Thomas G. Paterson. "Red Fascism: The Merger of Nazi Germany and Soviet Russia in the American Image of Totalitarianism, 1930s–1950s." *American Historical Review* 75 (April 1970):1046–64.

Almond, Gabriel A., and Sidney Verba. *The Civic Culture: Political Attitudes and Democracy in Five Nations*. Princeton NJ: Princeton University Press, 1963.

Alpers, Benjamin L. "This Is the Army: Imagining a Democratic Military in World War II." *Journal of American History* 85, no. 1 (June 1998):129–63.

Arbogast, William R. "An Analysis of Modernization in Army Newspapers." Master's thesis, University of Missouri, 1972.

———. "Issues and Answers: The U.S. Army Command Information Program." Master's thesis, U.S. Army Command and General Staff College, Fort Leavenworth KS, 1971.

Atwell, Lester. *Private*. New York: Simon and Schuster, 1958.

Baritz, Loren. *Backfire: A History of How American Culture Led Us into Vietnam and Made Us Fight the Way We Did*. New York: William Morrow, 1985.

Barson, Michael, and Steven Heller. *Red Scared!: The Commie Menace in Propaganda and Popular Culture*. San Francisco: Chronicle Books, 2001.

Bartov, Omer. *Hitler's Army: Soldiers, Nazis, and the War in the Third Reich*. New York: Oxford University Press, 1991.

Becker, Carl M., and Robert G. Theobaben. *Common Warfare: Parallel Memoirs by Two World War II GIs in the Pacific*. Jefferson NC: McFarland and Company, 1992.

Bell, Daniel. *The End of Ideology: On the Exhaustion of Political Ideas in the Fifties*. 2nd ed. New York: Free Press, 1960.

Bendersky, Joseph W. *The "Jewish Threat": Anti-Semitic Politics of the U.S. Army*. New York: Basic Books, 2000.

Bennett, Michael J. *When Dreams Came True: The GI Bill and the Making of Modern America*. Washington DC: Brassey's, 1996.

Bentley, Eric, ed. *Thirty Years of Treason: Excerpts from Hearings before the House Committee on Un-American Activities, 1938–1968*. New York: Viking Press, 1971.

Bernard, George W., John Beumer III, Andrea Herzberg-Morrison, and Bernard G. Sarnat. "Fred Herzberg, Oral Biology: Los Angeles, 1994, University of California: In Memoriam." *University of California History Digital Archives Collection*. http://sunsite.berkeley.edu/uchistory.

Biderman, Albert D. *March to Calumny: The Story of American POW's in the Korean War*. New York: Macmillan, 1963.

Blakey, George T. *Historians on the Home Front: American Propagandists for the Great War*. Lexington: University Press of Kentucky, 1970.

Blum, John Morton. *V Was for Victory*. New York: Harcourt Brace Jovanovich, 1976.

Bogle, Lori L. *The Pentagon's Battle for the American Mind: The Early Cold War*. Texas A&M University Military History Series. College Station: Texas A&M University Press, 2004.

Bohn, Thomas William. "An Historical and Descriptive Analysis of the 'Why We Fight' Series." PhD diss., University of Wisconsin, 1968.

Borowski, Tadeusz. *This Way to the Gas, Ladies and Gentlemen, and Other Stories*. Translated by Barbara Vedder. New York: Viking Press, 1959. English translation, 1967.

Brennan, Matthew. *Brennan's War: Vietnam 1965–1969*. Novato CA: Presidio Press, 1985.

Bristow, Nancy K. *Making Men Moral: Social Engineering during the Great War*. New York: New York University Press, 1996.

Burstyn, Varda. *The Rites of Men: Manhood, Politics, and the Culture of Sport*. Toronto: University of Toronto Press, 1999.

Camfield, Thomas M. "'Will to Win'—The U.S. Army Troop Morale Program of World War I." *Military Affairs: The Journal of Military History, Including Theory and Technology* 61, no. 3 (October 1977):125–28.

Capra, Frank. *The Name above the Title: An Autobiography*. New York: Macmillan, 1971.

Caute, David. *The Great Fear: The Anti-Communist Purge under Truman and Eisenhower*. New York: Simon and Schuster, 1978.

Cawthon, Charles R. *Other Clay: A Remembrance of the World War II Infantry*. Niwot CO: University Press of Colorado, 1990.

Chambers, John Whiteclay II. *To Raise an Army: The Draft Comes to Modern America*. New York: Free Press, 1987.

Chambers, Whittaker. *Witness*. New York: Random House, 1952.

Chomsky, Noam. *The Chomsky Reader*. Edited by James Peck. New York: Pantheon Books, 1987.

———. *For Reasons of State*. New York: Pantheon Books, 1973.

Coakley, Jay J. "Sport as Opiate." In *Sport in Contemporary Society: An Anthology*. Edited by D. Stanley Eitzen, 250–54. New York: St. Martin's Press, 1979.

Coffey, David. "African Americans in U.S. Forces in Vietnam." *Encyclopedia of the Vietnam War: A Political, Social, and Military History*. Edited by Spencer C. Tucker. Oxford: Oxford University Press, 1998.

Colegrove, Kenneth W. *Democracy versus Communism*. Edited by Hall Bartlett. Princeton NJ: D. Van Nostrand, 1957.

———. *International Control of Aviation*. Boston: World Peace Foundation, 1930.

———. *Militarism in Japan*. World Affairs Books no. 16. Boston: World Peace Foundation, 1936.

Collins, J. Lawton. *Lightning Joe: An Autobiography*. Baton Rouge: Louisiana State University Press, 1979.

Cortright, David. *Soldiers in Revolt: The American Military Today*. Garden City NY: Anchor Press/Doubleday, 1975.

Creel, George. *How We Advertised America*. New York: Harper and Brothers, 1920.

Cripps, Thomas, and David Culbert. "*The Negro Soldier* (1944): Film Propaganda in Black and White." *American Quarterly* 31, no. 5 (winter 1979):615–40.

Curtin, Michael. *Redeeming the Wasteland: Television Documentary and Cold War Politics*. New Brunswick NJ: Rutgers University Press, 1995.

Dennis, Jack. "Major Problems of Political Socialization Research." In *Socialization to Politics: A Reader*. Edited by Jack Dennis, 2–28. New York: John Wiley & Sons, 1973.

Dewey, John. *Democracy and Education: An Introduction to the Philosophy of Education*. New York: Macmillan, 1916.

Dollard, John. *Fear in Battle*. Washington DC: The Infantry Journal, 1944.

Doob, Leonard W. *Patriotism and Nationalism: Their Psychological Foundations*. New Haven: Yale University Press, 1964.

Dower, John W. *Embracing Defeat: Japan in the Wake of World War II*. New York: W. W. Norton/New Press, 1999.

———. *War without Mercy: Race and Power in the Pacific War*. New York: Pantheon Books, 1986.

Dudziak, Mary L. *Cold War Civil Rights: Race and the Image of American Democracy*. Princeton NJ: Princeton University Press, 2000.

Easton, David, and Jack Dennis. "The Child's Image of Government." In *Socialization to Politics: A Reader*. Edited by Jack Dennis, 59–81. New York: John Wiley and Sons, 1973.

———. "A Political Theory of Political Socialization." In *Socialization to Politics: A Reader*. Edited by Jack Dennis, 32–53. New York: John Wiley and Sons, 1973.

Ebenstein, William. *Two Ways of Life: The Communist Challenge to Democracy*. New York: Holt, Rinehart and Winston, 1964.

Ebert, James R. *A Life in a Year: The American Infantryman in Vietnam, 1965–1972*. Novato CA: Presidio Press, 1993.

Ellis, John. *The Sharp End: The Fighting Man in World War II*. New York: Charles Scribner's Sons, 1980.

Exoo, Calvin F. "Cultural Hegemony in the United States." In *Democracy Upside Down: Public Opinion and Cultural Hegemony in the United States*. Edited by Calvin F. Exoo. Westport CT: Praeger, 1987.

FitzGerald, Frances. *America Revised: History Schoolbooks in the Twentieth Century*. Boston: Little, Brown, 1979.

Foner, Eric. *The Story of American Freedom*. New York: W.W. Norton, 1998.

Foner, Philip S. *Morale Education in the American Army*. New York: International Publishers, 1944.

Ford, Nancy G. *Americans All! Foreign Born Soldiers in World War I*. College Station: Texas A&M University Press, 2001.

Fox, Victor J. *The Pentagon Case*. New York: Freedom Press, 1958.

Frank, Joseph Allen. *With Ballot and Bayonet: The Political Socialization of American Civil War Soldiers*. Athens: University of Georgia Press, 1998.

Freidel, Frank B., ed. *Union Pamphlets of the Civil War, 1861–1865*. 2 vols. Cambridge MA: The Belknap Press of Harvard University Press, 1967.

Fudge, Lt. Col. Robert Oliver. "The Armed Forces Radio Service." Master's thesis, George Washington University, 1949.

Fulbright, J. William. *Old Myths and New Realities*. New York: Random House, 1964.

———. *The Pentagon Propaganda Machine*. New York: Liveright, 1970.

Fussell, Paul. *Wartime: Understanding and Behavior in the Second World War*. New York: Oxford University Press, 1989.

George, Alexander L. *The Chinese Communist Army in Action: The Korean War and Its Aftermath*. New York: Columbia University Press, 1967.

George, Peter. *Red Alert*. New York: Ace, 1958. Published in Britain under the pseudonym Peter Bryant as *Two Hours to Doom* (London: Boardman, 1958).

Giangreco, D. M., and Kathryn Moore. *Dear Harry . . . Truman's Mailroom, 1945–1953: The Truman Administration through Correspondence with "Everyday Americans."* Mechanicsburg PA: Stackpole Books, 1999.

Gibson, James William. *The Perfect War: The War We Couldn't Lose and How We Did*. Boston: Atlantic Monthly Press, 1986.

Goedde, Petra. *GIs and Germans: Culture, Gender, and Foreign Relations, 1945–1949*. New Haven: Yale University Press, 2002.

Goldhamer, Herbert. *The Soviet Soldier: Soviet Military Management at the Troop Level*. New York: Crane, Russak and Company, 1975.

Goldman, Peter, and Tony Fuller, with Stryker McGuire, Wally McNamee, and Vern E. Smith. *Charlie Company: What Vietnam Did to Us*. New York: William Morrow, 1983.

Gray, J. Glenn. *The Warriors: Reflections on Men in Battle*. New York: Harper and Row, 1959.

Griese, Noel L. *Arthur W. Page: Publisher, Public Relations Pioneer, Patriot*. Atlanta: Anvil Publishers, 2001.

Griffith, Patricia. "Army Chaplains and the Program for Moral Build-Up" In

The Army Blue Book 1961—Volume I. Edited by Tom Compere, 183–86. New York: Military Publishing Institute, 1960.

Griffith, Robert. *The Politics of Fear: Joseph R. McCarthy and the Senate.* Lexington: University Press of Kentucky, 1970.

Haggis, Arthur George, Jr. "An Appraisal of the Administration, Scope, Concept, and Function of the United States Army Troop Information Program." PhD diss., Wayne State University, 1961. University Microfilms International Order Number 62–00909.

Hale, William Harlan. "'Militant Liberty' and the Pentagon." *The Reporter,* February 9, 1956, 30–34.

Hartz, Louis. *The Liberal Tradition in America: An Interpretation of American Political Thought since the Revolution.* New York: Harcourt Brace Jovanovich, 1955.

Heller, Joseph. *Catch-22.* New York: Simon and Schuster, 1955. Reprint, 1961.

Hersh, Seymour M. *My Lai 4: A Report on the Massacre and Its Aftermath.* New York: Random House, 1970.

Hesseltine, William B. *Lincoln and the War Governors.* New York: Alfred A. Knopf, 1948.

Hoffman, Alice M., and Howard S. Hoffman. *Archives of Memory: A Soldier Recalls World War II.* Lexington: University of Kentucky Press, 1990.

Hoover, J. Edgar. *Masters of Deceit: The Story of Communism in America and How to Fight It.* New York: Henry Holt, 1958.

Hovland, Carl I., Arthur A. Lumsdaine, and Fred D. Sheffield. *Experiments on Mass Communication.* Vol. 3 of *Studies in Social Psychology in World War II.* 4 vols. Princeton NJ: Princeton University Press, 1949.

Huntington, Samuel P. *The Soldier and the State: The Theory and Politics of Civil-Military Relations.* Cambridge MA: The Belknap Press of Harvard University Press, 1957.

———. *American Politics: The Promise of Disharmony.* Cambridge MA: The Belknap Press of Harvard University Press, 1981.

Hyman, Harold M. "The Election of 1864." In *History of American Presidential Elections,* vol. 3: 1155–1244. Edited by Arthur Schlesinger Jr. 4 vols. New York: Chelsea House, 1985.

Janowitz, Morris. "Civic Consciousness and Military Performance." In *The Political Education of Soldiers.* Edited by Morris Janowitz and Stephen D. Wesbrook, 55–80. Sage Research Progress Series on War, Revolution and Peace Keeping, vol. 11. Beverly Hills CA: Sage Publications, 1983.

———. *The Professional Soldier: A Social and Political Portrait.* New York: Free Press, 1960.

Jordan, Amos A., Jr. "Troop Information and Indoctrination." In *Handbook of Military Institutions.* Edited by Roger W. Little, 347–71. Sage Series on Armed Forces and Society. Beverly Hills CA: Sage Publications, 1971.

Jowett, Garth S., and Victoria O'Donnell. *Propaganda and Persuasion*. Newbury Park CA: Sage Publications, 1986.

Karsten, Peter. *Soldiers and Society: The Effects of Military Service on War and American Life*. Grass Roots Perspectives on American History no. 1. Westport CT: Greenwood Press, 1978.

Katz, Elihu, and Paul F. Lazarsfeld. *Personal Influence: The Part Played by People in the Flow of Mass Communications*. Glencoe IL: Free Press, 1955.

Kellet, Anthony. *Combat Motivation: The Behavior of Soldiers in Battle*. Boston: Kluwer-Nijhoff, 1982.

Kennedy, David M. *Over Here: The First World War and American Society*. New York: Oxford University Press, 1980.

Kent, Courtney, and Phoebe Kent. *The Case of General Edwin A. Walker*. New Orleans: Conservative Society of America, 1961.

Khruchchev, Nikita S. *Anatomy of Terror: Khrushchev's Revelations about Stalin's Regime*. Introduction by Nathaniel Weyl. Washington DC: Public Affairs Press, 1956.

Kinkead, Eugene. *In Every War But One*. New York: W.W. Norton, 1959.

———. "Reporter at Large: The Study of Something New in History." *New Yorker*, October 26, 1957, 102–53.

Klehr, Harvey, John Earl Haynes, and Fridrikh Igorevich Firsov. *The Secret World of American Communism*. New Haven: Yale University Press, 1995.

Knebel, Fletcher, and Charles Bailey II. *Seven Days in May*. New York: Harper and Row, 1962.

Koestler, Arthur. *Darkness at Noon*. New York: Macmillan, 1941.

Kovic, Ron. *Born on the Fourth of July*. New York: McGraw-Hill, 1976.

Krepinevich, Andrew, Jr. *The Army and Vietnam*. Baltimore: Johns Hopkins University Press, 1986.

Landing, Michael Lee. *The Only War We Had: A Platoon Leader's Journal of Vietnam*. New York: Ivy Books, 1987.

Lane, Jack C. "Ideology and the American Military Experience: A Reexamination of Early American Attitudes toward the Military." In *Soldiers and Civilians: The U.S. Army and the American People*. Edited by Garry D. Ryan and Timothy K. Nenninger, 15–26. Washington DC: National Archives and Records Administration, 1987.

Langton, Kenneth P., and M. Kent Jennings. "Political Socialization and the High School Civics Curriculum in the United States." In *Socialization to Politics: A Reader*. Edited by Jack Dennis, 365–90. New York: John Wiley, 1973.

Lasswell, Harold D. *Propaganda Technique in the World War*. New York: Knopf, 1927.

Lender, Mark Edward. *The New Jersey Soldier*. The New Jersey Revolutionary Experience, no. 5. Trenton: New Jersey Historical Commission, 1975.

Lewy, Guenter. "The American Experience in Vietnam." In *Combat Effectiveness: Cohesion, Stress, and the Volunteer Military.* Edited by Sam C. Sarkesian, 94–106. Sage Research Progress Series on War, Revolution, and Peacekeeping, vol. 9. Beverly Hills CA: Sage Publications, 1980.

Linderman, Gerald F. *The World within War: America's Combat Experience in World War II.* New York: Free Press, 1997.

Little, Roger W. "Buddy Relations and Combat Performance." In *The New Military: Changing Patterns of Organization.* Edited by Morris Janowitz, 195–223. New York: Russell Sage Foundation, 1964.

Loveland, Anne C. *American Evangelicals and the U.S. Military 1942–1993.* Baton Rouge: Louisiana State University Press, 1997.

Lovell, John P. "The Professional Socialization of the West Point Cadet." In *The New Military: Changing Patterns of Organization.* Edited by Morris Janowitz, 119–57. New York: Russell Sage Foundation, 1964.

Lynn, John A. *The Bayonets of the Republic: Motivation and Tactics in the Army of Revolutionary France, 1791–94.* Urbana: University of Illinois Press, 1984.

MacDonald, Charles B. *Company Commander.* Washington DC: Infantry Journal Press, 1947.

Manchester, William. *Goodbye, Darkness: A Memoir of the Pacific War.* Boston: Little, Brown, 1979.

Marchand, Roland. *Creating the Corporate Soul: The Rise of Public Relations and Corporate Imagery.* Berkeley: University of California Press, 1998.

Marshall, Samuel L. A. *Men against Fire: The Problem of Battle Command in Future War.* New York: William Morrow, 1947.

Maudlin, Bill. *Up Front.* New York: Henry Holt, 1944.

May, Elaine Tyler. *Homeward Bound: American Families in the Cold War Era.* New York: Basic Books, 1988.

McGirr, Lisa. *Suburban Warriors: The Origins of the New American Right.* Princeton NJ: Princeton University Press, 2001.

McPherson, James. *For Cause and Comrades: Why Men Fought in the Civil War.* New York: Oxford University Press, 1997.

Melzer, Richard. *Coming of Age in the Great Depression: The Civilian Conservation Corps Experience in New Mexico, 1933–1942.* Las Cruces NM: Yucca Tree Press, 2000.

Miller, Richard I. *Teaching about Communism.* New York: McGraw-Hill, 1966.

Millet, Allan R., and Peter Maslowski, *For the Common Defense: A Military History of the United States of America.* New York: Free Press, 1984.

Moïse, Edwin E. *Tonkin Gulf and the Escalation of the Vietnam War.* Chapel Hill: University of North Carolina Press, 1996.

Morrow, Curtis James. *What's a Commie Ever Done to Black People? A Ko-*

rean War Memoir of Fighting in the U.S. Army's Last All Negro Unit. Jefferson NC: McFarland, 1997.

Moskos, Charles C., Jr. *The American Enlisted Man: The Rank and File in Today's Military.* New York: Russell Sage Foundation, 1970.

Munson, Edward Lyman. *The Management of Men: A Handbook on the Systematic Development of Morale and the Control of Human Behavior.* Prepared with the literary assistance of Arthur H. Miller. New York: Henry Holt, 1921.

Murphy, William Thomas. "The Methods of *Why We Fight.*" *Journal of Popular Film* 1, no. 3 (summer 1972):185–96.

Myrdal, Gunnar, with Richard Sterner and Arnold Rose. *An American Dilemma: The Negro Problem and Modern Democracy.* 2 vols. New York: Harper and Brothers, 1944.

Nash, George H. *The Conservative Intellectual Movement in America since 1945.* New York: Basic Books, 1976.

Novick, Peter. *The Holocaust in American Life.* New York: Houghton Mifflin, 1999.

Orwell, George. *1984.* New York: Harcourt, Brace, 1949.

Osborn, Frederick. *Preface to Eugenics.* New York: Harper and Brothers, 1940.

Oshinsky, David M. *A Conspiracy So Immense: The World of Joe McCarthy.* New York: Free Press, 1983.

Paine, Thomas. *Collected Writings: Common Sense, The Crisis, and Other Pamphlets, Articles, and Letters, Rights of Man, The Age of Reason.* Compiled by Eric Foner. New York: Library of America, 1995.

Palmer, Thomas Alfred. "'Why We Fight,' A Study of Indoctrination Activities in the Armed Forces." PhD diss., Department of Political Science, International Law and Relations, University of South Carolina, 1971. University Microfilm International Order Number 71–21, 848.

Paret, Peter, Beth Irwin Lewis, and Paul Paret. *Persuasive Images: Posters of War and Revolution from the Hoover Institute Archives.* Princeton NJ: Princeton University Press, 1992.

Peterson, H. C., and Gilbert C. Fite. *Opponents of War, 1917–1918.* Madison: University of Wisconsin Press, 1957.

Prange, Gordon W., in collaboration with Donald M. Goldstein and Katherine V. Dillon. *At Dawn We Slept: The Untold Story of Pearl Harbor.* New York: McGraw-Hill, 1981.

Priscaro, Jerry L. "An Historical Study of the American Forces Korea Network and Its Broadcast Programming, 1957–1962." Master's thesis, Boston University, 1962.

Radine, Lawrence B. *The Taming of the Troops: Social Control in the United States Army.* Contributions in Sociology, Don Martindale, ed., no. 22. Westport CT: Greenwood Press, 1977.

Reeves, Richard. *President Kennedy: Profile of Power*. New York: Simon and Schuster, 1993.

Ridgway, Matthew B. *The Korean War: How We Met the Challenge, How All-Out Asian War Was Averted, Why MacArthur Was Dismissed, Why Today's War Objectives Must Be Limited*. New York: Doubleday, 1967.

Rishell, Lyle. *With a Black Platoon in Combat: A Year in Korea*. College Station: Texas A&M University Press, 1993.

Ross, Davis R. B. *Preparing for Ulysses: Politics and Veterans during World War II*. New York: Columbia University Press, 1969.

Ross, Stewart Halse. *Propaganda for War: How the United States Was Conditioned to Fight the Great War of 1914–1918*. Jefferson NC: McFarland, 1996.

Royster, Charles. *A Revolutionary People at War: The Continental Army and American Character, 1775–1783*. New York: W.W. Norton, 1979.

Rumer, Thomas A. *The American Legion: An Official History, 1919–1989*. New York: M. Evans, 1990.

Santoli, Al. *Everything We Had: An Oral History of the Vietnam War by Thirty Three American Soldiers Who Fought It*. New York: Random House, 1981.

Scherle, Victor, and William Turner Levy. *The Films of Frank Capra*. Secaucus NJ: Citadel Press, 1977.

Schrecker, Ellen. *Many Are the Crimes: McCarthyism in America*. Boston: Little, Brown, 1998.

"Scope and Content Note." Kenneth W. Colegrove Papers, *Herbert Hoover Presidential Library and Museum*. http://www.hoover.archives.gov./index.html.

Shirer, William L. *The Rise and Fall of the Third Reich*. New York: Simon and Schuster, 1960.

Simon, Robert L. *Fair Play: Sports, Values, and Society*. Boulder CO: Westview Press, 1991.

Spector, Ronald H. *After Tet: The Bloodiest Year in Vietnam*. New York: Free Press, 1993.

Spiegelman, Art. "Horton Hears a Heil." *New Yorker*, July 12, 1999, 62–63.

Spillane, Mickey. *One Lonely Night*. New York: Signet, 1952.

Stouffer, Samuel A., Arthur A. Lumsdaine, Marion Harper Lumsdain, Robin M. Williams Jr., M. Brewster Smith, Irving L. Janis, Shirley A. Star, and Leonard S. Cottrell Jr. *The American Soldier: Combat and Its Aftermath*. Vol. 2 of *Studies in Social Psychology in World War II*. 4 vols. Princeton NJ: Princeton University Press, 1949.

Stouffer, Samuel A., Edward A. Suchman, Leland C. DeVinney, Shirley A. Star, and Robin M. Williams Jr. *The American Soldier: Adjustment during Army Life*. Vol. 1 of *Studies in Social Psychology in World War II*. 4 vols. Princeton NJ: Princeton University Press, 1949.

Suid, Lawrence H. *Guts & Glory: The Making of an American Military Image in Film*. Revised and expanded edition. Lexington: University of Kentucky Press, 2002.

Summers, Harry G., Jr. *On Strategy: A Critical Analysis of the Vietnam War*. Novato CA: Presidio Press, 1982.

Terry, Wallace. *Bloods: An Oral History of the Vietnam War by Black Veterans*. New York: Random House, 1984.

Tomedi, Rudy. *No Bugles, No Drums: An Oral History of the Korean War*. New York: John Wiley, 1993.

Trett, Gerald L. "Remembering the Forgotten War." Post to *Korean War Project*, October 2, 2000. http://www.koreanwar.org/html/units/98en_photo.htm.

Urban, Wayne J., and Jennings L. Wagoner Jr. *American Education: A History*. New York: McGraw-Hill, 1996. Reprint, 2000.

Vaughn, Stephen. *Holding Fast the Inner Lines: Democracy, Nationalism, and the Committee on Public Information*. Chapel Hill: University of North Carolina Press, 1980.

Vorhees, Lt. Col. Melvin B. *Korean Tales*. New York: Simon and Schuster, 1952.

Weigley, Russell F. *History of the United States Army*. New York: Macmillan, 1967.

Welch, Robert H. W., Jr. *The Life of John Birch*. Boston: Western Islands, 1954.

Wells, Edward Stuart. "A Study of the United States Army's Internal Information Program." Master's thesis, New York University, 1958.

Wesbrook, Stephen D. *Political Training in the United States Army: A Reconsideration*. Mershon Center Position Papers in the Policy Sciences, no 3. Columbus: Mershon Center of the Ohio State University, 1979.

————. "The Potential for Military Disintegration." In *Combat Effectiveness: Cohesion, Stress, and the Volunteer Military*. Edited by Sam C. Sarkesian, 244–78. Sage Research Progress Series on War, Revolution, and Peacekeeping, vol. 9. Beverly Hills CA: Sage Publications, 1980.

Westbrook, Robert B. "Fighting for the American Family: Private Interests and Political Obligation in World War II." In *The Power of Culture: Critical Essays in American History*. Edited by Richard Wightman Fox and T. J. Jackson Lears. Chicago: University of Chicago Press, 1993.

Westin, Alan F. "The John Birch Society." In *The Radical Right*. Edited by Daniel Bell, 201–26. Garden City NY: Doubleday, 1963.

White, Bruce. "The American Military and the Melting Pot in World War I." In *War and Society in North America*. Edited by J. L. Granatstein and R. D. Cuff, 37–51. Toronto: Thomas Nelson, 1971. Reprinted in *The Military in America: From the Colonial Era to the Present*, edited by Peter Karsten (New York: Free Press, 1986).

Whitfield, Stephen J. *The Culture of the Cold War*. Baltimore: Johns Hopkins University Press, 1991.

Wiley, Bell Irvin. *The Life of Billy Yank: The Common Soldier of the Union*. Indianapolis: Bobbs-Merrill, 1951.

———. *The Life of Johnny Reb: The Common Soldier of the Confederacy*. Indianapolis: Bobbs-Merrill, 1943.

Williams, T. Harry. "Voters in Blue: The Citizen Soldier of the Civil War." *Mississippi Historical Review* 31, no. 2 (1944):187–204.

Williams, William Appelman. *The Tragedy of American Diplomacy*. Cleveland: World Publishing, 1959.

Wolfe, William Charles. *Frank Capra: A Guide to References and Sources*. Boston: G.K. Hall, 1987.

Woods, Randall Bennett. *Fulbright: A Biography*. Cambridge: Cambridge University Press, 1995.

Winkler, Allan. *The Politics of Propaganda: The Office of War Information, 1942–1945*. New Haven: Yale University Press, 1978.

Yang, Daqing. "Convergence or Divergence? Recent Historical Writings on the Rape of Nanjing." *American Historical Review* 104, no. 3 (June 1999):842–65.

Yarmolinsky, Adam. *The Military Establishment: Its Impacts on American Society*. New York: Harper and Row, 1971.

Yezzo, Dominic. *A G.I.'s Vietnam Diary, 1968–69*. New York: Franklin Watts, 1974.

INDEX

Ingram Content Group UK Ltd.
Milton Keynes UK
UKHW040438170723
425189UK00016B/215

9 780803 224865